The Roman Law of Inheritance

The Roman Law of Inheritance
The Evolution of the Roman Law of Inheritance during the Principate

Translated by Neophytos Christodoulides,
revised by Ulrike Babusiaux

EDINBURGH
University Press

Edinburgh University Press is one of the leading university presses in the UK. We publish academic books and journals in our selected subject areas across the humanities and social sciences, combining cutting-edge scholarship with high editorial and production values to produce academic works of lasting importance. For more information visit our website: edinburghuniversitypress.com

© Ulrike Babusiaux, 2024, 2026
English translation © Ulrike Babusiaux and Neophytos Christodoulides, 2024, 2026

Edinburgh University Press Ltd
13 Infirmary Street
Edinburgh EH1 1LT

First published in hardback by Edinburgh University Press 2024

Typeset in 11/13pt Adobe Garamond Pro
by Cheshire Typesetting Ltd, Cuddington, Cheshire, and
printed and bound by CPI Group (UK) Ltd, Croydon, CR0 4YY

A CIP record for this book is available from the British Library

ISBN 978 1 3995 3165 8 (hardback)
ISBN 978 1 3995 3166 5 (paperback)
ISBN 978 1 3995 3167 2 (webready PDF)
ISBN 978 1 3995 3168 9 (epub)

The right of Ulrike Babusiaux to be identified as the author of this work has been asserted in accordance with the Copyright, Designs and Patents Act 1988, and the Copyright and Related Rights Regulations 2003 (SI No. 2498).

Contents

List of Tables	vi
Preface	viii
1 Introduction	1
2 The General Historical and Legal Framework	13
3 The Rules of Intestacy	28
4 The Position of the Heir	60
5 The Protection of the Position of Heir	94
6 The Testamentary Order of Succession	109
7 Protecting Inheritance Expectations and the Rules of Disinheritance	158
8 The Law of Legacies	194
9 The Interpretation of Wills	248
10 Final Conclusions	274
Bibliography	279
Index of Sources	303
Index of Places and Persons	307
Index of Subjects	309

Tables

Overview 1:	*Corpus iuris civilis*	4
Overview 2:	Explaining a Fragment from the Digest	6
Overview 3:	The Law of Inheritance in The Institutes of Gaius	8
Overview 4:	Individual Titles of Chapters in the Sections treating Universal Acquisition in Gaius' Institutes	9
Overview 5:	A Chronological Table	13
Overview 6:	The Jurisprudence during the Empire	19
Overview 7:	The Temporal Frame of this Textbook	20
Overview 8:	The Imperial Layers of Law	27
Overview 9a:	The Order of Succession of the Children-in-Power	33
Overview 9b:	The Succeeding of the Descendants in the Male Line	34
Overview 9c:	No Succeeding after *filiae familias*	34
Overview 10:	The *nova clausula Iuliani*	50
Overview 11:	Order of Inheritance of a Mother after her Child	52
Overview 12:	Harmonised Application of the *ius novum* and the *ius antiquum*	54
Overview 13:	Layers of Law of the Rules of Intestacy during the Empire	58
Overview 14a:	Accrual in the Case of Varying Shares	65
Overview 14b:	Accrual in *coniunctio re et verbis*	66
Overview 15:	Comparison between General Usucaption and Hereditary Usucaption	70
Overview 16:	The Fiction to Grant an Action to the *bonorum possessor*	75
Overview 17:	The Evolution of the Guardianship of Women (*tutela mulieris*)	82
Overview 18:	The Distribution of the *caducum* to the Parents Appointed in the Will	87

Overview 19:	Prerequisites for the Position of Heir since the *lex Iulia et Papia*	88
Overview 20:	The Provisions of the *senatusconsultum Iuventianum*	106
Overview 21:	The Evolutionary Stages of the *hereditatis petitio*	108
Overview 22:	The Appointment of Heirs after the System of Asses	120
Overview 23:	Requirements for a Valid Will under the *ius civile*	131
Overview 24:	Grounds for Invalidating the Will under *ius civile* and *ius praetorium*	134
Overview 25:	The Four Categories of Codicils	144
Overview 26:	Possibilities of Reinterpreting a Will as a Codicil	147
Overview 27:	Consequences of the Formlessness of the Soldier's Will	151
Overview 28:	The Prohibition to Pass Over the *filius familias* under the *ius civile*	164
Overview 29:	Rules for the Disinheritance of Posthumously Born Children (*postumi*)	169
Overview 30:	Julian's Example of *collatio bonorum*	177
Overview 31:	Economical Reasons for the Claim of *bonorum possessio contra tabulas* by an *emancipatus*	177
Overview 32:	The Effects of the *nova clausula Iuliani*	180
Overview 33:	The System of *bonorum possessio contra tabulas*	185
Overview 34:	Stages in the Development of the Rules on Disinheritance	191
Overview 35:	Different Types of Legacies of the *ius civile*	201
Overview 36:	The Acquisition of a Legacy with Various Ancillary Provisions Attached	207
Overview 37:	The graduated Praetorian Protection of the Legatee	219
Overview 38:	Initial Differences between Legacies and *fideicommissa*	229
Overview 39:	The Rules of the *senatusconsultum Pegasianum* Creating a Balance between the Heir and the Fideicommissary	242
Overview 40:	Persisting Differences Between *Fideicommissa* and Legacies	244
Overview 41:	Rules for the Interpretation of Wills under the *ius civile*	259
Overview 42:	Reinterpreting the *ius civile* into *ius novum*	272

Preface

Preface to the English Edition

The realisation that English is about to become the lingua franca for Roman law has for some time prompted me to consider an English translation of my textbook on Roman inheritance law, the second edition of which was published in 2021. The concrete reason for the realisation of this idea was the need for academic support in English for my own teaching, due to an invitation to teach in an English-speaking environment.

The process of the translation has proved to be more difficult than I originally thought. It would not have been possible without the help of my team, namely Anna Elisa Stauffer and Nancy Rudolph, Lea Hugentobler, Anja Murer, Paula Giró, Stephanie Roth, Mert Kabranlar, Adrian Häusler and Jill Blumberg. They helped me to develop a suitable text, to correct formalities of the manuscript and to find appropriate terms for the many peculiar institutions of Roman inheritance law.

The bibliographical references in the appendix have been updated from the German edition.

The translation was supported by, among others, the Faculty of Law of the University of Zurich. I would also like to take this opportunity to express my sincere thanks to its Dean and his staff.

Ulrike Babusiaux
Zürich, November 2023

Translation of the Preface to the Second Edition in German

The positive reception of this book's first edition prompted the publishers to request a second edition. Preparing a second edition has allowed me to address some of the shortcomings of the previous one. However, the initial twofold purpose of this textbook remains the same. First, to provide a treatise that focuses on a single subject of Roman law, namely, the law of inheritance, in contrast to the usually compressed treatment of this topic in general works on Roman law; and second, to give Roman law of inheritance a place in the academic curricula called for by its historical importance, while making the historical layering of Roman private law more palpable to students.

Special thanks are due to my colleague Peter Oestmann, University of Münster, who had the idea of publishing a new series of textbooks and who played a decisive role in the whole project. It was his impetus that stimulated the creation of an instructional textbook with the aforementioned aims. It is also a sign of the importance of this endeavour that this book has been translated into Japanese by Minoru Tanaka, University of Nagoya, and Takeshi Sasaki, University of Kyoto. I am grateful to both of them. I am equally indebted to Ulrich Manthe, University of Passau, for pointing out the correct method of dating the SC Trebellianum, to Jens Peter Meincke, University of Cologne, for his remarks on the accurate reading of said senatusconsultum, and, again, to Minoru Tanaka for the interpretation of Papinian, D.35.1.102.

This edition has also benefited substantially from the many critical remarks of my team member, Thamar Xandry, who proofread the manuscript comprehensively and delved into the minutiae of the translation. Her linguistic and critical comments led to an extensive revision of most of the translated passages in this book. Published translations were consulted and reviewed (see footnote 6), but never adopted uncritically. Many thanks are also due to Alice Isepponi, who has provided valuable support in keeping the bibliography up to date, and to Yvonne Kastner, Silvan Schmid and Nicole Jaggi, who corrected various parts of this edition.

Finally, I am immensely grateful to my students at the University of Zurich, who have been using this textbook for more than five years, for their valuable feedback and questions, which always reveal new aspects of the same age-old questions.

Ulrike Babusiaux
July 2020

1

Introduction

1.1 A Roman Will Dating from AD142

In 1940, the French papyrologists Octave Guéraud and Pierre Jouguet published a Roman will, which remains the only specimen of a Roman will inscribed on wax tablets that has survived almost intact:

Antonius Silvanus eques alae primae
Thracum Mauretanae, stator praefecti,
turma Valeri, testamentum
fecit. Omnium bonorum meorum
castrensium et domes-
ticum Marcus Antonius Satrianus
filius meus ex asse mihi heres
esto. Ceteri alii omnes exheredes
sunto. Cernitoque hereditatem
meam in diebus centum proximis. Ni
ita creverit, exheres esto. Tunc
secundu gradu (Marcus?) Antonius
R...............lis frater
meus mihi heres esto cernitoque
hereditatem meam in diebus
sexaginta proximis. Cui do lego, si mihi
heres non erit, denarios argenteos septingentos
quinquaginta. [...]
[...] Do lego Anthoniae Thermutae
matri heredis mei supra scripti denarios argenteos
quingentos. Do lego praefecto meo
denarios argenteos quinquaginta. [...]
Hoc testamento dolus malus abesto. Familiam pecuniamque
testamenti faciendi causa emit Nemonius
duplicarius turmae Mari, libripende Marco Iulio

Tiberino sesquiplicario turnmae Valeri,
antestatus est Turbinium signiferum turmae
Proculi. Testamentum factum
Alexandreae ad Aegyptum in castris Augustis
hibernis legionis Secundae Traianae Fortis
et alae Mauretanae, sextas kalendas
Apriles Rufino et Quadrato consulibus [...][1]

Antonius Silvanus, knight of the first Mauritanian
cavalry wing of Thrace, attendant to the prefect,
from the squadron of Valerius, has made a will:
my son, Marcus Antonius Satrianus, shall be the sole
heir to my entire fortune,
both in the camp and at home.
Everybody else shall be disinherited.
He must decide whether to accept the inheritance
within the next one hundred days. If
he refuses, he shall be disinherited. Upon this,
my brother (Marcus?) Antonius R....lis,
shall be my heir on the second rank and must decide whether to
accept the inheritance within the next
sixty days. To the latter, if he
does not become my heir, I leave a legacy of seven hundred
and fifty silver denarii [...]
[...] I legate to Antonia Thermuta,
the mother of my heir, mentioned above,
five hundred silver denarii. I legate to my prefect
fifty silver denarii [...]
Evil intention may be absent from this will. Nemonius,
cavalryman with double pay to the squadron of Marius,
purchased the entire property to draw up a will, while Marcus Iulius
Tiberinus, cavalryman with one-and-a-half times pay in the squadron of
Valerius,

---

[1] I used the edition by Octave Guéraud and Pierre Jouguet, 'Un testament latin per aes et libram de 142 après J.-C. (Tablettes L. Keimer)' (1940) 6 Études de papyrologie 1, and Jean Macquéron, 'Le testament d'Antonius Silvanus, (Tablettes Keimer)' (1945) 23 RHD 123. I adhere to the emendations by Detlef Liebs, 'Das Testament des Antonius Silvanus, römischer Kavallerist in Alexandria bei Ägypten, aus dem Jahre 142 n. Chr.' in Klaus Märker and Christian Otto (eds), *Festschrift Weddig Fricke* (Alber 2000). For a German translation see Benedikt Strobel, *Römische Testamentsurkunden aus Ägypten vor und nach der Constitutio Antoniniana* (Beck 2014) 65–109.

acted as balance-holder. He called as witness Turbinius, standard-bearer of
the squadron
of Proculus. The will was drawn up
at Alexandria towards Egypt, in the imperial
winter camp of the second legion of Traian, the 'strong one',
and the Mauritanian wing on the twenty-seventh day
of March during the consulship of Rufinus and Quadratus [...]

The will of Antonius Silvanus, dated 27 March AD142, although only partially reproduced here, reveals the testator's meticulous planning. The testator named an heir, but also provided for a substitute heir in case the former was either unable or unwilling to accept the inheritance. The will also contained legacies. This unique piece of evidence offers an insight into Roman testamentary practice and a glimpse into the most important document a Roman citizen could draw up in the course of his life. And although it is here far from certain that the testator was a Roman citizen, his will clearly followed the rules that Roman law in the second century prescribed for drawing up a will. The rules for drawing up of a will, and the legal consequences for failing to comply with them, derive from the law of inheritance, which is part of the law of property that regulates the posthumous transfer of all that a person owes and is owed. The Roman rules of succession can be reconstructed from the writings of the Roman jurists.

However, neither the Roman testamentary documents nor the texts left to us by the jurists are intact or complete. Our main source of Roman law, as developed by jurists from the first century BC to the third century AD, is a collection of Roman legal sources published as legislation by the Byzantine Emperor Justinian I (AD527–565).

1.2 The Sources of the Roman Law of Inheritance

As part of his plan to restore the territorial and legal unity of the Roman Empire, Emperor Justinian collected excerpts for his code from both the writings of Roman jurists and the legislation of the Roman emperors. Since his collection was based mainly on the 'recycling' of the Roman legal tradition, it is also called a 'compilation' (*compilare,* literally 'to plunder', 'to pillage'). From the Early Modern Age, this collection was called *Corpus iuris civilis*, in contrast to the ecclesiastical law, the *Corpus iuris canonici.*

The first part of Emperor Justinian's compilation consists of a textbook for law students, the 'Institutes' (from *instituere*, literally 'to begin', 'to instruct;' hence, *institutiones*, 'instructions', 'teaching'). The second part, the 'Digest' (*digesta*), contains various excerpts (fragments) of the writings of the jurists, dating from the first century BC to the third century AD.

The third part, the 'Codex', contains the imperial legal pronouncements (*constitutione*s) of the emperors Hadrian (AD117–138) to Diocletian (AD284–305), thus providing a record of imperial legislation from the second to the fourth century AD. The Codex has only survived in its second, amended edition. Only the fourth part of this compilation is an original work of Emperor Justinian. It contains enactments for the reform of Roman law as it existed at the time. They are called 'Novels' (*novellae* from *novus*, 'new') and were written mainly in Greek because of their reformatory intent.

Overview 1: *Corpus iuris civilis*

Institutiones	textbook for first-year law students; modelled after the *Institutiones* of earlier jurists
Digesta	*ius* (law), excerpts from the writings of Roman jurists
Codex (*repetitae praelectionis*)	*leges* (legal pronouncements), a collection of *constitutiones* since Hadrian ('second edition')
Novellae	reformatory *constitutiones* by Justinian, written mainly in Greek

The collection of excerpts from the Roman jurists, known as the Digest, is the most important part of Justinian's compilation for our understanding of Roman law. It should be noted that already the Roman jurists themselves had used the word *digesta* (from *digerere*, literally 'to cut up', 'to arrange') for a thematically arranged collection of legal advice and opinions from a particular jurist. Justinian also used a Greek equivalent to describe the Digest. This term *Pandectae* (Greek, Πανδέκτης, literally 'all-encompassing') emphasises the comprehensive nature of the collection. Therefore, both titles of Justinian's work point to the rationale behind the compilation. It was intended to be a complete source of information on the state of the current law in order to provide a uniform and authoritative basis for legal education and practice in Justinian's time.

The instructions of Emperor Justinian (AD527–565) to the commission of legal experts ('compilers') appointed to compile the Digest reflect this aim. The commission was requested to select from the available material the most appropriate formulation for a legal opinion and to eliminate unnecessary repetition. Also, contradictions, in particular controversies between different Roman jurists were to be eliminated. The material thus selected was to be divided into fifty books and further subdivided into thematically arranged titles. This arrangement aimed at making the law both more accessible and more uniform. The price for this standardisation, however, was the omission of a significant part of the existing material. Emperor Justinian himself tells us that only about 5 per cent of the Roman legal writings available to his compilers found their way into the Digest, the rest being almost irretrievably lost.

We can get an idea of the richness of the material from the headings (*inscriptio,* 'heading', 'title') that the compilers have placed above each excerpt from the original material. Thus, in the heading of each fragment included in the Digest, we find the name of the jurist from whose work the fragment was taken and the title of the work, usually cited by the number of the book or scroll in which the text was found. The *inscriptio* thus provides information about the author, the occasion and the original date of the preserved text, often allowing us to guess at the original context of the fragment in question.[2]

1.2.1 An Example of a Fragment from the Digest

Each excerpt from the works of the Roman jurists will be cited according to its position in the Digest (D). The first number of the citation refers to the book of the Digest, the second to the part of the book and the third to the individual fragment. The latter contains the actual wording of the jurist's pronouncements, also called *lex*. In the Middle Ages, further subdivisions were added, traditionally called 'paragraphs', which can still be found in the margins of the editions used today. It is vital to observe the enumeration of the paragraphs. A paragraph begins with the introduction (*principium*), abbreviated as 'pr.'. The numbering begins only after the *principium,* so the numbers 1, 2, 3 etc. refer to the paragraphs after the *principium*. In the same vein, Justinian's institutiones are denoted as *Inst.* and the *Codex Iustinianus* as *C*; both are numbered accordingly. The headings of the *Codex Iustinianus* indicate the emperor or emperors responsible for the enactment, the date, if known, and the addressee of the enactment.

An excerpt from Book 28, Title 5, will illustrate this method of citing a fragment of Justinian's Digest. This passage deals with the requirements for the appointment of an heir (*institutio heredis*):

---

[2] A reconstruction of the jurists' writings was undertaken by Otto Lenel, *Palingenesia iuris civilis,* vol 2 (first published 1889, Akademische Druck- u. Verlagsanstalt. 1960 *with a supplement by Lorenz Edgar Sierl*; Aaalen 2000).

Overview 2: Explaining a Fragment from the Digest

D.28.5.1 pr.	source: Book 28 of the Digest (D.), Title 5, Fragment 1, introduction (*principium*)
Ulpianus libro primo ad Sabinum	heading: Ulpian, On Sabinus, Book 1
Qui testatur ab heredis institutione plerumque debet initium facere testamenti. licet etiam ab exheredatione, quam nominatim facit [...].	translation: He who draws up a will must usually begin by appointing an heir. It is also permitted [to begin] by disinheriting, which must be done by name [...].

Thus D.28.5.1pr. refers to the source of the fragment in Emperor Justinian's collection, while the heading '*Ulpianus libro primo ad Sabinum*', inserted by Justinian's compilers, reveals the original context of the sentence quoted. The text contains an elaboration from Book One of Ulpian's Commentary on Sabinus. The fragment deals with the order of the dispositions in a will. Following Ulpian's statement, the appointment of an heir must come first, and only in exceptional circumstances can the disinheritance of one person precede the appointment of an another as heir. However, any other provisions in the text which precede the appointment of an heir are invalid. Antonius Silvanus (Ch. 1.1) obviously followed this rule, since he began his will by naming his son as heir.

But how much trust can we place in Justinian's sources from the sixth century AD as an accurate reflection of the law from the first century BC to the third century AD? The debate about the authenticity of the writings of the Roman jurists as transmitted by the compilers of the Digest is less concerned with accidental loss or corruption of the text in the transmission, such as transcription errors or the loss of pages from books, than with deliberate alterations by Emperor Justinian's compilers. The debate about the extent and the ramifications of such changes is called, 'interpolation criticism'.

1.2.2 Interpolation Criticism

We use the term interpolation (*interpolare*, literally 'to distort', 'to alter') to describe the changes that the compilers made to the classical texts to bring them into line with Justinian's law, without indicating their modifications. The imperial enactments that frame the compilations confirm that Emperor Justinian instructed his compilers to make changes of this kind. There is therefore little doubt that the commission exercised this prerogative in compiling the Digest.

However, it is difficult to identify a specific interpolation in any given passage, as there is rarely any reference material that would shed sufficient light on the legal or textual conditions prior to Justinian. Interpolation criticism therefore remains largely speculative. Moreover, most allegations of interpolation are based on prejudices and assumptions that invariably depend on the amount of trust a scholar has placed in the authenticity of the Digest in general. Scholars of the late nineteenth and early twentieth centuries had little faith in the authenticity of the texts. They considered certain expressions and 'dubious' words to be alterations made by the compilers and proof of interpolation. Moreover, they assumed that an (alleged) erroneous argument or a terminological flaw could hardly stem from a Roman jurist. These arguments carried more weight when combined. Hence a 'demonstrably' interpolated passage was cited to prove that a hitherto unsuspected text was also interpolated, even though the latter contained no indications of an interpolation. This fallacy can be observed when a passage that is suspected of being interpolated because of flaws in its reasoning is cited as proof for the interpolation of another passage, even when the two texts are stylistically similar but different in content and show no similarities in their respective patterns of argumentation. These methodological shortcomings led to a counter-movement, the 'critique to interpolation criticism', which started at the beginning of the twentieth century. These critical voices pointed out that Justinian's instruction was primarily directed at eliminating superfluities, i.e. the deletion of repetitions and obsolete laws, and sought to eliminate contradictions between different Roman jurists.

Interpolation criticism did not end until after World War II. It was the Austro-German scholar Max Kaser, in particular, who stressed the need to focus textual criticism on the examination of the content of the text. Accordingly, it was necessary to examine carefully in each case whether the alleged interpolation could correspond to a rational motive on the part of Justinian. Moreover, suspicions of an interpolation based solely on stylistic considerations should be routinely dismissed. A comparison with the material that has survived outside the compilation of Emperor Justinian confirms this approach. As far as can be discerned, the alterations made by the compilers are limited to stylistic standardisation and, above all, abbreviations. Admittedly, most of the comparative texts survive only as fragments or excerpts in collected editions from the fourth and fifth centuries AD, and thus offer only limited possibilities for comparison. Moreover, these sources themselves are not free from alterations due to transmission.

Outside of the *Corpus iuris civilis*, only a single work has survived, the Institutes of Gaius (second century AD), discovered in 1816.

1.2.3 *The Institutes of Gaius*

The Institutes date from around AD160 and their author, Gaius, was probably a teacher of law and probably came from the eastern provinces of the

Empire, where Greek was the predominant language. The work is divided into four books. First, it introduces the law student to the law of persons (*personae*, 'persons'). Second, the law of property (*res*, 'object', 'property') and third, procedural law (*actiones*, 'actions'). The Institutes are subsequently cited as '*Inst.Gai.*', followed by the relevant book and chapter. The work significantly enhances our understanding of ancient Roman law, not only because it offers an insight into the way law was taught during the time of the Principate, but also because it contains jural institutes and legal pronouncements that were omitted from Justinian's compilation or had fallen into desuetude. This is also true of the law of inheritance, which Gaius treats in a separate section.

1.3 *De testamentis et de legatis*

Gaius divides the chapter on the acquisition of property into two sections:

Overview 3: The Law of Inheritance in The Institutes of Gaius[3]

C.	Property Law (*res*)	II, 1–III, 225
I.	Division of objects	II, 1–17
II.	Singular acquisition of property	II, 18–96
III.	Universal acquisition of property	II, 97–III, 87
	1. Division	II, 97–100
	2. Acquisition of inheritance under a will	II, 101–190
	3. Digression: Legacies (*legata*)	II, 191–289
	4. Acquisition of inheritance on intestacy	III, 1–76
	5. Remaining universal acquisition	III, 77–87
IV.	Obligations (*obligationes*)	III, 88–225

The first part deals with the singular acquisition of property over objects among living persons. In the second part, Gaius discusses the universal acquisition of property, of which inheritance is the main example (highlighted in Overview 3). Here, he mentions testamentary succession and succession as prescribed by law without a will, i.e. inheritance on intestacy (from *intestato*, 'without a will'). In particular, Gaius also discusses legacies (from *legare*, 'to legate', 'to bequeath'), which give the beneficiary (legatee) the right over a certain object after the testator's death. Following the structure of the textbook, we would expect to find the treatment of legacies in the section on 'singular

---

[3] Ulrich Manthe, *Gaius Institutiones* (2nd edn, Wissenschaftliche Buchgesellschaft 2010) 8.

acquisition', but the fact that Gaius chose to add this to the will and intestate succession shows that he considered hereditary succession as a unit, treating inheritances and legacies together. Thus, the law of succession is conceived as a separate body of law under the title 'On Wills and Legacies' (*De testamentis et de legatis*).

1.3.1 The Complexity of the Roman Law of Inheritance

The further division of the section *De testamentis et de legatis* in Gaius' Institutes (second century AD) reveals the complexity of the Roman inheritance law.

Overview 4: Individual Titles of Chapters in the Sections treating Universal Acquisition in Gaius' Institutes

2.		Acquisition of inheritance under a will	II, 100–190
	a.	Different types of wills	II, 101–108
	b.	Soldiers' wills	II, 109–113
	c.	Appointment of heirs	II, 114–151a
	d.	Family members as heirs and heirs from outside the family	II, 152–173
	e.	Substitute heirs	II, 174–184
	f.	Appointment of slaves as heirs	II, 185–190
3.		Digression: Legacies	II, 191–289
	a.	Justification of the digression	II, 191
	b.	Different types of legacies	II, 192–223
	c.	Legal limitations to legacies	II, 224–228
	d.	Invalid legacies	II, 229–234
	e.	Penal legacies	II, 235–237
	f.	Bequeathing to unspecified beneficiaries	II, 238–245
	g.	*fideicommissa*	II, 246–267
	h.	Differences between *fideicommissa* and legacies	II, 268–289
4.		Acquisition of inheritance without a will	III, 1–76
	a.	Order of intestacy under *ius civile*	III, 1–24
	b.	Praetorian law of inheritance (*bonorum possessio*)	III, 25–38
	c.	The estate of freedmen	III, 39–42

4.		Acquisition of inheritance without a will	III, 1–76
	d.	The estate of freedwomen	III, 43–44
	e.	The right to inherit of the patron's descendants, of a female patron, and of her descendants	III, 45–54
	f.	The estate of a Junian Latin	III, 55–76

Overview 4 shows that, in contrast to the general rules for making wills, special rules applied to the will of a soldier (see 2b). In addition, the possibility of setting up *fideicommissa* (see 3g) was added to the option of bequeathing legacies, since the testator could make legacies both according to a prescribed form and formlessly (*fideicommissa*). Finally, a special praetorian law of inheritance (*bonorum possessio*, see 4b) was created within the order of intestacy, alongside the *ius civile* inheritance law. There were also special regulations for the inheritance on intestacy of former slaves (see 4c–f). The very structure of Gaius' Institutes reveals two fundamental features of the Roman law of inheritance, namely the variety of legal institutions with a similar aim and a large number of special and particular laws for specific groups of people and specific situations. This heterogeneity of the Roman inheritance law has been perceived by scholars as a 'juristic shortcoming':

> Regarding its structure, the law of inheritance of this period [of classical law] lags behind most other areas of private law. Like the law of guardianship, it is complicated and convoluted. Numerous exceptions permeate the general rules and sometimes obscure them.[4]

However, we should remember that this complexity of the Roman inheritance law is the outcome of a historical development. Therefore, exactly this supposed 'weak spot' of Roman inheritance law can provide a lot of valuable information for legal historians. Namely, the Roman law of succession enables us to examine the origins, growth and the interplay of various legal stages of Roman private law. It is a telling feature of the development of Roman law that the various stages of its development do not supersede each other but, instead, accumulate. This is why the Roman law of inheritance proves such a fascinating topic for legal historians:

---

[4] Max Kaser, *Das römische Privatrecht. Erster Abschnitt* (Beck 1971) §157. III, 671. This view is already found in Fritz Schulz, *Classical Roman Law* (OUP 1951) 203 who points out that 'Classical jurisprudence discussed the law of succession on death with obvious predilection and at the same time admirable delicacy, but [...] This part of classical law was highly complicated and to a large extent perplexedly entangled, but the classical lawyers did little to simplify it. Their professional relish for details and for vexed questions was too strong for them and absorbed in the spinning of this fine network, they forgot the maxim *simplicitas legum amica*'.

> However, it is just this characteristic [the fine network] of the Roman succession law which renders it a particularly interesting field for legal historians. The labyrinthine law cries out for historical analysis; available materials are unusually rich; all factors in Roman legal evolution are clearly visible, particularly the strength of Roman jurisprudence and its limits and shortcomings.[5]

Like no other area of Roman private law, the Roman law of inheritance offers a wealth of material suitable for illustrating and observing in detail the legal evolution and the accumulation of the different layers of Roman private law.

The Romans stubbornly preserved the archaic, which explains why we find, especially in the Roman law of inheritance, an accumulation of different private law systems within one area of law. In fact, the proverbial 'traditionalism' of the Roman jurists prevented them from discarding or repealing age-old legal pronouncements. Instead, the newly fashioned law always took its place alongside the existing one, without replacing it. This tendency led to an almost inevitable layering of legal sources of different historical origins and divergent legal objectives, reflected in the legal reasoning of Roman jurists.

1.3.2 Legal Reasoning of Roman Jurists

The jurists' legal writing preserved in the Digest contain primarily case law, i.e. opinions and decisions on individual cases. For this reason, Roman law has been described as 'casuistic', i.e. developed on a case-by-case basis. In this process, new legal rules were created when a hitherto unforeseen case had to be solved or was brought forth by a jurist for the purpose of discussing a new legal problem. However, the jurists' newly created law required a foundation in the existing one; the legitimacy of the new law is derived from the continuity with the established legal order, which guarantees the approval of the new individual legal opinion by the legal peers. This is why the casuistic method of legal development is by its very nature conservative, allowing only gradual changes in perception. Legislation, by contrast, is always receptive to change, reform and new beginnings. Whenever a statute or an imperial enactment led to conflict or friction with the tradition, it was left to the jurists to reconcile the different requirements in each case. This adjustment, too, was the result of a case-law decision.

1.3.3 Three Main Questions

Given the peculiarities of the Roman legal order and Roman legal reasoning, Roman private law can only be presented and understood as an evolutionary process. And it is precisely this evolution of legal thought that this study of

---

[5] Schulz (n 4) 204.

Roman inheritance law will analyse. Therefore, all institutes of the Roman law of inheritance will be examined against the background of three main questions:

1. What stages of development can be identified and distinguished for a legal institute or for Roman inheritance law itself?
2. What principles govern each stage of development, and what characterises their specific nature?
3. How do Roman jurists draw from the different layers of law and how do they reconcile conflicting layers in each individual case?

The answers to these three guiding questions will be formulated separately for each institute of inheritance law at the end of each chapter ('Concluding considerations'). A general conclusion for the entire field of inheritance law and its development in Rome will be drawn in the final chapter (Ch. 10).

1.4 On the Structure of the Present Study

The individual chapters of the main part (Ch. 3 to 9) deal either with a single subject of the law of inheritance or with a separate legal institute, presented in its historical layers, thus revealing its multilayered structure. However, not all subjects of the Roman law of inheritance are dealt with. For example, the treatment of testamentary guardianship, manumission and gifts on account of death are left out because of the singularity of these topics. Instead, this book aims to present the basic concepts of the law of inheritance in all their complexity as revealed by the sources. In the course of the presentation, public and criminal law issues are also examined in terms of their relevance to the private law of inheritance. In addition, rules that seem excessively complex from today's perspective have been included in the interest of a complete historical reconstruction. To this end, the text of the sources has been reproduced (with translations) and commented on directly. For the reader, this exposure to the texts has the advantage of offering first-hand access to the legal reasoning of the Roman jurists.

Where it is deemed necessary, overviews have been included to summarise the detailed discussion, highlighting the main conclusions. In contrast, the discussion of scholarly controversies has been avoided; an updated bibliography is provided at the end of the book.

The following chapter (Ch. 2) provides the reader with key dates in Roman history and elementary information on the development of Roman law, which is necessary for the understanding of the subsequent chapters.

2

The General Historical and Legal Framework

More than any other area of law, the Roman law of inheritance is determined by the cultural imprint of its society. Therefore, a thorough understanding and a discussion of its historical evolution requires sufficient knowledge of the general historical and legal-historical framework within which the development of the law of inheritance took place. The historical development will be explained before discussing the different stages of the Roman legal evolution.

2.1 The General Historical Framework

The history of Rome can be divided into three periods: the Republic (510BC–27BC), the Principate (27BC–AD284) and Late Antiquity (AD306–565).

Overview 5: A Chronological Table

Roman Republic	510–27BC	Beginning: the deposition of the last king
		End: conferral of the *imperium* on Octavian
Principate (The Empire)	27BC–AD284	Beginning: Augustus (Octavian)
		End: the beginning of Diocletian's reforms
Late Antiquity	AD306–565	Beginning: Constantine I
		End: Justinian I

It remains to elucidate these key figures and to focus on specific events and some of the players who were instrumental in the evolution of Roman law.

2.1.1 The Roman Republic

According to Roman historians, the Roman Republic began with the deposition of the last king whose jurisdiction had extended over Rome and its surroundings (Latium). After the fall of the kings, power seemed to have fallen into the hands of the influential and powerful families (patricians), who would now occupy all of the political positions. The king was succeeded by the *praetor maximus* ('highest magistrate'). His name '*praetor*' (from *praeire*, literally 'to walk in front') suggests that he was also the leader of the army. Unlike the kingship, this office was reassigned annually and was thus held alternately by members of the patricians.

Those members of the population who did not have a share in political power gradually developed a sense of their own class status and were called 'plebeians' (from *plebs*, literally 'the mass'). As they had to fight in Rome's wars, they began to demand their share of political power, and the patricians gradually gave in to their demands. In 494BC the plebeians were able to appoint two magistrates from their ranks. This was meant to counterbalance the power of the patricians, which was wielded by the *praetor maximus*. These magistrates were elected as representatives of the *plebs* (*tribuni plebis*) and were considered sacrosanct (from *sacrosanctus*, 'most sacred') even by the patricians. As a result, the tribunes of the people could protect the plebeians from the despotism of the patrician magistrates by declaring their opposition (*veto*) to patrician power without being held accountable themselves. During the fifth century BC, the number of patrician high magistrates (*praetores*) doubled, as did the number of *tribuni plebis,* bringing them to four each. The law, however, remained firmly in the hands of the patrician families, who appointed the priests (*pontifices*) charged with interpreting the pronouncements of both divine and human law. According to Roman historiography, the priests used this prerogative to the advantage of their class.

This abuse of power led to another popular uprising. The revolt led to the first comprehensive compilation of legally binding rules, namely the law of the twelve tables (*lex duodecim tabularum*), enacted in 450BC.[1] Roman legal historians claim that this legislation was based on Greek models. A delegation is said to have travelled to various Greek cities and returned with ten tables of law. However, the story goes, there were gaps in the application of the law which were later filled by the enactment of two more tables. Although the original text was no longer available by the time of the Republic, the law of the twelve tables served as a reference and starting point for the legal development

---

[1] The law itself has not survived, but it can be reconstructed from citations, mainly from legal and annalistic sources. See now Olivero Diliberto, *Materiali per la palingenesia delle XII Tavole, I* (Edizioni universitarie della Sardegna 1992); Michel Humbert, Andrew D. E. Lewis and Michael H. Crawford, 'Lex duodecim tabularum' in Michael H. Crawford (ed), *Roman Statutes II* (Institute of Classical Studies 1996). Also noteworthy is the bilingual edition (German and Latin) by Dieter Flach and Andreas Flach (eds), *Das Zwölftafelgesetz. Leges XII tabularum* (WBG Academic 2004).

throughout the whole period under consideration. For example, the Roman historian Livy, who wrote between 27BC and AD17, famously declared that the law of the twelve tables was 'the source of all public and private law' (*fons omnis publici privatique est iuris*, Liv. 3.34.6).

However, the law did not resolve the ongoing disputes between the patricians and the plebeians. According to Roman historiography, it took further struggles before the plebeians gradually gained access to further offices, especially to high magistracies such as the praetorship and the consulship. After the sack and destruction of Rome by the Gauls in 387BC, it is said that the efforts to rebuild the city led to a decisive escalation between the two orders, resulting in a compromise between them. The *leges Liciniae Sextiae* of 367BC provided for two consuls, one of whom could be a plebeian, to exercise supreme power in the state. In return, the patricians were given the privilege of holding two newly created offices.

One of these was the praetorship, which was in charge for settling legal disputes between Roman citizens. This praetor, known as the *praetor urbanus*, had the power to adjudicate and therefore had judicial authority (*ius dicere*, 'to declare the law'). Originally, the judicial power of the praetor was intended to supervise enforcement measures, namely the seizure of the defendant himself and of the defendant's property. This supervision initially consisted of verifying whether the defendant had confessed to his obligation or whether his obligation was manifest, which later led to the praetor's review of the outcome of the proceedings. However, the praetor did not conduct the trial himself. Instead, he appointed a private judge (*iudex*) to preside over the parties and to issue the judgment to be enforced. The delegation of the litigation to a judge led to a division of the legal proceedings. The first stage of a trial was before the praetor (*in iure*), the second before the private judge (*apud iudicem*). This division remained in place until the Empire and must be considered a specific feature of Roman civil procedure.

The changes in the internal organisation of the state went hand in hand with military conquests by which Rome subjugated Italy before defeating Carthage in its quest for supremacy in the Mediterranean (First Punic War 264–241BC; Second Punic War 218–201BC). This expansion of Roman rule encouraged trade between Rome and non-Roman cities. It is in this context that we find the creation of a new praetorship. Its holder had jurisdiction over proceedings among non-Romans and between non-Romans and Romans. This office of the *praetor peregrinus* ('praetor for foreigners') was created in 242BC. From this point on, two different spheres of praetorian jurisdiction can be distinguished. The *praetor urbanus* ('praetor of the city') decided disputes between Romans, while the *praetor peregrinus* was responsible for disputes between Romans and non-Romans and for civil proceedings between non-Romans only. Subsequently, more praetorships were created for the provinces, i.e. the regions that Rome held in permanent custody, which were named after the term used for the jurisdiction of a magistrate (*provincia*). Eventually, under the dictatorship of Sulla (82–79BC), the number of praetors was fixed at eight. In 81BC it was also decided that both the *praetor urbanus* and the *praetor peregrinus*, after leaving their office in Rome, would serve for one year in the province, where a former praetor (*propraetor*) would assume the office of the governor of the province, exercising jurisdiction over all its inhabitants. The government of each praetor followed the rules laid down by the praetor himself at the beginning of his year in office (*edictum*, literally 'publication'; hence 'edict'). Initially, this edict was merely a 'guideline' for the administration of the praetor. He could therefore deviate from his edict in certain cases. However, since the enactment of the *lex Cornelia de iurisdictione* (67BC), the praetor was bound by his edict and had to grant the legal devices, actions and defences which were published in his edict to everyone. It is worth noting that the edict did not simply implement the content of the law of the twelve tables and statutes (*leges*). Rather, the praetor used his judicial authority to add formulas (*formulae*) of legal actions that he had created with the advice of Roman jurists.

In the last century BC, the Roman Republic was in a state crisis: Rome was ravaged by the internal upheavals of civil war and threatened by external forces. In the midst of these troubles, Octavian (63BC–AD14) was able to gain control of Rome by averting the external threat. The Senate then bestowed upon him the honorific title of 'Augustus' (27BC) and invested him with special powers to restore the republican order after the civil war. In this way, the Republic was formally restored, while essentially a new form of government was established: the Principate.

2.1.2 The Principate

The granting of special powers to Octavian in 27BC marked the beginning of a new era that lasted until the beginning of Diocletian's reign (AD284). The new form of government was called the 'Principate'. The name derives from '*princeps*' (literally 'the first man') and describes Octavian's special powers, initially granted to him personally, but later passed on to his successors by virtue of their status as emperors. This established a unique legal position for the emperor. Interestingly, although the emperor's self-perception and claim to power would change over the course of the Empire, as would the political circumstances, the legal construct remained essentially the same. This construction was based on two legal competences which had already existed during the time of the Republic but which, when combined, gave the *princeps* extraordinary powers. On the one hand, he possessed the unrestricted and temporally unlimited power of the tribune of the plebs (*tribunicia potestas*). On the other hand, he exercised the unrestricted powers of the governor (*imperium proconsulare*). Because the *princeps* was able to exercise these two competences without the institutional constraints of the republican offices that had existed before, he possessed extraordinary powers. With the powers of a tribune, the emperor could veto any order issued by a magistrate in order to protect a citizen from arbitrariness – the original rationale for this prerogative. Then again, the tribune was immune, i.e. sacrosanct, so no other veto would have any effects on him. Furthermore, since the emperor did not hold the office of the tribune, he could apply the *tribunicia potestas*, which released him from the restrictions and obligations of the office. The *imperium proconsulare*, conversely, was of paramount importance for foreign policy, especially for the administration of the provinces; all the more so because the power (*imperium*) granted to Octavian was unlimited in time and scope (*maius et infinitum*), unlike the power usually held by governors during the Republic. As a result, the *princeps* had permanent command of the troops and jurisdiction over all the inhabitants of the provinces. He also controlled the governors, whose jurisdiction over their assigned provinces had to yield to his overarching *imperium*.

The outlined form of government under the Principate admittedly lacked a secure order of succession, as the power would always revert to the people upon the death of the *princeps*. This made it necessary for him to choose a successor during his lifetime and to allow the latter to participate in the two main offices that comprised the position with a view to the future. Furthermore, the *princeps* relied on the Empire's elite to secure the position of his successor. The jurists played an important role in assisting the *princeps* in this respect, and received a special imperial promotion in return. Reforms under the Emperors Augustus (27BC–AD14), Hadrian (AD117–138) and Septimius Severus (AD193–211) turned the Roman jurists into the main actors of imperial law and legislation.

When Octavian took office, he is said to have granted certain jurists the *ius respondendi* ('right to give authoritative opinions'). The purpose of this privilege was to allow its holder to issue *responsa* (legal opinions, literally 'answers') in the emperor's name in order to reinforce his opinion with special authority. Therefore, the fact that the emperor privileged the jurist's authority to deliver *responsa*, strengthened the standing of such legal opinions in legal proceedings. Whereas the previously privately commissioned *responsa* of Roman jurists had been consulted by the praetor and the *iudex* merely as private opinions on the law, *responsa* in the name of the emperor were considered legally binding (*lex*, literally 'legislation'). As a result, if several jurists agreed on a particular opinion and issued it in the emperor's name, the judge had to follow that opinion and could not base his judgment on dissenting legal opinions. The judge was only free to choose which opinion to adopt if the individual *responsa* differed from each other. In conclusion, the imperial intervention in the practice of the jurists brought about legal uniformity and resulted in imperial control over the law applied by the courts.

Emperor Hadrian's proclamation of an *edictum perpetuum* ('perpetual edict'), binding on the urban praetors and the governors of the provinces, reveals the same rationale. The annual edicts of the magistrates had been the result of their personal judicial authority, although their content was based on the edict of their predecessor. But now Emperor Hadrian commissioned the jurist Julian (second century AD) to draw up a generally applicable version of the praetor's edict. This edict was enacted by a *senatusconsultum* around AD130 and became the immutable basis for the administration of justice in Rome and the provinces. The jurists, however, continued to have the power to interpret and develop the provisions of the edict. But the inflexibility of the edict now significantly limited the legislative power of the magistrates and, above all, placed it under the control of the *princeps*.

In many ways, the era of the Severan emperors (AD193–235) marked the culmination of the influence of the Roman jurists in the affairs of state. As early as the time of Emperor Hadrian (AD117–138), jurists were directly involved in the *princeps's* legislative process, both in the imperial council (*consilium*) and in the imperial chancellery. The Severan era produced three jurists whose writings established them as the most influential exponents of their profession and who held positions as imperial civil servants and members of the imperial council. These were Aemilius Papinianus (Papinian), Iulius Paulus (Paul) and Domitius Ulpianus (Ulpian). All three held the office of the *praefectus praetorio* and were the emperor's direct representatives in matters of civil administration and justice. They were thus in charge of both civil and criminal adjudication, and could also carry out appeal proceedings (*appellationes*) against decisions of lower instances. But even those Roman jurists in less elevated positions influenced imperial legislation by preparing, as civil servants, imperial *rescripta* (from *rescribere*, literally 'to write back', 'to reply in writing') to legal questions from across the Empire and by advising the imperial court. The jurist's dual role was characteristic of the entire imperial period and is also evident in their 'private' scholarly production (legal writings), which has been collected in Justinian's Digest.

Overview 6 provides a chronological account of the most frequently quoted jurists in the context of the respective imperial dynasty:

Overview 6: The Jurisprudence during the Empire

27BC–AD96 Augustus 27BC–AD14, successive Julio-Claudian emperors 27BC–AD68, Flavian emperors AD69–96	**Labeo** **Sabinus/Nerva/Cassius** **Proculus**
AD96–193 Adopted emperors: • Trajan AD98–117 • Hadrian AD117–138 • Antoninus Pius AD138–161 • Marcus Aurelius AD161–180	**Javolenus** **Neratius/Celsus** **Julian** **Gaius/Pomponius** **Marcellus/Q. Cervidius Scaevola**
AD193–235 Severan emperors: • Septimius Severus AD193–211 • Antoninus Caracalla AD211–217 • Elagabalus AD218–222 • Alexander Severus AD222–235	**Papinian** **Paul** **Ulpian** **Modestinus**

The assignment of a jurist to a particular imperial reign can shed light on the framework conditions of his legal writing and allow us to place him in the genealogy of jurists. However, the details of this part of the history of Roman jurisprudence, as well as the individual biographies and the description of the writings of the different jurists of the time of the Principate, will not be covered in this book. It must be emphasised that the Principate, characterised by the proximity of the emperor to jurisprudence created the preconditions for the establishment of legal writing as a separate branch of scholarship. This development came to an end in the period following the Severan dynasty, known as the age of the 'barracks emperors' (AD235–284) because of the frequent changes of rulers, mainly through military coups. During this period, Roman jurisprudence lost the prominent and influential position it had held since the time of Octavian. As a result of the violent changes of government, the military became the dominant aspect of imperial administration, although the imperial chancellery continued to issue legal opinions and advise the emperor on legal matters. Moreover, the jurists of the Principate continued to exert influence through their legal writings, which were still read and applied by their less prominent successors. This echo of the earlier law is particularly noticeable during the reigns of the Emperors Diocletian (Eastern Roman Empire AD284–305) and Maximian (Western Roman Empire AD286–305). They sought to consolidate their power over the Roman Empire by reorganising the state, while consciously following the paradigm of the Principate in their administration of justice.

2.1.3 Late Antiquity

The rise of Christianity as a state religion under Emperor Constantine I (AD306–337) marked the beginning of Late Antiquity. The invocation of divine legitimation altered the justification of power and changed its manifestations. Moreover, Christianity had an impact on the content of the law. Nevertheless, the writings of the jurists of the Principate and the enactments of previous Roman emperors were still known by the fourth century AD and continued to be transmitted and disseminated. The Migration Period (fourth and fifth centuries AD) caused the disintegration of the legal and administrative unity of the Empire. While the ancient world survived in the East of the Empire, the Western Roman Empire ended with the death of Emperor Julius Nepos (AD474–480), the last Western emperor recognised by Byzantium.

2.1.4 The Temporal Framework of the Study

The time span for which the development of Roman inheritance law is to be examined is limited in comparison with the time frame outlined. It lies mainly between the first century BC and the third century AD (highlighted in Overview 7), if only because of the availability of sources (Ch. 1.2). From a historical perspective, the presentation thus covers the late Republic and the Empire (Principate).

Overview 7: The Temporal Frame of this Textbook

The Roman Republic	510–27BC	Beginning: the deposition of the last king
		End: conferral of the *imperium* on Octavian
The Principate (The Empire)	27BC–AD284	Beginning: Augustus (Octavian)
		End: the beginning of Diocletian's reforms
Late Antiquity	AD306–565	Beginning: Constantine I
		End: Justinian I

As the historical sketch has shown, this period of almost four hundred years is not a homogeneous epoch. However, Justinian's compilation of Roman legal writings (Digest) has almost exclusively preserved texts from this period, with the emphasis on the tradition of the second and third centuries AD. Our perception of Roman law has therefore been shaped by the jurists of these two centuries.

2.2 The Different Layers of Roman Private Law

The Roman jurists of the second and third centuries AD distinguished between different layers of law, or more precisely between legal rules at the same stage of development. The presentation of the different layers of law with regard to their respective origin and legal character can be considered as an essential part of Roman legal writing. The Roman jurists did not classify the different legal sources hierarchically, but described them 'genetically' in order to highlight the changes that a new layer of law brought to the existing rules. Scholars have used the wording of the Roman jurists to characterise the Roman legal order. It is customary in research to speak of the 'layers of Roman law' (German: *Rechtsschichten des römischen Rechts*). The term is used to describe the historical accumulation of rules of different origins and differing aims as a distinctive feature of Roman private law (Ch. 1.3.1). Since the different layers of law also shape the institutions of the law of inheritance, their delineation, as discerned in the writings of the jurists, will be discussed in due course.

2.2.1 Ius naturale

The *ius naturale* ('natural law') forms the theoretical point of departure for any reflection on the different layers of law. It should not be confused with the modern concept of 'natural law', as the following text shows:

> *Ulpianus, libro primo institutionum: Ius naturale est, quod natura omnia animalia docuit: Nam ius istud non humani generis proprium, sed omnium animalium, quae in terra, quae in mari nascuntur, avium quoque commune est. Hinc descendit maris atque feminae coniunctio, quam nos matrimonium appellamus, hinc liberorum procreatio, hinc educatio: Videmus etenim cetera quoque animalia, feras etiam istius iuris peritia censeri. (D.1.1.1.3.)*

> Ulpian, Institutes, book 1: Natural law is what nature has taught to all living beings, since it is not peculiar to humankind, but is common to all animals, whether born on land or in the sea, even to birds. It is from this law that the union of husband and wife, which we call marriage, and the procreation and the raising of children, are derived. We see, indeed, that all other animals, even wild beasts, are also covered by the knowledge of this law. (D.1.1.1.3.)

Ulpian (third century AD) defines *ius naturale* as what is given by nature, i.e. found in its primary state, as opposed to man-made law. The fact that man-made law can differ from the original *ius naturale* is a point of reference for critical legal theory:

> *Paulus, 14 ad Sabinum: Ius pluribus modis dicitur: Uno modo, cum id quod semper aequum ac bonum est ius dicitur, ut est ius naturale. Altero modo,*

quod omnibus aut pluribus in quaque civitate utile est, ut est ius civile. [...]
(D.1.1.11.)

Paul, Sabinus, book 14: The term 'law' is used in different ways. On the one hand, when it describes what is always just and good, it is called law, i.e. *ius naturale*. On the other hand, when it describes what is expedient for all or for the majority in a given society, it is called *ius civile* [...]. (D.1.1.11.)

Whereas *ius naturale* adheres to the precepts of general justice (*aequitas*), the *ius civile*, the law made for the members of a particular local community, serves the purpose of utility (*utilitas*). Therefore, the *ius civile* may privilege certain groups or individuals, which goes against the idea of universal justice, hence the *ius naturale*. Therefore, the layer of *ius naturale*, like *aequitas*, can be invoked to adjust existing rules or to request their modification.

2.2.2 Ius civile

The *ius civile* forms the fundamental, man-made layer of law:

> *Inst.Gai.1.1.: Omnes populi, qui legibus et moribus reguntur, partim suo proprio, partim communi omnium hominum iure utuntur: Nam quod quisque populus ipse sibi ius constituit, id ipsius proprium est vocaturque ius civile, quasi ius proprium civitatis; [...].*

> Inst.Gai.1.1.: All peoples governed by laws and customs use a law which is partly their own and partly common to humankind. For what each people establishes for itself as law is its own and is called *ius civile*, as if it were peculiar to that (local) community; [...].

The *ius civile* is the law applicable within a community (*civitas*); therefore, the protection of this law was granted only to those who were citizens of that particular community.[2] With regard to the city of Rome, the law of the twelve tables (*ca.* 450BC) and other statutes (*leges*) from the time of the Republic are the primary sources of the Roman *ius civile*. The *ius gentium* (literally 'law of the peoples') formed the counterpart of the *ius civile*. It extended beyond the borders of Rome and constituted a separate layer of law. Unlike today's public international law, *ius gentium* was not limited to relations between different states, but also included private law, i.e. legal contacts between citizens of different polities, such as commercial transactions. The law of inheritance under consideration does not make use of the *ius gentium*. This can be explained by its close connection with family law, which is normally restricted to persons

---

[2] A more archaic term for *ius civile* is *ius Quiritium*, 'the law of the *Quirites*'. *Quirites* was the ancient name for Roman citizens.

of the same citizenship. Consequently, since the law of inheritance in many respects served to perpetuate family ties after death, there was little room for its application to non-Romans (*peregrinus*, 'alien', 'foreigner'). To the extent that the law of inheritance later became relevant to non-Romans, the gaps in the *ius civile* were filled by praetorian law (*ius praetorium*) and imperial legislation.

2.2.3 Ius praetorium *and* ius honorarium

The *ius praetorium*, or *ius honorarium*, forms the second layer of man-made law:

> *Papinianus, 2 definitionum: Ius praetorium est, quod praetores introduxerunt adiuvandi vel supplendi vel corrigendi iuris civilis gratia propter utilitatem publicam. Quod et honorarium dicitur ad honorem praetorum sic nominatum. (D.1.1.7.1.)*

> Papinian, Definitions, book 2: Praetorian law is what the praetors have introduced to aid, supplement or correct the *ius civile* for the public good. This is also called 'honorary law', named after the office of the praetors. (D.1.1.7.1.)

The term *ius praetorium* is derived from the office of the magistrate (*praetor*, or more generally, *honor*, 'office', hence 'honorary law') and refers to the fact that the law is based on the praetor's edict. Its purpose stemmed from the purpose of the praetorian edict, which was to enforce the law. The edict provided the formulas for the actions and exceptions necessary to grant legal protection. For this reason, the *ius praetorium* is understood mainly in its relation to the *ius civile*, as the sum of all the legal principles and institutions applicable to a Roman citizen. From this perspective, praetorian law served primarily to enforce the *ius civile* and to fill in its statutory gaps by means of edictal provisions. However, the legal protection granted by the praetor could also contradict the *ius civile*. This 'corrective' function, like the entire *ius praetorium*, could be justified by the public office of the praetor.

The praetor's interventions inevitably led to tensions between the *ius civile* and the *ius praetorium*. The competitive relation between the two jural layers outlasted the Principate. Although the edict had been promulgated by Emperor Hadrian (AD117–138) as part of the imperial legislation (Ch. 2.1.2), Roman jurists continued to refer to its provisions as *ius praetorium*. In the same vein, imperial jurists perceived the traditional *ius civile* as a separate layer of law, even though imperial law ordered new tenets and directly modified it.

2.2.4 Ius civile *and* ius novum *under the Principate*

Imperial law is considered the third layer of man-made law, consisting of *senatus consulta* and imperial constitutions (*constitutiones*). Imperial jurists held that both types of imperial pronouncement had the force of law:

Inst.Gai.1.4.: Senatus consultum est, quod senatus iubet atque constituit; idque legis vicem optinet, quamvis [de ea re] fuerit quaesitum.

Inst.Gai.1.4.: A *senatusconsultum* is what the Senate issues and enacts. And this too has the force of a legislative act, although this is disputed.

A *senatusconsultum* is a decree issued by the Senate. Gaius (second century AD) considers its normative value equivalent to statutory law, but acknowledges that his view is controversial. His succinct comment refers to the evolution of the Senate during the Principate from an advisory role to a legislative body. In the Republic, the Senate had been an assembly of former high magistrates (praetors and consuls). Its main competences included the constitutional approval (*auctoritas patrum*) of laws (*leges*) and the consultation (*consultum*, from *consulere*, 'to ask for advice') of the magistrates. At the request of the supreme magistrates, the Senate met to deliberate on their demands. Under the Empire, this right to submit motions to the Senate (*ius agendi cum senatu*) fell to the *princeps* by virtue of his *tribunicia potestas* (Ch. 2.1.2). As the emperors' power grew and the right of the emperor to address the Senate (*oratio principis*) carried more weight against senatorial deliberations, the *senatusconsultum* became a source of law, i.e. generally binding legislation.

The enactments of the *princeps*, grouped under the collective term 'constitutiones' (from *constitutum, constituere*, 'to set up'), also became legally binding:

Ulpianus, 1 institutionum: pr. Quod principi placuit, legis habet vigorem: Utpote cum lege regia, quae de imperio eius lata est, populus ei et in eum omne suum imperium et potestatem conferat.
(1) Quodcumque igitur imperator per epistulam et subscriptionem statuit vel cognoscens decrevit vel de plano interlocutus est vel edicto praecepit, legem esse constat. Haec sunt quas volgo constitutiones appellamus. (D.1.4.1pr.-1)

Ulpian, Institutes, book 1: pr. Whatever pleases the *princeps* has the force of law, since the people have conferred upon him all authority and power by a royal ordinance (*lex regia*), which was enacted with regard to his *imperium*.
(1) Therefore, whatever the emperor decrees, whether by letter or by signature, whether he declares after deliberation, whether he decides formlessly in an interlocutory decision, or whether he orders through an edict, has the force of law. We commonly call these decrees 'constitutions'. (D.1.4.1pr.-1)

Ulpian (third century AD) explains the binding nature of the constitutions by the fact that the *princeps* himself was appointed to his position by a royal ordinance (*lex regia*). This royal law was probably linked to a law confirming the right of higher magistrates to assume power (*lex de imperio*). Such a law has been preserved on a bronze tablet for Emperor Vespasian (AD69–79) and is thought to have existed for other emperors as well. With this inaugural law, the people and the Senate conferred imperial prerogatives on the new *princeps*. According to Ulpian, since the people and the Senate could enact statutes, the *princeps* also had the right to make laws.

With regard to the different kinds of imperial enactments (*constitutiones*), let us turn first to the edicts (*edicta*). Under the Republic, an edict was an order issued by a magistrate within his jurisdiction to lay down the general rules of his office (Ch. 2.1.1). Under the Empire, the *princeps,* as holder of the *imperium proconsulare maius et infinitum,* was given the power to issue edicts of general application. The most famous and perhaps most important of these was the *Constitutio Antoniniana,* issued by Emperor Caracalla in AD212 (after Antonius 'Caracalla'), which granted Roman citizenship to all free inhabitants of the Roman Empire.

In contrast to the edict, the remaining constitutions dealt with individual cases. The most important of these were the *rescripta* (from *rescribere,* 'to write back', 'to answer in writing'), which were legal opinions issued by the imperial chancellery at the request of a petitioner. The specific form of the rescript depended on its addressee. If addressed to dignitaries, imperial magistrates or a community, it was a letter (*epistula*). If addressed to a private individual, however, the imperial rescript was written under the original request without any formal requirements; hence, the name *subscriptio* (literally 'underwriting'; hence, 'signature'). Initially, this legal advice was only binding for the specific case referred to in the petition. Thus, if a judge, as a civil servant of the imperial administration, was confronted with an imperial rescript in a case, he was bound by it for reasons of hierarchy. In addition, rescripts also acquired normative force in that they were cited in other disputes raising a legal question similar to the original issue. Similarly, imperial judgments (*decreta*) or interlocutory decisions (*interlocutiones*) were applied to other cases by virtue of the emperor's authority.

The perception of the imperial pronouncements as equivalent to legislation enacted by the people (*lex*) explains why the imperial law was even considered a source of the *ius civile*:

> *Papinianus 2 definitionum: Ius autem civile est, quod ex legibus, plebis scitis, senatus consultis, decretis principum, auctoritate prudentium venit. (D.1.1.7pr.)*

> Papinian, Definitions, book 2: The *ius civile,* however, comprises all that stems from laws, plebiscites, *senatusconsulta,* imperial decrees, and the authority of eminent jurists. (D.1.1.7pr.)

According to Papinian, the laws of the Republic (*leges*), the plebiscites (*plebiscita*), the *senatusconsulta* and the imperial judgments (*decreta principum*) were all sources of the *ius civile*. Finally, he mentions the authority of distinguished jurists (*auctoritas prudentium*) as a source of the *ius civile*. The latter refers to the opinions given by jurists to litigating parties, to praetors and even to the emperor, or defended in their legal writings. The scholarly consensus among different jurists on the correct application of the law in a particular case or on an abstract question formed the basis for the validity of these opinions. At the same time, the privilege of the *ius respondendi*, first granted by Augustus, added strength to the opinions of such distinguished jurists (Ch. 2.1.2).

Papinian's catalogue of legal sources shows that, despite its archaic origins, the *ius civile* continued to change until the third century AD, and that the imperial law was an important factor in this change. When Papinian cites imperial judgments (*decreta*) as an example of *ius civile*, he is referring to this continuity. The close connection between *ius civile* and imperial law is also evident in the fact that imperial constitutions mainly contain applications of the existing *ius civile* and only rarely introduce abrupt changes and completely new principles. Only when the need arose in a specific case was the existing law modified and adapted to the given requirements. Obviously, the case-law method of the Roman jurists (Ch. 1.3.2) had set a precedent for the emperor's gradual application of the law. We do, however, also find the *senatusconsulta*, by which the emperor pronounced a new and diverging law (*ius novum*), which openly repealed the traditional *ius civile*.

In sum, the imperial law, cannot be seen merely as a third layer of law added to the established *ius civile* and *ius praetorium*. Rather, in its quest for comprehensiveness, the imperial law embraces the existing legal order and incorporates it insofar as it conforms to the ruler's legal policy. This self-conception of imperial law reflects the constitutional form of the Principate. In the same way that the *princeps* appropriated the prerogatives of certain offices of the Republic in order to legitimise his power and thus exceed republican authority (Ch. 2.1.2), the imperial law absorbed its republican predecessor and extended it according to its own imperial rationale.

The Roman emperor's adherence to republican legal concepts is striking, even when the imperial legislation deliberately created *ius novum* (new law). The vectors of *ius novum* were, on the one hand, the *senatusconsulta* and, on the other hand, the imperial courts. Although the decree of the Senate already existed in the Republic, it acquired force of law only under the Principate. Similarly, a procedural competence from republican times, '*cognitio*', originally referred to an ad hoc judicial inquiry in special circumstances. In imperial times, the republican model was used to set up special courts that applied a *cognitio extra ordinem* (literally 'a special procedure') on a permanent basis.

The very term '*cognitio extra ordinem*' indicates that in this procedure the courts did not follow the praetorian edict, but only the rules laid down by the emperor. The particularities of the *cognitio extra ordinem* concerned both the procedural aspect of the proceedings and the substantive law applied by the courts.

Although the extraordinary powers of the emperor became an important source of the *ius novum* throughout the Empire, it remained officially limited to specific issues and imperial jurisdiction. However, since the imperial *cognitio extra ordinem* coexisted with existing forms of adjudication, it forced the latter to compete and adapt. As a result, the *ius novum* created by the *cognitio* gradually replaced the legal order established by the *ius civile* and the *ius praetorium*, without even formally abolishing them.

Overview 8: The Imperial Layers of Law

Roman Republic	statutes (*leges*), mainly the law of the twelve tables and its interpretation by the older jurists	*ius civile*
Roman Republic	edicts by the praetors and governors of the provinces; interpretation of the edict by contemporary jurists	*ius praetorium*
Empire (Principate)	*constitutiones* *senatusconsulta* *cognitio extra ordinem*	application, interpretation and emendation of the existing *ius civile* and *ius praetorium* introduction of new laws (*ius novum*)
ius naturale as a constitutive legal entity concerning all layers of law		

The following chapters will examine the different stages of development of Roman law, i.e. the different layers of private law, with a focus on the Roman law of inheritance.

3

The Rules of Intestacy

We already find a distinction between testamentary and statutory succession in the law of the twelve tables (*ca.* 450BC). Statutory succession is subsidiary; hence, it applied if the decedent died intestate (V. 4): *Si intestato moritur, cui suus heres nec essit, agnatus proximus familiam pecuniamque habeto.*[1] ('If a person dies intestate and without a direct heir, the household and the estate shall pass to the agnate next-of-kin.'). By 'intestacy' (*intestatus*, 'without a testament,' 'without a will'), Roman jurists meant the following:

> *Paulus, 67 ad edictum: 'Intestatus' est non tantum qui testamentum non fecit, sed etiam cuius ex testamento hereditas adita non est. (D.50.16.64.)*
>
> Paul, Edict, book 67: Someone is said to be 'without a will' (*intestatus*) not only if he has not made a will, but also if his estate has not been taken under a will. (D.50.16.64.)

Thus, the legal rules governing intestacy applied when the decedent had not left a valid will in the first place or if a will had failed for any other reason. This was the case, e.g., if the designated heir predeceased the testator or did not accept the estate. Then the decedent's next-of-kin and relatives moved up in the line of succession. Therefore, these rules of intestacy are also called, 'the rules of family inheritance'.

The legal position thus attained by the heir is described in the law of the twelve tables as 'ownership of property' whereas 'property' is defined by the compound synonym *familia pecuniaque*; thus, encompassing both the slaves of the decedent's household (*familia*, 'household'), as well as its financial assets (*pecunia*, 'money'):

> *Ulpianus, 46 ad edictum: 'Familiae' appellatio qualiter accipiatur, videamus. Et quidem varie accepta est: Nam et in res et in personas deducitur. In res, ut*

---

[1] The reconstruction adheres to Michel Humbert, Andrew D. E. Lewis and Michael H. Crawford, 'Lex duodecim tabularum' in Michael Crawford (ed) *Roman Statutes II* (Institute of Classical Studies 1996) 580.

puta in lege duodecim tabularum his verbis 'adgnatus proximus familiam habeto'. [...] (D.50.16.195.1.)

Ulpian, Edict, book 46: Let us consider how we understand the term 'household' (*familia*). It is indeed understood in various ways since it refers both to objects and persons; to objects, as in the law of the twelve tables, where it says, 'Let the agnate next-of-kin have the estate'. [...] (D.50.16.195.1.)

Ulpian (third century AD) points out that in the rules of intestacy of the law of the twelve tables, the term '*familia*' referred to objects, not persons. Hence '*familia*' did not only denote the legal relationship between family members but could also refer to property.

Since the hierarchical structures of the family determined the rules of intestacy, I will outline here the principles underlining the Roman family law and gauge their importance for the rules of intestacy.

3.1 The Hierarchical Structure of Family

Like the *civitas* (Ch. 2.2.2), the Roman family, i.e. the household, is perceived as a hierarchically structured legal community:

Ulpianus, 46 ad edictum: [...] iure proprio familiam dicimus plures personas, quae sunt sub unius potestate aut natura aut iure subiectae, ut puta patrem familias, matrem familias, filium familias, filiam familias quique deinceps vicem eorum sequuntur, ut puta nepotes et neptes et deinceps. Pater autem familias appellatur, qui in domo dominium habet, recteque hoc nomine appellatur, quamvis filium non habeat: non enim solam personam eius, sed et ius demonstramus. [...] (D.50.16.195.2.)

Ulpian, Edict, book 46: [...] according to our civil law, we call a 'household' several persons who, either by nature or by law, have been subjected to the authority of a single man, namely, the *pater familias*, the *mater familias*, a son under the paternal power (*filius familias*), a daughter under the paternal power (*filia familias*) and those who succeed them in order, such as grandsons, granddaughters and so on. We call '*pater familias*', however, somebody who has the power over the household. And he is correctly called thus, even if he has no child because we do not merely refer to his person but also to his legal status. [...] (D.50.16.195.2.)

According to the *ius civile*, the family is as a group subjected to the power of one head. The head of the Roman family was the *pater familias*, who controlled the rest of the family. Notably, the power of the *pater familias* stretched over the descendants of each son still in his power (*filius familias*) and could thus extend across generations. In other words, for as long as the grandfather lived, his sons and their children remained in his power. Since a *filius familias* could become the head of a family in his own right, he was called *pater familias* once he ceased to be in his father's power. He was called thus even if he was not married or had no children, as the term '*pater familias*' merely described the status of independence from the father's power. However, the grandchildren came into their father's power upon their grandfather's death. Therefore, after their grandfather's death, they did not become legally independent (*sui iuris*) but merely were subjected to somebody else's power.

The power of the *pater familias* over his family (*patria potestas*, literally 'paternal power') initially entailed the right to decide over the life and death of his offspring. It allowed him to expose a newborn child even in the time of the Principate. As regards property, persons under the *potestas* were incapable of owning property. Children-in-power could only acquire for their *pater familias* as the latter's 'extended arm', in his name, but not for themselves. With this information about the *patria potestas* in mind, one can explain why the *familia* in the broadest sense includes slaves as well, for they too were in the power of the *pater familias* and, similar to his children-in-power, could acquire property and rights for him:

> Inst.Gai.2.87.: *Igitur liberi nostri, quos in potestate habemus, item quod servi nostri [...] nanciscuntur [...] id nobis adquiritur [...]; et ideo si heres institutus sit, nisi nostro iussu hereditatem adire non potest; et si iubentibus nobis adierit, hereditas nobis adquiritur, proinde atque si nos ipsi heredes instituti essemus; et convenienter scilicet legatum per eos nobis adquiritur.*
>
> Inst.Gai.2.87.: Therefore, we acquire what our children that we have in our power, and our slaves [...] obtain [...] And so, where he [who is under *patria potestas*] is appointed heir, he cannot accept the inheritance if we do not tell him to do so. Then, when he accepts, on our command, we acquire the inheritance, just as if we had been made heirs ourselves. Correspondingly, a legacy to him accrues to us.

Slaves and children-in-power acquired property and rights for the *pater familias*. This also applies to acquisition through inheritance. Suppose a son under the paternal power or daughter under the paternal power was appointed heir by a third party's will or made the beneficiary of a legacy. In that case, the *pater familias* decided if the inheritances or the legacy would be accepted. Thus, the children-in-power did not acquire the inheritance for themselves but for the *pater familias*, as the proprietor of the family estate.

Establishing *patria potestas* over the children presupposed a legally valid marriage of the parents under Roman law:

Inst.Gai.1.55.: Item in potestate nostra sunt liberi nostri, quos iustis nuptiis procreavimus, quod ius proprium civium Romanorum est. [...]

Inst.Gai.1.55.: In the same manner, we have under our *potestas* our children, born in a legally valid marriage. This right belongs to Roman citizens only. [...]

A legally valid marriage required that both spouses held Roman citizenship. However, women who did not have Roman citizenship could, as an exception, enter a legal marriage under Roman law if they were granted the privilege to enter a Roman marriage, the *conubium*.

The child-in-power ceased to be under the *patria potestas* and gained legal capacity only upon the death of the *pater familias*:

Ulpianus, 46 ad edictum: [...] Et cum pater familias moritur, quotquot capita ei subiecta fuerint, singulas familias incipiunt habere: Singuli enim patrum familiarum nomen subeunt. [...] (D.50.16.195.2.)

Ulpian, Edict, book 46: [...] once the *pater familias* dies, each person formerly under his *potestas*, begins to have a separate household. For each is called '*pater familias*'. [...] (D.50.16.195.2.)

Upon the death of the *pater familias*, his children-in-power became *sui iuris* (legally independent) and received the capacity to own property. There was no distinction in this regard between a son and daughter under the paternal power. However, they differed between them in as much as the *filius familias* could obtain power over his lawful offspring, while the *filia familias* merely obtained power over herself (Ch. 3.1.4).

This succession of the children-in-power to the position of the head of the family upon the latter's death forms the first stage of the Roman rules of intestate succession under the *ius civile*. The extract from the law of the twelve tables, cited above (V.4), states that if somebody dies intestate, his *sui heredes* ('direct heirs') will inherit his estate: 'If a person dies intestate and without a direct heir [...]' (*si intestate moritur, cui suus here nec essit* [...]). The order of succession of the children-in-power to the estate of the *pater familias* was thus not prescribed, but implied.

3.1.1 Intestate Entitlement of Children-in-Power

The natural succession of children as direct heirs into the position of the *pater familias* occurs because the children-in-power lack the legal capacity to own property while their *pater familias* is alive:

Paulus, 2 ad Sabinum: In suis heredibus evidentius apparet continuationem dominii eo rem perducere, ut nulla videatur hereditas fuisse, quasi olim hi domini essent, qui etiam vivo patre quodammodo domini existimantur. Unde etiam filius familias appellatur sicut pater familias, sola nota hac adiecta, per quam distinguitur genitor ab eo qui genitus sit. Itaque post mortem patris non hereditatem percipere videntur, sed magis liberam bonorum administrationem consequuntur. [...] (D.28.2.11.)

Paul, Sabinus, book 2: As regards the direct heirs, it seems quite evident that a continuation of ownership leads to the assumption that no inheritance has occurred. Instead, it is as if they [the direct heirs] had already been owners for a long time since they were supposedly regarded as such during their father's lifetime. Therefore, the *filius familias* is named like the *pater familias*, and it is only by the added title that the *progenitor* is distinguished from his offspring. Hence, after the father's death, the children are not considered to have inherited but to have obtained free administration of the property. [...] (D.28.2.11.)

During the life of the *pater familias*, his children-in-power lack the capacity to own property but have a share in the family property on account of the power structures in the family. Therefore, they cannot transact but are subject to the power of the *pater familias*. Conceived thus, the death of the *pater familias* entails the devolution of the administration of the property on the already co-entitled children. Since the *pater familias* and the children-in-power belong to the household, the death of the *pater familias* does not mean the end of the family property, but only the change of the power to administer it:

Inst. Gai.3.2.: Sui autem heredes existimantur [...] liberi, qui in potestate morientis fuerunt, veluti filius filiave, nepos neptisve ex filio, pronepos proneptisve ex nepote filio nato prognatus prognatave. [...] ita demum tamen nepos neptisve et pronepos proneptisve suorum heredum numero sunt, si praecedens persona desierit in potestate parentis esse, sive morte id acciderit sive alia ratione, veluti emancipatione; nam si per id tempus, quo quis moriatur, filius in potestate eius sit, nepos ex eo suus heres esse non potest. Idem et in ceteris deinceps liberorum personis dictum intellegemus.

Inst.Gai.3.2.: The direct heirs [...] are the children who were in his power at the time of his death, such as a son or daughter, a grandson or a granddaughter through a son, a great-grandson or great-granddaughter through a grandson, who is the son of a son. [...] However, grandchildren or great-grandchildren only count as direct heirs if those preceding in degree have ceased to be under the *potestas* of the *pater familias*. This can happen because of death or for another reason, like *emancipatio*. For, if a man has a son in his power on his death, a grandson by the said son cannot be a direct heir. The same applies to the other children-in-power.

The position of the direct heirs is not limited to the decedent's children. Instead, all descendants, through the male line, subjected to the power of the (grand-)

father, are considered direct heirs. However, more remote offspring, e.g., grandchildren and great-grandchildren, are displaced by those closer in line, e.g., sons and grandsons, for as long as the latter are alive. Only when a son or grandson is released from the *potestas* of his father, do their children assume their father's position (stirpital representation, from *per stirpes*, literally 'by the stem'). But as long as the *filius familias* is alive and not emancipated, he displaces the offspring.

Naturally, this displacement concerns only the person's offspring:

> Inst.Gai.3.7.: *Igitur cum filius filiave et ex altero filio nepotes neptesve extant, pariter ad hereditatem vocantur; nec qui gradu proximior est, ulteriorem excludit. Aequum enim videbatur nepotes neptesve in patris sui locum portionemque succedere. Pari ratione et si nepos neptisque sit ex filio et ex nepote pronepos proneptisve, simul omnes vocantur ad hereditatem.*

> Inst.Gai.3.7.: Therefore, if a son, a daughter, grandsons, or granddaughters by the other son survive, they are equally called to inherit, and the nearer degree does not exclude the more remote. For it seemed just to let grandsons and granddaughters succeed to their father's place and share. By the same reasoning, if a grandson or granddaughter through a son or a great-grandson or great-granddaughter by a grandson, survive they all are called upon to inherit equally.

Under the stirpital representation, the descendants of a predeceased son or grandson are in the line of succession next to the sons and grandsons who are closer in line. Thus, the offspring of the predeceased son, or grandson, is equally entitled, as direct heirs, with the son's siblings, i.e., their uncles and aunts. *Filiae familias*, on the other hand, who as, direct heirs, are equally entitled with their brothers while alive, do not form a 'stem' (*stirps*). Therefore, their descendants will not become direct heirs of their grandfather on their mother's side. Instead, if born in wedlock, they are entitled to inherit from their father's family.

Following the principles discussed above, we have the first class of heirs on intestacy under the *ius civile* in Overview 9a–9c:

Overview 9a: The Order of Succession of the Children-in-Power

grandfather (decedent)			
father 1		father 2	daughter/sister
son 1	son 2	son 3	
grandson 1	granddaughter	grandson 2	
great-granddaughter		great-grandson	
1/3		1/3	1/3

If the grandfather deceases during the lifetime of father 1, father 2 and their sister, the three inherit jointly according to *per capita*; thus, only these three each receive one third of the estate.

Overview 9b: The Succeeding of the Descendants in the Male Line

grandfather (decedent)			
~~father 1~~		father 2	daughter/sister
son 1	son 2	son 3	
1/6	1/6	1/3	1/3

If father 1 is predeceased, his son 1 and son 2 succeed him. In this way, they share their father's third and get one sixth each; father 1 and his sister inherit one third each.

Overview 9c: No Succeeding after *filiae familias*

grandfather (decedent)			
father 1		father 2	~~daughter/sister~~
son 1	son 2	son 3	
1/2		1/2	
grandson 1	grandson 2	granddaughter 1	grandson 3

If the sister is predeceased, while fathers 1 and 2 are still alive, the latter share the estate; thus, they receive one-half each. The sister's descendent, however, receives nothing because she is a woman and does not form a *stirps*. The male offspring, in contrast, form *stirps*. Hence, grandsons 1 and 2 succeed son 1, granddaughter 1 succeeds son 2 and grandson 3 succeeds son 3 if the respective son has died. But whereas the male offspring form a stem, the stem of son 2 ends with granddaughter 1 since she cannot hold *patria potestas*.

Nevertheless, the *patria potestas* of the *pater familias* over his children, which establishes the position of the statutory heirs, does not only end with the former's death, but can also be terminated during his life.

3.1.2 The emancipatio *of Children-in-Power*

Termination of the *patria potestas* by a legal act is called *emancipatio* ('release from the *patria potestas*'). The term refers to the act of mancipation (*mancipatio*), which in this context is performed for granting freedom. The mancipation is an act per *aes et libram*, i.e., a quasi-purchase transaction carried out with 'bronze and scales' (*per aes at libram*). The origin of the transaction per *aes et libram* can be found in the weighing of the sale price, being, thus, a cash transaction. In the period that is of interest here, the transaction *per aes et libram* served as a conveyance through which ownership of *res mancipi* and power over *alieni iuris* (slaves and children-in-power) was transferred. The original formalities of the sale, *per aes et libram* became merely a ritual. To obtain ownership or power, the transferee strikes the scales with a bronze coin and hands this over to the transferor, 'instead of the sale price' (*quasi pretii loco*, Inst.Gai.1.119.). This 'mancipation for one piece of money' (*mancipatio nummo uno*) has eventually dissociated itself from the original nature of the transaction as one of purchase. Hence, *mancipatio* could be used for other purposes:

> Inst.Gai.1.132.: Praeterea emancipatione desinunt liberi in potestate parentum esse. Sed filius quidem tribus mancipationibus, ceteri vero liberi sive masculini sexus sive feminini una mancipatione exeunt de parentium potestate: Lex enim XII tabularum tantum in persona filii de tribus mancipationibus loquitur his verbis: 'Si pater ter filium venum duit a patre filius liber esto.' [...]

> Inst.Gai.1.132.: Moreover, children-in-power cease to be under *patria potestas* through *emancipatio*, but a son is only free from *patria potestas* after three mancipations. Other children, however, of either sex, are free of *patria potestas* after one mancipation, for the law of the twelve tables speaks of three mancipations only for a son, as follows: 'If a father sells his son three times, the son is to be free of the father' [...]

To be released from the *patria potestas*, the *filius familias* must be transferred three times into the power of a third party and be released by the latter. The same applies for all other offspring (daughters, grandsons, granddaughters), except that it is sufficient that their transfer took place once. Gaius (second century AD) deduces this heightened difficulty for the emancipation of a son from a sentence in the law of the twelve tables (*ca.* 450BC), by which a son shall be free from the father's power if the latter has sold him three times. It is suspected that the law of the twelve tables initially foresaw a son's freedom as punishment for the *pater familias*, who abused his *patria potestas* by selling his son into foreign servitude too often. However, this penalty is used in the period that concerns us to dissolve the *patria potestas* upon mutual agreement. Ernst Rabel described *emancipatio*, therefore, as a 'legal transaction conceived in imitation,' by which the recognised legal consequences for the paternal act of *mancipatio* (freedom of the son) are deflected from its intended purpose (and thus led to the intentional release from the *patria potestas*).

Regarding the intestacy rules of the *ius civile* the *emancipatio* removes the child-in-power from the class of direct heirs. Furthermore, if a son is released, his offspring will succeed him. A child-in-power released from *patria potestas* lost his family, and, consequently, his status (*capitis deminutio*). As a result, under the law of inheritance, the emancipated child was like a predeceased one.

If the intestate father had no (other) children in his power, then the law of the twelve tables (V. 4) foresaw that the agnate next-in-line shall become heir: '[...] the nearest agnate shall have the household and the estate' (*agnatus proximus familiam pecuniamque habeto*).

3.1.3 Intestate Entitlement of the adgnatus proximus

The term *adgnatus* (*adgnatus*, literally 'to enter by birth', thus: agnate) describes a blood relative who descends from a common ancestor in the uninterrupted male line:

> *Inst.Gai.3.10.: Vocantur autem adgnati, qui legitima cognatione iuncti sunt. Legitima autem cognatio est ea, quae per virilis sexus personas coniungitur. Itaque eodem patre nati fratres agnati sibi sunt, qui etiam consanguinei vocantur, nec requiritur, an etiam matrem eandem habuerint. Item patruus fratris filio et invicem is illi agnatus est. [...]*

> Inst.Gai.3.10.: 'Agnates' means relatives through a legal relationship. 'Legal relationship,' again, means the connection through males. Hence, brothers born to one father are related as agnates, also called '*consanguinei*' (siblings from the father's side). And it is irrelevant whether they also have the same mother. Likewise, a paternal uncle and his brother's son are each other's agnate. [...]

Agnatic kinship is defined as a relationship between persons who are or would be under the power of one and the same *pater familias*, if the latter were still alive. Due to the restriction of paternal power to men, this form of kinship is only mediated through them. Women can only be agnatically related insofar as they are or would be under a common paternal power with others, i.e., as daughters, granddaughters or cousins.

The degree of agnatic kinship depends on the number of births between relatives under the same *patria potestas*. In the first degree, the agnatic relatives of the decedent are his father and his children-in-power until his death. His agnatic relations of the second degree are his siblings, who are under the paternal power of the same father or would have been, as well as the grandfather and the grandchildren through a son. Finally, the third degree of agnatic kinship is formed between the decedent and his nephews and nieces who descend from a brother, but not a sister, as well as uncles and aunts, who are siblings of the father.

Only the nearest agnate, is entitled to inherit on intestacy under the *ius civile*:

Inst.Gai.3.11.: Non tamen omnibus simul agnatis dat lex XII tabularum hereditatem, sed his, qui tum, cum certum est aliquem intestatum decessisse, proximo gradu sunt.

Inst.Gai.3.11.: The law of the twelve tables, however, does not grant all agnates the inheritance simultaneously, but only those of the nearest degree, once it is certain that someone has died intestate.

The nearest agnate precludes the more remote agnatic relations. Therefore, the moment when intestacy occurs is decisive for ascertaining the degree of agnatic kin, i.e., when it becomes clear that the decedent left no valid will. In contrast to the direct heirs, stirpital representation does not apply to the *proximus agnatus*:

Inst.Gai.3.12.: Nec in eo iure successio est. Ideoque si agnatus proximus hereditatem omiserit vel, antequam adierit, decesserit, sequentibus nihil iuris ex lege competit.

Inst.Gai.3.12.: And in this area of law, there is no succeeding. Thus, if the nearest agnate renounces the inheritance or dies before accepting it, the law gives no right to those agnates who come next.

There is no provision for descendants to succeed to the position of heir as *agnatus proximus*. If many agnates are simultaneously next in line, the inheritance falls to them *per capita*:

Inst.Gai.3.16.: Quod si defuncti nullus frater extet, sed sint liberi fratrum, ad omnes quidem hereditas pertinet; sed quaesitum est, si dispari forte numero sint nati, ut ex uno unus vel duo, ex altero tres vel quattuor, utrum in stirpes dividenda sit hereditas, sicut inter suos heredes iuris est, an potius in capita. Iam dudum tamen placuit in capita dividendam esse hereditatem. Itaque quotquot erunt ab utraque parte personae, in tot portiones hereditas dividetur, ita ut singuli singulas portiones ferant.

Inst.Gai.3.16.: Hence, if the decedent has no surviving brother, but there are children of brothers, the inheritance goes to all of them. But it has been asked if by chance the children were born unequal in number (so that one brother had one or two and the other three or four), the inheritance should be divided *per stirpes*, as is the law where direct heirs are concerned, or *per capita*. However, it has already been decided a long time ago that the inheritance should be divided *per capita*. Thus, the inheritance will be divided into as many portions as there will be persons on either side, so that each gets a share.

The predeceased agnates of the first and second degrees (siblings of the deceased) are succeeded by the agnates of the third degree. If five children stem from two predeceased brothers, i.e., nephews or nieces of the decedent, they are all called upon to inherit as nearest agnates. If stirpital representation had applied here, as it had been the case with direct heirs, the nephews and nieces would have to divide their father's share. But, since the agnatic relations do not inherit *per stirpes* but *per capita*, every nephew and niece receive their *per capita* share, i.e., one-fifth of the estate.

3.1.4 Intestate Entitlement of Women

Daughters under the paternal power have an equal share in the estate with the brothers. As we saw, however, the former's offspring is not entitled to inherit from the father's family. Similarly, women could inherit on intestacy but could not establish agnatic relations as they could not exert *patria potestas* (Ch. 3.1.1). A *filia familias* who is released from *patria potestas* becomes *sui iuris* but has no depending relatives:

> *Ulpianus, 46 ad edictum: Mulier autem familiae suae et caput et finis est. (D.50.16.195.5.)*

> Ulpian, Edict, book 46: The woman, however, is both the beginning and end of her household. (D.50.16.195.5.)

Ulpian (third century AD) put it in a nutshell. The family of the woman was limited to herself. Since (legitimate) children were under the father's power, they were, as far as the *ius civile* was concerned, only related to the husband's family. A woman could initially only establish a family tie with her offspring if she was herself under the marital power of her husband (*in manu*):

> *Inst.Gai.3.3.: Uxor quoque, quae in manu eius est, sua heres est, quia filiae loco est. Item nurus, quae in filii manu est, nam et haec neptis loco est. Sed ita demum erit sua heres, si filius, cuius in manu est, cum pater moritur, in potestate eius non sit. [...]*

> Inst.Gai.3.3.: A wife *in manu* to her husband is also his direct heir upon death because she stands in the position of a daughter to him. The same applies to a daughter-in-law, who is *in manu* of his son, for she too stands in the position of a granddaughter to him. But she will be direct heir only if the son, to whom she is *in manu*, is not under the paternal power of his father at the time of the latter's death. [...]

A wife *in manu* of her husband has the legal position of a daughter and can inherit from her children as their sister. If she is in the power of her father-in-law, she can inherit from him as a granddaughter. Thus, she only inherits if her husband, a *filius familias*, predeceases his father. Although the *manus*-marriage fell into disuse by the end of the Republic, it is treated by Gaius (second century AD) for didactic purposes. Referring to legal history, he shows that originally, the disadvantageous position of the wife under inheritance law could be avoided by entering a *manus*-marriage. If, however, a woman entered a marriage without coming under the power of her husband, as was customary during the Principate, she was either *sui iuris* or under the *patria potestas* of her father. In the latter case, she was entitled to inherit from her birth family, i.e., as direct heir (of her father) or as *agnata proxima* (feminine of *agnatus proximus*), e.g., to her brother or uncle.

Interestingly, we find that at an unknown time after the law of the twelve tables the rules of intestacy concerning women were further curtailed:

> *Inst.Gai.3.14.:* [...] *nostrae vero hereditates ad feminas ultra consanguineorum gradum non pertinent. Itaque soror fratri sororive legitima heres est, amita vero et fratris filia legitima heres esse non potest; sororis autem nobis loco est etiam mater aut noverca, quae per in manum conventionem apud patrem nostrum iura filiae nancta est.*

> Inst.Gail.3.14.: [...] but our inheritances do not pertain to women beyond the degree of siblings from the father's side. And so, a sister is a statutory heir to her brother or sister, while a father's sister and a brother's daughter cannot be a statutory heir. However, a mother or a stepmother who has acquired the rights of a daughter through *manus*-marriage to our father stands in the position of a sister to us.

According to this interpretation, women who were further removed than siblings from the father's side (*consanguinei*) could not inherit as *agnatae proximae*. Therefore, women related to the decedent in the third degree were not called upon to inherit under the rules of intestacy.

Thus, a sister of the decedent could inherit as an agnatic relation, whereas an aunt from the father's side was excluded, as was a niece of the decedent, even though an uncle and a nephew from the father's side could inherit as agnates.

3.1.5 Intestate Entitlement of the gentiles

The *gentiles* (persons of the same *gens*, 'kin') form the third class in the intestacy rules:

> *Inst.Gai.3.17.: Si nullus agnatus sit, eadem lex XII tabularum gentiles ad hereditatem vocat. Qui sint autem gentiles, primo commentario rettulimus; et cum illic admonuerimus totum gentilicium ius in desuetudinem abisse, supervacuum est hoc quoque loco de eadem re curiosius tractare.*

> Inst.Gai.3.17.: If there are no agnates, the same law of the twelve tables gives the inheritance to the members of the *gens*. I have explained who the

members of the *gens* are in the first commentary. And since I have already pointed out that the entire *ius gentilicum* went out of use, it is pointless to discuss it further here.

This law of inheritance of the *gens* law had already fallen into desuetude by the time of Gaius (second century AD). Since the law of the twelve tables had never been abolished, the jurist had to refer to the change in the legal situation in his textbook.

The praetorian law introduced a sweeping change to the rules of the *ius civile* governing intestacy, which developed parallel to the latter.

3.2 The Praetorian Rules of Intestacy

Like the law of inheritance of the *ius civile*, the praetorian edict differentiated between the law of wills and the rules of intestacy. Whereas the heir under the *ius civile*, became the owner of the estate, the *ius praetorium* initially granted the entitled person only possession of the estate. This specific praetorian remedy is called *bonorum possessio* and provides its holder with possession of the estate as well as all the economic benefits of the inheritance. Nonetheless, the praetor cannot 'make somebody an heir' (Ch. 4.2.2). The granting of the *bonorum possessio ab intestato* ('without a will') follows the praetor's edict: '*Si tabulae testamenti nullae extabunt*'[2] (if there is no testamentary document). In this edict, the praetor mentions the persons entitled to claim *bonorum possessio* in the absence of a will. The heirs on intestacy are divided into various classes:

> *Ulpianus, 44 ad edictum: Sed successionem ab intestato in plures partes divisit: Fecit enim gradus varios, primum liberorum, secundum legitimorum, tertium cognatorum, deinde viri et uxoris. (D.38.6.1.1.)*
>
> Ulpian, Edict, book 44: The praetor, however, divided succession on intestacy into several classes. For he set them up in various degrees: first are the children, second, statutory heirs, third, the blood kin, and then, husband and wife. (D.38.6.1.1.)

The first class of the praetorian edict comprises the descendants (*liberi*), the second, the statutory heirs (*legitimi*), the third, the blood kin (*cognati*) and the fourth consists of the spouses (*vir et uxor*). The jurists add to these classes aforementioned the word '*unde*' ('whence') to denote the reason for their respective entitlement to *bonorum possessio*. The four classes mentioned are entitled to claim *bonorum possessio* successively. It must be noted that the claim of each class is only possible within a limitation period. It is one year for

---

[2] Otto Lenel, *Das Edictum Perpetuum* (3rd edn, Tauchnitz 1927) 355.

parents and children and one hundred days in all other instances. Once this deadline passes, the next class is eligible for application.

The classes created by the praetor are partly based on the *ius civile*; however, we also find that persons were included in the praetorian order of succession on intestacy who would not have been entitled under the *ius civile*.

3.2.1 The First Class of the Praetorian Heirs

In the first class *unde liberi*, all descendants of the deceased are called by the praetor:

> Inst.Gai.3.26.: Nam liberos omnes, qui legitimo iure deficiuntur, vocat ad hereditatem, proinde ac si in potestate parentis mortis tempore fuissent, sive soli sint, sive etiam sui heredes, id est qui in potestate patris fuerunt, concurrant.

> Inst.Gai.3.26.: For he calls all descendants who have been abandoned under *ius civile* to apply for the inheritance in the same way as if they had been under the paternal power, at the time of his death. This applies regardless of whether they are sole survivors or compete with direct heirs, namely, descendants under the *patria potestas*.

This group of descendants (*liberi*) comprises the direct heirs, already entitled under the *ius civile* and the descendants released from the *patria potestas* through *emancipatio* during the decedent's lifetime (Ch. 3.1.2). Like the *ius civile*, both male and female descendants are entitled. The question of how to proceed within a stem arose if several generations survived, e.g., grandchildren next to children. Under the *ius civile*, the *emancipatio* of a *filius familias* led to the succeeding of the grandchildren (Ch. 3.1.3). But since the *ius praetorium* also allowed the emancipated son to inherit on intestacy rules, stirpital representation could not be applied similarly:

> Pomponius, 4 ad Sabinum: Si filius emancipatus non petierit bonorum possessionem, ita integra sunt omnia nepotibus, atque si filius non fuisset, ut quod filius habiturus esset petita bonorum possessione, hoc nepotibus ex eo solis, non etiam reliquis adcrescat. (D.38.6.5.2.)

> Pomponius, Sabinus, book 4: If an emancipated son has not applied for *bonorum possessio*, all the rights of the grandsons remain intact, just as if there was no son. Therefore, what the son would have been entitled to, had he applied for *bonorum possessio*, accrues solely to the grandsons who descend from him, not the others. (D.38.6.5.2.)

The grandchildren, therefore, can only succeed the emancipated son under the *ius praetorium* if the latter has yet to claim *bonorum possessio ab intestato*. Suppose the grandchildren are still under the *patria potestas* of their grandfather and hence, direct heirs under the *ius civile*. In this case, a conflict arises between the rules of intestacy of the *ius civile* and the *ius praetorium*. According to the former only the grandchildren inherit, according to the latter, only the emancipated son. This conflict between the heirs on intestacy, who have priority under the *ius civile*, and the heirs on intestacy of the first class under the *ius praetorium*, was repealed by an imperial innovation to the praetor's edict, called *nova clausula Iuliani* (Ch. 3.3.2).

3.2.2 The Second and Third Class of the Praetorian Heirs

The second class of the praetorian rules of intestacy (*unde legitimi*) refers to the *ius civile*:

> *Ulpianus, 46 ad edictum: Haec autem bonorum possessio omnem vocat, qui ab intestato potuit esse heres, sive lex duodecim tabularum eum legitimum heredem faciat sive alia lex senatusve consultum. [...] (D.38.7.2.4.)*

> Ulpian, Edict, book 46: However, this kind of *bonorum possessio* includes everyone who can inherit on intestacy, whether the law of the twelve tables, any other law, or a decree of the Senate (*senatusconsultum*), make him a statutory heir. [...] (D.38.7.2.4.)

Within the second class, all persons who inherit by intestacy under the *ius civile* are eligible for *bonorum possessio ab intestato*. Thus, direct heirs and nearest agnates are entitled to claim. Therefore, the praetorian provision results in the possibility for the children under the *potestas* of the testator to claim the estate *ab intestato* in both the first (as *liberi*) and second class (as *legitimi*). Only after them, just as according to *ius civile*, can the *proximus agnatus* claim the *bonorum possessio ab intestato*, in the class *unde legitimi*. The *gentiles*, however, have no claim as the *ius praetorium* regarded their entitlement as obsolete. Instead, in imperial times, *senatusconsulta* established statutory rights of inheritance. The beneficiaries of this legislation were considered legitimate heirs and had just as much right to claim the *bonorum possessio ab intestato* as any other person entitled to inherit through the law of the twelve tables (Ch. 3.4).

The emancipated children-in-power were excluded from the second class of praetorian heirs by intestacy, since herein only those entitled under the *ius civile* could claim the inheritance. After all, the emancipated children-in-power had lost their family ties because of *capitis deminutio* and thus could not inherit by intestacy under *ius civile*, either as direct heirs or as agnates. Likewise, the praetor excluded those women who were agnatically related beyond the second degree of *consanguinitas*, following the established interpretation of the *ius civile* (Ch. 3.1.4).

These persons, who were excluded from the second class of praetorian heirs, could be entitled to claim in the third class (*unde cognati*). In this class, the praetor granted *bonorum possessio ab intestato* to relatives by blood (*cognati*, from *cognatus*, 'blood kin'). It is important to distinguish cognatic from agnatic relations:

> *Modestinus, 12 Pandectarum: Cognationis substantia bifariam apud Romanos intellegitur: Nam quaedam cognationes iure civili, quaedam naturali conectuntur, nonnumquam utroque iure concurrente et naturali et civili copulatur cognatio. Et quidem naturalis cognatio per se sine civili cognatione intellegitur quae per feminas descendit, quae vulgo liberos peperit. Civilis autem per se, quae etiam legitima dicitur, sine iure naturali cognatio consistit per adoptionem. Utroque iure consistit cognatio, cum iustis nuptiis contractis copulatur. [...] (D.38.10.4.2.)*

> Modestinus, Encyclopaedia, book 12: The Romans understand the nature of kinship in two different ways. For some kinships are established by the *ius civile*, some by the *ius naturale*. At times, kinship is established by the coincidence of both *ius naturale* and *ius civile*. Specifically, natural (cognatic) kinship by itself without civil (agnatic) kinship is understood as that mediated by women who have brought children into the world outside marriage. Civil kinship, however, which is also called legitimate, arises through adoption without *ius naturale*. Kinship under both laws exists if it is established on the basis of a legally valid marriage. [...] (D.38.10.4.2.)

The two types of kinship are paradigmatic for differing layers of law. On the one hand, Modestinus (third century AD) mentions *cognatio* as an example of *ius naturale* (Ch. 2.2.1). *Agnatio*, on the other hand, is perceived as belonging to the *ius civile*. The said types of kinship could appear separately or together. For example, a mother and her children are only related as cognates because an *agnatio* cannot be established due to the lack of *potestas*. In contrast, *agnatio* without *cognatio* occurs when adopting a child because the *pater familias* gains *potestas* over the former.[3] Last, we have both cognatic and agnatic ties when a child is born from a Roman marriage, because the father's *potestas*

---

[3] Adoption occurs, like *emancipatio*, through the *mancipatio* of a child-in-power to a fiduciary third party who subsequently releases the former. Suppose the *mancipatio* of a *filius familias* is thus conducted thrice or once for another child-in-power. In that case, the child is released from the power of his *pater familias*. Through a fictional procedure (*in iure cessio*), the designated adoptive father claims *patria potestas* over the child. The previous *pater familias* does not object, and the child comes under the *potestas* of the adoptive father.

establishes the agnatic, whereas the blood relations between the child with the mother and the father establish the cognatic kinship.

The praetorian rules of intestacy *unde cognati* apply to the cognatic relatives, the decedent's 'natural' kin:

> *Inst.Gai.3.27.: Adgnatos autem capite deminutos non secundo gradu post suos heredes vocat, id est, non eo gradu vocat, quo per legem vocarentur, si capite minuti non essent, sed tertio proximitatis nomine. Licet enim capitis deminutione ius legitimum perididerint, certe cognationis iura retinent. [...]*

> Inst.Gai. 3.27.: Agnates, however, who have suffered *capitis deminutio*, qualify not in the second class after direct heirs, that is, the class in which they would have qualified by statute if they had not undergone *capitis deminutio*, but under the third class because of close kinship. Though they have lost their statutory rights through *capitis deminutio*, they certainly retain their cognatic rights. [...]

A son ceased to be under the *patria potestas* of his father if he underwent *emancipatio* and, thus, lost the agnatic ties to his family. This loss of status (*capitis deminutio minima*) concerns only the agnatic relations. The blood kinship, however, remained intact. Therefore, emancipated children could receive *bonorum possessio ab intestato* under the third class, *unde cognati*.

Also, women, who could not be included as heirs on intestacy as agnates under the *ius civile* because they were further removed from the testator, were protected by the praetor under the class *unde cognati*:

> *Inst.Gai.3.29.: Feminae certe agnatae, quae consanguineorum gradum excedunt, tertio gradu vocantur, id est, si neque suus heres neque agnatus erit.*

> Inst.Gai.3.29.: Undoubtedly, female agnates, who are beyond the degree of siblings on the father's side qualify in the third class, namely, if neither a direct heir nor a male agnate is available.

As we saw, women beyond the third degree were no longer seen as agnates entitled to inherit under the *ius civile* (Ch. 3.1.4). But they could receive *bonorum possessio unde cognati*. Thus, they only received *bonorum possessio ab intestato* after the direct heirs and the *agnatus proximus*, but were at least not entirely excluded, as they were under the *ius civile*. Even more significant was the recognition of kinship mediated by women in the class *unde cognati*:

> *Inst.Gai.3.30: Eodem gradu vocantur etiam eae personae, quae per feminini sexus personas copulatae sunt.*

> Inst.Gai.3.30.: In the same class are also called those persons who are [related] through women.

The third class of the praetorian rules of intestacy allowed persons not related to the testator through the male line but descending from a female relative of his, to claim *bonorum possessio*. Therefore, contrary to the order of the *ius civile*, descendants of women were recognised as relatives, entitled to inherit on intestacy. The consideration of cognatic kinship marked a paradigm shift in the Roman family and inheritance law:

> *Ulpianus 46 ad edictum: Haec bonorum possessio nudam habet praetoris indulgentiam neque ex iure civili originem habet: Nam eos invitat ad bonorum possessionem, qui iure civili ad successionem admitti non possunt, id est cognatos. (D.38.8.1pr.)*

> Ulpian, Edict, book 46: This kind of *bonorum possessio* depends entirely on the leniency of the praetor and does not originate from the *ius civile*. He grants *bonorum possessio* to those who cannot become heir under the *ius civile*; hence, the *cognati*. (D.38.8.1pr.)

Ulpian points out that only praetorian law recognises and allows a succession on intestacy, based on cognatic ties. He considers this a significant innovation compared to the *ius civile*. The praetorian order of succession also significantly alters the law of husband and wife.

3.2.3 Intestate Entitlement between Spouses under Praetorian Law

As we saw, husband and wife could only inherit from each other *ab intestato* under the *ius civile* if their marriage was *in manu* (Ch. 3.1.4). If the spouses were married *sine manu*, as was customary from the end of the Republic, neither kinship nor a surviving spouse's right to inherit *ab intestato* existed under the *ius civile*.

To complete this picture, the regulation about *dos* ('dowry') needs to be mentioned. Dowry was given by the bride's family to the bridegroom and was meant to provide sustenance for the wife and financial security during and after the marriage. The absence of a hereditary claim by the widow who survived her husband was partly compensated through the action for the return of the dowry (*actio rei uxoriae*, literally 'action for the wife's assets'). In this way, the widow secured her alimony but could not receive her late husband's property. The widower, too, stood to inherit nothing under the *ius civile* if his *sine manu* wife had died intestate.

The praetorian law remedies this by granting the spouses a claim of *bonorum possessio ab intestato*; thus, adding their claim to the three classes of the praetorian rules of intestacy aforementioned:

> *Ulpianus, ad edictum 47: pr. Ut bonorum possessio peti possit unde vir et uxor, iustum esse matrimonium oportet. [...]*

(1) Ut autem haec bonorum possessio locum habeat, uxorem esse oportet mortis tempore. [...] (D.38.11.1pr.-1.)

Ulpian, Edict, book 47: The application for *bonorum possessio unde vir et uxor* requires a legally valid marriage. [...]
(1) For *bonorum possessio* of this kind to be granted, she must be his wife at the time of his death. [...] (D.38.11.1pr.-1.)

The only requirement for *bonorum possessio ab intestato* in the class *unde vir et uxor* was a marriage recognised by the *ius civile* at the time of death. By accepting a right of inheritance between spouses, the praetor waived a hitherto indispensable inheritance requirement: kinship.

The jurists justified this modification of praetorian law compared to the *ius civile* with the principle of equity (*aequitas*):

Paulus, 41 ad edictum: Bonorum possessionis beneficium multiplex est: Nam quaedam bonorum possessiones competunt contra voluntatem, quaedam secundum voluntatem defunctorum, nec non ab intestato habentibus ius legitimum vel non habentibus propter capitis deminutionem. Quamvis enim iure civili deficiant liberi, qui propter capitis deminutionem desierunt sui heredes esse, propter aequitatem tamen rescindit eorum capitis deminutionem praetor [...] (D.37.1.6.1.)

Paul, Edict, book 41: The benefits of *bonorum possessio* are multifold. Because some kinds of *bonorum possessio* are obtained against the wishes of the testators and others in accordance with it, and *bonorum possessio* certainly belongs to those, who have a statutory right to it on the grounds of intestacy, but also to those who have no such right because of a loss of status (*capitis deminutio*). Although children are excluded from direct inheritance under the *ius civile* because of their *capitis deminutio*, the praetor can reverse the *capitis deminutio* for reasons of equity [...] (D.37.1.6.1.)

The most important innovation of the praetorian inheritance law, compared to the *ius civile*, is the entitlement of emancipated children to inherit under the rules of intestacy. This is considered 'equitable and just' by Paul (third century AD) because the praetor treats all descendants equally, whether they are under *potestas* or not, and allows them to succeed their father. The connection between *patria potestas* and inheritance, so fundamental under the *ius civile*, thus becomes obsolete. What matters from now on is the (both natural or legal) kinship between the testator and his heir.

The differing prerequisites for the succession by intestacy of *ius civile*, on the one hand, and *ius praetorium*, on the other, can, in certain instances, lead to contradictions between the two layers of law.

3.3 Conflicts between *ius civile* and *ius praetorium*

Although there was no formal conflict between the law of succession developed under the *ius praetorium* and the *ius civile* because the praetor, as we saw (Ch. 3.2), could not create a civil heir, the granting of *bonorum possessio*, however, made it possible for the grantee to become an heir under the *ius civile* through prescriptive acquisition (Ch. 4.1.4). If the praetor therefore admits an applicant to *bonorum possessio* who is not entitled to the inheritance under the *ius civile*, this might endanger the legal position of the civil heir, as he can lose his status after the *bonorum possessor* has completed the acquisition period and thus acquired the inheritance. Because the rights to inherit per *ius civile* and *ius praetorium* diverge from each other, it must be assessed for each case whether the *bonorum possessio* should lead to prescriptive acquisition of the inheritance or if the heir of *ius civile* should have priority over the *bonorum possessor*.

The Roman jurists referred to this question by distinguishing *bonorum possessio 'cum re'* (literally, 'with access to property'), i.e., possession of the estate including the right to obtain the inheritance via prescriptive acquisition, and *bonorum possessio 'sine re'* (literally, 'without access to property'), that did not allow for prescriptive acquisition of the position as heir.

3.3.1 Bonorum possessio sine re – cum re

Bonorum possessio ab intestato sine re means that the praetor recognises the precedence of the *ius civile* over the *ius praetorium*. This is pre-eminently the case when the person entitled under the *ius civile* is also given priority under the *ius praetorium*:

> Inst.Gai.3.36.: *Nam si verbi gratia iure facto testamento heres institutus creverit hereditatem, sed bonorum possessionem secundum tabulas testamenti petere noluerit, contentus eo, quod iure civili heres sit, nihilo minus ii, qui nullo facto testamento ad intestati bona vocantur, possunt petere bonorum possessionem; sed sine re ad eos hereditas pertinet, cum testamento scriptus heres evincere hereditatem possit.*

> Inst.Gai.3.36.: For example, if an heir has been appointed in a valid will, and has formally declared his acceptance of the inheritance, but did not wish to apply for *bonorum possessio secundum tabulas*, being content as heir under the *ius civile*. Now, if no will was left, then those who would have been entitled to the estate on intestacy, can still apply for *bonorum possessio ab intestato*, but the grant will be *sine re*, as the testamentary heir may deprive them of the inheritance.

Suppose the testamentary heir under the *ius civile* is satisfied with his position and waives his right to claim *bonorum possessio secundum tabulas*. In that case, the praetorian heir on intestacy can claim *bonorum possessio ab intestato*. Since the preferred claim of *bonorum possessio* because of a will has not been brought forward, the praetor will grant a claim to the heir on intestacy. The praetor will, however, only grant the heir on intestacy *bonorum possessio sine re* because also under the *ius praetorium* the testamentary heir ranks before the statutory heir.[4]

The praetor also gives priority to the *ius civile* heir if the *bonorum possessor ab intestato* competes with an heir on intestacy of a higher rank:

> Inst.Gai.3.37.: *Idem iuris est, si intestato aliquo mortuo suus heres noluerit petere bonorum possessionem, contentus legitimo iure. Nam et agnato competit quidem bonorum possessio, sed sine re, quia evinci hereditas a suo herede potest. Et illud convenienter: si ad agnatum iure civili pertinet hereditas et is adierit hereditatem, sed si bonorum possessionem petere noluerit, et si quis ex proximis cognatis petierit, sine re habebit bonorum possessionem propter eandem rationem.*

> Inst.Gai.3.37.: The law is the same when a person dies intestate, and his direct heir refuses to claim *bonorum possessio*, being content as statutory heir. An agnate, too, will have a right to *bonorum possessio*. But the grant will be *sine re* because he can be evicted from the estate by the direct heir. Similarly, if the estate comes to an agnate under the *ius civile* and he accepts it but fails to demand *bonorum possessio*, a cognate in the nearest degree can demand it. Still, he will have *bonorum possessio sine re* for the same reason.

This conflict also occurs if the heir on intestacy is satisfied with the position under *ius civile*, thus, waving his claim for *bonorum possessio ab intestato*. Gaius' example deals with direct heirs, who are also entitled to *bonorum possessio* under the *ius praetorium*, both in the first and second classes. As they have not claimed the possession, the *agnatus proximus* of subsequent rank is entitled to request the *bonorum possessio ab intestato*. Since no priority claim has been submitted, *bonorum possessio* can be granted to him. The praetor will, nonetheless, consider the priority of the direct heir under *ius civile*, and the agnate's *bonorum possessio ab intestato* will be *sine re*.

Whereas the aforementioned cases demonstrate the precedence of the *ius civile* over the *ius praetorium* heir, we see that the coincidence of the decedent's direct heirs (grandchildren) and the *emancipatus* (son), who are next in line, causes a split between the succession on intestacy under the *ius civile*

---

[4] *Bonorum possessio sine re* is without effect regarding the *ius civile* heir but affords its holder protection against third parties who claim the estate or remove items from it.

and the *ius praetorium* (Ch. 3.2.2). This conflict would be resolved under the Empire through Emperor Hadrian's drafting of the edict (AD130). Following the Roman jurists' terminology, this imperial innovation must still be considered a rule of *ius praetorium* (Ch. 2.2.3).

3.3.2 The nova clausula Iuliani *and the Rules of Intestacy*

The section of the praetor's edict added during Emperor Hadrian's reform is called *nova clausula Iuliani* ('Julian's new clause'), referring to its author, the jurist Julian (second century AD):

> *Pomponius, 4 ad Sabinum: Si quis ex his, quibus bonorum possessionem praetor pollicetur, in potestate parentis, de cuius bonis agitur, cum is moritur, non fuerit, ei liberisque, quos in eiusdem familia habebit, si ad eos hereditas suo nomine pertinebit neque nominatim exheredes scripti erunt, bonorum possessio eius partis datur, quae ad eum pertineret, si in potestate permansisset [...]. (D.38.6.5pr.)*

> Pomponius, Sabinus, book 4: If any of those to whom the praetor promises *bonorum possessio*, were not under the *potestas* of the father, whose estate is at issue, at the time of the latter's death, the *bonorum possessio* shall be granted to him and to the children he will have in the family of the same [father], if they were entitled to the inheritance in his name and have not been expressly disinherited, for that share which would have belonged to him if he had remained under the paternal power [...]. (D.38.6.5pr.)

This edictal clause provides that if an emancipated son, who has priority under the *ius praetorium*, coincides with grandchildren still under the *potestas* of their grandfather (direct heirs under the *ius civile*), the son's (fictional) share in the estate should be divided between him and his children. Thus, the different heirs on intestacy under *ius praetorium* and *ius civile* will inherit at the same time. This innovative solution can only be conceived as a division of *bonorum possessio ab intestato* between grandchildren and son and is a trade-off between the exigencies of the *ius civile* and the *ius praetorium*. The *ius civile* is observed in as far as the grandchildren, who succeed to the position of direct heirs, get a share in their father's estate. In contrast, the *ius praetorium* is observed to the extent that the *emancipatus* is treated as equal to the descendants under the *potestas*. At the same time, the *nova clausula Iuliani* safeguards the interests of additional descendants, e.g., siblings of the *emancipatus*, by granting the *emancipatus* and his children only the fictional share of a son. Hence, the participation of the son's children does not change the stirpital representation, applicable to both *ius civile* and *ius praetorium*.

Overview 10: The *nova clausula Iuliani*

grandfather (decedent)			
son 1	son 2	*emancipatus*: 1/8		daughter
		grandson 1: 1/16	grandson 2: 1/16	
1/4	1/4	1/4		1/4

The *nova clausula Iuliani* shows that the jurists of the Empire did not solely decide individual cases but strove to establish a coherent system of intestacy rules and to resolve contradictions between the *ius civile* and *ius praetorium*.

In addition to the corrections of the *ius praetorium*, we find two instances of a reform of the imperial law that regulated the inheritance on intestacy of the mother after her children and that of the children after their mother.

3.4 Imperial Reforms

According to the *ius civile*, a mother and her children are not agnatically related, hence, not entitled to inherit from each other (Ch. 3.1.4). Per the *ius praetorium*, they can only claim *bonorum possessio* under the third class as blood kin (*unde cognati*) (Ch. 3.2.2). This option is, however, not useful if there are *ius civile* heirs who have priority under the first (*unde liberi*) or second class (*unde legitimi*) of the *ius praetorium*. The absence of succession on intestacy between mother and child was repealed by two *senatusconsulta* in the second century AD.

3.4.1 The Senatusconsultum Tertullianum

The first, the *senatusconsultum Tertullianum*, dating from the time of Emperor Hadrian, regulates the succession of a mother from her children:

> Inst.3.3.2: *Postea autem senatusconsulto Tertulliano, quod divi Hadriani temporibus factum est, plenissime de tristi successione matri, non etiam aviae deferenda cautum est: Ut mater ingenua trium liberorum ius habens, [...] ad bona filiorum filiarumve admittatur intestatorum mortuorum, licet in potestate parentis est, ut scilicet, cum alieno iuri subiecta est, iussu eius adeat cuius iuri subiecta est.*
>
> Inst.3.3.2.: And afterwards, the *senatusconsultum Tertullianum*, enacted in the time of the deified Hadrian, comprehensively provided for the succession of children from their mothers, though not from their grandmothers, whereby it was provided that a freeborn woman who had the *ius trium liberorum* [...] should be entitled to succeed to the estate of her children who died intestate, even though she is under paternal power; though, in this latter

case, she cannot accept the inheritance except by the authority of the person in whose power she is.

A mother could inherit from her child, who was not under *potestas* and, thus, capable of owning property, if she was a free Roman, *sui iuris*, and had already given birth to three children. The *ius trium liberorum* ('right of three children') was enshrined in the Augustan marriage laws (27BC–AD14) and secured the testamentary rights of women (Ch. 4.3). Women who gave birth to fewer than three (legitimate) children and who had not been awarded the *ius trium liberorum* as a privilege lost their testamentary share. Emperor Hadrian's *senatusconsultum* moved beyond this rule and granted the free, freeborn woman with three children a right to her child's intestate succession.

However, this newly created rule of intestacy of the mother came second to higher-ranking inheritance claims:

> Inst.3.3.3.: *Praeferuntur autem matri liberi defuncti, qui sui sunt [...]. Sed filiae suae mortuae filius vel filia opponitur ex constitutionibus matri defunctae, id est aviae suae. Pater quoque utriusque, non etiam avus vel proavus, matri anteponitur, scilicet cum inter eos solos de hereditate agitur. Frater autem consanguineus tam filii quam filiae excludebat matrem: Soror autem consanguinea pariter cum matre admittebatur: Sed si fuerat frater et soror consanguinei et mater liberis honorata, frater quidem matrem excludebat, communis autem erat hereditas ex aequis partibus fratri et sorori.*

> Inst.3.3.3.: Children of the decedent who are direct heirs, are preferred to the mother [...]. And even where the deceased is a woman, her son or daughter have, by imperial constitutions, a prior claim to the mother, that is, to their grandmother. Again, the decedent's father is preferred to the mother, but not the paternal grandfather or great-grandfather, at least when it is between them only that the question arises who is entitled. However, a brother from the father's side excluded the mother from the succession to both sons and daughters, but a sister by the same father came in equally with her mother. Where there were both a brother and a sister from the father's side, as well as a mother who was entitled by the number of her children, the brother excluded the mother, and divided the inheritance into equal parts with his sister.

Preferment over the mother is given to the decedent's direct heirs and the daughter's descendants, who are entitled to claim first. The father of the deceased child comes next. The decedent's brother from the male line also excludes the mother, whereas the sister from the male line can claim simultaneously with the mother. In case of a conflict between brother and sister from the father's side, the mother is excluded, and the estate is divided between the siblings equally. This rule applies especially if the decedent's siblings are descendants of the father only, i.e. born from their father's marriage to another woman.

The exclusion of the mother in case of the survival of a brother from the father's side shows anew the desire not to mix the property of different families. Since the brother from the father's side continued the agnatic family to which the testator belonged, the testator's mother, who would typically not be part of that family, was only allowed to inherit on intestacy next to a brother, as fourth in line. The mother could inherit on intestacy only as third in line with the sister of a testator from the father's side (*consanguinitas*).

Overview 11: Order of Inheritance of a Mother after her Child

			the paternal side			the maternal side
child (decedent)	direct heirs: descendants	father	paternal brother	paternal sister		**mother**
			paternal sister	mother		
	1.	2.	3.			4.

The order of inheritance on intestacy from a child, as foreseen in the *senatusconsultum* is based on an innovative combination of already-known principles. The priority of the children under *potestas* of the deceased son follows the *ius civile*. So does the priority given to the decedent's father, as (former) *proximus agnatus*, over the merely cognatically related mother.[5] Moreover, the preference of siblings from the father's side (*consanguinei*) can be explained in the light of the interpretation of the *ius civile* that limits the women's right to inherit beyond the second grade (Ch. 3.1.4). Considering the children of a deceased daughter (descendants of a female decedent) and accepting the mother's right to inherit are obvious innovations. The level of protection they grant to cognatic kin goes even further than the praetorian edict because the senate recognises the ties with the mother as kin under the *ius civile*. However, the mother would have been entitled under the *ius praetorium* in the class *unde cognati* to *bonorum possessio* (Ch. 3.2.2). Therefore, the importance of the *senatusconsultum Tertullianum* lay pre-eminently in the fact that it granted the mother the position of heir under the *ius civile*. This expansion of the *ius*

---

[5] We must bear in mind that the 'child' is not agnatically related once released from the *patria potestas*. Therefore, the father's position can be explained from his role as an *emancipator* from the *patria potestas*. Only later did jurists interpret the *senatusconsultum Tertullianum* in such a way that it also applied to children born out of wedlock, i.e., free from *potestas*.

civile order of intestacy had the consequence for the *ius praetorium* that the mother moved up from the class *unde cognati* into the class of statutory heirs (*unde legitimi*).

The conflicting tendencies show that the *senatusconsultum Tertullianum* did not completely displace the rules of intestacy of the *ius civile* and *ius praetorium*; but merely complemented them. The jurists of the Empire were therefore discussing the harmonisation between the new (*ius novum*) of the *senatusconsultum* and the pre-existing rules of intestacy, the old law (*ius antiquum*).

3.4.2 The Application of ius novum and ius antiquum

The *senatusconsultum Tertullianum* regulated the mother's right to inherit only partially; it thus only granted the author the position of heir wheras her competitors were referred to the existing rules of intestacy. Hence, the jurists examined the mother's right to inherit on intestacy in a twofold manner.

They first examined if the mother was an heir on intestacy under the *senatusconsultum Tertullianum*; thus, they applied, the *ius novum*. As we saw, however, the *senatusconsultum* prioritised other persons entitled to inherit over the mother's claim. The priority of a person was examined under the *ius novum* only as a prerequisite for the mother's right to inherit; hence, hypothetically. If the jurist in this hypothetical examination eventually concluded that there was a priority, the *senatusconsultum Tertullianum* no longer applied, and the order of succession would be decided following the *ius civile* and *ius praetorium*. Only if nobody entitled under the *ius antiquum* accepted the estate could the jurist examine again if the mother could receive the inheritance under the *senatusconsultum Tertullianum*. If the mother accepted the inheritance after her right to inherit had been confirmed under the *senatusconsultum Tertullianum*, the procedure was finished. If, however, she did not accept, the old law revived:

> Ulpianus, 13 ad Sabinum: Si mater hereditatem filii filiaeve non adierit ex senatusconsulto Tertulliano, in bonorum possessione antiquum ius servandum est: Cum enim cesset praelatio matre omittente senatusconsulti beneficium, ius succedit vetus. (D.38.17.2.20.)
>
> Ulpian, Sabinus, book 13: If the mother did not accept the inheritance of a son or a daughter under the *senatusconsultum Tertullianum*, the ancient law (*antiquum ius*) regarding *bonorum possessio* must be observed. Indeed, the preference granted to the mother ended when she gave up the advantage of the *senatus consultum*, which is why the ancient law now takes its place. (D.38.17.2.20.)

Following the *ius antiquum*, those entitled to inherit on intestacy, both under the *ius civile* and the *ius praetorium*, could accept the estate. If the mother could inherit as a cognatic relation following the *bonorum possessio ab intestato*, she could have again another claim under this law. Her right to inherit, however, was limited to the class *unde cognati*. Therefore, she lost her right under the *senatusconsultum Tertullianum* to claim the *bonorum possessio* in the class *unde legitimi* by waiving her right to inherit under the *ius civile*.

Conversely, if she merely refrained from claiming *bonorum possessio ab intestato*, her right to inherit under the *ius civile* remained intact:

> *Ulpianus, 13 ad Sabinum: Sed si mater repudiaverit bonorum possessionem, de adeunda autem hereditate deliberet, dicendum erit adgnatum non succedere, quoniam nondum verum est non adisse matrem. (D.38.17.2.21.)*
>
> Ulpian, Sabinus, book 13: But if the mother has renounced *bonorum possessio* but is deliberating whether to accept the inheritance under the *ius civile*, we must state that the agnate will not succeed because it is not yet true that the mother has not accepted the inheritance. (D.38.17.2.21.)

The mother has repudiated the *bonorum possessio ab intestato* (in the class *unde legitimi*) but has not renounced the inheritance under the *ius civile*. Hence, she had not yet forfeited her rights from the *senatusconsultum*, but it remained unclear if her right to inherit followed the *ius novum* or the right of intestacy under *ius antiquum*. This is why the *agnatus proximus*, who under the *ius civile* would have had a right to inherit after the children-in-power, was excluded from the inheritance in the meantime. As soon as the mother's renunciation of the inheritance was final, the agnatic succession of *ius civile* would come into effect.

The different alternatives in the application of the *senatusconsultum Tertullianum* are summarised in Overview 12:

Overview 12: Harmonised Application of the *ius novum* and the *ius antiquum*

senatusconsultum Tertullianum: is the mother entitled to inherit as heir *ab intestato*?	yes: she can accept or renounce.
	no: the *ius antiquum* applies.
ius antiquum: who is called upon under the *ius antiquum*?	*ius civile:* • direct heirs • *agnatus proximus* *ius praetorium:* • descendants • statutory heirs • *cognati*
	the mother can also be called upon under the *bonorum possessio ab intestato* as a *cognata*.

ius antiquum: is there an heir willing to accept the inheritance?	yes: if the heir is willing to accept, he will take the inheritance.
	no: if the mother was hitherto not entitled, she can inherit under the *senatusconsultum Tertullianum*.

3.4.3 The Senatusconsultum Orfitianum

A similar mixture of rules applies to the children's right to inherit after their mother, introduced by the *senatusconsultum Orfitianum* in AD178:

> Inst.3.4pr.: Per contrarium autem ut liberi ad bona matrum intestatarum admittantur, senatusconsulto Orfitiano effectum est, quod latum est Orfito et Rufo consulibus, divi Marci temporibus. Et data est tam filio quam filiae legitima hereditas, etiamsi alieno iuri subiecti sunt: Et praeferuntur et consanguineis et adgnatis defunctae matris.

> Inst.3.4pr.: Conversely, children were admitted to inherit from their deceased mother on intestacy by the *senatusconsultum Orfitianum*, accomplished in the time of the deified Emperor Marcus when Orfitus and Rufus were consuls. And a legal right of succession was conferred on both sons and daughters, even though in the power of another, in preference to their deceased mother's blood-related brothers and sisters and other agnates.

This *senatusconsultum*, enacted under Emperor Marcus Aurelius (AD161–180), allowed children to inherit upon intestacy from their mother, with priority over the right on intestacy of agnates (under the *ius civile*) and cognates (under the *ius praetorium*). Thus, this imperial ruling displaced the existing order of succession on intestacy under the *ius civile*:

> Ulpianus, 12 ad Sabinum: 'Si nemo filiorum eorumve, quibus simul legitima hereditas defertur, volet ad se eam hereditatem pertinere, ius antiquum esto.' Hoc ideo dicitur, ut, quamdiu vel unus filius vult legitimam hereditatem ad se pertinere, ius vetus locum non habeat: Itaque si ex duobus alter adierit, alter repudiaverit hereditatem, ei portio adcrescet. [...] (D.38.17.1.9.)

> Ulpianus, Sabinus, book 12: 'Let the ancient law be observed, if none of the children, or those simultaneously entitled to the estate as statutory heirs, wishes to obtain the estate.' This clause was enacted so that the ancient law might not apply if only one son wished the statutory inheritance to belong to him. Hence, if one of the two sons accepts the estate, but the other rejects it, the share of the latter will accrue to the former. [...] (D.38.17.1.9.)

Ulpian (third century AD) discusses the wording of the *senatusconsultum* according to which the old law only applies if no heir accepts under the *ius novum*. It is suspended, as long as at least one child is willing to take the mother's inheritance. Only after all children have renounced their right can the heir on intestacy under the *ius civile* and *ius praetorium* claim the inheritance. The fact that the child is given priority in inheriting after his mother, i.e., a position resembling a direct heir, makes the balancing act between *ius antiquum* and *ius novum* easier for the *senatusconsultum Orfitianum* than for the *senatusconsultum Tertullianum*. The imperial right of inheritance concerning children is prioritised until all children have renounced the estate.

Finally, the rules of the *senatusconsultum Orfitianum* were considered as being *ius civile*, and hence changed the order of succession of the *ius civile*, which in turn affected the *ius praetorium*:

> *Paulus, liber singularis ad senatusconsultum Orfitianum: Filius, qui se nolle adire hereditatem matris dixit, an potest mutata voluntate adire, antequam consanguineus vel adgnatus adierit, videndum propter haec verba, 'si nemo filiorum volet hereditatem suscipere,' quia extensiva sunt. Et cum verba extensiva sint, paenitentia eius usque ad annum admittenda est, cum et ipsa filii bonorum possessio annalis est. (D.38.17.6.1.)*

> Paul, *senatusconsultum* Orfitianum, sole book: Let us consider whether a son who has said that he does not accept his mother's estate can inherit after he has changed his mind and before a blood kin from the father's side or an agnate has inherited. The latter is possible because of the following words: 'if none of the children desires to accept the estate.' And because these words have a broader meaning, he should be allowed to change his mind, but only for one year, because the *bonorum possessio* of the child itself is also limited to one year. (D.38.17.6.1.)

Paul discusses a case where a son, having renounced his right to inherit under the *ius civile* following the *senatusconsultum*, claimed *bonorum possessio ab intestato* from his mother. Since the claim to *bonorum possessio* in the class *unde legitimi* is based on law of inheritance of the *senatusconsultum Orfitianum*, we must ask whether the renunciation under the *ius civile* also affects the claim of *bonorum possessio*. Paul (third century AD) decides that renouncing the right to inherit under the *ius civile* does not preclude a claim of *bonorum possessio ab intestato* because the *senatus consultum* excludes the child only if it has renounced both its entitlement under the *ius civile* and *ius praetorium*. Hence, the *ius antiquum* revives only if the son repudiates both his right to inherit under the *ius civile* and, perhaps merely through omission to raise a claim, the *bonorum possessio ab intestato*.

Thus, the son who wants to obtain *bonorum possessio*, following the *senatusconsultum Orfitianum* under the class *unde legitimi*, succeeding his mother, has an advantage compared to the mother who claims, as her child's heir, the *bonorum possessio* under the *senatusconsultum Tertullianum* in the same class. As we saw (Ch. 3.4.2), the mother is excluded from the *bonorum possessio ab intestato* in the class *unde legitimi* if she refuses to accept the inheritance (*aditio hereditatis*) according to the *ius civile*. In contrast, the child who has waived his right to inherit under the *ius civile*, following the *senatusconsultum Orfitianum*, is granted the *bonorum possessio ab intestato* in the class *unde legitimi*. Paul bases the different outcomes on the wording of the two *senatusconsulta*. His view might be further supported by the fact that the mother's right to inherit depends in other situations (under the *ius civile* and *ius praetorium*) on the renunciation by a person with priority, while the children inheriting from the mother on intestacy displace all remaining heirs. The *ius antiquum* and the derogation of the *senatusconsultum* only come into force under the *senatusconsultum Orfitianum* once all children have waived all their open and possible claims to intestacy. Contrary to this, the *senatusconsultum Tertullianum*, in examining the mother's right to inherit, presupposes that a claimant with priority did not claim the *bonorum possessio ab intestato*. Even though jurists clearly distinguished between the spheres of the *ius novum* and the *ius antiquum*, we see that the two layers of law cannot be separated under the *senatusconsultum Tertullianum*, while their distinction under the *senatusconsultum Orfitianum* was possible due to the rule of priority.

The rule about the conflict of claims between the children of the daughter and the mother entitled under the *senatusconsultum Tertullianum* (Ch. 3.4.1) demonstrates that a mother's children are in a privileged position against the mother as heir on intestacy of her children. As we saw, children entitled to inherit from a daughter under the *senatusconsultum Orfitianum*, have priority over the mother, who is entitled under the *senatusconsultum Tertullianum*. As a result, the *senatusconsultum Orfitianum* has priority over the *senatusconsultum Tertullianum*.

The two *senatusconsulta* form the pinnacle of the evolution of the ancient Roman intestacy rules, though subsequent rescripts and case law further refined the system discussed. In conclusion, the two *senatusconsulta* allow a review of the layers of the law on intestacy and their evolution in a nutshell.

3.5 Concluding Considerations on the Rules of Intestacy

1. Toward the end of the Empire, the Roman rules of intestacy presented themselves as a mixture of differing forms of regulation. The intestacy rules for children-in-power and for agnates, which were laid down in the law of the twelve tables of *ca.* 450BC, still form the basis of the imperial inheritance law. Taking this as a starting point, the praetor granted those entitled

per classes of the edict the *bonorum possessio ab intestato*. The two imperial *senatusconsulta* enacted to regulate the law of inheritance between mother and child intervened directly in the order of succession of the *ius civile* and supplemented the existing rules as *ius novum*.

Overview 13: Layers of Law of the Rules of Intestacy during the Empire

ius antiquum:		*ius novum:*	
ius civile:	*ius praetorium*:	*ius civile*:	*ius praetorium*:
direct heirs	+ *emancipati*	+ the wife's children	*nova clausula Iuliani*
proximus agnatus		+ the wife's children + The mothers	
	cognati		
	spouses		

Overview 13 shows that the various layers of law accumulate and permeate each other. This interdependence is demonstrated by the fact that the *ius novum* initially created rules on the level of *ius civile*. Thus, it interacted with one of the previous layers of law. The interdependence is also visible in the reception of the imperial intervention into the *ius praetorium*, thus conditioning an innovation of the praetorian law of succession.

2. Despite this interdependence, however, the various layers of law are not the result of a coherent legal policy. On the one hand, the law of inheritance of the *ius civile* preserves a continuation of the agnatic family structure after the death of the head of the family. On the other hand, the rules of intestacy of the *ius praetorium* aim for equal treatment of all descendants, regardless of whether they are under the *patria potestas* or only related as cognates. At the same time, the procedural nature of the praetorian rules prevents them from achieving any formal revision of the order of succession of the *ius civile*. An actual modification of the archaic *ius civile* only occurs during the Empire through the *senatusconsulta*, which repeal the old and create a new *ius civile*. This new law improves the position of a woman as heir of her children. Hence, a decisive shift to a cognatic family paradigm occurred.

3. The antiquated agnatic family paradigm is not abandoned but survives through the entitlement of the *agnatus proximus*, who is also protected under the *ius praetorium* (*unde legitimi*). The order of succession on intestacy of the *ius civile* remains intact next to the praetorian, except for the rules of inheritance of the *gentiles*, and this coexistence creates contradictions; namely, between the *ius civile* and the *ius praetorium* when children under

the *potestas* are emancipated. As we saw (Ch. 3.3.2), these contradictions would be harmonised through a more comprehensive imperial intervention during the Empire. The *nova clausula Iuliani* was a balancing act between *ius praetorium* and *ius civile*. The said edict fused both layers by allowing *ius civile* and *ius praetorium* heirs to inherit on intestacy in parallel. The edict thus proves the tendency of the imperial law to even out tensions between *ius civile* and *ius praetorium* for the sake of a unified law on which the *princeps* has left his mark.

4

The Position of the Heir

The legal rules governing intestacy under the *ius civile* and the position of the direct heirs, more specifically, show that the position of the heir follows the statutory pattern of the law of the twelve tables; thus, taking the agnatic family as its paradigm. The latter is based on the power structure of the *pater familias* over his children. The fact that the position of the heir depends on the succession in the power structure explains why the heir, as a successor, assumes the rights and obligations of the decedent in their totality:

> *Iulianus, 6 digestorum: Hereditas nihil aliud est, quam successio in universum ius quod defunctus habuerit. (D.50.17.62.)*

> Julian, Digest, book 6: Inheritance is nothing but the succession to every right and obligation of the decedent. (D.50.17.62.)

This perception of the position of an heir as a successor to all rights and obligations (universal succession, from *successio in universum ius*) was also applied to the testamentary order of succession at a date that remains unknown to us (Ch. 6.1). Hence, the heir inherits the rights and obligations of the decedent; as a legal successor to the latter he can sue and he can be sued in the decedent's name:

> *Inst.Gai.4.112.: Non omnes actiones, quae in aliquem aut ipso iure conpetunt aut a praetore dantur, etiam in heredem aeque conpetunt aut dari solent. Est enim certissima iuris regula ex maleficiis poenales actiones in heredem nec conpetere nec dari solere, velut furti, vi bonorum raptorum, iniuriarum, damni iniuriae. Sed heredibus [eiusdem videlicet] actoris huiusmodi actiones competunt nec denegantur, excepta iniuriarum actione et si qua alia similis inveniatur actio.*

> Inst.Gai.4.112.: Not all actions that lie against somebody by *ius civile* or are granted against him by the praetor, also lie against the heir, nor are they usually granted against him. For it is an undisputed rule that penal actions based on delictual liability that arise from wrongdoings, neither lie against the heir

nor are granted against him. These are, for instance, the actions for theft, robbery, infringements of personality rights, or unlawful damage. But heirs of the claimant will have these actions and will not be denied them, apart from the action for infringements of personality rights and similar actions.

The transfer of rights and obligations to the heir included the transfer of all actions that could have been initiated by a decedent or that could have been initiated against the latter. Only penal actions which are based on delictual liability (*actiones poenales*) are passively non-inheritable upon death. However, they are actively transmissible, so that the heir can bring all delictual actions, except for the action for infringements of personality rights (*actio iniuriarum*). This can be explained by the nature of the action, as it protects highly personal rights and sanctions, e.g., insults and minor bodily harm. This rule of transfer of rights (and obligations) to the heir applies to actions under *ius civile* as well as those under *ius praetorium*.

Despite the consistent definition of the position of heir under the *ius civile*, there is a strict alternativity between inheritance by will and intestacy in this layer of law:

> *Pomponius, 3 ad Sabinum: Ius nostrum non patitur eundem in paganis et testato et intestato decessisse: Earumque rerum naturaliter inter se pugna est 'testatus' et 'intestatus'. (D.50.17.7.)*

> Pomponius, Sabinus, book 3: Our law does not allow anybody, who is not a soldier, to die both testate and intestate. For there is a natural antagonism between the concepts 'testate' and 'intestate'. (D.50.17.7.)

Apart from the special imperial rules for soldiers (Ch. 6.4.2), the legal rules governing intestacy could not be applied if a testamentary heir accepted the inheritance. The principle applied was: *nemo pro parte testatus pro parte intestatus decedere possit* ('nobody can dispose part of his property in a will and the rest on intestacy'). Only if no testamentary heir came forth, could succession upon intestacy be applied.

We will now examine the individual aspects of these principles concerning the acquisition of inheritance under the *ius civile*. Then we will review the additions and modifications of the *ius praetorium*. Finally, we will compare the personal requirements relating to the heir under the *ius civile*, *ius praetorium*, and *ius novum*.

4.1 The Acquisition of an Inheritance under the *ius civile*

The consequences of universal succession as a feature of the position of heir under the *ius civile* can be observed most clearly in the association of heirs, already found in the law of the twelve tables.

4.1.1 The Association of Co-Heirs

The community of co-heirs (*consortium*) emerges by operation of law among the direct heirs:

> Inst.Gai.3.154a: [...] Olim enim mortuo patre familias inter suos heredes quaedam erat legitima simul et naturalis societas quae appellabatur ercto non cito, id est dominio non diviso: Erctum enim dominium est, unde erus dominus dicitur: Ciere autem dividere est: unde caedere et secare et dividere dicimus.

> Inst.Gai.3.154a: [...] Once, there was, however, a kind of partnership between the direct heirs of a deceased *pater familias* that was both statutory and natural, called '*ercto non cito*', namely, 'society by undivided ownership'. For '*erctum*' means ownership, from which stems '*erus*', owner. '*Ciere*', on the other, means 'to divide', from which we say, '*caedere*' both for, 'to cut' and 'to divide'.

In a historical overview, Gaius (second century AD) explained that direct heirs formed a statutory 'partnership by undivided ownership' (*societas ercto non cito*). However, the meaning of a *societas ercto non cito* seemed no longer evident to Gaius' contemporaries. Thus, he explained that the word *erus* (from *erctum*, 'patrimony') denotes the owner and *ciere* (to cut, thus, *non cito*) means the division. The analysis of the expression shows that the legal position of the decedent passed undivided to the direct heirs and that only they could divide the property. Since the acquisition of the inheritance was a natural process for the direct heirs (Ch. 3.1.1), their community was a natural one, because it emerged automatically from the termination of the *potestas* of the *pater familas*, leading to the simultaneous succession of all the direct heirs into the position of the *pater familias*. The common assumption of a power to dispose, previously belonging to a single person, accounts for the special powers of disposal of the individual members of the *consortium*:

> Inst.Gai.3.154b: [...] in hac autem societate fratrum [...] illud proprium erat, [unus] quod vel unus ex sociis communem servum manumittendo liberum faciebat et omnibus libertum adquirebat: Item unus rem communem mancipando eius faciebat, qui mancipio accipiebat.

> Inst.Gai.3.154b: [...] But in this partnership of brothers [...] it was characteristic that even one of the partners could manumit a slave held in common and made him the freedman of all. So also, one partner transferred an item held in common ownership to a third party through *mancipatio*.

Each co-heir had the authority to bind the other partners legally. Thus, no joint action by the co-heirs was necessary to dispose of the estate. Since the share in the family estate was a manifestation of family ties, and of the succession into the legal position of the common father, no conflict of interest among the family members was anticipated. However, the law of the twelve tables already provided the option to end the partnership and to divide the estate.

V. 9-10 Familiam erciscunto ciento. Si petit, iudicem arbitrumve postulato.[1]

V. 9-10: They shall summon the household and divide. If he sues, he shall demand a judge or an arbitrator.

This rule presumed that the co-heirs initially divided the estate on their own. If necessary, however, a co-heir could ask a judge or an arbitrator to proceed with the distribution of the property. This division of inheritance by court included, until the Empire, only the existing assets, not the liabilities of the deceased's estate. These liabilities continued to be subject to the principle of universal succession:

C.3.36.6 Gord. (s.a.): Ea quae in nominibus sunt non recipiunt divisionem, cum ipso iure in portiones hereditarias ex lege duodecim tabularum divisa sunt.

C.3.36.6. Gord. (s.a.): What consists of debts claims cannot be divided, for, under the law of the twelve tables, it is divided by the law itself into inheritance shares.

The decisive factor for the liability from the estate and for the acquisition of claims of the deceased is the share of the inheritance. This legal position allotted to each co-heir can neither be renounced nor lost through adjudication. Therefore, agreements about the division of the estate's debts are also excluded:

C.2.3.26. Diocl./Maxim. (a. 294): Pactum successorum debitoris ex lege duodecim tabularum aes alienum hereditarium pro portionibus quaesitis singulis ipso iure divisum in solidum unum obligare creditori non potest: [...].

C.2.3.26. Diocl./Maxim. (a. 294): An agreement entered into by the debtor's heirs, by which the estate's indebtedness was divided in proportion to the shares, that each of them obtained, cannot bind one of the debtors to the creditor for the entire amount because under the law of the twelve tables the estate's debts were divided in proportion to the shares, by operation of law [...].

---

[1] Cited after Michel Humbert, Andrew D. E. Lewis and Michael H. Crawford, in Michael H. Crawford (ed), *Roman Statutes II* (Institute of Classical Studies 1996).

In the case decided here, the co-heirs agreed in the course of the dispute not only on the division of the estate's property, but also on the distribution of debts. The rescript stresses that the agreement is only valid concerning the allocation of property to individual heirs. The consensus regarding the distribution of debts contravenes the law of the twelve tables, and cannot be imposed on the estate's creditors. Regarding the estate's creditors, liability remains per share in the estate; hence, the creditors can pursue every co-heir up to the amount of his share.

The rule whereby the descendants of the direct heirs succeed into the position of the predeceased *filius familias* (Ch. 3.1.1) must be understood against this background. The liabilities of the direct heir devolve to his descendants within his stem.

The rules regarding the association of statutory co-heirs also apply to testamentary heirs. However, if one testamentary heir does not acquire his part or if he predeceases his descendants, the latter do not succeed him. His share, instead, falls to the remaining co-heirs.

4.1.2 The Accrual for Testamentary Heirs

The accruing (from *accrescere*, 'to increase') among co-heirs leads to the entitlement of testamentary heirs as long as they exist, while excluding intestate succession. Hence, testamentary succession and succession on intestacy are mutually exclusive, and the jurists call this the principle: '*nemo pro parte testatus pro parte intestatus decedere potest*' (Ch. 4). Like the joint liability of the heirs, accrual is not discretionary, but occurs by operation of law:

> *Gaius, 14 ad legem Iuliam et Papiam: Qui semel aliqua ex parte heres exstitit, deficientium partes etiam invitus excipit, id est tacite ei deficientium partes etiam invito adcrescunt. (D.29.2.53.1.)*

> Gaius, Lex Iulia et Papia, book 14: Once someone has accepted the inheritance to any share of an estate, he will also, even without his consent, acquire the shares of his co-heirs who refuse to accept them. That is to say; their shares will tacitly accrue to him, even contrary to his will. (D.29.2.53.1.)

Accrual merely requires that the heir who stands to benefit, has accepted the inheritance. He neither needs to know that the other heir has failed nor does he need to accept the accrued share formally. If the remaining share accrues to several heirs, they accrue proportionately to their share, as Overview 14a shows:

Overview 14a: Accrual in the Case of Varying Shares

testator			
co-heir 1: 1/8	co-heir 2: 1/8	co-heir 3: 1/2	co-heir 4: 1/4
does not accept	predeceased	accrual: 1/6	accrual: 1/12
		accrual of 1/4 of the estate in total	

Since, under the testator's will, co-heir 3 is to get double of what co-heir 4 will get, they will also accrue through the failure of co-heirs 1 and 2 the remaining share of one-fourth in proportion to this internal distribution. In other words, the co-heir 3 receives one-sixth by accrual (2/12) and the co-heir 4 only 1/12 of the share from the failure.

Special accrual rules applied if the testator had provided for groups in the testamentary succession for which an accrual was to be preferred:

Paulus, 6 ad legem Iuliam et Papiam: Triplici modo coniunctio intellegitur: Aut enim re per se coniunctio contingit, aut re et verbis, aut verbis tantum. Nec dubium est, quin coniuncti sint, quos et nominum et rei complexus iungit, veluti 'Titius et Maevius ex parte dimidia heredes sunto,' vel ita 'Titius Maeviusque heredes sunto,' vel 'Titius cum Maevio ex parte dimidia heredes sunto.' Videamus autem, ne etiam si hos articulos detrahas 'et' 'que' 'cum,' interdum tamen coniunctos accipi oporteat, veluti 'Lucius Titius, Publius Maevius ex parte dimidia heredes sunto,' vel ita 'Publius Maevius, Lucius Titius heredes sunto. Sempronius ex parte dimidia heres esto,' ut Titius et Maevius veniant in partem dimidiam et re et verbis coniuncti videantur. [...] (D.50.16.142.)

Paul, Lex Iulia et Papia, book 6: 'A joinder of heirs' can have three meanings: it can be made through the institution itself, by using the institution and words contained in the will, or by the words alone. There is no doubt that those are joined who are connected both by the linking of their names and by the object, e.g.: 'let Titius and Maevius be heirs to half a share', or: 'let Titius and Maevius be my heirs', or: 'let Titius, with Maevius, be heirs to half a share.' Let us see, however, if we omit the 'and' and 'with', whether the parties can be considered to be joined, for instance, 'let Lucius Titius, Publius Maevius be heirs to half a share', or: 'let Publius Maevius, Lucius Titius, be my heirs to a half. Let Sempronius be the heir to half a share.' Thus, Titius and Maevius are entitled to half of the estate and are understood to be joined concerning the institution and the words. [...] (D.50.16.142.)

The group of heirs is called a 'joinder of heirs' (*coniunctio*). It can occur in two ways: through the appointment to a common share (*coniunctio re*), or through the joint nomination in the case of appointment to a common share (*coniunctio re et verbis*). It is neither necessary nor sufficient to use link words, as Paul (third century AD) demonstrates through several examples where the heirs are not explicitly but implicitly appointed to the same share. Thus, the substantive appointment to the same share is crucial. Whether a joinder of heirs was intended, depends on the interpretation of the will:

> *Pomponius, 1 ad Quintum Mucium: Si ita quis heredes instituerit: 'Titius heres esto: Gaius et Maevius aequis ex partibus heredes sunto,' quamvis et syllaba coniunctionem faciat, si quis tamen ex his decedat, non alteri soli pars adcrescit, sed et omnibus coheredibus pro hereditariis portionibus, quia non tam coniunxisse quam celerius dixisse videatur. (D.28.5.67.)*

> Pomponius, on Quintus Mucius, book 1: If someone appoints heirs as follows: 'let Titius be my heir and let Gaius and Maevius be heirs to equal shares.' If either [of Gaius and Maevius] dies, his share will not accrue to the other alone, but to all co-heirs in proportion to their share, although the word 'and' is a conjunction, because it appears that the testator did not mean to join the two heirs together, but rather spoke in haste. (D.28.5.67.)

According to the example provided by Pomponius (second century AD), the true joinder of the co-heirs, i.e. a connection actually intended by the testator, must be distinguished from the merely joint naming of co-heirs in the will. Not every 'and' in a will leads to a *coniunctio* following the rules of accrual. Rather, it is decisive that the interpretation of the testament shows that the heirs were appointed to a common share of the estate. Overview 14b illustrates the outcome of forming joinders of heirs based on an example:

Overview 14b: Accrual in *coniunctio re et verbis*

'Titius and Maevius shall be heirs'/'Titius and Maevius shall each be heirs to one half'/ 'Lucius Titius, Publius Maevius shall be heirs to half a share'			
[Lucius Titius]	Publius Maevius	[co-heir 3]	co-heir 4
predeceased		predeceased	
	5/8		3/8

Suppose four persons are appointed heirs to equal shares, and only Lucius Titius and Publius Maevius form a joinder of heirs. In that case, the share of the predeceased Lucius Titius passes to Publius Maevius alone. The share of the predeceased co-heir 3, however, who does not form a joinder with the other co-heirs, accrues to the remaining co-heirs, i.e., both to Publius Maevius and co-heir 4, per their respective share. Hence, Publius Maevius acquires one-fourth (his share), an additional one-fourth (the share of Lucius Titius) and the one-eighth of the co-heir 3. In total, he gets five-eighths of the estate. The co-heir 4, however, receives, in addition to his share of one-fourth, only the part of the share of the co-heir 3; hence, three-eighths of the estate in total. In comparison: if Lucius Titius and Publius Maevius were not a joinder of heirs, then Publius Maevius and co-heir 4 would have acquired half of the estate each, since Lucius Titius and co-heir 3 would not be considered.

An heir can drop out of the order of succession due to death, but also because he refused to accept. Different rules apply for acquiring an estate, depending on whether we have direct heirs or *extranei* (from *extraneus* = 'extraneous'), i.e. 'heirs from outside the family'.

4.1.3 The Acceptance of the Inheritance

Only direct heirs receive the inheritance by operation of law:

> *Inst.Gai.2.157.: Sed sui quidem heredes ideo appellantur, quia domestici heredes sunt et vivo quoque parente quodam modo domini existimantur; unde etiam si quis intestatus mortuus sit, prima causa est in successione liberorum. Necessarii vero ideo dicuntur, quia omni modo, velint nolint, tam ab intestato quam ex testamento heredes fiunt.*

> Inst.Gai.2.157.: But they are called 'direct heirs' because they are heirs from the household, and even during the lifetime of their *pater familias* somehow, considered co-owners of the estate. Hence, where anyone dies intestate, the first right to his succession belongs to his children under the paternal power. They are even called 'necessary heirs' because under all circumstances, willing or not, they become heirs both on intestacy and under a will.

Since direct heirs were already considered entitled to the household's assets during the *pater familias'* lifetime (Ch. 3.1.1), they acquired the inheritance by operation of law when the head of the household died. Moreover, the direct heirs were initially not free to accept the estate since they were *heredes necessarii*. Eventually, they would become free from this compulsory inheritance under the *ius praetorium* (Ch. 4.2.1).

But all other heirs, who were not direct heirs but *extranei*, acquired the estate only through (formal) acceptance:

> *Inst.Gai.2.162.: Extraneis autem heredibus deliberandi potestas data est de adeunda hereditate vel non adeunda.*

> Inst.Gai.2.162.: The *extranei*, however, are given the option to deliberate whether to accept or to refuse the inheritance.

The *extranei* can, therefore, choose whether to accept or renounce the inheritance. To determine the acquisition of the estate on their part, it remains crucial to distinguish between the decedent's death and the inheritance's accession. The act of accepting can take various forms. Hence, the testator can ask for a solemn acceptance by the heir:

> Inst.Gai.2.165.: *Cum ergo ita scriptum sit: 'Heres Titius esto,' adicere debemus: 'Cernitoque in centum diebus proxumis, quibus scies poterisque. Quodni ita creveris, exheres esto.'*

> Inst.Gai.2.165.: Therefore, if it was written: 'Titius shall be my heir', we must add, 'and within a hundred days after you learn of your appointment and can do so, you must decide whether to accept, and if you don't solemnly accept thus, you shall be disinherited.'

Through the testamentary appointment, the testator requested that Titius must solemnly accept the estate (*cretio*) within one hundred days of becoming aware of the inheritance. Otherwise, he shall be disinherited. Here, Titius must solemnly declare that he accepts the inheritance within the prescribed time limit in front of witnesses to receive the estate. If the testator has, however, not requested a *cretio*, the acceptance can occur formlessly:

> Inst.Gai.2.167.: *At is, qui sine cretione heres institutus sit aut qui ab intestato legitimo iure ad hereditatem vocatur, potest aut cernendo aut pro herede gerendo vel etiam nuda voluntate suscipiendae hereditatis heres fieri: Eique liberum est, quocumque tempore voluerit, adire hereditatem; [...]*

> Inst.Gai.2.167.: But if someone is appointed heir without the requirement to solemnly accept or if he is statutory heir on account of intestacy, he can, either by solemn acceptance, by acting as heir, or simply by expressing his formless desire to be an heir, become an heir. And he can decide at whatever time he wishes to accept the inheritance [...]

The designated heir acquires the estate formlessly by acting intentionally as heir (*pro herede gestio*), or through a formless declaration of acceptance. There was an acceptance as long as the heir's words or deeds demonstrate that he wishes to accept the inheritance. These principles also apply in the case of heirs by intestacy.

Until the estate was accepted by the *extranei* or after it had been renounced by the direct heirs, a period could pass during which the inheritance remained vacant. Roman jurists called this situation: the *hereditas iacens* ('lying estate').

4.1.4 Acquiring an Inheritance through Prescriptive Acquisition

Initially, the *ius civile* foresaw that the position of heir could be obtained through prescriptive acquisition (or usucaption) by taking possession of the *hereditas iacens*:

> Inst.Gai.2.52.: *Rursus ex contrario accidit, ut, qui sciat alienam rem se possidere, usucapiat, velut si rem hereditariam, cuius possessionem heres nondum nactus est, aliquis possederit; nam ei concessum est usucapere, si modo ea res est, quae recipit usucapionem. Quae species possessionis et usucapionis pro herede vocatur.*

> Inst.Gai.2.52.: Conversely, it can happen that someone who knows that the property he possesses belongs to another can acquire it by usucaption. For instance, if someone possesses property belonging to an estate of which the heir has not yet obtained possession. Then he is permitted to acquire, provided the property is of a sort that permits usucaption. This kind of possession and usucaption is called '*pro herede*' (in place of the heir).

If someone took hold of an *hereditas iacens* in place of the heir (*pro herede*), and had it in his possession, he could become heir through prescriptive acquisition, even if he knew he was not entitled to the inheritance. Hence, whereas usucaption of ownership under Roman law required that the *usucaptor* was in 'good faith' (*bona fide*) when obtaining possession, the usucaption of the position of an heir (*usucapio pro herede*) initially did not require 'good faith'.

The time limit prescribed for a prescriptive acquisition of an estate also differed from the one required for usucaption in general:

> Inst.Gai.2.53–54.: *(53) Et in tantum haec usucapio concessa est, ut et res, quae solo continentur, anno usucapiantur.*
> *(54) Quare autem etiam hoc casu soli rerum annua constituta sit usucapio, illa ratio est, quod olim rerum hereditariarum possessiones ut ipsae hereditates usucapi credebantur, scilicet anno: lex enim XII tabularum soli quidem res biennio usucapi iussit, ceteras vero anno: Ergo hereditas in ceteris rebus videbatur esse, quia soli non est [quia neque corporalis est]; [...]*

> Inst.Gai.2.53–54.: (53) The nature of this usucaption is such that even immovable property may be acquired within a year.
> (54) The reason here why assets that belong to the land can also be acquired by usucaption in a single year is that in ancient times it was believed that the rights to possess the property belonging to an estate were acquired in the same way as the estate itself, that is to say, in one year. For the law of the

twelve tables prescribed two years for the usucaption of land and one year for other property. Hence, an inheritance was considered part of the latter, as it is neither part of the land nor corporeal [...]

Whereas immovables could be acquired by prescriptive acquisition after two years, immovables from an inheritance could thus be acquired within a year, like movable goods since the time limit for usucaption of an estate applied to all items belonging to the estate. Hence, the one-year limitation period for movable goods applied because the inheritance itself could not be seen as immovable.

Therefore, usucaption of an estate was easier than usucaption of property in general. Overview 15 sums up the specific rules of this particular kind of usucaption:

Overview 15: Comparison between General Usucaption and Hereditary Usucaption

general prescriptive acquisition (*usucapio*)	hereditary prescriptive acquisition (*usucapio pro herede*)
transfer (*traditio*)	taking the estate
just cause for usucaption (*causa*)	intention to possess in place of the heir
good faith (*bona fides*)	good faith not necessary
possession of the object for oneself (*possessio*)	possessing the estate, objects of the estate, for oneself (*possessio*)
expiry of time limit for usucaption: **1 year** for movable property **2 years** for immovable property	expiry of time limit for usucaption: **1 year**
usucaption is excluded in case of theft or robbery (*res furtiva*)	usucaption is excluded in case of theft or robbery (*res furtiva*)

The reason given for privileging the *usucaptor* of an estate was a concern for the uninterrupted continuation of the household cult and the protection of the estate's creditors:

> Inst.Gai.2.55.: *Quare autem omnino tam inproba possessio et usucapio concessa sit, illa ratio est, quod voluerunt veteres maturius hereditates adiri, ut essent, qui sacra facerent, quorum illis temporibus summa observatio fuit, ut et creditores haberent, a quo suum consequerentur.*
>
> Inst.Gai.2.55.: The reason why such an unlawful kind of possession and usucaption [of the estate] were allowed in the first place was that the old jurists wanted heirs to accept inheritances very soon so that they could perform the

domestic cult whose observation was of the utmost importance at that time. Moreover, the creditors should have someone from whom to claim what was due.

Enabling someone to become heir by usucaption was meant as an incentive for the designated heir to accept the inheritance, to preserve the domestic cult and to secure the claims of the estate's creditors. Thus, either the designated heir accepted and met the religious and liability obligations or another person appropriated the estate or parts of it, and took over the responsibilities attached to what he had obtained.

However, the jurists of the Empire conceived this kind of usucaption as an anomaly, as it allowed a foreign object to be acquired despite the usucaptor's knowledge that he was not entitled. By the time of Gaius (second century AD), this expedited usucaption was formally abolished:

> *Inst.Gai.2.57.: Sed hoc tempore iam non est lucrativa: Nam ex auctoritate Hadriani senatusconsultum factum est, ut tales usucapiones revocarentur; et ideo potest heres ab eo, qui rem usucepit, hereditatem petendo proinde eam rem consequi, atque si usucapta non esset.*

Inst.Gai.2.57.: At present, however, such a profitable usucaption no longer exists. For a *senatusconsultum* by the deified Hadrian said that usucaption of this kind could be revoked. And, therefore, an heir can recover the object from the person who acquired it by usucaption, by claiming the inheritance, as if the usucaption had never happened.

The final blow to this peculiar kind of usucaption came from a *senatusconsultum* from the reign of Emperor Hadrian that granted the heir an action for recovery of the estate against the possessor after the time limit for usucaption (Ch. 5). Apparently, in the second century AD, the need to grant the creditors of an estate a secure footing of liability for their claims was less pressing than when the initial rule of *usucapio pro herede* was passed. Hence, the anomalous outcome of a *usucapio pro herede* in bad faith was repealed.

The fact that the *ius praetorium* eased the creditor's access to the decedent's estate could be a reason why this form of usucaption became obsolete.

4.2 The Acquisition of an Inheritance under the *ius praetorium*

Through *bonorum possessio*, the praetor not only developed a distinct praetorian law of inheritance (Ch. 3.2) but also regulated the acquisition of an estate under the *ius civile*. Thus, providing legal security to the heir and the creditors of the estate.

4.2.1 Praetorian Rules on the Acquisition of an Estate under the ius civile

While a declaration of acceptance of an estate is bound by a time limit under the *ius civile* only if the testator has requested one, the praetor can set a deadline for any designated heir:

> Inst.Gai.2.167.: [...] Sed solet praetor postulantibus hereditariis creditoribus tempus constituere, intra quod, si velit, adeat hereditatem, si minus, ut liceat creditoribus bona defuncti vendere.

> Inst.Gai.2.167.: [...] If the estate's creditors apply for it, the praetor usually sets a time limit for the designated heir to decide whether to accept the inheritance. And if he does not, the creditors can sell the decedent's estate.

This happened mainly when the estate's creditors requested it, as they wished to sue him for the estate's debts and therefore wanted certainty about the heir. The praetor treated the designated heir, who had missed the set deadline, as ineligible to accept the estate. Even though he was heir under the *ius civile*, the *bonorum possessio*, i.e. the position of heir under praetorian law, was denied to him.

Conversely, the praetor allowed the direct heirs, who were not permitted to renounce the estate under the *ius civile*, to do so:

> Inst.Gai.2.158.: Sed his praetor permittit abstinere se ab hereditate [...]

> Inst.Gai.2.158.: The praetor, however, permits them to renounce the inheritance [...]

Under praetorian law, the direct heirs could thus renounce the inheritance so that the successors of lower rank could obtain *bonorum possessio*. However, the right of the direct heir to renounce (Ch. 3.1.1) and the right of the *extraneus* not to accept the inheritance were forfeited if the designated heir interfered with the estate:

> Inst.Gai.2.163.: Sed sive is, cui abstinendi potestas est, inmiscuerit se bonis hereditariis, sive is, cui de adeunda deliberare licet, adierit, postea relinquendae hereditatis facultatem non habet, [...]

> Inst.Gai.2.163.: If, however, someone who is allowed to renounce an inheritance interferes with the assets of the estate, or someone permitted to deliberate whether to accept an estate, does so, he has no ability to reject it afterwards [...]

If the heir had already dealt with matters of the estate, he could no longer renounce it. It would have been a contradiction to profit from the estate but to refuse to assume the responsibilities of the inheritance. This rule shows that the rationale behind the praetorian regulation on the acceptance of inheritances lies in the heir's liability to the creditors of the estate.

Equally, *bonorum possessio* was designed to forestall a prolonged vacant succession.

4.2.2 The bonorum possessor *as praetorian heir*

As we have seen (Ch. 3.2), *bonorum possessio* can only be acquired within a certain time limit. Moreover, different persons are called upon to claim the estate one after the other:

> *Ulpianus*, 49 ad edictum: Successorium edictum idcirco propositum est, ne bona hereditaria vacua sine domino diutius iacerent et creditoribus longior mora fieret. E re igitur praetor putavit praestituere tempus his, quibus bonorum possessionem detulit, et dare inter eos successionem, ut maturius possint creditores scire, utrum habeant, cum quo congrediantur, [...] *(D.38.9.1pr.)*
>
> Ulpian, Edict, book 49: An edict concerning sequence of successors was promulgated to prevent estates from remaining too long without owners; thus, burdening creditors with prolonged delays in payment. Therefore, the praetor thought that a time limit should be prescribed for those to whom he granted *bonorum possessio*, and that a sequence should be established among those so that creditors might sooner ascertain against whom they take action, [...] (D.38.9.1pr.)

According to Ulpian (third century AD), this graduated entitlement of several praetorian heirs to *bonorum possessio ab intestato* avoided a vacant succession for a prolonged period. The aim was to protect the estate from unauthorised interference by third parties and to increase legal certainty for the creditors of the estate. For this reason, the application of a respective class had to be lodged within a certain period of time. If one of those entitled decided to submit such an application, *bonorum possessio* was granted to him, and the vacancy was filled. If nobody applied by the relevant deadline, the next class of praetorian heirs was called upon. As a consequence, even if only members of a subsequent class decided to apply for *bonorum possessio*, the creditors of the estate suffered a shorter delay in payment overall.

Since, under this rule, the position of the heir under *ius civile* did not have to correspond to the position of the *bonorum possessor* under *ius praetorium*, it could happen that the *bonorum possessor* was not identical with the heir's civil successor. Therefore, the praetor had to take comprehensive measures to align the position of the *bonorum possessor* with that of the heir under *ius civile*:

> *Inst.Gai.4.34: Habemus adhuc alterius generis fictiones in quibusdam formulis, velut cum is, qui ex edicto bonorum possessionem petit, ficto se herede agit. Cum enim praetorio iure et, non legitimo, succedat in locum defuncti, non habet derectas actiones et neque id, quod defuncti fuit, potest intendere suum esse neque id, quod ei debebatur, potest intendere dari sibi oportere; itaque ficto se herede intendit, [...] et si illi debeatur pecunia, praeposita simili fictione heredis ita subicitur: 'Tum si pareret Numerium Negidium Aulo Agerio sestertia x milia dare oportere.'*
>
> Inst.Gai.4.34.: We also use other kinds of fictions in certain procedural formulas. E.g., if someone who claims *bonorum possessio* under the edict, sues on the fiction that he is heir. As he succeeds the decedent under the *ius praetorium* and not under the *ius civile*, he is not entitled to a direct action. Hence, he cannot claim that the decedent's property is his, nor can he demand that what was due to the latter should be paid to him. So, he claims by the fiction that he is the heir [...] or if, in the case of a debt, a similar fiction is used, thus: 'If it then turned out, that Numerius Negidius (the defendant) had to give to Aulus Agerius (the plaintiff) ten thousand.'[2]

The most important support given to the *bonorum possessor* by the praetor was to grant him all available actions on inheritance as if he had become an heir under *ius civile*. However, if the *bonorum possessor* was not simultaneously heir under the *ius civile* he could only use these actions with the help of a legal fiction. The particular structure of the formula allowed to treat the *bonorum possessor* as a fictitious heir. The formula was composed of an *intentio* (*intentere*, 'to claim', 'to prove'), containing the plaintiff's statement of claim, and a *condemnatio* (*condemnare*, 'to condemn', 'to convict') that allowed the judge to condemn the defendant. A judge could only condemn a defendant if the requirements stated in the *intentio* were met, i.e., if the plaintiff had proven his claim. Since the *intentio* was a condition precedent to the *condemnatio*, the judge's task was only to examine whether the condition was met or not. Namely, the judge had neither discretion to alter the condition nor competence to deviate from the plaintiff's claim as formulated in the *intentio*.

The praetor used the judge's dependence on the formula to link the *condemnatio* to merely hypothetical prerequisites. The fiction, therefore, was to impose an additional requirement on the judge. In the case of *bonorum possessio* this requirement was the following: 'provided that he, the *bonorum*

---

[2] *Aulus Agerius* and *Numerius Negidius* are generic names for the parties to a lawsuit. *Aulus Agerius* (literally 'the wealthy claimant') refers to the plaintiff, and *Numerius Negidius* (literally 'the refuser to pay') refers to the defendant. See Leopold Wenger, *Institutionen des römischen Zivilprozessrechts* (Huber 1925) 127, fn 7.

possessor, were an heir.' Thus, the judge not only had to examine whether the plaintiff had proved his claim, but also had to link his examination to the plaintiff's unproven claim that he was heir. Through this interlinking, the praetor created a legal fiction: if a debt actually existed in favour of the heir, the mechanism of the formula meant that the debtor (i.e. the defendant), also had to be judged in favour of the *bonorum possessor*, even though the latter was not an heir.

Overview 16: The Fiction to Grant an Action to the *bonorum possessor*

	intentio	*fictio*	*condemnatio*
heir's claim:	'if it is proven that the heir is owed money (100),'	not required	'then you, judge, must condemn the defendant for the amount (100).'
action of *bonorum possessor*:	'if it is proven that the *bonorum possessor* is owed money (100),'	'provided that he would be an heir.'	'then you, judge, must condemn the defendant for the amount (100).'

By granting the *bonorum possessor* all the actions available to the heir under the *ius civile*, the praetor places him on an equal economic footing with the heir. This equality ultimately serves the interests of the creditors of the estate, since it is only in this way that the *bonorum possessor* can pursue the debtors of the estate and replenish the estate. Moreover, in the reverse case, the praetor allows the creditors of the estate to sue the *bonorum possessor*.

Finally, the praetor can force the 'sale of the estate' (*venditio bonorum*) in order to satisfy the creditors.

4.2.3 Venditio bonorum

The *venditio bonorum* primarily applies when there are no heirs to an estate:

> Inst.Gai.3.78: *Bona autem veneunt aut vivorum aut mortuorum: [...]. Mortuorum bona veneunt velut eorum, quibus certum est neque heredes [...] neque ullum alium iustum successorem existere.*

> Inst.Gai.3.78.: The property of both the living and the dead can be sold: [...]. The property of a decedent is sold, for example, when it is certain that he has left no heirs [...] or any other legal successor.

If every direct heir had renounced the estate and no *extraneus* accepted it, the praetor could allow the creditors to sell the estate to pay off all debts. The forced sale of an estate involved the following steps: first, the praetor seized it; second, he granted the creditors *bonorum possessio*; third, the property (*bona*) was sold to the highest bidder (*bonorum emptor*); finally, the buyer satisfied the registered creditors with what each of them was entitled to from the proceeds of the estate.

The *venditio bonorum* further applied when the heir who was willing to take was over-indebted. In this case, the praetor protected the creditors of the estate from the competing claims from the heir's creditors, who would gain new liability assets as a result of the inheritance. The protection of the creditors of the estate was twofold:

> Ulpianus, 2 de omnibus tribunalibus: Si creditores heredem suspectum putent, satisdationem exigere possunt pro suo debito reddendo. Cuius rei gratia cognoscere praetorem oportet nec statim eum satisdationis necessitati subicere debet, nisi causa cognita constiterit prospici debere his, qui suspectum eum postulaverunt. (D.42.5.31pr.)

> Ulpian, All Seats of Judgment, book 2: If the creditors suspect the heir [of being overindebted], they can request surety to secure payment of the debt. The praetor must investigate this matter and shall not immediately force him [the heir] to give surety unless, after investigating the matter, it has been found that those who have requested the praetor to treat him [the heir] as suspicious must be safeguarded. (D.42.5.31pr.)

If the creditors of the estate feared that the heir was over-burdened with debts, they could request that the praetor grant the heir *bonorum possessio* only against surety (*satisdatio*). However, before the praetor required the heir to provide a surety, he investigated the matter (*cognitio*) to determine, whether the creditors' assertions were justified. The praetor had to make sure that the creditors' claims were well-founded and that the heir was truly insolvent. The surety (*satisdatio*) was given by a promise of a third party who would act as a guarantor for the claims of the creditors of the estate if they were endangered by the over-indebtedness of the heir. This kind of surety (*fideiussio*) was given as a *stipulatio*, i.e., a formal promise.

If the indebted heir could not find a guarantor, he would not receive *bonorum possessio*. The estate would then be divided among the creditors:

> Ulpianus, 2 de omnibus tribunalibus: Quod si suspectus satisdare iussus decreto praetoris non obtemperaverit, tunc bona hereditatis possideri venumque dari ex edicto suo permittere iubebit. (D.42.5.31.3.)

> Ulpian, All Seats of Judgment, book 2: But if an heir who is suspected [to be over-indebted] is ordered by decree of the praetor to give surety and does not obey, the praetor will order [the creditors] to take possession of the estate following his edict and allow them to sell it. (D.42.5.31.3.)

If the praetor had verified over-indebtedness and the heir had failed to provide the requested surety, the magistrate would not grant the estate to the heir but to the creditors of the estate. The aim of this appointment was again the utilisation, i.e., the sale of the estate (*venditio bonorum*) to satisfy the creditors.

If the heir's property was already under administration, i.e. ready to be sold, the creditors could request a 'separation between the estate of the testator and the heir's property' (*separatio bonorum*):

> *Ulpianus, 64 ad edictum: Solet autem separatio permitti creditoribus ex his causis: ut puta debitorem quis Seium habuit: Hic decessit: Heres ei extitit Titius: Hic non est solvendo: Patitur bonorum venditionem: Creditores Seii dicunt bona Seii sufficere sibi, creditores Titii contentos esse debere bonis Titii et sic quasi duorum fieri bonorum venditionem [...] (D.42.6.1.1.)*

> Ulpian, Edict, book 64: It is customary to grant the creditors the application for separation for the following reasons: let us assume that someone has Seius as a debtor. The latter dies, leaving Titius as his heir. Titius is not solvent and his property is sold. The creditors of Seius claim that the estate of Seius satisfies them and that the creditors of Titius should be satisfied with the property of Titius. Hence, the sale of the two properties takes place, as it were [...] (D.42.6.1.1.)

The debtor Seius is dead, and Titius is his heir. Titius is insolvent. Hence, his property goes into administration. The estate's creditors can now demand the separation of the properties to prevent the liquidation of the estate in favour of the creditors of the insolvent heir (Titius). If the praetor allowed the separation, the estate's creditors could put the estate of Seius under administration without sharing it with the creditors of the heir Titius.

All cases of *venditio bonorum* by the creditors, i.e. the forced utilisation of the estate by the creditors, entailed a social degradation for the decedent. The testator could, however, avoid this by providing for this eventuality in his will.

4.2.4 The Slave as heres necessarius

In cases of over-indebtedness of an estate, the usual practice was to appoint one's slave as heir. But the appointment of a slave could only be valid if the slave was previously manumitted by will:

> *Inst.Gai.2.186.: Sed noster servus simul et liber et heres esse iuberi debet, id est hoc modo: 'Stichus servus meus liber heresque esto,' vel: 'heres liberque esto'.*

> Inst.Gai.2.186.: Our slave must be ordered simultaneously to be free and an heir. This must be done thus: 'Stichus, my slave shall be free and my heir' or: 'my heir and he shall be free'.

Only if a slave had been manumitted did he cease to be part of the estate and could himself inherit. The appointment of a slave as an heir was advantageous to the testator because the freedmen, like the children-in-power (Ch. 4.1.3), were considered *heredes necessarii*:

> *Inst.Gai.2.153: Necessarius heres est servus cum libertate heres institutus, ideo sic appellatus, quia sive velit sive nolit, omni modo post mortem testatoris protinus liber et heres est.*

> Inst.Gai.2.153.: A *heres necessarius* is a slave appointed as heir and given his freedom. He is called thus, because, whether he wants or not, he becomes immediately free and heir after the testator's death.

A slave appointed as heir and released by will received the inheritance by operation of law without being allowed to refuse it. The praetor did not grant him the option of renouncing the estate, which was available to children-in-power. Appointing and freeing a slave by will was therefore a reliable means of avoiding the *venditio bonorum* of an over-indebted inheritance, since the slave would become heir in any event:

> *Inst.Gai.2.154.: Unde qui facultates suas suspectas habet, solet servum suum primo aut secundo vel etiam ulteriore gradu liberum et heredem instituere, ut si creditoribus satis non fiat, potius huius heredis quam ipsius testatoris bona veneant, id est, ut ignominia, quae accidit ex venditione bonorum, hunc potius heredem quam ipsum testatorem contingat; [...]*

> Inst.Gai.2.154.: Therefore, anyone who suspects he is insolvent usually appoints his slave as heir, either of the first, the second or a further degree while giving him his freedom, so that if the creditors are not satisfied, it is rather the heir's property than the estate of the testator that is sold. In other words, so that the loss of honour that occurs due to the sale of property affects this heir rather than the testator himself [...]

Since the former slave would, in any case, become an heir to the over-indebted estate, he was often appointed as heir of a subsequent rank to avoid the estate becoming vacant after all the heirs with priority had renounced the inheritance. In this way, the testator avoided the consequences of the *venditio bonorum* of his estate, since the creditors would now pursue the former slave, instead of trying to liquidate it. If there was sale of the freedman's assets, it would not be a *venditio bonorum* of the estate but of the heir's property. The testator was therefore spared the public disgrace of selling the estate; the freedman, however, lost his civic honour (*infamia*) due to the *venditio bonorum*. *Infamia* i.a. meant that he could not appear as a witness or be a party to a lawsuit in his name.

The praetor sought to mitigate these unavoidable consequences for the *heres necessarius* by exceptionally limiting his liability for the debts of the estate to the extent of the estate's assets:

> *Inst.Gai.2.155.: Pro hoc tamen incommodo illud ei commodum praestatur, ut ea, quae post mortem patroni sibi adquisierit, sive ante bonorum venditionem sive postea, ipsi reserventur; et quamvis pro portione bona venierint, iterum ex hereditaria causa bona eius non venient, nisi si quid ei ex hereditaria causa fuerit adquisitum [...]*

> Inst.Gai.2.155.: As compensation for this burden, he [the slave as heir] will be granted the following benefit: what he acquired after his master's death, either before or after the sale of property, he will be allowed to keep. And even though only a part of the debts may have been paid by the proceeds of the sale, property subsequently acquired by him cannot again be sold on account of the debts, unless he acquired something because he was the heir [...]

While the heir was in principle burdened with unlimited liability for the debts of the estate, the slave, as *heres necessarius*, was allowed to separate his property from the decedent's estate and to protect it from the actions of creditors. This separation of properties (*separatio bonorum*) allowed the slave who had received the inheritance, even against his will, to keep it separate from his property and to avoid *infamia*.

4.3 The Capacity to Inherit (*testamenti factio*) under the *ius civile* and *ius praetorium*

The legal capacity to inherit comprised the ability to legally accept the inheritance and to exercise the rights of an heir. Any Roman citizen not under the *potestas* of his father possessed the full capacity to inherit under the *ius civile*. Women, children under the paternal power and slaves only had a limited capacity to inherit.

4.3.1 The Guardianship over Women

Women's limited legal capacity to inherit resulted from the general restriction on their capacity to act:

> *Inst.Gai.1.189–190.: (189) Sed inpuberes quidem in tutela esse omnium civitatium iure contingit; quia id naturali ratione conveniens est, ut is, qui perfectae aetatis non sit, alterius tutela regatur, [...]. (190) Feminas vero perfectae aetatis in tutela esse fere nulla pretiosa ratio suasisse videtur: nam quae vulgo creditur, quia levitate animi plerumque decipiuntur et aequum erat eas tutorum auctoritate regi, magis speciosa videtur quam vera; mulieres enim*

quae perfectae aetatis sunt, ipsae sibi negotia tractant, et in quibusdam causis dicis gratia tutor interponit auctoritatem suam [...]

Inst.Gai.1.189–190.: (189) The law of every community provides that persons who are not of age shall be under guardianship because it stands to natural reason that the guardianship of another should control one who was not yet of age [...]. (190) However, no valid reason appears for the guardianship over adult women. For the commonly held view that their spirit's fickleness easily deceives them and that they thus need the guidance of their guardians, seems to be more of a pretence than a real reason. This is because women who are of age conduct their own affairs and in some cases a guardian gives his consent only as an act of formality [...]

Under Roman law, children, who were not of age (*pupilli*), and women, were placed under guardianship (*tutela*). Thus, women under guardianship required their guardian's consent (*auctoritas*) for any transaction that created an obligation or a legal burden. Guardianship over women was limited to giving consent and did not include a relation of authority over the person or their property, unlike guardianship over children under age. Nonetheless, it substantially limited the women's ability to act. This also affected the law of inheritance, since a woman who was appointed as an heir could only accept the inheritance with the consent of her guardian, because of possible debts of the estate:

Inst.Gai.1.176.: Sed aliquando etiam [...] permittitur tutorem petere, veluti ad hereditatem adeundam.

Inst.Gai.1.176.: Also, sometimes [...] it is allowed to request a guardian, as, for example, to accept an inheritance.

Gaius' comment on the guardian's consent needed to accept the inheritance refers to the woman's right to demand a substitute guardian in the absence of her regular guardian. Hence, if the latter was unavailable or prevented, the woman could find a new guardian to obtain the consent necessary to accept the inheritance. A woman's right to request a substitute guardian was evidence of the dwindling of the institution of guardianship of women, mainly since the last century of the Republic. Under the law of the twelve tables (*ca.* 450BC), the woman *sui iuris* was initially under either a testamentary or a statutory guardianship. A testamentary guardian was appointed by will, and the statutory guardian was the next-of-kin agnate (*agnatus proximus*). If no agnates were present, a guardian was appointed from the *gentiles*. Whereas both statutory guardianship of the gentiles and the gentilian rules of intestacy became defunct (Ch. 3.1.5), statutory guardianship of agnates was only later repealed:

> *Inst.Gai.1.157.: Sed olim quidem, quantum ad legem XII tabularum attinet, etiam feminae agnatos habebant tutores. Sed postea lex Claudia lata est, quae, quod ad feminas attinet, <tales> tutelas sustulit; [...]*

> Inst.Gai.1.157.: In former times, however, as far as the law of the twelve tables was concerned, women too had their agnates as guardians. But, afterwards, the *lex Claudia* was enacted and lifted guardianships concerning women [...]

A *lex Claudia*, dating from around AD44–49, lifted the statutory agnatic guardianship over women. This left only the option of appointing a guardian for the woman in her father's will (testamentary guardianship), or having a guardian appointed on application to the magistrate (magisterial guardianship). The magistrate appointed a guardian if the will of the father, or of the husband, did not provide for a guardian or if the designated person could not act as guardian:

> *Inst.Gai.1.185.: Si cui nullus omnino tutor sit, ei datur in urbe Roma ex lege Atilia a praetore urbano et maiore parte tribunorum plebis, qui Atilianus tutor vocatur; in provinciis vero a praesidibus provinciarum lege Iulia et Titia.*

> Inst.Gai.1.185.: If someone has no guardian, one is appointed under the *lex Atilia*, in Rome by the *praetor urbanus* and the majority of the tribunes of the people and is called, 'Atilian' guardian; in the provinces, however, he is appointed by the governor under the *lex Iulia et Titia*.

The magistrate appointed a guardian only upon request, as was the case for the *bonorum possessio* granted by the praetor or praefect. The basis for magisterial guardianship were the *lex Atilia* (approx. 210BC) for Rome, and the *lex Julia et Titia*, probably from 31BC, for the provinces. As we saw, a woman could apply for a guardian if she needed the latter's consent for certain transactions, such as the acceptance of an inheritance.

The development discussed here shows that the guardianship over women evolved during the Republic from a means of exercising power over women to a legal formality required only for certain transactions. Whereas the initial rule of the law of the twelve tables entailed the control of the agnatic family over its female members, we find in the creation of a *tutela* by the magistrate a watering down of the family-bound guardianship of women. This applied even more when guardians were appointed at the woman's request if the testamentary, or statutory, guardian was unavailable.

In the Empire, the Augustan marital laws further diminished the importance of the *tutela* over women (Ch. 4.4). These laws were designed to promote marriage and the procreation of children. One incentive for procreation was the promise of freedom from guardianship for married women with three children:

Inst.Gai.1.194.: Tutela autem liberantur ingenuae quidem trium liberorum iure [...]

Inst.Gai.1.194.: But freeborn women are exempt from guardianship if they have given birth to three children [...]

If a freeborn Roman woman bore three children, or was granted the *ius trium liberorum*, she could freely dispose of her property. By the time of the Empire, therefore, the *tutela* of women became a simple legal formality. The development discussed here is summarised in Overview 17.

Overview 17: The Evolution of the Guardianship of Women (*tutela mulieris*)

statutory guardianship	testamentary guardianship	magisterial guardianship
law of the twelve tables: *proximus agnatus* and *gentiles*	law of the twelve tables: the prerogative of the *pater familias*	*lex Atilia* (210BC): prerogative of the praetor *lex Iulia et Titia* (31BC): prerogative of the praefect
repealed by the *lex Claudia* (AD44–49)	can also be ordered with the woman's choice of the guardian	only upon request (by the woman or another entitled person)
	lex Iulia et Papia (18BC, AD9) women with three children or the *ius liberorum* are exempt from guardianship	

Bearing in mind that the *tutela* as a means of control over a woman became defunct, as observed before, it is unsurprising that women often appear in legal texts as both heiresses and testators who arrange for their property after their death (Ch. 6.1).

In contrast, we do not find any relaxation of the restrictions imposed by the *ius civile* on children under the paternal power in the period under consideration. As we saw above (Ch. 3.1), children-in-power are often compared to slaves in terms of their inability to own property; the latter lacked legal capacity altogether. Both children-in-power and slaves lack the passive capacity to inherit.

4.3.2 The Capacity to Inherit of those under the Paternal Power

The fact that only the *pater familias* possessed capacity to own property (Ch. 3.1) meant that there were two very different legal situations for the child under the paternal power who was to inherit. In the simplest situation, the child became *sui iuris* and inherited from its *pater familias*, either by will or on intestacy. However, if the child under the paternal power inherited from a third party, it continued to be subject to the *potestas*, and could not decide whether to accept or not; the *pater familias* decided:

> *Ulpianus, 6 ad Sabinum: Qui in aliena est potestate, non potest invitum hereditati obligare eum in cuius est potestate, ne aeri alieno pater obligaretur. (D.29.2.6pr.)*

> Ulpian, Sabinus, book 6: Someone under the *patria potestas* cannot burden the person under whose power he is with the estate's debts, without the latter's consent. This is to prevent the father from being burdened with somebody else's debt. (D.29.2.6pr.)

Since the *pater familias* was liable for any debts of the estate he incorporated into the household's property, he had to decide whether the child under the paternal power should accept the inheritance. In other words, he had to consider whether the benefits of the inheritance outweighed its burden. Therefore, the acceptance of an inheritance by a child under the paternal power needed the *pater familias'* consent; without his authorisation, the acceptance was invalid under the *ius civile*. However, the situation was different when the child under the paternal power applied for *bonorum possessio*:

> *Ulpianus, ad Sabinum 6: Sed in bonorum possessione placuit ratam haberi posse eam, quam citra voluntatem adgnovit is qui potestati subiectus est. (D.29.2.6.1.)*

> Ulpianus, Sabinus, book 6: It is established about *bonorum possessio* that it can be approved if a claim was made by someone under *patria potestas*, against the wishes of the latter. (D.29.2.6.1.)

The application of a child under the paternal power for *bonorum possessio*, even though the child lacked legal capacity to own property, was not completely void, but only provisionally ineffective, and could be validated with the consent of the *pater familias*.

A slave, unlike a child under *potestas*, lacked any legal capacity, and even if Roman jurists recognised that slaves were human beings, from a legal point of view they were regarded as objects.

This also affected their treatment in the law of inheritance. The law of inheritance perceived the slave as part of the estate, the *familia* (Ch. 3.1). In contrast, the slave could be deployed by the owner to carry out transactions and draft wills. As we saw (Ch. 4.2.4), the testamentary manumission and appointment of one's slave as heir could prevent a sale of the estate in the case of over-indebtedness of the inheritance. If the testator appointed another person's slave, the said appointment would benefit the slave's owner:

> *Gaius, 17 ad edictum provinciale: Non minus servos quam liberos heredes instituere possumus, si modo eorum scilicet servi sint, quos ipsos heredes instituere possumus, cum testamenti factio cum servis ex persona dominorum introducta est. (D.28.5.31pr.)*

> Gaius, Provincial Edict, book 17: We can appoint slaves as heirs no less than children-in-power, but only if they are slaves to those we can appoint as heirs. For *testamenti factio* with slaves is derived from capacity of their masters. (D.28.5.31pr.)

The appointment of the slave as heir was done with the master in mind. The diversions via the slave served to mobilise the economic advantage conveyed by the appointment as heir. In fact, the beneficiary of the appointment was always the respective owner of the slave. Even if the will's wording did not change, the beneficiary changed when the slave was passed to somebody else. The testator would use this effect when appointing a slave to secure the validity of his will. Suppose, that the designated heir predeceases the testator, thereby rendering the will obsolete. If the slave is appointed as heir and his owner dies, his heirs will succeed him and become heirs through the slave, which means that there is no need to amend the will.

The rules of the *ius civile* and *ius praetorium*, examined here, remained valid under the law of the Empire, which, as we saw (Ch. 2.2.4), maintained the distinction between these two layers of law. Nonetheless, the law of inheritance remained an area significantly shaped by the legal reforms of the Empire.

4.4 The Capacity to Obtain and the Worthiness to Inherit under the *ius novum*

The law of inheritance was fundamentally reshaped by the 'Augustan marital laws'. Namely, they were a series of laws enacted to promote marriage and the procreation of children among Roman citizens. At the same time, they sought to combat non-marital relationships and marriages that were not between persons of equal rank. The Augustan marital laws included: a law on the punishment of adultery (*lex Iulia de adulteriis coercendis*, of 18BC); a law on the ordering of marriage (*lex Iulia de maritandis ordinibus*, of 18BC); a law on marriage within the social order (*lex Papia Poppea nuptialis*, of AD9).[3]

---

[3] For a textual reconstruction, see Eric C. Green, Andrew D. E. Lewis and Michael H. Crawford, '*Lex Iulia de maritandis ordinibus/lex Papia Poppea*' in Michael H Crawford (ed) *Roman Statutes II* (Institute of Classical Studies 1996) 801–809.

The *lex Iulia de adulteriis* was a criminal law that made adultery (*adulterium*), i.e., the extramarital intercourse of a married woman, a capital offence. The *lex Iulia de maritandis ordinibus* and the *lex Papia Poppea* regulated marriage by obliging citizens to marry and sought to strengthen and broaden the existing restrictions on certain unions. Roman citizens were not allowed to marry certain women who were considered 'disreputable'. These included prostitutes and women convicted of adultery (*adulterium*) under the *lex Iulia de adulteriis*. Moreover, senators were not allowed to marry actresses and former slaves, i.e. freedwomen. The *lex Iulia de maritandis ordinibus* introduced the obligation to marry between the ages of twenty-five and sixty for men and between twenty and fifty for women. This was coupled with the obligation to remarry if a marriage was dissolved by divorce or death, but exemption was granted if there were children (from a previous marriage). Freeborn parents with three children were not required to remarry. Freed persons needed four children to obtain this privilege. This exemption was called *ius liberorum* ('right of children'). The right could also be granted as a privilege in the case of childlessness through no fault of one's own.

The laws were relevant for inheritance law because the *princeps* used the economic importance of inheritances as a means of exerting pressure for his politically and legally controversial aims.

4.4.1 The Consequences of Caducum *under the* lex Iulia et Papia

The *lex Iulia de maritandis ordinibus* and the *lex Papia Poppea*, which were collectively referred to by the Roman jurists as *lex Iulia et Papia*, ordered that persons who failed to fulfil the obligation to marry and bear children were either restricted or unable to inherit by testament.

> Inst.Gai.2.111.: *Caelibes quoque, qui lege Iulia hereditatem legataque capere vetantur, item orbi, id est qui liberos non habent, quos lex [Papia plus quam dimidias partes hereditatis legatorumque capere vetat, ex militis testamento solidum capiunt].*[4]

> Inst.Gai.2.111.: The unmarried, whom the *lex Iulia* prohibits from inheriting or receiving legacies, and also those who have no children, whom the *lex* [*Papia* forbids to take more than half an estate or legacy, are not barred from inheriting in full under a soldier's will].

---

[4] I adhere to the textual emendations of Ulrich Manthe, *Gaius Institutiones* (2nd edn, WBG Academic 2010) 148 fn 1, with further references.

The new sanction rendered unmarried (*caelibes*) and childless (*orbi*), who were appointed as heirs under a will or were considered as legatees, disallowed from keeping what they had obtained through the will (*incapacitas*). It should be noted that a person who married below rank, and thus entered into a forbidden marriage, was also considered to be unmarried. Due to the *lex Iulia et Papia*, the unmarried lacked the capacity to keep what they had obtained under a will, while the childless inherited only half of the inheritance or legacy left to them. The remainder therefore lapsed as a *caducum* (from *cadere*, 'to lapse').

This legal consequence applied not only for testamentary appointments under the *ius civile* but also for the *bonorum possessio secundum tabulas*:

> *Paulus, 4 ad legem Iuliam et Papiam: 'Hereditatis' appellatione bonorum quoque possessio continetur. (D.50.16.138.)*

> Paul, Lex Iulia et Papia, book 4: *Bonorum possessio* is included in the term 'inheritance'. (D.50.16.138.)

In his commentary on the *lex Iulia et Papia*, Paul (third century AD) considered inheritance (*hereditas*) and *bonorum possessio* equivalent. Hence, the *lex Iulia et Papia* also applied to the *bonorum possessor* who was not heir under the *ius civile*. The legal consequences of the *lex Iulia et Papia* were determined for each individual heir or *bonorum possessor*, so that heirs and legatees who had fulfilled their duties to marry and procreate (and thus had capacity to obtain) could inherit by will, even if other co-heirs or co-legatees were excluded due to their *incapacitas* following the statutory provision. In accordance with the provisions on the loss of co-heirs (Ch. 4.1.1), the lapsed share fell to the persons named in the will who had the capacity to obtain under the *lex Iulia et Papia*:

> *Inst.Gai.2.206: [...] post legem vero Papiam deficientis portio caduca fit et ad eos pertinet, qui in eo testamento liberos habent.*

> Inst.Gai.2.206.: [...] but after the enactment of the *lex Papia*, a lapsed share of the legacy is considered ownerless, and belongs to those mentioned in the will who have children.

Those with capacity to obtain under the *lex Iulia et Papia*, i.e. the appointed heirs who were married and had children, also got a bonus for their 'good behaviour' in that they received the lapsed part of the share of the childless and the entire share of the unmarried. Overview 18 illustrates this redistribution on the basis of a fictious case:

Overview 18: The Distribution of the *caducum* to the Parents Appointed in the Will

testator			
co-heir 1	**co-heir 2**	**co-heir 3**	**co-heir 4**
1/4	1/4	1/4	1/4
unmarried	married (childless)	married (childless)	married father
no capacity to obtain (*incapacitas*)	half of the testamentary share	half of the testamentary share	capacity to obtain 'reward for children' (+1/8+1/8+1/4)
0	1/8	1/8	3/4

The testator has appointed four friends as co-heirs to one-fourth each. Co-heir 1 is unmarried and, therefore, as a *caelebs* lacks the capacity to obtain under the will. His share lapses as a *caducum*. Co-heirs 2 and 3 are childless, and this affects their position differently: as *orbi*, they receive only half of the share provided for in the will, namely, one-eighth. In contrast, co-heir 4, a married father, inherits not only his part of one-fourth but receives the lapsed 1/8 + 1/8 of co-heirs 2 and 3 as well as the lapsed share of one-fourth of Co-heir 1. As a result, co-heir 4 receives three-quarters of the estate, co-heirs 2 and 3 share the remaining quarter, and co-heir 1 is entirely excluded.

If no heirs with legal capacity to obtain were mentioned in the will, the *caducum* passed to the state. Under Emperor Augustus (27BC–AD14), the estate's assets passed to the *aerarium populi Romani* (public treasury) and under Emperor Caracalla (AD211–217) to the *fiscus*, i.e. the imperial treasury. From a procedural aspect, the *fiscus* claimed the lapsed share through an action (*vindicatio caducorum*) to ascertain the heir's *incapacitas* under the *lex Iulia et Papia*.

It must be stressed that the controversial legal consequence of the *lex Iulia et Papia* applied only to testamentary heirs, so that childless or unmarried heirs could still inherit *ab intestato*. In addition, exceptions for the nearest of kin were in place:

> C.6.51.1.1b Iustinianus (a. 534): *Et cum lex Papia ius antiquum, quod ante eam in omnibus simpliciter versabatur, suis machinationibus et angustiis circumcludens solis parentibus et liberis testatoris usuque ad tertium gradum, si scripti fuerant heredes, suum imponere iugum erubuit antiquum intactum eis conservans, nos omnibus nostris subiectis sine differentia personarum concedimus.*

C.6.51.1.1b Justinian (a. 534): And as the *lex Papia*, by its contrivances and technicalities, practically invalidated the ancient law, which was strictly enforced before the former's enactment, and did not hesitate to impose its yoke upon the ascendants and descendants of the testator; as far as the third degree, only preserving for them the benefits of the ancient law, if they had been appointed heirs, we grant all our subjects this advantage without discrimination.

Emperor Justinian (AD527–565), who abolished the *lex Papia*, stated that the reasons for the lapse did not apply to parents (in ascending order) and children (in descending order) of the decedent, up to the third degree. These persons were therefore exempted from the limitations imposed on passive testamentary capacity. This seems to be in line with the stated aim of the Augustan marital laws to strengthen the family. As in other cases (Ch. 3.1.4), the degrees of kinship depended on the number of births between the testator and the beneficiary. As only relatives in the direct line could benefit, children, grandchildren, parents and grandparents were exempt from the disadvantages of the marital laws. Overview 19 summarises all prerequisites for the legal capacity to take an estate, under the *ius civile* and *ius novum*, that were in force during the Empire:

Overview 19: Prerequisites for the Position of Heir since the *lex Iulia et Papia*

	without limitation:	limited:	excluded:
legal capacity to inherit:	- *pater familias* - also on behalf of children-in-power or - slaves	women *sui iuris* (*lex Voconia*)	non-Romans (*peregrini*)
capacity to obtain (*capacitas*):	married Roman citizens with three children or the *ius liberorum*	married but childless (*orbi*)	unmarried without the *ius liberorum* (*caelibes*)

The *lex Iulia et Papia* also contained a special rule for spouses of great practical importance.

4.4.2 Spousal inheritance law of the lex Iulia et Papia

Since the traditional rules of intestacy allowed spouses to inherit only in exceptional cases (Ch. 3.1.5) or only subsidiarily (Ch. 3.2.3), the surviving spouse was often appointed as heir or beneficiary by will. The *lex Iulia et Papia* penalised celibacy and childlessness, which already entailed disadvantages concerning the law of inheritance, and spouses in an illegitimate marriage. Since Emperor

Justinian had repealed the *lex Iulia et Papia*, we can only derive these penalties from a work that has survived outside the *Corpus iuris civilis*, the Epitome of Ulpian (UE):[5]

> *UE 16.2: Aliquando nihil inter se capiunt: Id est, si contra legem Iuliam Papiamque Poppaeam contraxerint matrimonium, verbi gratia si famosam quis uxorem duxerit, aut libertinam senator.*

> UE 16.2: Sometimes, they [the spouses] do not inherit anything from each other. This is when they enter a marriage against the *lex Iulia et Papia Poppaea*, e.g., if someone married a disreputable woman or if a senator married a freedwoman.

Spouses whose marriage was illegitimate under the *lex Iulia et Papia* could not appoint each other as heirs or legatees. If spouses did not procreate, i.e. were *orbi*, they partly lacked the capacity to keep what they had obtained:

> *UE 15.1: Vir et uxor inter se matrimonii nomine decimam capere possunt. Quod si ex alio matrimonio liberos superstites habeant, praeter decimam, quam matrimonii nomine capiunt, totidem decimas pro numero liberorum accipiunt.*

> UE 15.1: Husband and wife inherit from each other one-tenth on account of marriage. If they have surviving children from previous marriages, they receive as many one-tenths as they have children above and beyond the said one-tenth they receive on account of their marriage.

Spouses, who were legally married could only appoint each other as heirs to a tenth part of each of their properties by will. If the beneficiary had children from a previous marriage, he or she could receive another tenth part for each child. There were exceptions to the limitations on the capacity to obtain where the aim of the *lex Iulia et Papia* was unaffected:

> *UE 16.1: Aliquando vir et uxor inter se solidum capere possunt, velut si uterque vel alteruter eorum nondum eius aetatis sunt, a qua lex liberos exigit, id est si vir minor annorum XXV sit aut uxor annorum XX minor; item si utrique lege Papia finitos annos in matrimonio excesserint, id est vir LX annos, uxor L; [...]*

---

[5] See Fritz Schulz (ed), *Die Epitome Ulpiani des Codex Vaticanus Reginae 1128* (Markus und Weber's Verlag 1926); Martin Avenarius, *Der pseudo-ulpianische liber singularis regularum. Entstehung, Eigenart und Überlieferung einer hochklassischen Juristenschrift* (Wallstein 2005), with a review by Wolfgang Kaiser (2005) 127 Zeitschrift der Savigny Stiftung, Romanistische Abteilung 560.

> UE 16.1.: Sometimes husband and wife can accept the inheritance in full from each other, e.g., if either or both are not yet of the age when children are requested by law, i.e. the man below twenty-five or the wife below twenty. The same applies if both have exceeded the age prescribed by the *lex Papia* while their marriage is intact, i.e. if the man is sixty and the wife fifty.

Spouses who could not have children because of their very young or old age were exempted from the restrictions of the *lex Iulia et Papia*. This applied namely to men under twenty-five and over sixty, and women under twenty and over fifty. The exception took into account the biological limits of reproductive capacity, which were already known in Antiquity. It also applied when childlessness was due to the death of an infant. Neither case was considered a violation of the law:

> UE 16, 1a: *Libera inter eos testamenti factio est, si ius liberorum a principe inpetraverint [...]*
>
> UE 16, 1a: They have the *testamenti factio* if they have obtained the *ius liberorum* by the emperor

Accordingly, childless spouses who had received the *ius liberorum* as a privilege from the *princeps* had full capacity to obtain. They were treated as if they had three children (together) and thus, as if they had fulfilled the procreation requirement of the *lex Iulia et Papia*.

The requirement of moral suitability for the testamentary heir, introduced by the Augustan marital laws, further nuanced the requirements for an heir during the Empire. The imperial court practice requested an heir to be worthy of the estate (*dignus*) and disqualified him if he was proven unworthy (*indignus*).

4.4.3 Unworthiness to Inherit (*indignitas*)

Unworthiness to inherit led to the loss of the legal capacity to obtain the inheritance, similar to *incapacitas* under the *lex Iulia et Papia*. The unworthy person's share of the estate went to the imperial treasury (*fiscus*) and could therefore be claimed by the *fiscus*, like a *caducum*. Unlike legal incapacity, however, unworthiness to inherit was not based on a law, but was developed by the imperial courts on a case-by-case basis. The initial aim was to close gaps in the criminal confiscation by transferring the inheritance to the imperial treasury.

> *Paulus, liber singularis de portionibus: Praeterea ex his, quae per flagitium damnatus adquisiit, portiones liberorum non augentur: Veluti si cognatum suum interemi curaverit et eius hereditatem adiit vel bonorum possessionem accepit: Nam ita divus Pius rescripsit. Cui consequenter illud idem princeps*

constituit, cum filia familias veneno necasse convinceretur eum, a quo heres instituta erat: Quamvis iussu patris, cuius in potestate erat, hereditatem eam adiisset, tamen fisco eam vindicandam esse. (D.48.20.7.4.)

Paul, Shares, sole book: Moreover, any property which the convicted father has acquired through crime does not increase the share of the children. For instance, if he was responsible for the death of a relative and entered upon his estate or has obtained *bonorum possessio* of the same as the deified Pius stated in a rescript. Consistently with this, he held that if a *filia familias* was convicted of killing a person by whom she had been appointed as an heir by poison. Even though she had entered the inheritance by order of her *pater familias*, it should escheat to the treasury. (D.48.20.7.4.)

In both rescripts of Emperor Antoninus Pius (AD138–161), the testator was killed by a person close to the heir, though the heir was not considered criminally responsible. If the heir were convicted of aiding or abetting in any way, the criminal law would allow the share to be revoked. This criminal consequence did not apply to the children of the person who had the heir killed nor to the *pater familias* of the daughter-in-power who killed the testator by poison. The emperor therefore provided a remedy for these cases through a private-law lapse of the estate to the *fiscus*. The estate could escheat to the imperial treasury even without any criminal responsibility. Crucial was that the heir was considered unworthy (*indignus*) because of his family connection to the perpetrator. Accordingly, the claim of the *fiscus* (*vindicatio caducorum*) would be successful.

Unworthiness to inherit did not have to be the result of another's crime, but could also be the result of one's own failure, as another decision of Antoninus Pius shows:

Marcianus, 5 regularum: Indignum esse divus Pius illum decrevit, ut et Marcellus libro duodecimo digestorum refert, qui manifestissime comprobatus est id egisse, ut per neglegentiam et culpam suam mulier, a qua heres institutus erat, moreretur. (D.34.9.3.)

Marcian, Rules, book 5: The deified Pius decreed that a person was unworthy, as Marcellus reports in the twelfth book of his Digest, who was manifestly proven to have caused the death of the woman, who had appointed him as heir, through his negligence and fault. (D.34.9.3.)

A woman appointed a man as heir. He took the risk that she would die because of his negligence. Roman criminal law did not apply if a free person was killed by negligence; Antoninus Pius also allowed a private-law remedy, namely, the *vindicatio caducorum* by the imperial treasury. The careless heir was considered unworthy (*indignus*), so the estate lapsed to the *fiscus* and could be forfeited.

Not only the actions of the heir, but also those of the testator, could prove the unworthiness of the heir:

> *Papinianus, 16 quaestionum: Cum quidam scripsisset heredes quos instituere non potuerat, quamvis institutio non valeret neque superius testamentum ruptum esset, heredibus tamen ut indignis, qui non habuerunt supremam voluntatem, abstulit iam pridem senatus hereditatem [...] (D.34.9.12.)*
>
> Papinian, Questions, book 16: If somebody had appointed [in a second will] persons as heirs he was not allowed to; although the appointment of this kind was not valid, and the first will was not broken in consequence, the Senate has, nonetheless, since long decreed that the heirs [under the first will of the testator] should be deprived of the same as unworthy because their appointment was not the testator's last wish. (D.34.9.12.)

The testator had made two valid wills and appointed a different heir in each. As a rule, the most recent will replaced the previous one, so that the heirs named in the second will took the inheritance (Ch. 6.2). However, if the heirs named in the second will did not have *testamenti factio*, the second will became invalid. The first will therefore remained valid and the heir named in it was called upon to take the estate. Papinian (third century AD) mentioned a decision by the Senate that the heir named in the first will was unworthy. The estate would not go to any of the heirs named in the two wills, but would instead belong to the imperial treasury. In this case, the heir named in the first will was unworthy because the testator no longer wished him to be heir. If, however, the heir accepted the estate despite the testator's wish to the contrary, he would have disregarded the testator's will, which would have been punished by the estate being forfeited.

Although the cases on *indignitas* discussed here were not comprehensively and systematically regulated, they reveal that the scrutiny of ethical suitability in inheritance law, introduced by the *lex Iulia et Papia*, became stricter during the Empire. If the heir was deemed morally unsuitable, he might not have been permitted to inherit. The imperial treasury benefited from this development, as it could claim the shares that had lapsed.

4.5 Concluding Considerations on the Position of Heir

The rules on the position of heir clearly reveal the various operating principles of the different layers of law.

1. The *ius civile* bases the position of the heir on succession, the latter following the paradigm of the direct heirs of the *pater familias*. The *heres extraneus*

can decide whether to become an heir, but if he chooses to do so, the legal consequences, such as the joinder of heirs, the accrual and the liability for a debt, will apply without any further actions on his part. The creditor of an estate is protected by the *ius civile*, since the liabilities pass automatically to the heir and through the simplified procedure of prescriptive acquisition of the estate.

2. By contrast, the desire to quickly obtain an heir in the interests of the creditors characterises the rules of *ius praetorium*. For this purpose, the praetor sets a time limit for the entitled person to accept the estate and to apply for *bonorum possessio secundum tabulas*. If the designated heirs miss these deadlines, lower-ranking beneficiaries will be allowed to claim the *bonorum possessio secundum tabulas*. Finally, if no heir is willing to take the estate, the praetor will sell the goods of the estate at the request of the creditors of the estate (*venditio bonorum*).

3. The *ius novum*, for which the Augustan marriage laws (27BC–AD14) were the starting-point, attempted to 'moralise' the law of inheritance by making the general conduct of the heir relevant for the acquisition of an estate. According to the *lex Iulia et Papia*, only married persons with a certain number of children could become testamentary heirs without restrictions. The lapse of a share led initially to the accumulation of the share for those with the legal capacity to obtain under the *lex Iulia et Papia*, and later to the acquisition by the imperial treasury. The treasury also benefited from the creation of special cases of unworthiness to inherit (*indignitas*) by collecting the inheritance of unworthy heirs. These rules existed in addition to the passive testamentary capacity under the *ius civile* and *ius praetorium*, which was determined by the legal capacity to act. This meant that not only were persons without *testamenti factio* under the *ius civile*, i.e. persons without the legal capacity to act, excluded from the inheritance, but also those who did not adhere to the imperial precept of marriage and childbearing under the *ius novum*.

5

The Protection of the Position of Heir

A functioning system of inheritance law requires that the heir be protected against unlawful possession of the estate by third parties. The heir's protection is achieved through a special claim, the *hereditatis petitio* (literally 'the seeking of the inheritance'). This action *in rem* allows the heir to claim the delivery of the estate from anyone who holds it. During the period examined here, the *hereditatis petitio* has been adapted and extended. The transformation of the claim corresponds to the general development of procedural law, which forms the counterpoint to the historical emergence of the different layers of law. In the traditional *ius civile*, emerging from the law of the twelve tables and its subsequent juridical interpretation, we find the first known system of Roman civil procedure: the *legis actiones* procedure (*legis actio* from *lege agere*, 'to sue under the law'). This earliest form of civil procedure was characterised by a limited number of *legis actiones*, formulated with painstaking precision and, like the *ius civile*, only available to Roman citizens. Although the *leges Iuliae iudiciorum publicorum et privatorum* (17BC) of Augustus almost completely repealed the *legis actiones*, they are still explained in Gaius' textbook dating from the second century. The *legis actiones* system was obviously perceived as the basis and the starting point for later procedural systems of Roman law. By the time of the Republic, the *legis actiones* procedure had to compete with the more flexible formulary procedure (*agere per formulas*, 'to sue through procedural formulas'), which had mostly been developed by the praetor's edict. The edict collected procedural formulas that were either introduced to enforce claims of the *ius civile* or had been created by the praetor himself as part of the *ius praetorium* (Ch. 2.1.1). The formula of the *hereditatis petitio* belonged to the latter. From the Principate onwards, however, the formulary procedure had to compete with the imperial *cognitio extra ordinem* (literally, 'the extraordinary procedure' as opposed to the ordinary formulary procedure) (Ch. 2.2.4). Initially, the imperial jurisdiction was only introduced for a singular legal question and was merely intended to supplement the existing formulary procedure. However, as imperial law created new possibilities for legal protection that the traditional civil procedure did not provide for, the *cognitio extra ordinem* gradually superseded the formulary procedure. This is particularly true in the law of inheritance, as from Augustus onwards both the formless additions to wills (codicils, Ch. 6.4.1) and the enforcement of formless bequests (*fideicommissa*, Ch. 8.5) were legally valid under imperial law.

The general development of the Roman civil procedure can be exemplified in the *hereditatis petitio* as a claim of the formulary procedure, its precursors in the *legis actiones* and its modifications through the *cognitio extra ordinem*.

5.1 The *legis actiones* and *sponsio* Procedures

A concrete point of departure for the development of the *hereditatis petitio* is a precursor claim of the *legis actiones* procedure, which made it possible to claim possession of an object or a set of objects. This *legis actio sacramento in rem* was a real action (*in rem*, 'to recover an object') carried out by means of a procedural oath (*sacramentum*, 'penalty,' 'oath', 'solemn declaration'). Strict ritualism and the fact that a movable object in dispute had to be carried or brought to court were peculiar features of this claim:

> *Inst.Gai.4.16.: Si in rem agebatur, mobilia quidem et moventia, quae modo in ius adferri adducive possent, in iure vindicabantur ad hunc modum: Qui vindicabat, festucam tenebat; deinde ipsam rem adprehendebat, velut hominem, et ita dicebat: 'Hunc ego hominem ex iure Quiritium meum esse aio, secundum suam causam sicut dixi, ecce tibi, vindictam imposui,' et simul homini festucam imponebat. Adversarius eadem similiter dicebat et faciebat. Cum uterque vindicasset, praetor dicebat: 'Mittite ambo hominem'. Illi mittebant. Qui prior vindicaverat, sic dicebat: 'Postulo, anne dicas, qua ex causa vindicaveris.' Ille respondebat: 'Ius feci, sicut vindictam imposui.' Deinde qui prior vindicaverat, dicebat: 'Quando tu iniuria vindicavisti D aeris sacramento te provoco'; adversarius quoque dicebat similiter: 'Et ego te D aeris sacramento provoco', aut si res infra M assess erat scilicet L asses sacramenti nominabant [...]*

> Inst.Gai.4.16.: When a real action was brought forth, chattels and animals that could be moved or be brought or led to court were claimed before the praetor in such way: The party making the claim held a rod (*festuca*), and, while seizing the object in dispute, for example, a slave, said, 'I claim that this slave belongs to me as mine by due acquisition, according to the law of the *Quirites*; see, as I have said, behold, I have laid my rod (*vindicta*) on him,' and, while he touched the man with the rod, his opponent said and did the same. And when both had vindicated him, the praetor said: 'Both of you, release the man!' and they did so. Then, the first claimant said, asking the other thus: 'I demand that you tell me on what legal basis you have claimed your property.' And the latter replied: 'I exercised my ownership over him as

I laid my rod upon him.' The first claimant said: 'Since you have wrongfully vindicated him, I challenge you to stake five hundred asses as *sacramentum*.' In turn, his opponent said similarly: 'I too, challenge you to stake five hundred asses as *sacramentum*.' If the object was worth less than a thousand asses, only fifty asses would be staked as *sacramentum* [...]

Gaius' discussion of the *vindicatio* for the delivery of possession of an individual object also applies to the claim for the delivery of the estate. The *legis actio sacramento in rem* for the delivery of the estate required that items from the estate be brought before the praetor to symbolise the inheritance. Then, both parties, the plaintiff and the defendant, had to assert that they were entitled to the estate, i.e., were the true and rightful heirs. This claim was underlined by touching the items in question. The praetor then ordered both parties to abandon possession of the item. After each party challenged the other party's claim, the plaintiff pledged a sum of money (*sacramentum*) to counter the defendant's claim. In turn, the defendant also 'pledged' against the plaintiff's claim. This procedural wager led to the peculiarity that the judge appointed by the praetor did not decide directly on the parties' entitlement to the estate, but on whose *sacramentum* was just and whose *sacramentum* was not. From this perspective, the status of an heir was merely a preliminary question to the decision on the forfeiture of the pledge. The party who could prove that he was the heir would be successful and could keep his pledge or demand the pledge from his opponent. If a party did not oppose the opponent's claim by asserting his own entitlement, the opponent could immediately take the estate as heir.

The ritual of the *legis actio sacramento in rem* shows that the claim for the delivery of the estate was initially conceived as a competition between two claimants to the estate. The judge's limited discretionary powers were a peculiar feature of this procedure. The judge did not rule directly on the claimants' respective entitlements, but could only decide on the wager.

The *legis actio per sponsionem* (*per sponsionem*, 'by mutual agreement', 'a wager'), which is a later development of the *legis actio sacramento*, is also characterised by the judge's implicit decision-making:

> Inst.Gai.4.93.: *Per sponsionem vero hoc modo agimus: Provocamus adversarium tali sponsione: 'Si homo, quo de agitur, ex iure Quiritium meus est, sestertios XXV nummos dare spondes?,' deinde formulam edimus, qua intendimus sponsionis summam nobis dari oportere; qua formula ita demum vincimus, si probaverimus rem nostram esse.*

> Inst.Gai.4.93.: But in a procedure by *sponsio* we challenge the other party to such a wager as follows: 'If the disputed slave is mine under the law of the *Quirites*, do you promise to pay me twenty-five sesterces?' And then, we

deliver a formula by which we claim that the sum mentioned in the wager should be paid to us. However, we only obtain judgment by this formula if we prove that the object belongs to us.

The procedure *per sponsionem* had the character of a bet that the plaintiff asked the defendant to make. Again, the judge only decided who was to receive the wager. The question of who had become the heir was conceived as a preliminary question, and was therefore a condition for accepting or rejecting the wager.

To sum up, the two earlier claims for the delivery of the estate gave the judge only limited decision-making powers. As a lay judge, he could only decide on the placement of the wager, but he had no authority to answer directly who had become the heir. However, from the perspective of legal evolution, it should be noted that the procedure *per sponsionem* was already less formal than the original *legis actio sacramento in rem*. In addition, the procedure *per sponsionem* allowed the plaintiff to choose the formula by which the wager was to be claimed. The procedure thus forms a conceptual link to the more flexible formulary procedure that brought forth the *hereditatis petitio*.

5.2 The *hereditatis petitio* of the Formulary Procedure

In the formulary procedure, the plaintiff had two options for filing the *hereditatis petitio*. He could still use the procedure *per sponsionem*. In addition, the praetorian edict offered him the new option of claiming the estate directly:

> Inst.Gai.4.92.: *Petitoria autem formula haec est, qua actor intendit rem suam esse.*

> Inst.Gai.4.92.: The *formula petitoria*, however, is the one, by which the plaintiff claims that the item is his own.

For the first time, this formula introduced a direct claim to be the owner or to be the heir to the estate. It allowed the judge to decide whether the plaintiff's main assertion was justified, i.e. whether he was entitled as owner or heir. The wording of the *formula petitoria* ('formula for delivery') has been reconstructed as follows:

> *Si paret hereditatem Publi Maevi ex iure Quiritium Auli Ageri esse, si arbitratu tuo res Aulo Agerio non restituetur, quanti ea res est, tantam pecuniam Numerium Negidium Aulo Agerio condemnato; si non paret, absolvito.*[1]

---

[1] Otto Lenel, *Das Edictum Perpetuum* (3rd edn, Tauchnitz 1927) 177.

If it is proved that the estate of Publius Maevius belongs to Aulus Agerius (the plaintiff) according to the law of the *Quirites*, and if the objects have not been delivered to Aulus Agerius after your [the judge's] arbitration, then you shall order Numerius Negidius (the defendant) to pay Aulus Agerius the amount equivalent to the objects' value. If the assertion is not proven, then you shall discharge him.

This formula, addressed to the judge (*iudex*), provided for several steps in the procedure *apud iudicem*. First, the judge had to examine the position of the plaintiff as heir, i.e., he had to assess the evidence produced to prove the claimant's entitlement. Second, once the judge had determined that the claimant was heir, he would turn to the defendant and ask him to satisfy the plaintiff by handing over the objects claimed. In fact, the *formula petitoria* (*si arbitratu tuo...non restituetur*) contains an *arbitrium*-clause (*arbitrium*, 'margin of discretion'). Based on this clause, the judge could, by an interlocutory order, ask the defendant to 'voluntarily' hand over the objects to the claimant. The final outcome of the trial would then depend on the defendant's response to the court's order. If he complied and the claimant obtained the claimed objects, the judge would acquit the defendant. If the defendant chose to keep the objects, he was sentenced to compensate the claimant for the value of his loss.

The *arbitrium*-clause is the most obvious sign, that, unlike earlier claims, the *formula petitoria* allowed the judge to examine the central question of the claimant's entitlement. Despite this significant change, the *hereditatis petitio* still does not allow the judge to compel the defendant to perform in kind. In fact, it is a general feature of the formulary procedure that, following the formula, only monetary compensation is awarded. This is the expression of the limited judicial power of Roman judges and is known as the principle of pecuniary condemnation (*condemnatio pecuniaria*).

The shift in the judge's competence from the *legis actio* to the formulary procedure has also changed the way in which the parties present their case. Whereas in the *legis actio* procedure there were two claimants, each claiming to be the heir, in the formulary procedure only the plaintiff claimed to be the heir. As the *arbitrium*-clause shows, the *hereditatis petitio* could also be brought against the possessor of the estate:

Ulpianus, 15 ad edictum: Regulariter definiendum est eum demum teneri petitione hereditatis, qui vel ius pro herede vel pro possessore possidet [...] (D.5.3.9)

Ulpian, Edict, book 15: As a rule, it should be noted that only someone who is either entitled as heir or as possessor can be sued with the *hereditatis petitio*. (D.5.3.9)

The defendant could be in possession because he believed himself to be an heir to the estate (*pro herede*), but it was no longer necessary to claim heirship to become a defendant. It was sufficient to be in possession (*pro possessore*) of the estate or of objects belonging to it, e.g., if the possessor did not know that the owner had died or if he had received the object during the decedent's lifetime.

But the requirement of possession has also been relaxed over time:

> *Ulpianus, 15 ad edictum: Non solum autem ab eo peti hereditas potest, qui corpus hereditarium possidet, sed et si nihil, et videndum, si non possidens optulerit tamen se petitioni, an teneatur. Et Celsus libro quarto digestorum scirbit ex dolo eum teneri: Dolo enim facere eum qui se offert petitioni [...]* (D.5.3.13.13.)

> Ulpian, Edict, book 15: The *hereditatis petitio* can be brought not only against the person who actually possesses an object that belongs to the estate, but even if he does not possess anything, one must examine whether he is liable if he nevertheless offers to take the role of the defendant. And Celsus writes in the fourth book of the Digest that he is liable for fraud, because anyone who offers to defend a suit of this kind acts fraudulently [...] (D.5.3.13.13.)

Ulpian explains that the possessor and anyone who offers to participate in the proceedings can be sued with the *hereditatis petitio*. Since the latter took part in the proceedings, he led the plaintiff to believe that he was the *possessor*, which must be a qualified deceit if he was not. His malice would be used against him by treating him as a possessor. Similarly, someone who has fraudulently abandoned possession of the estate in order to avoid litigation could be sued with the *hereditatis petitio*.

If this praetorian action was also intended to protect the heir under *ius civile*, what protection was given to the praetorian heir (*bonorum possessor*)?

5.3 The Protection of the *bonorum possessor*

The praetor who had granted *bonorum possessio* to an eligible applicant protected him by a special interdict (*interdictum*, literally 'prohibition'). Interdicts were provisional measures taken by the praetor to protect factual situations. The interdict to protect a *bonorum possessio* was called '*quorum bonorum*' (literally 'of which estate'):

> *Ulpianus, 67 ad edictum: pr. Ait praetor: 'Quorum bonorum ex edicto meo illi possessio data est, quod de his bonis pro herede aut pro possessore possides possideresve, si nihil usucaptum esset, quod quidem dolo malo fecisti, uti desineres possidere, id illi restituas.'*

(1) Hoc interdictum restitutorium est et ad universitatem bonorum, non ad singulas res pertinent et appellatur 'quorum bonorum' et est apiscendae possessionis universorum bonorum. (D.43.2.1pr.–1.)

Ulpian, Edict, book 67: The praetor says: 'Whatever of this estate, the *bonorum possessio* of which has been granted to him by my edict, you possess or would possess, either as heir or as possessor, if nothing had been acquired by usucapion, and whatever you have done fraudulently to give up the possession, you will restore to him.'
(1) This interdict is restitutionary and applies to the estate as a whole, not to individual objects. It is called *'quorum bonorum'* (of which estate) and is an interdict for obtaining possession of the entire estate. (D.43.2.1pr.–1.)

The praetor protected the *bonorum possessor* by ordering the restitution of the estate or of objects belonging to the estate that had been taken by an heir or a third party. As Ulpian stresses, the aim of the interdict was not only to preserve the *bonorum possessor's* existing possessions, but also to ensure that the possession were returned to him by third parties and even by the civil heir himself.

In turn, the heir of *ius civile* could sue the *bonorum possessor* with the *hereditatis petitio*. These conflicting claims are evidence of the latent competition between an heir of *ius civile* and a praetorian *bonorum possessor*:

Ulpianus, 15 ad edictum: Pro herede possidet, qui putat se heredem esse. Sed an et is, qui scit se heredem non esse, pro herede possideat, quaeritur: Et Arrianus libro secundo de interdictis putat teneri, quo iure nos uti Proculus scribit. Sed enim et bonorum possessor pro herede videtur possidere. (D.5.3.11pr.)

Ulpian, Edict, book 15: A person possesses as an heir if he believes himself to be an heir. But we might ask, what if someone knows that he is not the heir and yet possesses as an heir? Arrian, in the second book 'On Interdicts', believes that he is liable and, as Proculus states, this is the law we apply. But the *bonorum possessor* is also considered to possess as heir. (D.5.3.11pr.)

The *hereditatis petitio* was properly directed against the possessor who held the estate *pro herede* (as heir) or *pro possessore* (as possessor). This raised the question of whether the claim could also be directed against those who knew that they were not heirs under the *ius civile*, but held *bonorum possessio* under praetorian law. Ulpian, citing Arrian and Proculus (first century AD), noted that the *bonorum possessor* could also be sued with the *hereditatis petitio*, since as a praetorian heir, he also possessed *pro herede*.

The coexistence of two contradictory remedies, the *hereditatis petitio* and the interdict *quorum bonorum*, is the result of the overlapping of the *ius civile* and the *ius praetorium* regarding the position of the heir. Whose position takes precedence, i.e., whether the *ius civile* heir has to return the estate according to the interdict or whether, on the contrary, the *bonorum possessor* has to deliver the estate according to the *hereditatis petitio*, depends on the individual case. The criteria for distinguishing between *bonorum possessio sine re* and *bonorum possessio cum re* also apply in this respect. (Ch. 3.3.1).

During the Empire, the *bonorum possessio* was gradually consolidated against the competing position of the heir of *ius civile* (Ch. 3.3.2), leading to a clarification of their respective scopes. The stronger institutionalisation of the *bonorum possessio* explains why jurists of the Empire also granted the *hereditatis petitio* to the *bonorum possessor*:

> *Ulpianus, 15 ad edictum: Ordinarium fuit post civiles actiones heredibus propositas rationem habere praetorem etiam eorum quos ipse velut heredes facit, hoc est eorum quibus bonorum possessio data est. (D.5.5.1.)*

> Ulpian, Edict, book 15: It was in accordance with the order that the praetor, having set out the civil actions to heirs under the *ius civile*, also considered those whom he himself makes heirs, so to speak, that is, also to those who have received the *bonorum possessio*. (D.5.5.1.)

The equal treatment of the praetorian and civil heir can be justified by the fact that their positions had already been assimilated. For one, the praetor granted the *bonorum possessor* all actions for and against the estate 'as if he were heir'; moreover, the *bonorum possessor* of the estate could acquire the position of civil heir through prescriptive acquisition (Ch. 4.2.2). Ultimately, this convergence of the two positions allowed the *bonorum possessor* to choose between the interdict and the *hereditatis petitio* for his legal protection.

The imperial law further modified the *hereditatis petitio*.

5.4 Imperial Law: The *senatusconsultum Iuventianum*

The imperial legislation did not immediately interfere with the *hereditatis petitio*. Instead, the jurists decided to apply some of the provisions governing the *vindicatio caducorum* of the imperial treasury (Ch. 4.4.1) to the *hereditatis petitio*. The most important imperial ruling in this respect was a *senatusconsultum* passed under Emperor Hadrian (AD129). Since the jurist Juventius Celsus is named as consul of the year in which it was passed, scholars call it the *senatusconsultum Iuventianum*:

> *Ulpianus, 15 ad edictum: 6) [...] de quibus cum forma senatus consulto sit data, optimum est ipsius senatus consulti interpretationem facere verbis eius relatis. 'Pridie idus Martias Quintus Iulius Balbus et Publius Iuventius Celsus Titius Aufidius Hoenius Severianus consules verba fecerunt de his, quae imperator caesar Traiani Parthici filius divi Nervae nepos Hadrianus*

Augustus optimus maximusque princeps pater patriae quinto nonas Martias quae proximae fuerunt libello complexus esset, quid fieri placeat, de qua re ita censuerunt.

6a) Cum, antequam partes caducae ex bonis Rustici fisco peterentur, hi qui se heredes esse existimant, hereditatem distraxerint, placere redactae ex pretio rerum venditarum pecuniae usuras non esse exigendas idemque in similibus causis servandum.

6b) Item placere, a quibus hereditas petita fuisset, si adversus eos iudicatum esset, pretia, quae ad eos rerum ex hereditate venditarum pervenissent, etsi eae ante petitam hereditatem deperissent deminutiaeve fuissent, restituere debere.

6c) Item eos qui bona invasissent, cum scirent ad se non pertinere, etiamsi ante litem contestatam fecerint, quo minus possiderent, perinde condemnandos, quasi possiderent: Eos autem, qui iustas causas habuissent, quare bona ad se pertinere existimassent, usque eo dumtaxat, quo locupletiores ex ea re facti essent.

6d) Petitam autem fisco hereditatem ex eo tempore existimandum esse, quo primum scierit quisque eam a se peti, id est cum primum aut denuntiatum esset ei aut litteris vel edicto evocatus esset. censuerunt' [...] (D.5.3.20.6-6d.)

Ulpian, Edict, book 15: 6 [...] Since regulations have been issued on these matters in a *senatusconsultum*, it is best to render the contents of the *senatusconsultum* verbatim and then to interpret it: 'On the fourteenth of March, the consuls Quintus Julius Balbus and Publius Juventius Celsus Titius Aufidius Hoenus Severianus, introduced a motion to vote on that, what the emperor and mighty prince, the Emperor Hadrianus Augustus Caesar, son of Trajanus Parthicus, grandson of the deified Nerva, the greatest and best princeps, Father of the Country, had presented in a speech on the third of March, concerning what he thought should be decided. Thereupon they [the senators] voted as follows:

6a. Since those who believed themselves to be heirs have disposed of the inheritance before the imperial treasury brought suit for those parts of the estate of Rusticus that were forfeited as *bona caduca*, we decree that no interest should be charged on the money obtained as the price for the objects sold, and that the same rule should be observed in similar cases.

6b. Similarly, we decree that when judgment is given against parties who have been sued for the delivery of an estate, the price obtained for the sale of any object belonging to the estate must be refunded by them, even if these objects were destroyed or alienated before the claim for the delivery of the estate was filed.

6c. Similarly, if those have taken possession of an estate knowing that it does not belong to them, and even if they have acted before the *litis contestatio* to free themselves from the possession, they are to be condemned just as if they had been in possession. Still, those who had good reason to believe that they were entitled to the estate are only liable to the extent that they were enriched as a result of this.

6d. The imperial treasury shall be deemed to have brought the suit for the delivery of the estate from the time when anyone first knew that it was being claimed from him, that is, from the time when he was notified or summoned either by an official letter or by a public notice [...]' (D.5.3.20.6–6d.)

According to Ulpian (third century AD), four main points of the *senatusconsultum Iuventianum* need to be stressed:

1. The possessor of the estate who considers himself entitled to it and has sold it does not have to pay interest on the money he has received as the price.
2. The possessor of the estate has to hand over the sale proceeds of the items belonging to the estate, even if the items themselves have perished before the action is brought forth.
3. Concerning the liability, a distinction must be made between the possessor in bad faith, who knew that he was not entitled to the estate, and the possessor in good faith, who could assume that he was. The possessor in bad faith is treated as if he still were in possession of the estate's items. The possessor in good faith must restore only to the extent that he was actually enriched.
4. An estate is considered as 'claimed' when it is pursued in court.

5.4.1 The Different Legal Consequences of the senatusconsultum Iuventianum

Let us now consider each of the individual points on which Ulpian commented. First, the obligation to pay interest on pecuniary obligations (above point 1), then the question of when an estate can be considered as 'claimed' (above point 4):

> *Ulpianus, 15 ad edictum: 'Petitam autem hereditatem' et cetera: Id est ex quo quis scit a se peti: Nam ubi scit, incipit esse malae fidei possessor. 'Id est cum primum aut denuntiatum esset': Quid ergo si scit quidem, nemo autem ei denuntiavit, an incipiat usuras debere pecuniae redactae? Et puto debere: Coepit enim malae fidei possessor esse [...] (D.5.3.20.11.)*

Ulpian, Edict book 15: The words 'an estate has been claimed', refer to the time from which anyone knows that the estate is demanded of him; for as soon as he knows, he immediately becomes a possessor in bad faith, that is, 'as soon as he was notified'. What would be the case, however, if he was aware of the fact and still no one notified him? Would he begin to owe interest on the sale proceeds? And I think he will, for he has become a possessor in bad faith [...] (D.5.3.20.11.)

The possessor of an estate who legitimately believed he was entitled to it was generally not obliged to pay interest on monetary claims under a *hereditatis petitio*. Interest was due only from the moment when the possessor became aware that he was not entitled. This occurred at the latest when the defendant was summoned by the magistrate (*denuntiatio litis*). The obligation to pay interest on monetary debts is linked with the possessor's liability to surrender the sale proceeds (above, point 1):

> *Ulpianus, 15 ad edictum: [...] Bonae fidei possessor si vendiderit res hereditarias, sive exegit pretium sive non, quia habet actionem, debebit pretium praestare: Sed ubi habet actionem, sufficiet eum actiones praestare. (D.5.3.20.17.)*

> Ulpian, Edict, book 15: [...] If a possessor in good faith has sold items belonging to an estate, he must refund the price whether he has received the payment or not, because he has the right to bring an action [against the buyer for payment]. But where he has a right of action, it is sufficient to grant him [the claimant] the actions. (D.5.3.20.17.)

If the possessor has sold the estate and received a sale price, this price replaces the sold items from the estate (*surrogatio*). Hence, even the possessor in good faith must surrender the sales proceeds. If he has not yet obtained the sum, he can transfer his claim against the buyer to the heir.

In contrast, the possessor in bad faith is held to a high standard of liability:

> *Ulpianus, 15 ad edictum: Restituere autem pretia debebit possessor, etsi deperditae sunt res vel deminutae. Sed utrum ita demum restituat, si bonae fidei possessor est, an et si malae fidei? Et si quidem res apud emptorem extent nec deperditae nec deminutae sunt, sine dubio ipsas res debet praestare malae fidei possessor aut, si recipere eas ab emptore nullo modo possit, tantum quantum in litem esset iuratum. At ubi deperditae sunt et deminutae, verum pretium debet praestari, quia si petitor rem consecutus esset, distraxisset et verum pretium rei non perderet. (D.5.3.20.21.)*

> Ulpian, Edict, book 15: The possessor must restore the sale proceeds even if the items have been destroyed or alienated. But is he obliged to restore them if he is the possessor in good faith or also the possessor in bad faith? If the items are still in the possession of the purchaser, and have not been destroyed or alienated, the possessor in bad faith must undoubtedly hand over the

actual items, or, if he cannot recover them from the purchaser, he must pay as much as the items are sworn [by the plaintiff] to be worth in court. If the items have been destroyed or alienated, the real value must be paid, because if the plaintiff had obtained possession of the items, he would not have disposed of them and would not have lost their real value. (D.5.3.20.21.)

The possessor in bad faith, i.e. someone who knew he was not the heir, had to hand over the sale proceeds to the claimant, even if the items sold had since been destroyed or lost. In other words, the possessor in bad faith is liable for the original value of the item belonging to the estate. The amount due depends on whether the item has been destroyed or alienated. If the buyer is still in the possession of the item, the possessor of the estate will be condemned to pay the subjective value that the item has for the heir. In this case, the possessor in bad faith must compensate the claimant for his inability to restore the item himself. If the item has been destroyed, the possessor must restore the objective value of the object and is therefore liable for its accidental loss.

In contrast, the possessor of the estate who acted in good faith had only limited liability for the sale price of the items from the estate:

Ulpianus, 15 ad edictum: Utrum autem omne pretium restituere debebit bonae fidei possessor an vero ita demum, si factus sit locupletior, videndum: Finge pretium acceptum vel perdidisse vel consumpsisse vel donasse. Et verbum quidem pervenisse ambiguum est, solumne hoc contineret, quod prima ratione fuerit, an vero et id quod durat. Et puto [...] ut ita demum competat, si factus sit locupletior. (D.5.3.23pr.)

Ulpian, Edict, book 15: It should be considered whether a possessor in good faith is required to restore the full sales price, or only if he is still enriched. Suppose that, having obtained the sales price, he has either lost it, spent it or given it away. And the word 'obtained' is actually ambiguous. Does it only apply to what was there in the beginning, or to what remains? And I think [...] that it should only apply if he is still enriched. (D.5.3.23pr.)

If the possessor of the estate, who was in good faith, lost the money he had received from the sale, or spent it or gave it away, he would not be liable. This follows from the *senatusconsultum Iuventianum*, which required that the possessor had 'obtained' (*pervenire*) the item from the estate. A possessor in good faith was only considered to have 'obtained' if the money was still in his possession. In order to protect the possessor in good faith who believed in his entitlement, his liability was limited to the existing enrichment. The different standards of liability between the possessor in good faith and the possessor in bad faith corresponded to point 3 above of the *senatusconsultum Iuventianum*. While the possessor in bad faith was liable for every eventuality, the possessor in good faith was only liable for his enrichment. Thus, the *senatusconsultum Iuventianum* introduced a differentiated liability, depending on whether the possessor of the inheritance knew that he was not entitled to it. This differentiation corresponded to a trend already observed in Hadrian's reforms regarding the prescriptive acquisition of estates (Ch. 4.1.4), whereby the possessor in bad faith was disadvantaged in relation to the possessor in good faith. Overview 20 compares the liability standards of the *senatusconsultum Iuventianum* for both categories of possessors.

Overview 20: The Provisions of the *senatusconsultum Iuventianum*

	monetary debts to be returned with interest:	restitution of the sale price:	extent of the obligation to restore:
possessor of the estate in good faith:	does not apply if there is no knowledge of the action (notice)	only if still among the assets (enrichment)	only if still among the assets
possessor of the estate in bad faith:	from the time of taking possession	always; liability even for force majeure, i.e. if items of the estate are lost	liability for everything acquired in connection with the estate, liability even for force majeure

The differentiation of the obligation to restore, according to the good or bad faith of the possessor of the estate led to a 'moralisation' of the claim for the delivery of the estate. It was no longer a dispute between claimants to the inheritance. The aim was now to prevent unjust possession of the estate.

5.4.2 Fiscal and Private Litigation

The observed differentiation of the liability standards for the estate possessor in the *hereditatis petitio* follows the *vindicatio caducorum* of the imperial treasury, which gave rise to the *senatusconsultum Iulianum*. However, the application of this rule from the fiscal procedure to the *hereditatis petitio* of private law was not a matter of course for the Roman jurists:

> *Ulpianus, 15 ad edictum: In privatorum quoque petitionibus senatusconsultum locum habere nemo est qui ambigit, licet in publica causa factum sit.* (D.5.3.20.9.)

> Ulpian, Edict, book 15: When a private party brings an action, no one doubts that the *senatusconsultum* also applies, even though the latter was issued as a public matter. (D.5.3.20. 9.)

Ulpian (third century AD) highlighted that the situation in a fiscal procedure was different from that in a private proceeding. He did not doubt, however, that the rationale of the *senatusconsultum Iuventianum* could be applied to the rules of the *hereditatis petitio*.

This view illustrates the primacy of imperial law over *ius civile* and *ius praetorium* (Ch. 2.2.4). As long as the imperial law merely developed the traditional layers of law, imperial novations or concretisations were to be accepted as legally binding. Moreover, the paradigmatic position of imperial ordinances in the *cognitio extra ordinem* should not be underestimated. Even if these provisions initially applied only to the particular sphere of imperial jurisdiction, they were to be regarded as binding (*lex*). Therefore, these provisions had to be incorporated into existing law as far as possible. This was especially the case when the reception of imperial provisions did not pose any difficulties. Since the *vindicatio caducorum* of the imperial treasury corresponded to the *hereditatis petitio* of private law, the interpretation of the latter in the light of the former did not pose any difficulties. Hence, the obligation to pay interest on monetary debts (1) as well as the obligation to return the sale proceeds (2) could be incorporated without difficulty into the provision of *quanti ea res est* of the *hereditatis petitio*. For, the word '*res*' (thing) does not only describe a corporal item of the estate, but refers to the entire object in dispute and could therefore include all the benefits that the heir had lost through the deprivation of possession.

In addition, the distinction between a possessor of the estate in good faith and a possessor in bad faith (3) is already found in the traditional formula, which distinguishes between the possessor *pro herede* and the possessor *pro possessore*. Following the reasoning of the *senatusconsultum Iuventianum*, the possessor *pro herede* is in good faith and the possessor *pro possessore* is in bad faith.

The fact that the notification of the defendant (*denuntiatio*) could cause his bad faith showed that the *senatusconsultum Iuventianum*, unlike the *hereditatis petitio*, was related to the imperial *cognitio* (Ch. 2.2.4). At this point it was necessary to transfer the rationale of the new procedure to the existing modalities of the formulary process. Thus, for the *hereditatis petitio*, the summons of the defendant by the praetor were considered the decisive moment for the presumption of bad faith.

In conclusion, the interpretation of the *hereditatis petitio*, following the precepts of the *senatusconsultum Iuventianum*, is an example of the scope of the imperial law, which modified the *ius civile* and *ius praetorium* not only directly, through statutes, but also through juristic interpretation.

5.5 Concluding Considerations on the Protection of the Position of Heir

1. The three procedures mentioned were different stages in the development of the claim for the delivery of the estate: the *legis actio* procedure for *ius civile*; the formulary procedure for *ius civile* and the *ius praetorium*; the *cognitio extra ordinem* for the *ius novum*.
2. The procedure of *legis actio* was characterised by a strict formalism, visible in the *legis actio sacramento in rem*. The capacity to bring an action or be sued depended on the law of inheritance. In contrast, the praetor's *formula petitoria* was very flexible and open to interpretation. Therefore, the *formula petitoria* was very receptive to the additional requirements of the *senatusconsultum Iuventianum* regarding the liability of the possessor of an estate under the *cognitio extra ordinem*.
3. The analysis of the claim for the delivery of the estate in its various procedural manifestations reveals the interdependence of the different stages of development and the legal continuity observed from the law of the twelve tables to the Empire. And even though we can trace a development from a dispute between two claimants over an estate (procedural bet) to an action for the restitution of the heir against the estate's possessor, we can also discern an endeavour to integrate each amendment into the existing law. Consequently, even the imperial novation did not abolish the law, but was understood as an improvement of the existing law, as far as possible (Ch. 6.4.4).

Overview 21: The Evolutionary Stages of the *hereditatis petitio*

law of the twelve tables ca. **450BC**	the *legis actio* procedure: procedural wager	capacity to sue: claiming to be heir	capacity to be sued: claiming to be heir
Republic from 367BC	formulary procedure: *formula petitoria*	capacity to sue: claiming to be heir	capacity to be sued: possession *pro herede/pro possessore*
Empire *senatusconsultum* ***Iuventianum*,** **AD129**	formulary procedure/*cognitio extra ordinem*	capacity to sue: claiming to be heir	capacity to be sued: possession, agreement (*dolus*), dereliction (*dolus*)

6

The Testamentary Order of Succession

The Latin *testamentum* derives from *testari* ('to witness'), indicating that the testator's last will had to be declared in the presence of witnesses. The role of the witnesses was to guarantee the authenticity and integrity of the will after the testator's death. In the Republic and the Empire, the will was considered the most important legal act of a Roman citizen (Ch. 1.1). Family members eagerly awaited the opening of the will because the content of the last judgement (*supremum iudicum*) could reveal the testator's secret opinions; at the same time, we can perceive the testator's intention to provide for very vulnerable family members and secure their livelihood. The variety of the testator's intentions in wills is reflected in the different legal contents of Roman testaments. They can provide for the appointment or disinheritance of heirs; the testator can bequeath legacies; he can free slaves and also appoint guardians. The legal basis for these final dispositions was, until the Empire, contained in a single sentence of the law of the twelve tables (V.3): 'As he disposed over his household, property and guardianship, so shall it be lawful' *(uti legassit super familia pecuniave tutelave sua, ita ius esto)*:[1]

> *Pomponius, 5 ad Quintum Mucium: Verbis legis duodecim tabularum his 'uti legassit suae rei, ita ius esto' latissima potestas tributa videtur et heredis instituendi et legata et libertates dandi, tutelas quoque constituendi. [...] (D.50.16. 120.)*
>
> Pomponius, Quintus Mucius, book 5: By the following words of the law of the twelve tables, 'As a man has the right to dispose of his estate by his will, so shall it be lawful', an exceedingly far-reaching force is considered to have been granted to appoint heirs, to bequeath legacies and to grant liberty, and also to establish guardianships. [...] (D.50.16.120.)

---

[1] Cited after Michel Humbert, Andrew D. E. Lewis, Michael H. Crawford, in Michael H. Crawford (ed), *Roman Statutes II* (Institute of Classical Studies 1996) 635–640.

This sentence from the law of the twelve tables is the legal basis for the power to appoint an heir, to bequeath legacies, to free slaves and to appoint guardians. Therefore, the testator had to make extensive provisions by appointing a successor, bequeathing legacies, manumitting deserving slaves so that they do not become part of the estate, and by appointing a guardian (*tutor*) for women and children to help them with their legal transactions. The granting of such powers to the testator requires the observance of a certain formalism:

> *Inst.Gai.2.101.: Testamentorum autem genera initio duo fuerunt: Nam aut calatis comitiis testamentum faciebant, quae comitia bis in anno testamentis faciendis destinate erant, aut in procinctu, id est, cum belli causa arma sumebant: Procinctus est enim expeditus et armatus exercitus. Alterum itaque in pace et in otio faciebant, alterum in proelium exituri.*

> Inst.Gai.2.101.: Initially, there were two kinds of wills. For testators either made a will at the popular assembly, which met twice a year for that purpose or in the face of the enemy, that is to say, when the testator took up arms to make war. The term '*procinctus*' refers to an army set up and ready. Hence, one form of will was made in peace and leisure, and another in the face of battle.

In his historical review, Gaius presents two forms of wills of the *ius civile* that had fallen into disuse by his time (second century AD): The will drawn up before the public assembly (*testamentum calatis comitiis*) and the will drawn up 'on the eve of battle' (*testamentum in procinctu*).

As military service and participation in the assembly were only available to men, these forms of drawing a will were also only open to men. Also, these two early forms of testaments are based on the public witnessing of the last will in front of the other citizens. By contrast, for the late Republic and the Empire, which are historically better documented, the making of a will was a private legal act.

6.1 The Will under *ius civile*

The power to independently dispose of one's estate beyond one's death through a will conflicts with the precept of family succession (Ch. 3). This visible tension has led to the scholarly assumption that the freedom of testation was initially limited to bequeathing legacies, thus preserving the intestate succession of children under the paternal power. The word '*legare*' in the cited sentence of the law of the twelve tables (V.3: *uti legassit super familia pecuniave* [...]) supports this view. In the Empire, the term '*legare*' referred to the singular acquisition upon death; hence, it referred to the bequest (*legatum*). While the heir, as legal successor of the testator, acquired the latter's rights and obligations, the legatee acquired only a right to an individual object or a group of objects. If the words cited originated from the law of the twelve tables and the word '*legare*' meant bequests only, it is likely that a will was initially limited to leaving bequests. Such a 'testamentary legacy' entailed a mixture of statutory succession order and voluntary order of succession, because the intestate heirs had to fulfil the legacies. As a result, this early form of private will would present a compromise between the principle of family succession and the testator's freedom of testation. The better-documented law of the late Republic and the Empire decisively favoured freedom of testation by also allowing the testator to appoint heirs from outside the family and to disinherit children under his paternal power. The main application of a will is the mancipatory will (*testamentum per aes et libram*).

6.1.1 The Mancipatory Will

The mancipatory form of a will derives its name from the fact that it is made by *mancipatio*, i.e. by a symbolic sale in front of five witnesses. Generally, *mancipatio*, originally a cash purchase, was performed to transfer ownership over an object or a person under the paternal power (slave or child under the *potestas*). But as shown in the case of release from power (*emancipatio*), this ritual was also used for other purposes, such as releasing children from the *patria potestas* (Ch. 3.1.2). Similarly, the mancipatory will resulted from separating *mancipatio* from its initial purpose, namely, the intention to acquire; it is – to cite a well-known expression coined by Ernst Rabel – 'a legal transaction conceived in imitation' (*nachgeformtes Rechtsgeschäft*):[2]

> *Inst.Gai.2.103: [...] Sane nunc aliter ordinatur, quam olim solebat; namque olim familiae emptor, id est, qui a testatore familiam accipiebat mancipio, heredis locum optinebat, et ob id ei mandabat testator, quid cuique post mortem suam dari vellet; [...]*

> Inst.Gai.2.103.: [...] It is now arranged differently indeed from what was previously the custom. For formerly the buyer of the estate, that is to say, the party who received it by *mancipatio* from the testator had the position of heir, which is why the testator commissioned him concerning what he desired to be given to anyone after his death; [...]

The original purpose of the mancipatory will was to transfer the estate and the position of heir to a trustee (*familiae emptor*, literally 'the buyer of the estate'),

---

[2] The term was coined by Ernst Rabel, 'Nachgeformte Rechtsgeschäfte' (1906) 40 Zeitschrift der Savigny Stiftung für Rechtsgeschichte, Romanistische Abteilung 290 and (1907) 41 Zeitschrift der Savigny Stiftung für Rechtsgeschichte, Romanistische Abteilung 311.

so that the instructions as to how the estate should be distributed could be made with binding effect for the heir. In Gaius' time, however, the *familiae emptor* no longer acted as an heir himself. Rather, the transfer of the estate to him served the purpose of formally appointing a third party as heir:

> *Inst.Gai.2.103: [...] nunc vero alius heres testamento instituitur, a quo etiam legata relinquantur, alius dicis gratia propter veteris iuris imitationem familiae emptor adhibetur.*

> Inst.Gai.2.103: [...] Now, however, in the will one is appointed heir and tasked with fulfilling legacies, the other one acts as the purchaser of the estate, only for the sake of form, in imitation of the ancient law.

In this situation of the mancipatory will, the heir and the *familiae emptor* are separate. The estate is still transferred to the latter, but the 'sale', i.e., the *mancipatio*, is now a mere formality. Hence, the testamentary document (*tabulae testamenti*)[3] is central to the process of making a will. The *mancipatio* is thus a ritual that validates the written will:

> *Inst.Gai.2.104.: [...] qui facit testamentum, adhibitis, sicut in ceteris mancipationibus, V testibus civibus Romanis puberibus et libripende, postquam tabulas testamenti scripserit, mancipat alicui dicis gratia familiam suam; in qua re his verbis familiae emptor utitur: 'Familiam pecuniamque tuam endo mandatela tua custodelaque mea esse aio, eaque, quo tu iure testamentum facere possis secundum legem publicam, hoc aere, et' ut quidam adiciunt, 'aeneaque libra, esto mihi empta'; deinde aere percutit libram idque aes dat testatori velut pretii loco; deinde testator tabulas testamenti tenens ita dicit: 'Haec ita ut in his tabulis cerisque scripta sunt, ita do ita lego ita testor, itaque vos, quirites, testimonium mihi perhibetote,' et hoc dicitur nuncupatio: Nuncupare est enim palam nominare, et sane quae testator specialiter in tabulis testamenti scripserit, ea videtur generali sermone nominare atque confirmare.*

> Inst.Gai.2.104.: [...] Someone who makes a will, as in the case of other *mancipationes,* calls together five Roman citizens of the age of puberty as witnesses, and a balance-holder and, having written down his will, transfers his household by *mancipatio* as a matter of form to a certain person. And the said purchaser speaks thus: 'let your family and money pass into my charge and custody, and, so that you may make your will properly following the public law, let me purchase them with this bronze,' or as some authorities add, 'with this bronze scale." Then he strikes a balance with the piece of

---

[3] *Tabulae* were tablets covered with wax upon which the text of the will was inscribed. For the usual form of will see (Ch. 6.3.1). See Ch. 1.1 for an example of such a wax tablet.

bronze and delivers the latter to the testator as purchase money. Then the testator, holding the will, says, 'I do give and bequeath, and declare that I do so, everything written in these wax tablets, and do you, *Quirites* (Roman citizens) bear witness to my act.' This ritual is called *nuncupatio*, for this term means to declare publicly. And, indeed, what the testator specifically stated in writing in his will is considered to have been declared and confirmed by this general affirmation.

The mancipatory will, literally 'the will by scales and bronze' (*testamentum per aes et libram*), adheres to the usual procedure for *mancipatio*, i.e. it requires five witnesses and a balance-holder who formally weighed the coins. The inheritance is the object of the *mancipatio*. The *emptor familiae*, however, merely agrees to buy the estate in order to enable the testator to make a will. Therefore, the *emptor familiae* stresses that the testator has the power of disposal over his estate while he merely acts as a guardian over it. So, the *emptor familiae* does not permanently receive the estate but merely exerts temporary control. In this legal 'limbo', the testator declares: 'as it was written on the tables, thus I give, I legate, I call upon the witnesses, and, thus, *Quirites*, be my witnesses'.

This declaration is called '*nuncupatio*,' i.e. a binding disposition over a mancipated object, as is customary for *mancipationes* to transfer property. This *nuncupatio* is the central aspect of the making of a testament, while the act of *mancipatio* merely forms the ritual against which the *nuncupatio* takes place. This shift from the actual transfer of the property by *mancipatio* to a purely ritual determination of the heir is also evident in the legal consequences. Although the *emptor familiae* takes control of the property and declares having purchased the inheritance, the sole purpose of this symbolic transfer is the making of a will by the 'selling' testator. The point of reference of the *testaementum per aes et libram* is no longer the *mancipatio* as an act of transfer, but the possibility to dispose freely of the estate at the moment of the transfer.

The mancipatory will was a simplification in comparison to the previous forms of testament that were public because it could be made privately. The testator did not have to rely on the meeting of the public assembly or the gathering of the army. Instead, he could arrange his affairs anytime if he could assemble the necessary number of witnesses.

In the following, we will only deal with the mancipatory will. Its shape followed the precepts of cautelary jurisprudence, i.e. jurists advising the parties in arranging legal transactions (*cautela*, from *cavere*, 'provide for'). Rules that were initially recommendations for good practice were considered as binding precepts by the jurists of the Empire:

> *Gaius, 2 institutionum: Si quaeramus, an valeat testamentum, in primis animadvertere debemus, an is qui fecerit testamentum habuerit testamenti factionem, deinde, si habuerit, requiremus, an secundum regulas iuris civilis testatus sit. (D.28. 1. 4.)*
>
> Gaius, Institutes, book 2: If we inquire whether a will is valid, we must first ascertain if the testator had the *testamenti factio*, and then, if he had, we must determine if it was drawn up under the rules of the *ius civile*. (D.28.1.4.)

Gaius mentions two requirements for the validity of a will: Firstly, the capacity to draw up a will (*testamenti factio*);[4] secondly, compliance with the rules of *ius civile*. Whereas the capacity to draw up a will is a specific form of the capacity to legally act, hence, linked to a person's status, the *regulae iuris civilis* entail the particular requirements that jurisprudence has developed for drawing up wills.

6.1.2 The testamenti factio

The capacity of a person to draw up a will (*testamenti factio*) as the ability to dispose of one's property for the time after one's death must be present without interruption from the time the will is drawn up until the time of inheritance by the heir.[5] Only persons capable of owning property for themselves, i.e. *sui iuris*, were capable of making a will (Ch. 3.1.2):

> *Gaius, 17 ad edictum provinciale: Qui in potestate parentis est, testamenti faciendi ius non habet, adeo ut, quamvis pater ei permittat, nihilo magis tamen iure testari possit. (D.28.1.6pr.)*
>
> Gaius, Provincial Edict, book 17: Someone under the *patria potestas* has no *testamenti factio*. And this is even so if the father permitted him, for he could not legally make a will. (D.28.1.6pr.)

Hence, children under the paternal power could not make valid wills, even if authorised by their *pater familias*, because they did not have the capacity to own property. A child under the paternal power acquires the capacity to draw up a will only after it was released from the *patria potestas*, thus, becoming *sui iuris* (Ch. 3.1.2).

Women had a limited capacity to draw up a testament, even after they had become *sui iuris*, i.e. if they were not *in manu* of their husband or his

---

[4] *Testamenti factio activa* refers to the capacity to draw up a will whereas *testamenti factio passiva* is the capacity to be instituted as heir or to be granted a legacy in accordance to *ius civile*.

[5] The *testamenti factio* must not be confounded with the capacity to obtain through a will, cf. Ch. 4.4.

father and not under *patria potestas* (Ch. 3.1.4). As we saw above (Ch. 4.3.1), women *sui iuris* were placed under guardianship and therefore had limited capacity to draw up a will. In fact, they needed the consent of their guardian to make a will. The *testamenti factio* of the female testator thus depended on the guardian, i.e. whether he had an interest and therefore wanted to have a say in the making of the will, or whether he decided to allow the woman to draw up her will as she wished.

When examining this question, as with the institute of guardianship in general (Ch. 4.3.1), we find a tendency for the female testator to gain more freedom of disposal over time. Following the law of the twelve tables, women *sui iuris* were under the statutory guardianship of their agnates:

> *Inst.Gai.1.155.: Quibus testamento quidem tutor datus non sit, iis ex lege XII tabularum agnati sunt tutores, qui vocantur 'legitimi'.*

> Inst.Gai.1.155.: Those who do not have a guardian appointed by will receive their agnates as guardians, called 'guardians-at-law' under the law of the twelve tables.

Like the rules of intestacy, the guardianship of the agnates was applied where the will did not make a relevant provision or where no will was left. The purpose of this legal guardianship was obviously to keep family property within the agnatic family and to minimise the risks that women posed to these assets. The main risk in question was that the woman would transfer the property to her children, who, if they were legitimate, were under the *patria potestas* and would be succeeded by the man's family. The hereditary transfer of her property to her children was perceived as an undesirable consequence by the woman's birth family, especially if the woman did not come under the *manus* of her husband or his *pater familias* and thus remained eligible to inherit from her family of origin. This constellation bore the danger that the property was transferred from her family of origin to her husband's family through the woman and her descendance. Also, from the perspective of the husband's family, there was the risk that property could pass to another family if, e.g. she married her first husband *in manu* and then married her second husband in a free marriage and had children with the latter. One way to prevent this undesirable transfer of assets between families was to limit the women's capacity to make wills and, therefore, to make dispositions for the benefit of their children dependent on the consent of their agnates only.

The placing of women under the guardianship of the agnates was, as we have seen (Ch. 4.3.1), abolished in the first century AD by the *lex Cornelia* (AD44–49). But even before this law, a woman could get rid of a troublesome guardian by appointing another guardian. The appointment of a new tutor following the woman's wishes was made through a 'marriage by purchase' (*coëmptio*). The *coëmptio* was a sale formed after the *mancipatio* that could be used to enter into a marriage or to prepare the appointment of a guardian.

Through *coëmptio*, a woman was transferred to the buyer and thus came under his power:

> *Inst.Gai.1.115.: Quod est tale: Si qua velit quos habet tutores deponere et alium nancisci, illis auctoribus coemptionem facit; deinde a coemptionatore remancipata ei, cui ipsa velit, et ab eo vindicta manumissa incipit eum habere tutorem, a quo manumissa est; qui tutor fiduciarius dicitur, [...]*

> Inst.Gai.1.115.: It is done thus: If a woman wishes to release her present guardians and obtain another, she enters a *coëmptio* with the consent of her guardians; and then the other party to the sale re-emancipates her to whom she chooses as guardian, and the latter manumits her through the ritual of the rod, and thus he becomes her guardian and is called a fiduciary guardian [...]

If the aim of the *coëmptio* was to appoint a guardian, the woman entered into a *coëmptio* with a third party with the consent of her former guardians. The third party acquirer obtained a power similar to that of a spouse (*manus*), but exercised it in a fiduciary capacity. This is shown by the fact that he was to give the woman to another man, who would then become her guardian. The latter, by releasing her from his power, would become her guardian. If a woman was not already exempt from guardianship by virtue of the Augustan marriage laws (Ch. 4.3.1), she could choose a guardian whom she trusted and make a will with the content she desired.

In the past, the *coëmptio* gave the woman the legal capacity to make a will:

> *Inst.Gai.1.115a: Olim etiam testamenti faciendi gratia fiduciaria fiebat coemptio: Tunc enim non aliter feminae testamenti faciendi ius habebant, exceptis quibusdam personis, quam si coemptionem fecissent remancipataeque et manumissae fuissent; sed hanc necessitatem coemptionis faciendae ex auctoritate divi Hadriani senatus remisit.*

> Inst.Gai.1.115a.: In the past, a fiduciary *coëmptio* was performed to make a will. For at that time, women, with some exceptions, did not have *testamenti factio* unless they had performed a *coëmptio* and, after being resold, were manumitted. But the Senate, at the suggestion of the deified Hadrian, abolished this necessity of making a *coëmptio*.

Initially, only women released from statutory guardianship could draw up a will. This requirement was entirely abolished by a *senatusconsultum* under Emperor Hadrian (AD117–138):

> Inst.Gai.2.112.: *Postea vero ex auctoritate divi Hadriani senatusconsultum factum est, quo permissum est sui iuris feminis etiam sine coemptione testamentum facere, si modo non minores essent annorum XII; scilicet ut quae liberatae non essent, tutore auctore testari deberent.*

> Inst.Gai.2.112.: Afterwards, a *senatusconsultum* was enacted under the deified Hadrian, by which women were permitted to make a will even without *coëmptio*; provided, however, they were not under twelve years of age; and if they had not been released from guardianship, they were required to establish their wills with the consent of their guardians.

The *senatusconsultum* allowed a woman who had reached puberty to make a will with the consent of her guardian without prior *coëmptio*. The aim of the *senatusconsultum* was not to generally free women from guardianship, but to regulate women's legal capacity to make wills. Before Hadrian's reforms, a woman could make a valid will only if (1) she was *sui iuris*, (2) she had reached the age of puberty, i.e. was older than twelve, (3) she had been bought by *coëmptio*, mancipated and emancipated again, (4) her guardian consented or she had been released from guardianship (*ius trium liberorum*). It was not until the time of Hadrian that a woman could make a will if she was *sui iuris*, had reached the age of puberty, had the consent of her guardian, or was exempt from it because she had the required number of children.

6.1.3 The Appointment of an Heir

The rules governing the appointment of heirs result, on the one hand, from the act of appointing an heir and the mancipatory will and, on the other hand, from the requirements developed by the cautelary practice of the Republic with regard to the formal declaration. The form of appointment reveals a clear division of roles:

> Ulpianus, 1 ad Sabinum: *Qui testamento heres instituitur, in eodem testamento testis esse non potest. [...] (D.28.1.20pr.)*

> Ulpian, Sabinus, book 1: Someone appointed testamentary heir cannot be a witness to the same will. [...] (D.28.1.20pr.)

The designated heir cannot be a witness to the making of a testament. The role of the witness to a will makes this clear. If a witness is also a party, his testimony is worthless because it may be influenced by personal interests. Furthermore, the appointment of an heir in a will is only valid if it is made in the prescribed manner:

> Inst.Gai.2.116.: *Ante omnia requirendum est, an institutio heredis sollemni more facta sit; nam aliter facta institutione nihil proficit familiam testatoris*

ita venire testesque ita adhibere aut ita nuncupare testamentum, ut supra diximus.

Inst.Gai.2.116.: Most of all, we must ask whether the appointment of the heir followed the traditional formalities. For if the appointment were made otherwise, it would not matter if the estate of the testator was sold, the witnesses assembled, and the will publicly declared, as we stated above.

The form of appointment follows custom (*mos*). Preserving this form is a condition for the validity of the will. Even if the act of *mancipatio* was duly performed, but the appointment was not made in the customary manner, the will would be invalid:

Inst.Gai.2.117.: Sollemnis autem institutio haec est: 'Titius heres esto;' sed et illa iam conprobata videtur: 'Titium heredem esse iubeo;' at illa non est conprobata: 'Titium heredem esso volo,' sed et illae a plerisque inprobatae sunt: 'Titium heredem instituo,' item: 'heredem facio'.

Inst.Gai.2.117.: The heir is formally appointed thus: 'let Titius be my heir.' But it also seems commonly accepted to say, 'I order that Titius be my heir.' However: 'I desire Titius to be my heir' is not accepted. Also not accepted by most are 'I appoint Titius my heir' and 'I make Titius my heir'.

The traditional wording was: 'Titius shall be my heir' (*Titius heres esto*). In the time of Gaius the command: 'I order Titius to be my heir,' was also acceptable. However, not acceptable were statements such as: 'I want Titius to be my heir', 'I appoint Titius as my heir', or 'I make Titius my heir'. This comparison shows that the appointment requires a command to the heir to accept the position. This command must be free from temporal limitations:

Papinianus, 1 definitionum: Hereditas ex die vel ad diem non recte datur, sed vitio temporis sublato manet institutio. (D.28.5.34.)

Papinian, Definitions, book 1: An inheritance cannot legally be given from a certain time or until a certain time, but since the defect about the time is ignored, the appointment of the heir will stand. (D.28.5.34.)

For this reason, an heir cannot be appointed temporarily or subject to a (resolutive) condition. The appointment of a pre-, or post-heir is excluded. Once appointed, the heir remains an heir (*semel heres, semper heres* = 'once an heir, always an heir'). Any temporal limitation of the position as heir is void. This kind of appointment must be distinguished from an appointment subject to a suspensive condition, which lasts until the heir's death once the condition has been fulfilled (Ch. 7.1.2). Unlike the resolutory condition, the suspensive condition is possible and valid. Impossible conditions are considered unwritten:

> *Ulpianus, ad Sabinum 5: Sub impossibili condicione vel alio mendo factam institutionem placet non vitiari. (D.28.7.1.)*

> Ulpian, Sabinus, book 5: It is established that an appointment made under an impossible condition, or through mistake, is not void. (D.28.7.1.)

The impossible or otherwise defective condition may be cancelled without affecting the appointment. The appointed person becomes an unconditional heir. Whether the condition is considered impossible depends on the individual circumstances:

> *Ulpianus, 9 ad Sabinum: Si quis ita institutus sit, si monumentum post mortem testatoris in triduo proximo mortis eius fecisset: Cum monumentum in triduo perfici non possit, dicendum erit condicionem evanescere quasi impossibilem. (D.28.7.6.)*

> Ulpian, Sabinus, book 9: If an heir has been appointed on the condition that he should erect a tomb for the testator within three days of the testator's death, and since a tomb cannot be completed in three days, it must be said that the condition lapses as impossible. (D.28.7.6.)

If the testator had appointed an heir on the condition that he should build a tomb for him, but had set an unrealistic time limit for the completion of the edifice, it would be impossible to fulfil the condition. Ulpian therefore decided to delete the condition and treat the heir as having been appointed unconditionally.

The appointment of the heir can be made either orally or verbally, in accordance with the dual form of the mancipatory will. The oral appointment follows the form of *nuncupatio*:

> *Ulpianus. 2 ad Sabinum: Heredes palam ita, ut exaudiri possunt, nuncupandi sint: licebit ergo testanti vel nuncupare heredes vel scribere: Sed si nuncupat, palam debet. Quid est palam? Non utique in publicum, sed ut exaudiri possit: Exaudiri autem non ab omnibus, sed a testibus: Et si plures fuerint testes adhibiti, sufficit sollemnem numerum exaudire. (D.28.1.21pr.)*

> Ulpian, Sabinus, book 2: The names of the heirs should be announced publicly so that they could be heard. Therefore, the testator is permitted to either name the heirs orally or write down their names. If he mentions them orally, however, he must do so publicly. What does the term 'publicly' mean? It does not mean that this shall be done in general publicly, but so that the names may be heard clearly, not by everyone, but only by the witnesses to the will. And where there are several witnesses, it will be sufficient for them to be heard by the number prescribed by law. (D.28.1.21pr.)

The *nuncupatio* of the heir required for the act of *mancipatio* (*palam nuncupare*) that the mancipatory witnesses to the *mancipatio* heard and understood the *nuncupatio*. However, a general public announcement was not required. Ulpian's discussion is nevertheless noteworthy because it shows that the act of *mancipatio* was still practised at the beginning of the third century AD; it had therefore not yet been completely replaced by the written will (Ch. 6.1.1).

6.1.4 The Appointment of Co-Heirs

There were precise rules for appointing several persons as heirs (co-heirs; Ch. 4.1.1). It was customary to call and calculate the shares of an estate after the division of the coins of an As, hence, into twelves or ounces (*unciae*):

> *Ulpianus, 7 ad Sabinum: Pater familias distribuere hereditatem in tot partes potest quot voluerit: Sed sollemnis assis distributio in duodecim uncias fit. (D.28.5.13.1.)*

> Ulpian, Sabinus, book 7: The *pater familias* can divide his estate into as many portions as he wishes, but the regular division of an estate is made into twelve shares, called *unciae*. (D.28.5.13.1.)

Ulpian (third century AD) described the division of the estate into twelve ounces as 'formal'(*sollemnis*). If the testator wished to appoint several heirs, he had to designate the individual shares according to the system of *unciae*. Thus, an appointment could be made to a sixth (*sextans*), a quarter (*quadrans*) or a third (*triens*). Accordingly, the sole heir appointed to the entire estate was called '*heres ex asse*' ('out of the entire As'); those appointed to half as co-heirs were called '*heres ex semisse*' ('out of half an As'). The appointments in asses and their calculation are summarised in Overview 22:

Overview 22: The Appointment of Heirs after the System of Asses

one As	1/2 As	1/3 As	1/4 As	1/6 As	1/12 As
twelve parts	six parts	four parts	three parts	two parts	one part
sole heir	heir to half	heir to a third	heir to a fourth	heir to a sixth	heir to a twelfth

The concept of inheritance as a unit, ideally divided into twelve parts, had legal implications. This became apparent when the testator divided more than 12/12 among the heirs:

> *Ulpianus, 7 ad Sabinum: Sed si excesserit in divisione duodecim uncias, aeque pro rata decrescet: Ut puta me ex duodecim unciis heredem, te ex sex scripsit: ego hereditatis habeo bessem, tu trientem. (D.28.5.13.4.)*

Ulpian, Sabinus, book 7: If a testator divides his estate into more than twelve shares, a diminution will then be made *pro rata* as if he appointed me heir to twelve shares, and yourself heir to six. Then, I will be entitled to two thirds (=eight) of the estate shares and you to a third (=four). (D.28.5.13.4.)

The testator's miscalculation should not be confused with the overburdening of the heir (Ch. 8.2.2), or with the problem of a lack of assets in the estate. It is not a financial problem but a problem of calculation. The testator, perhaps because he had appointed more heirs than originally planned, had divided the estate into eighteen parts, with one heir receiving twelve ounces and the other six ounces. Although the allocation of eighteen parts in total was incorrect, it became clear that the first heir should receive two-thirds of the estate and the second heir one-third. Therefore, the distribution could be brought down to twelve ounces, so that the first one would receive three-quarters (8/12) and the second one-quarter (4/12). The simple example given by Ulpian was intended to illustrate the principles of the calculation for more difficult cases. The estate should be brought to twelve in order to achieve a perfect division.

The same applies if the testator has disposed of less than 12/12 of his estate:

Ulpianus, 7 ad Sabinum: Denique si minus distribuit, potestate iuris in hoc revolvitur: Ut puta si duos heredes ex quadrante scripserit: Nam hereditas eius residua accedit, ut ex semissibus videantur scripti. (D.28.5.13.2.)

Ulpian, Sabinus, book 7: Hence, if the testator divides his estate into a smaller number than this, one comes back to this division [into 12 ounces] automatically. If, for example, a testator appoints two heirs, each to a fourth of his estate because, in this case, the remainder of the estate is apportioned so that each heir is held to have been appointed for six shares. (D.28.5.13.2.)

Ulpian applies the principle of accrual among co-heirs already discussed above (Ch. 4.1.2) also to cases where the testator had disposed of only part of his estate. According to the rules of separation between testamentary and intestate succession, the remaining part of the estate does not go to the heirs on intestacy, but to the testamentary heirs. The principle '*nemo pro parte testatus, pro parte intestatus decedere potest*' is based on the need for the heirs to join together (Ch. 4). Only if there are no testamentary heirs, or if all the appointed heirs renounce, is the testator considered to have died intestate and is succeeded by order of intestacy.

6.1.5 Substitute Heirs *(substitutiones)*

The strict separation between the testamentary and the statutory order of succession explained the need to appoint substitute heirs (*substitutiones*).

Their appointment prevented the share of a lapsing heir from passing to the remaining heirs, or the will from becoming void if all the heirs had died before the testator. Substitute heirs could be appointed in the event that the heir had died before the inheritance. They could also be appointed if the appointed heir renounced the inheritance:

> Inst.Gai.2.174.: Interdum duos pluresve gradus heredum facimus, hoc modo: 'Lucius Titius heres esto cernitoque in diebus <C> proximis, quibus scies poterisque. Quodni ita creveris, exheres esto. Tum Maevius heres esto cernitoque in diebus centum et reliqua'; et deinceps in quantum velimus, substituere possumus.

> Inst.Gai.2.174.: Sometimes, we appoint heirs of two or more degrees thus: 'Lucius Titius shall be my heir, and you must declare formally within the next hundred days after you know your appointment and can accept. But if you do not declare thus, you shall be disinherited. Then you, Maevius, be my heir, and declare your decision within a hundred days, etc.' And accordingly, we can appoint as many substitutes as we desire.

Gaius discusses a case where the testator has appointed an heir and a substitute heir and has requested both to formally declare within one hundred days (*cretio*) if they wish to accept the inheritance (Ch. 4.1.3). The formal acceptance of the inheritance is a condition for being established as an heir. It is therefore provided that after the expiry of the limitation period, the heir is disinherited and the substitute heir is appointed. For his part, the substitute heir must observe the deadline for the formal declaration if he does not want to miss out on the inheritance of the heirs by intestate succession. The heir or substitute heir who has not accepted the testamentary inheritance is not further considered in the will. This rule also shows that the substitute heir inherits directly from the testator and not from the appointed heir.

A different rule applies to a special form of appointment of a substitute heir, i.e. the appointment of a substitute heir for a minor child (*substitutio pupillaris*) who has died before coming of age (*pubertas*):

> Inst.Gai.2.179.: Liberis nostris inpuberibus, quos in potestate habemus, non solum ita [...] substituere possumus, id est, ut si heredes non extiterint, alius nobis heres sit; sed eo amplius ut, etiamsi heredes nobis extiterint et adhuc inpuberes mortui fuerint, sit iis aliquis heres, velut hoc modo: Titius filius meus mihi heres esto. Si filius meus mihi heres non erit, sive mihi heres erit et hic prius moriatur quam in suam tutelam venerit, tunc Seius heres esto.

> Inst.Gai.2.179.: We can not only appoint a substitute heir for our children under the age of puberty who are under our power [...] that is if they did not become our heirs and another might be our heir; but even more so if they

become our heirs and die before reaching the age of puberty; another may be their heir. For example: 'let my son Titius be my heir and if my son does not become my heir, or if he should do so and die before he becomes his guardian, then let Seius be my heir'.

The *pater familias* could make a will for his son who was still an *impubes*, i.e. a *filius familias* under the age of fourteen, by appointing a substitute heir for him. This was in case the *impubes* died before the inheritance passed to him, or he became the heir of the *pater familias* but died before reaching *puberty*. The power of the *pater familias* to make a valid will on behalf of his son was justified by the fact that the son did not have the capacity to make a valid will (Ch. 6.1.2). The question arose as to whether the appointed substitute heir inherited from the *pater familias* or from the deceased *filius familias*:

> *Inst.Gai.2.180.: Quo casu si quidem non extiterit heres filius, substitutus patri fit heres; si vero heres extiterit et ante pubertatem decesserit, ipsi filio fit heres substitutus. Quam ob rem duo quodam modo sunt testamenta, aliud patris, aliud filii, tamquam si ipse filius sibi heredem instituisset; aut certe unum est testamentum duarum hereditatum.*

> Inst.Gai.2.180.: In this instance, if the son does not become the heir, the substitute heir will be the heir to the father; but if the son should become the heir and die before reaching puberty, the substitute will become the heir to the son himself. On this account there are, as it were, two wills, one of the father, the other of the son, just as if the son had appointed an heir; or there is one will which disposes of two estates.

In order to answer this question, the following situations must be distinguished: If the *impubes*, for whom the *pater familias* has appointed a substitute heir, has died before his father, the substitute heir will be the father's heir, since the son has never been an heir to the estate. The opposite is true if the son, who has become the heir, has died before reaching the age of majority. In this case, the substitute heir appointed by the *pater familias* becomes the son's heir. Gaius justified this distinction by arguing that if the son became his father's heir, then the father had made two wills, or at least had disposed over two different estates. In any case, the making of a will for the son depended on the valid making of a will for the father.

> *Ulpianus, ad Sabinum 6: Quisquis autem impuberi testamentum facit, sibi quoque debet facere: Ceterum soli filio non poterit, [...] (D.28.6.2.1.)*

> Ulpian, Sabinus, book 6: If someone makes a will for the benefit of a child who has not reached puberty, he must also make one for himself. Otherwise, he cannot establish a will for his son alone, [...] (D.28.6.2.1.)

A *pater familias* can make a valid will on behalf of his son only if he has made a valid will himself. If the will of the father is ineffective due to the lack of heirs and the intestate succession occurs, the son's testament will be ineffective as well. This dependency manifests itself in the form of the son's will:

> *Ulpianus, 6 ad Sabinum: Prius autem sibi quis debet heredem scribere, deinde filio substituere et non convertere ordinem scripturae: Et hoc Iulianus putat prius sibi debere, deinde filio heredem scribere: ceterum si ante filio, deinde sibi testamentum faciat, non valere. [...] (D.28.6.2.4.)*

> Ulpian, Sabinus, book 6: The testator should first mention his heir. And then, he can appoint a substitute heir for his son. Also, he must not reverse this order of appointment. Iulianus also thinks that one should first select an heir for oneself and, afterwards, one for one's son. If one were to make a will for one's son first, and after that one for oneself, it would be void. [...] (D.28.6.2.4.)

Since the will for the son depended on the father's will, the *pater familias* had to appoint his heir before appointing a substitute heir to inherit in place of or from the son. The *substitutio pupillaris* was therefore only valid if the father left a valid will, i.e. appointed an heir.

The cautelary practice was concerned with the risks that the *substitutio pupillaris* entailed for the *impubes*, namely the disposition of the substitute heir, who might be inclined to cause the contingency of substitution:

> *Inst.Gai.2.181.: Ceterum ne post obitum parentis periculo insidiarum subiectus videretur pupillus, in usu est vulgarem quidem substitutionem palam facere, [...] illam autem substitutionem, per quam, etiamsi heres extiterit pupillus et intra pubertatem decesserit, substitutum vocamus, separatim in inferioribus tabulis scribimus easque tabulas proprio lino propriaque cera consignamus et in prioribus tabulis cavemus, ne inferiores tabulae vivo filio et adhuc inpubere aperiantur. Sed longe tutius est utrumque genus substitutionis separatim in inferioribus tabulis consignari, quia si ita consignatae vel separatae fuerint substitiones, ut diximus, ex priore potest intellegi in altera quoque idem esse substitutus.*

> Inst.Gai.2.181.: However, in order to ensure that the minor is not subject to reprisals after his parent's death, it is customary to make the ordinary substitution publicly [...] But when we appoint a substitute heir upon the contingency that the minor becomes an heir but he dies before coming of age, we write the substitution separately on subsequent tablets and seal them with a different thread and wax. Furthermore, in the first tablets, we provide that the later tablets must not be opened while the son is still alive and a

minor. But it is much safer if both kinds of substitution are sealed separately in the subsequent tablets because, if the said appointments have been sealed or separated, as we said, one can deduce from the first tablet that the person appointed as substitute heir therein is also appointed in the second.

The documentary practice on which Gaius advised sought to protect the *pubes* from attacks by the substitute heir by concealing the identity of the substitute heir appointed in the event of the death of the *impubes*. A first measure of confidentiality is taken by making a son's will in a separate document. According to the instructions of the *pater familias*, this document could only be opened after the death of the *impubes*. A second option, favoured by Gaius, was to remove any mention of a substitute heir from the father's will. The father's will (the first document) instructed that the son's will (the second document) should not be opened until after the son's death. In this way, the identity of the substitute heir remained confidential as long as the son was alive. Keeping the identity of the substitute heir secret limited the risk that a greedy substitute heir would try to harm the son. When the son came of age, the father's will is no longer valid and the son was required to make his own will.

6.2 The Invalidity and Revocation of the Will under the *ius civile*

The will was invalid under the ius *civile* if the form prescribed for the *mancipatio* was not observed, if the requirements for the institution were not met, or if the testator either lacked the *testamenti factio* or subsequently lost it. In addition, the testator might wish to adapt the will to changed circumstances and therefore revoke the old will in favour of a new one.

6.2.1 The Loss of the testamenti factio

Since the *testamenti factio* was a special form of the legal capacity, the *pater familias* lost his *testamenti factio* as soon as he became legally incapacitated. Legal incapacity occurred when the *pater familias* became insane (*furiosus*), but could also be the result of a change of status (*capitis deminutio*):

> Inst.Gai.2.145.: *Alio quoque modo testamenta iure facta infirmantur, velut cum is, qui fecerit testamentum, capite deminutus sit; [...]*

> Inst.Gai.2.145.: Wills legally made may become void in another way. For example, if somebody, having drawn up a will, suffers *capitis deminutio* [...]

The most glaring example of a change in status is the complete loss of legal capacity (*capitis deminutio maxima*), for example as a result of war captivity. The Roman citizen who became a prisoner of war not only lost his freedom de facto, he also became a slave in law. According to the Roman *ius civile*, he was neither free, nor a citizen, nor a member of his family. When he returned from captivity, his rights were restored. This restoration was called the *ius postliminium* ('right of return'):

> Pomponius, 37 ad Quintum Mucium: In bello, cum hi, qui nobis hostes sunt, aliquem ex nostris ceperunt et intra praesidia sua perduxerunt: Nam si eodem bello is reversus fuerit, postliminium habet, id est perinde omnia restituuntur ei iura, ac si captus ab hostibus non esset. Antequam in praesidia perducatur hostium, manet civis. Tunc autem reversus intellegitur, si aut ad amicos nostros perveniat aut intra praesidia nostra esse coepit. (D.49.15.5.1.)
>
> Pomponius, Quintus Mucius, book 37: If our enemies seize one of us in war and take him into their fortifications and he returns during the same war; he will have the right of *postliminium*. Hence, all his rights are restored to him, just as if he had not been captured by the enemy. However, he remains a citizen before he is taken into the enemy's fortifications. He is understood to have returned if he comes to our allies or is about to enter our fortifications. (D.49.15.5.1.)

The right of return restored the former rights of the returned prisoner of war as if he had never been captured. While the loss of rights occurred at the moment of separation from the area under Roman jurisdiction, the return to the Roman territory caused the restoration of those rights. Thus, only while a Roman citizen was under foreign jurisdiction was he treated as a slave under Roman law. As soon as he returned to an area under Roman jurisdiction, all the rights of a free Roman citizen were restored. At the same time, it was fictitiously assumed that he had never been in enemy territory and had never been a slave. This fiction was only useful if the Roman returned from captivity. If he died in captivity, however, his will was invalid because the *ius civile* required the *testamenti factio* both at the time of drawing up a will and at the time of death. The *lex Cornelia*, enacted under the dictatorship of Sulla (AD82–79), was intended to prevent this outcome:

> Iulianus, 42 digestorum: Lege Cornelia testamenta eorum, qui in hostium potestate decesserint, perinde confirmantur, ac si hi qui ea fecissent in hostium potestatem non pervenissent, et hereditas ex his eodem modo ad unumquemque pertinet [...] (D.28.1.12.)
>
> Julian, Digest, book 42: Following the *lex* Cornelia, the wills of those who died in captivity are confirmed as if the enemy had never captured them. And in the same way, their inheritance passes to those who are entitled [...] (D.28.1.12.)

The *lex Cornelia* treated the wills of Romans captured in war as valid if they died in captivity without regaining their status. To this end, the *lex Cornelia* applied a fiction whereby the moment of captivity was considered the moment of death. In this way, the rule under *ius civile* that the *testamenti factio* had to be given both at the time of making the will and at the time of death was preserved. The Roman who died in captivity could be considered as having the *testamenti factio*, since only the moment of captivity was relevant.

However, this fiction was not helpful if the captive had not drawn up a will and would, therefore, be inherited on intestacy. Since enslavement dissolved family ties (*status familiae*), the order of intestacy could not apply. The estate was therefore treated as vacant (*bona vacantia*) and passed to the treasury. The *lex Cornelia* also rectified this:

> *Iulianus, 62 ad digestorum: Bona eorum, qui in hostium potestatem pervenerint atque ibi decesserint, sive testamenti factionem habuerint sive non habuerint, ad eos pertinent, ad quos pertinerent, si in potestatem hostium non pervenissent: Idemque ius in eadem causa omnium rerum iubetur esse lege Cornelia, quae futura esset, si hi, de quorum hereditatibus et tutelis constituebatur, in hostium potestatem non pervenissent. (D.49.15.22pr.)*

> Iulian, Digest, book 62: The estate of those who have fallen into the hands of the enemy and have died there, whether they had the *testamenti factio* or not, belongs to those to whom it would have belonged, had they not been captured by the enemy. And it is required by the *lex* Cornelia that there should be the same law with regard to all matters which there would have been if the persons, for whose inheritances and guardianships arrangements had been made, had not fallen into the hands of the enemy. (D.49.15.22pr.)

Following the *lex* Cornelia, a Roman citizen who was taken captive should be succeeded by those who would have been his heirs, had he not been taken captive. It did not matter whether he had the *testamenti factio* at the time of his capture or whether he went into captivity as a *filius familias*. Even if he did not make a will, the *lex Cornelia* made it possible for the captive Roman to be succeeded by his relatives.

6.2.2 Institutio ex certa re

As we have seen (Ch. 6.1.3), the appointment of an heir required the use of certain words. An appointment which did not use the words prescribed by the *ius civile* was invalid and rendered the will ineffective. The most important content requirement of the appointment of the heir was the prohibition to appoint for a specific asset (*institutio ex certa re*). Based on the idea of universal succession (Ch. 4), the heir could only inherit in shares. It is only when the property is divided that the specific assets can be distributed to the co-heirs. In spite of this, we find many wills in the Digest which appoint an heir to a specific asset. This shows that the imperial jurists were lenient in dealing with this prohibition:

> *Ulpianus, 1 ad Sabinum: Si ex fundo fuisset aliquis solus institutus, valet institutio detracta fundi mentione. (D.28.5.1.4.)*

> Ulpian, Sabinus, book 1: If someone is appointed sole heir to a parcel of land, the appointment is valid, without any mention of the land. (D.28.5.1.4.)

According to a solution of Sabinus, the appointment to an asset was invalid, but was saved by not considering the asset, but the appointment itself as valid. Thus the heir appointed to the land became the sole heir. This solution also applied where two co-heirs were appointed to different assets:

> *Ulpianus, 5 ad Sabinum: Si duo sint heredes instituti, unus ex parte tertia fundi Corneliani, alter ex besse eiusdem fundi, Celsus expeditissimam Sabini sententiam sequitur, ut detracta fundi mentione quasi sine partibus heredes scripti hereditate potirentur, [...] (D.28.5.9.13.)*

> Ulpian, Sabinus, book 5: If two heirs are appointed, one to a third of the Cornelian estate, and the other to two-thirds, Celsus follows the almost unchallenged opinion of Sabinus, of leaving the mention of the land aside, that the heirs whose names appear in the will are entitled to the estate just as if their respective shares had not been indicated [...] (D.28.5.9.13.)

In this example, the testator has appointed the two co-heirs to different parts of the same asset. If we ignore the appointment of the asset, both are co-heirs. However, if we disregard the proportional appointment, the two co-heirs could inherit in equal shares. However, this does not take into account which parts the testator had in mind when choosing the assets. In the Empire, it was also possible to interpret the appointment to an asset as a directive for the division of the estate:

> *Papinianus, 6 responsorum: Qui [...], bonorum maternorum, quae in Pannonia possidebat, libertum heredem instituit, paternorum, quae habebat in Syria, Titium. Iure semisses ambos habere constitit, sed arbitrum dividendae hereditatis supremam voluntatem factis adiudicationibus [...] sequi [...]. (D.28.5.79pr.)*

> Papinian, Replies, book 6: Someone [...] appointed his freedman as heir to the property from his mother, which he possessed in Pannonia, and appointed Titius heir to his property from his father, which he held in Syria. The law establishes that each heir would be entitled to half of the estate, but the judge having the right to adjudicate property in the claim of the division of the inheritance will follow the testator's last wishes [...]. (D.28.5.79pr.)

In this case the testator has appointed a freed slave to the land from his mother in Pannonia. He then appointed Titius as heir to the land from his father in Syria. Papinian initially applied the solution of Sabinus (first century AD) by considering the two heirs appointed to a given asset as co-heirs (*heredes ex semisse*). At the same time, he stressed that in the procedure of the division, the intention of the testator had to be respected. This is why the judge should grant property of the individual assets in accordance with the testator's wishes.

6.2.3 The Revocation of a Will

The formalism of the mancipatory will made it necessary that any change relevant to the will required the drawing up of a new will:

> *Ulpianus, ad Sabinum 2: Si quid post factum testamentum mutari placuit, omnia ex integro facienda sunt. Quod vero quis obscurius in testamento vel nuncupat vel scribit, an post sollemnia explanare possit, quaeritur: Ut puta Stichum legaverat, cum plures haberet, nec declaravit de quo sentiret: Titio legavit, cum multos Titios amicos haberet [...] (D.28.1.21.1.)*

> Ulpian, Sabinus, book 2: If the testator wishes to change his will after it has been established, everything must be done over again from the beginning. The question, however, arises whether, after the legal formalities have been complied with, he can clarify anything in words or writing that might be rather obscure. For instance, if he had bequeathed Stichus when he had several slaves of that name and did not mention which one he meant; or if he bequeathed a legacy to Titius when several of his friends were called Titius [...] (D.28.1.21.1.)

Any adjustment of a will to changed circumstances required a new will to be made. This must be distinguished from a will that was imprecise or incomplete (Ch. 9.1). Here the existing will could be supplemented by the manifested will of the testator. The revocation of an earlier will by a later one is permanent; if the later one lapses, the earlier one cannot take effect again:

> *Inst.Gai.2.144.: Posteriore quoque testamento, quod iure factum est, superius rumpitur; nec interest, an extiterit aliquis ex eo heres an non extiterit: Hoc enim solum spectatur, an existere potuerit: Ideoque si quis ex posteriore testamento, quod iure factum est, aut noluerit heres esse aut vivo testatore aut post mortem eius, antequam hereditatem adiret, decesserit aut per cretionem exclusus fuerit [...] aut propter caelibatum ex lege Iulia summotus fuerit ab hereditate, quibus casibus pater familias intestatus moritur: Nam et prius testamentum non valet ruptum a posteriore, et posterius aeque nullas vires habet, cum ex eo nemo heres extiterit.*

> Inst.Gai.2.144.: A will is also invalidated by one duly made subsequently. And whether an heir takes under it or not does not make any difference.

It only matters that he can take. Therefore, if the heir appointed by the last will, which was legally drawn up, is unwilling to take under the said will or if he has died during the lifetime of the testator, or after the death of the latter, and before he has entered upon the estate; or if he is excluded for not having accepted the estate within the limitation period [...] or by the *lex Iulia* on account of being unmarried. In all these cases, the *pater familias* dies intestate; for the first will being revoked by the subsequent one is not valid, and the last will also fails since nobody becomes heir under it.

A later will revoked the previous one entirely. This was the case even if the wills were only partially contradictory, so that they could remain in force side by side. This rigidity stems from the link between the will and the ritual of *mancipatio*. Since the ritual is decisive, in cases where the latter will revokes the former, it does not matter whether the person named in the second will is really an heir. It was sufficient that he had *testamenti factio* at the time of the making of the will; he therefore had the capacity to inherit under the *ius civile*. If the second will was duly drawn up in accordance with these requirements, it permanently displaced the previous one. Thus, neither the renunciation of the inheritance by the heirs named in the second will, nor their death, nor the lack of capacity to keep what one had obtained (*incapacitas*) under the *lex Iulia et Papia* will revive the previous will. Instead, the order of intestacy applies.

Because of its formalism, the duly made mancipatory will cannot be revoked formlessly.

> Inst.Gai.2.151.: *Potest, ut iure facta testamenta nuda voluntate infirmentur. Apparet non posse ex eo solo infirmari testamentum, quod postea testator id noluerit valere, usque adeo, ut si linum eius inciderit, nihilo minus iure civili valeat. Quin etiam si deleverit quoque aut combusserit tabulas testamenti, non ideo minus desinent valere, quae ibi fuerunt scripta, licet eorum probatio difficilis sit.*

> Inst.Gai.2.151.: A will duly drawn up can be invalidated by the expression of a contrary intention, but clearly it cannot become inoperative alone because afterwards the testator was unwilling that it should stand, and even if he went so far as to cut the thread with which it was tied, it will, nonetheless remain valid under the *ius civile*. Even if he should erase or burn the document of the will, what he wrote will still be valid, albeit difficult to prove.

Under the *ius civile*, the mancipatory will remained valid if the testator opened the testamentary document, destroyed it, or broke its seal. As long as the content of the will, in particular the appointment of an heir, could be proved, the latter remained the heir, and the original will, duly made, remained in force.

Overview 23 summarises the main requirements for the validity of the will under the *ius civile*. They form the point of reference for the testamentary rules under the *ius praetorium*.

Overview 23: Requirements for a Valid Will under the *ius civile*

mancipatio:	testamenti factio:	appointment of heir:
sale of the estate to a *familiae emptor* in front of five witnesses *nuncupatio* of the testamentary document	*pater familias* *mater familias* (with her guardian's consent, and if she has *testamenti factio*, since Hadrian without *coëmptio*)	solemn command '*Titius heres esto*' to a part (12/12 of one as) substitution possible substitutions must precede other dispositions
will can be made orally (*nuncupatio*) or in writing (document) *mancipatio* is obligatory	loss of *testamenti factio* insanity captivity	prohibition of appointment to a single asset (*institutio ex certa re*).
rescinded only through a new mancipatory will	validity in case of captivity in war through *fictio legis Corneliae*	as an exception, *substitutio pupillaris*, will for a minor

In what follows, we will examine the ways in which the praetorian interventions modified the rules of the *ius civile* of testamentary law.

6.3 The Will under the *ius praetorium*

As we have seen (Ch. 3.2), the praetor in his edict, under the heading *de bonorum possessionibus*, adopted the distinction between the testamentary order and the order of intestacy that was so crucial for the *ius civile*. The claim of the testamentary heirs of the *bonorum possessio secundum tabulas* was based on the first subtitle of the edict on *bonorum possessio*. The existence of a will was therefore required:

> *Ulpianus, ad edictum 39: Exigit praetor, ut is, cuius bonorum possessio datur, utroque tempore ius testamenti faciendi habuerit, et cum facit testamentum et cum moritur. Proinde si impubes vel furiosus vel quis alius ex his qui testamentum facere non possunt testamentum fecerit, deinde habens testamenti factionem decesserit, peti bonorum possessio non poterit. Sed et si filius familias putans se patrem familias testamentum fecerit, deinde mortis tempore pater familias inveniatur, non potest bonorum possessio secundum tabulas peti. [...]* (D.37.11.1.8.)

Ulpian, Edict, book 39: The praetor requires that anyone, of whose estate the *bonorum possessio* is attributed [by the praetor], to have possessed the *testamenti factio*, not only when he has made the will, but also at the time of his death. But, if a minor, an insane or anyone without the *testamenti factio*, makes a will and afterwards becomes competent to do so and dies, the *bonorum possessio* of his estate cannot be claimed. But also if a *filius familias*, believing to be *pater familias*, has made a will, but is found to be *pater familias* at the time of his death, there can be no application for *bonorum possessio secundum tabulas*. [...] (D.37.11.1.8.)

Like the acceptance of an inheritance under the *ius civile*, the claim of *bonorum possessio secundum tabulas* required that the testator had the *testamenti factio* at the time of drawing his will. The *ius praetorium* also presumed that minors, lunatics and children under the paternal power could not leave a valid will. This applied even if the *testamenti factio* returned afterwards, i.e., during the will's vesting. For example, the minor came of age, or the *filius famlias* became the *pater familias*. However, the *bonorum possessio secundum tabulas*, unlike the position of heir under the *ius civile*, could be obtained if the will was duly made and the *testamenti factio* was only lost afterwards. Under the *ius praetorium*, it was sufficient that the *testamenti factio* existed at the time the will was made:

Inst.Gai.2.147.: *Non tamen per omnia inutilia sunt ea testamenta, quae vel ab initio non iure facta sunt vel iure facta postea inrita fact aut rupta sunt. Nam si septem testium signis signata sint testamenta, potest scriptus heres secundum tabulas bonorum possessionem petere, si modo defunctus testator et civis Romanus et suae potestatis mortis tempore fuerit. Nam si ideo inritum fiat testamentum, quod puta civitatem vel etiam libertatem testator amisit [...] non potest scriptus heres secundum tabulas bonorum possessionem petere.*

Inst.Gai.2.147: Nevertheless, those wills are not invalid in all respects which either were not lawfully made in the first place or were lawfully made but later became invalid or were overturned. For when they have been sealed with the seals of seven witnesses, the appointed heir can claim *bonorum possessio secundum tabulas* if the decedent was a Roman citizen and *sui iuris* at the time of his death. But if the will became inoperative, e.g., because the testator lost his citizenship or even his freedom [...], he cannot claim *bonorum possessio secundum tabulas*.

After the will had been duly sealed, the testator became insane. Since insanity only affected the capacity to act, but not his legal capacity in general, the appointed heir could claim the *bonorum possessio secundum tabulas*.

Although the appointed heir did not become the heir under the *ius civile*, the praetor considered the originally valid appointment sufficient for the granting of the *bonorum possessio secundum tabulas*. The grant required a duly sealed will and the legal capacity of the testator. If the testator suffered *capitis deminutio maxima* after having made his will, and thus lost his legal capacity, the will could not be valid even under the *ius praetorium*, because the latter closed the door to the testamentary succession of an incapable person.

The order of the *bonorum possessio secundum tabulas* claims follows the order of the testamentary appointments:

Ulpianus, 41 ad edictum: Defertur bonorum possessio secundum tabulas primo gradu scriptis heredibus, mox illis non petentibus sequentibus, non solum substitutis, verum substituti quoque substitutis, et per seriem substitutos admittimus. Primo gradu autem scriptos accipere debemus omnes, qui primo loco scripti sunt: Nam sicuti ad adeundam hereditatem proximi sunt, ita et ad bonorum possessionem admittendam. (D.37.11.2. 4.)

Ulpian, Edict, book 41: *Bonorum possessio secundum tabulas* is granted at the first stage to the appointed heirs, and afterwards, if they do not claim it, to the following [heirs], not only the substitute heirs, but also to the substitute heirs of the substitutes; and thus, we admit the substitute heirs according to their rank. We consider those appointed first as heirs of the first degree; as they have the prior right to accept the estate, they should also be the first entitled to *bonorum possessio*. (D.37.11.2.4.)

First, the principal heir is called upon to claim the *bonorum possessio secundum tabulas*. If he does not claim it, then the substitute heir of the first order is called upon; if he also does not claim it, then the substitute heir next in line is called upon. Thus, the substitution that the testator can arrange under the *ius civile* is also observed under the *ius praetorium*. Unlike the *ius civile*, the *ius praetorium* applies the rule of substitute heirs not only when the principal heir has died or renounced the estate, but also when the priority heir has not claimed *bonorum possessio*.

The differences between the requirements of the will under the *ius civile* and those under the *ius praetorium* are summarised in Overview 24. It shows that, in contrast to the *ius civile*, the praetor gave priority to the testamentary document and considered a will duly drawn up and sealed before seven witnesses to be sufficient for the grant of *bonorum possessio secundum tabulas*.

Overview 24: Grounds for Invalidating the Will under *ius civile* and *ius praetorium*

	Subsequent insanity of the testator:	Loss of status (*capitis deminutio maxima*):	Temporary loss of *testamenti factio*:
ius civile:	invalidation of the will	invalidation of the will	invalidation of the will
ius praetorium:	a duly made will entitles to *bonorum possessio secundum tabulas*	no claim of *bonorum possessio secundum tabulas*	if the *testamenti factio* was regained until the time of death: claim for *bonorum possessio secundum tabulas*

The praetorian concept of the will gradually separated from the tenets of *ius civile*. The main stages of this development are discussed below.

6.3.1 The Importance of the Testamentary Document

Wills under the *ius civile* (Ch. 6.1.1) were inscribed on tables (*tabulae*), i.e. wooden tablets covered on one side with wax (Ch. 1.1). The text was inscribed in the wax. When the text was finished, the two tables were placed with the writing surfaces facing each other. They were then tied together with a thread placed in a furrow (*sulcus*) on the back of the second tablet. At this point, the document was sealed by the witnesses. In order to read the text, the seals had to be broken or the thread cut. The testator declared this will valid during the *mancipatio* by *nuncupatio*. The witnesses of the *mancipatio*, five Roman citizens, the buyer of the estate and the balance-holder confirmed that the testament had been drawn up in the course of a mancipatory ritual. A document sealed in this way could be presented by the heir to claim *bonorum possessio secundum tabulas*:

> Inst.Gai.2.119.: *Praetor tamen, si septem signis testium signatum sit testamentum, scriptis heredibus secundum tabulas testamenti bonorum possessionem pollicetur, si nemo sit, ad quem ab intestato iure legitimo pertineat hereditas, velut frater eodem patre natus aut patruus aut fratris filius, ita poterunt scripti heredes retinere hereditatem: Nam idem iuris est et si alia ex causa testamentum non valeat, velut quod familia non venierit aut nuncupationis verba testator locutus non sit.*

> Inst.Gai.2.119.: The praetor, however, if the will is attested by the seals of seven witnesses, promises the heirs mentioned in the will to place them in possession of the estate, if there is no one to whom the inheritance will belong as statutory heir under the rule of intestacy, as, for example, a brother

by the same father, or a paternal uncle, or the son of a brother. In this way, the heirs mentioned in the will can retain the estate, for the same rule of law applies when a will is not valid for some other reason, for instance, because the estate was not sold [by *mancipatio*], or the testator did not pronounce the words required for the public declaration (*nuncupatio*).

To grant *bonorum possessio secundum tabulas*, the praetor required a will sealed by seven witnesses. But unlike the *ius civile*, the *ius praetorium* did not require the *mancipatio* ritual. A will sealed by seven witnesses and the testator's *testamenti factio* were sufficient for a valid appointment. The testamentary document thus formed the basis of the *bonorum possessio secundum tabulas*, which was in principle suitable as proof of the making of a will by *mancipatio*. The praetor, however, did not examine whether the document was made by *mancipatio*, but merely required proof that the will had been sealed by seven witnesses.

Gaius (second century AD) now deals with the case where the recorded will is shown to have been made without *mancipatio*, so that the form of the *ius praetorium* is satisfied, but not the ritual required by the *ius civile*. Hence, the order of intestacy applies. But as long as the heirs on intestacy do not claim, the *ius praetorium* respects the prima facie duly made will, and the praetor grants the *bonorum possessio secundum tabulas* to the heir appointed in the testament sealed by seven witnesses. Although the *bonorum possessio secundum tabulas* is visibly linked to the requirements of the *ius civile*, these are partly superseded by the fact that the *mancipatio* only had to be recorded, but did not need to have actually taken place. The fact that the praetor treated a will that is invalid under the ius *civile* as valid under the *ius praetorium* had only subsidiary consequences at first, i.e. if the heirs on intestacy did not claim *bonorum possessio ab intestato*. However, a rescript of Emperor Antoninus Pius (AD138–161) gave the praetorian testamentary heir priority over the heir on intestacy under the *ius civile*:

> Inst.Gai.2.120.: *Sed videamus, an etiam si frater aut patruus extent, potiores scriptis heredibus habeantur; rescripto enim imperatoris Antonini significatur eos, qui secundum tabulas testamenti non iure factas bonorum possessionem petierint, posse adversus eos, qui ab intestato vindicant hereditatem, defendere se per exceptionem doli mali.*

> Inst.Gai.2.120.: But let us consider whether even if there is a brother or a paternal uncle, they are considered more entitled than the heirs appointed in the will. For it is stated in a rescript of Emperor Antoninus that parties who have obtained *bonorum possessio secundum tabulas* because of a will that was not properly drawn up, can, through an exception based on fraud (*dolus malus*), defend themselves against parties that claim the estate on intestacy.

The rescript granted the testamentary heir, who could rely on a sealed will with seven witnesses, the objection of fraud (*exceptio doli*) in case the *agnati*, as statutory heirs (Ch. 3.2.2), raised the claim for the delivery of the inheritance (*hereditatis petitio*) against the *bonorum possessor* (Ch. 5.3). The objection of fraud is a remedy to protect the defendant against fraudulent behaviour (*dolus*) of the claimant. It blocks the claim if the praetor or the presiding judge decides that the plaintiff has acted fraudulently. The accusation of fraud is established here because the praetor would grant the *hereditatis petitio* to a testamentary heir, appointed in a sealed will before seven witnesses, against the heirs on intestacy. Therefore, the heirs under the *ius civile* – even if they obtained the estate – would have to restore it immediately under *ius praetorium*. As their entitlement to claim the inheritance is a purely formal position, their endeavour to enforce it must be considered as *dolus*. According to the terminology already applied to conflicts of actions between *ius civile* heirs and *ius praetorium* heirs on intestacy (Ch. 3.3.2), the praetorian heir was hence entitled to the *bonorum possessio cum re*. In other words, he succeeded against the *ius civile* heir.

It is, however, uncertain whether this priority of the *ius praetorium* over the *ius civile* also extends to other formal defects of the will:

> Inst.Gai.2.121.: *Quod sane quidem ad masculorum testamenta pertinere certum est; item ad feminarum, quae ideo non utiliter testatae sunt, quod verbi gratia familiam non vendiderint aut nuncupationis verba locutae non sint: [...]*

> Inst.Gai.2.121.: This certainly concerns, in any case, the wills of male persons; likewise those of women who have ineffectively made a will because, for example, they have not sold the property or have not spoken the words of *nuncupatio* [...]

The *ius praetorium* displaces the *ius civile* in instances where the ritual of *mancipatio* was not performed, although the *mancipatio* had been attested. In contrast, Gaius left open the question of whether the imperial reinforcement of the seven-witness will also applied to wills of women that were made without their tutor's consent:

> Inst.Gai.2.121–122: (121) *[...] An autem et ad ea testamenta feminarum, quae sine tutoris auctoritate fecerint, haec constitutio pertineat, videbimus.*
> (122) *Loquimur autem de his scilicet feminis, quae non in legitiam parentium aut patronorum tutela sunt, sed [de his quae] alterius generis tutores habent, qui etiam invite coguntur auctores fieri. Alioquin parentem et patronum sine auctoritate eius facto testament non summoveri palam est.*

> Inst.Gai.2.121–122.: (121) [...] but it remains to be seen if this constitution also applies to the wills of women established without their guardians' authority.
>
> (122) We are speaking, however, of those women who are not under the legal guardianship of their parents or patrons, but of those who have guardians of another kind and who are compelled, even if unwilling, to grant their consent. That otherwise a parent or a patron is not removed by a will made without his authority is evident.

The fact that a will made by a woman without her guardian's consent but which adhered to the requirement of seven witnesses could form the basis of a *bonorum possessio secundum tabulas*, supports the view that the consent of the guardian could be seen as a mere ritual like the *mancipatio*, which was disposable under *ius praetorium*. However, the guardian's consent could also be seen as an essential requirement for the woman's legal capacity to make a will. Gaius leaves the question open and the texts transmitted in the Digest do not provide an answer either. Since guardianship over women had already lost its importance during the Roman Republic (Ch. 6.1.2), it is conceivable that the consent of the guardian was only considered a requirement for a valid will under *ius civile*, but a mere formality under the *ius praetorium* of the Empire. However, this question cannot be settled with certainty.

With regard to the relationship between the praetorian will and the *ius civile* will, we must remember that the *bonorum possessio secundum tabulas* was originally a means of ensuring compliance with the *ius civile* by granting the estate to the heir under the *ius civile*. Conflict with the *ius civile* only arose when the praetor decided the entitlement according to standards that deviated from this layer of law. Thus, the praetor granted the *bonorum possessio secundum tabulas* even if the testator subsequently lost his legal capacity to make a will, or if there was no *mancipatio* at all. The importance of the testamentary document, which took on a life of its own as opposed to the ritual of *manicpatio*, explains the praetor's diverging approach.

The fundamentality of the document also sets the rules applicable to the revocation of the will under *ius praetorium*.

6.3.2 The Revocation under the ius praetorium

Whereas under the *ius civile* an existing will could only be revoked by carrying out a new *mancipatio* (Ch. 6.2.3), revocation under *ius praetorium* required the destruction of the document:

> Inst.Gai.2.151a: *Quid ergo est? Si quis ab intestato bonorum possessionem petierit et is, qui ex eo testamento heres est, petat hereditatem, potest eum per exceptionem doli mali summovere, si modo ea mens testatoris fuisse probetur,*

ut ad eos, qui ab intestato vocantur, perveniat hereditas: Et hoc ita rescripto imperatoris Antonini significatur.

Inst.Gai.2.151a.: So what applies? If anyone has demanded *bonorum possessio* on intestacy, and the person who is heir by virtue of that will has filed a claim for the estate, he [the heir on intestacy] can exclude him [the claimant] by an objection on the ground of fraud, provided it is proved that the intention of the testator was that the estate should go to those who could be called to the inheritance in case there was no will; and this is made clear by a rescript of the Emperor Antoninus Pius.

If the testator had destroyed the testamentary document, the praetor granted the heirs on intestacy the *bonorum possessio ab intestato*. Thus, the magistrate accepts that the destruction of the written will sufficiently manifested the testator's intention. However, this raises the question of whether the praetorian heir on intestacy would prevail against the testamentary heir, i.e. whether he could obtain the *bonorum possessio cum re* (Ch. 3.3.1). This question was not conclusively settled until the Empire, but was decided on a case-by-case basis. Following a rescript of Emperor Antoninus Pius (AD138–161), the *bonorum possessor* generally held the objection of fraud against the testamentary heir (*exceptio doli*). In this way, the *bonorum possessor ab intestato* generally had priority over the testamentary heir under the *ius civile*. The allegation of *dolus* is based on the fact that the heir appointed in the will relies on a purely formal legal position. Since he disregards the testator's manifested will, he is considered 'unworthy' (*indignus*, Ch. 4.4.3), so that the estate belongs to the *bonorum possessor* and not to him.

If the document itself is not destroyed, but only the thread that held the tables together, a distinction must be made:

Ulpianus, 39 ad edictum: Si linum, quo ligatae sunt tabulae, incisum sit, si quidem alius contra voluntatem testatoris inciderit, bonorum possessio peti potest: Quod si ipse testator id fecerit, non videntur signatae et ideo bonorum possessio peti non potest. (D.37.11.1.10)

Ulpian, Edict, book 39: If the thread that joins the tablets of the will is cut, even though this was done by a third party, against the testator's wish, *bonorum possessio [secundum tabulas]* can be demanded. If, however, the testator himself cut it, the will is not considered to have been sealed [anymore], and, therefore, *bonorum possessio [secundum tabulas]* cannot be claimed. (D.37.11.1.10)

The destruction of the material document can only be considered as a revocation of the will if the testator himself has cut the thread that binds the two tables together. If, however, this intervention is the act of a third party, the testator's will remains intact and can be upheld by granting the *bonorum possessio secundum tabulas* to the appointed heir.

Under the *ius praetorium*, the documentary testament gained in importance, which increased the interest in protecting this type of document against forgery. Thus, several laws contained provisions aimed at protecting legal documents in general and wills in particular. I will briefly outline these rules in so far as they are relevant to the *bonorum possessio secundum tabulas*.

6.3.3 Legal Protection against Forgery

The *senatusconsultum Neronianum* (AD61) combated the forgery of legal documents. To this end, it laid down rules for the establishment of documents to ensure the preservation of the original wax tables, commonly used for transactions and wills (Ch. 6.3.1). In particular, the tables were no longer to be tied with a thread, but pierced so that the thread could be passed through the hole and sealed. This was to prevent the threads from coming loose and the internal text of the tablets from being altered afterwards, as was possible with the original form of the tablets with wrapped threads. This requirement was of particular importance to the *ius praetorium*, since only a document drawn up in accordance with the requirements of the *senatusconsultum Neronianum* was recognised as a valid testamentary document.

A statute enacted under Emperor Augustus (27BC–AD14) to reform inheritance tax (*lex Iulia de vicesima hereditatum*, AD6) went even further by forcing the praetor to prove the identity of the witnesses to the sealing:

> *Ulpianus, ad edictum 50: Cum ab initio aperiendae sint tabulae, praetoris id officium est, ut cogat signatores convenire et sigilla sua recognoscere. (D.29.3.4.)*

> Ulpian, Edict, book 50: When the will is about to be opened for the first time, the praetor must require the witnesses to appear and acknowledge their seals. (D.29.3.4.)

When a will was opened, the witnesses had to be summoned before the praetor to verify the authenticity of the seals attached. Since the granting of *bonorum possessio secundum tabulas* required a duly sealed document in the presence of seven witnesses, this requirement directly affected the *ius praetorium*. *Bonorum possessio* could only be granted if the appointment was made in a verifiable, duly sealed document.

The praetor's obligation to verify the identity of the witnesses to a will is linked to the increased public control of the opening of wills during the Empire. The purpose of this control was not only to ensure the effective collection of the inheritance tax of 5 per cent levied by Augustus, but also to facilitate the monitoring of compliance with the rules on *caducum* of the *lex*

Iulia et Papia (Ch. 4.4.1). When the reading of the will was carried out by a public official, heirs without the capacity to obtain or who were unworthy of inheriting could quickly be identified and the claims of the *fiscus* could be asserted immediately.

The legislation of the Republic already recognised criminal measures to protect the authenticity of wills. The most important law that lasted into the Empire was the *lex Cornelia de falsis* or *lex Cornelia testamentaria nummaria* (81BC), enacted under the dictatorship of Sulla. This law provided for the establishment of a permanent criminal court (*quaestio perpetua*) to prosecute the removal of testamentary seals, the production of forged seals or the sealing of forged wills. The *lex Cornelia* survives only in fragments, but its primary aim seems to have been to protect the sealing of wills, so crucial to the *bonorum possessio secundum tabulas*:

> *Paulus, 5 sententiarum: Qui vivi testamentum aperuerit recitaverit resignaverit, poena Corneliae tenatur: [...] (D.48.19.38.7.)*
>
> Paul, Sentences, book 5: Anyone who opens the will of someone still living, reads it out and reseals it, is punished under the *lex Cornelia*: [...] (D.48.19.38.7.)

Someone has broken the seal of the duly sealed will. While the destruction of the testamentary will by a third party did not prevent the claim of *bonorum possessio secundum tabulas* (Ch. 6.3.2), the breaking of the seal invalidated the will, since the praetor would only accept a document sealed by seven witnesses as a valid will. If the seal has been broken, the testamentary document must be duly sealed again before seven witnesses:

> *Ulpianus, disputationum 4: Si testamentum quod resignaverit testator iterum signatum fuerit septem testium signis, non erit imperfectum, sed utroque iure valebit tam civili quam praetorio. (D.28.1.23.)*
>
> Ulpian, Disputations, book 4: If the testator has broken the seals of a will, and it has been sealed a second time by him and seven witnesses, it will not be void, but will be valid both under the *ius civile* and *ius praetorium*. (D.28.1.23.)

In this case, the testator removed the seal from his will in order to have it sealed again. While a will opened in this way remains valid under the *ius civile*, the breaking of the seal is considered a revocation under *ius praetorium*. This revocation can be reversed if the testator 'restores' the damaged seal by resealing it.

In the Empire, the *lex Cornelia* was supplemented by the *senatusconsultum Libonianum* (AD16), issued under Emperor Tiberius (AD14–37) and an edict of Emperor Claudius (AD41–54):

> *C.9.23.3. Imperator Alexander Severus (a.223): Senatusconsulto et edicto divi Claudii prohibitum est eos, qui ad scribenda testamenta adhibentur, quamvis dictante testatore aliquid emolumentum ipsis futurum scribere, et poena legis Corneliae facienti inrogata est. [...]*

> C.9.23.3. Emperor Alexander Severus: It was forbidden by a *senatusconsultum* and by the edict of the deified Claudius that those who write the wills of others, even though at the dictation of the testators, should include in them any advantage to themselves, and the punishment of the *lex Cornelia* is imposed upon anyone who does so. [...]

The *senatusconsultum* and the edict forbade the scribe of the will to include himself as an heir or legatee, even if the testator had dictated it. If the scribe broke this rule, he was punished under the *lex Cornelia*, i.e. he would be exiled (as a Roman citizen) or executed (as a slave).

The criminal prosecution of the scribe did not, however, affect the validity of the will. Only the jurists of the Empire drew consequences for private law from this criminal prohibition:

> *Iulianus, 78 digestorum: Si quis hereditatem [...] sibi adscripserit, quaeritur, an hereditas [...] pro non scripto habeatur. Et quid, si substitutum habeat huiusmodi institutio? Respondit: Pars hereditatis, de qua me consuluisti, ad substitutum pertinent: Nam senatus cum poenas legis Corneliae constitueret adversus eum, qui sibi hereditatem [...] scripsisset, eodem modo improbasse videtur, [...], ut perinde haberentur, ac si insertae testamento non fuissent. (D.34.8.1.)*

> Julian, Digest, book 78: If someone [a scribe] has appointed himself [...] in a [someone else's] will, we may ask if the appointment [...] must be considered as not written. And also, whether an heir can have a substitute under an appointment made in this way? The answer was that the portion of the estate concerning which you have asked advice belongs to the substitute, for when the Senate fixed the penalties of the *lex Cornelia* against a person who appointed himself heir [...] it seems to have disapproved of such appointments, in the same way [...] so that provisions of this kind are considered as if they had not been inserted in the will. (D.34.8.1.)

Here, the scribe to whom the testator had dictated his will seized the opportunity to appoint himself as heir. After the *senatusconsultum Libonianum*, the scribe could be punished under the *lex Cornelia de falsis* for forging a will. Punishment under the *senatusconsultum Libonianum* also affected the position of the heir. According to Julian, the sentence giving rise to the criminal penalty was to be regarded as 'not written' (*pro non scripto habetur*), so that the substitute heir replaced the scribe. Since both the will under *ius civile* and under *ius praetorium* required a genuine testamentary document, the application of the *lex Cornelia* led to partial invalidity under both layers of law. In contrast to the imperial rules on the opening and sealing of wills, criminal protection is indispensable not only for the praetorian will but also for the will under *ius civile*.

While the testamentary forms of *ius civile* and *ius praetorium* are closely intertwined, we find that the imperial law overturned the traditional tenets by granting the hitherto unimaginable possibility of making a will without any formal requirements.

6.4 The Formless Will of the Imperial Law

The creation of a special procedure of imperial jurisdiction (*cognitio extra ordinem*, Ch. 2.2.4) was the prerequisite for this groundbreaking change to the Roman will by imperial law. Within the framework of this special jurisdiction, Emperor Augustus (27BC–AD14) was the first to recognise as enforceable formless additions to wills (codicils) and formless bequests (*fideicommissa*). From the time of Trajan (AD98–117), privileges for soldiers were also gradually introduced, known as the 'soldier's will' (*testamentum militis*), which was equally enforceable only by *cognitio extra ordinem*. The three creations of the *ius novum* are marked by a total disregard for the precepts of *ius civile* and *ius praetorium*: The codicils (from *codicilli*, literally 'little letters', formless additions to a will), which were considered as legally binding since Augustus, were additions made by the testator outside the formal will, because the testator had no opportunity to amend his will, or to draw it up again by *mancipatio* or by deed. Moreover, the *fideicommissa* (*fideicommissum*, from *fidei committere*, literally 'to put in trust'), which became enforceable under Augustus, referred to requests that the testator had made to his heir independently of a will. Finally, the term 'a soldier's will' refers to the formless will of a soldier, which could be executed without *mancipatio* or the drawing up of a document.

In the following, only the codicil and the soldier's testament will be considered as special features of the *ius novum* on the law of wills; the *fideicommissa* will be discussed in more detail in the law of legacies due to their similarities with the latter (Ch. 8.5). As far as wills are concerned, it is sufficient to point out that *fideicommissa* were formless and could be imposed on any beneficiary of a will. The testator could therefore impose a *fideicommissum* on anyone who was to receive anything from the estate.

The Institutes of the Emperor Justinian (AD527–565) inform us about the enforceability of codicils introduced by Emperor Augustus:

> Inst.2.25pr.: *Ante Augusti tempora constat ius codicillorum non fuisse, sed primus Lucius Lentulus, ex cuius persona etiam fideicommissa coeperunt,*

codicillos introduxit. Nam cum decederet in Africa scripsit codicillos testamento confirmatos, quibus ab Augusto petiit per fideicommissum ut faceret aliquid: Et cum divus Augustus voluntatem eius implesset, deinceps reliqui auctoritatem eius secuti, fideicommissa praestabant, [...]. Dicitur Augustus convocasse prudentes, inter quos Trebatium quoque, cuius tunc auctoritas maxima erat, et quaesisse, an possit hoc recipi nec absonans a iuris ratione codicillorum usus esset: Et Trebatium suasisse Augusto, quod diceret, utilissimum et necessarium hoc civibus esse propter magnas et longas peregrinationes, quae apud veteres fuissent, ubi, si quis testamentum facere non posset, tamen codicillos posset. [...]

> Inst.2.25pr.: It is certain that the legal institutions of codicils did not exist before the time of Augustus, but that Lucius Lentulus, who was also the originator of trusts, was the first to introduce codicils. For, when he was on the point of death in Africa, he wrote 'little letter' (codicils), confirmed by his will, by which he begged Augustus to do something for him as a *fideicommissum*. Once the deified emperor Augustus had fulfilled his wishes, others followed the precedent and fulfilled *fideicommissa* in the same manner [...]. Augustus is said to have summoned jurists, among them Trebatius, who at that time enjoyed the highest reputation, and asked them whether the new usage could be adopted and whether the use of codicils did not run counter to the received principles of law. And Trebatius is said to have recommended their admission, remarking how highly convenient and even necessary they were to the citizens, on account of the great and prolonged journeys in those early days, upon which a man might often be able to make codicils when he could not make a will [...]

The reason for allowing formless amendment of the will by codicil was due to a particular case: Lucius Lentulus, shortly before his death in Africa, had written additions to his will in codicils and called upon Augustus, who was mentioned in the will, to fulfil the *fideicommissum*. Since Augustus respected the decedent's wishes, these additions were subsequently treated as binding and generally adhered to. Since codicils could be left formless, Augustus asked the jurists of the imperial *consilium* whether the recognition of these formless additions was contrary to legal principles (*nec absonans a iuris ratione codicillorum usus esset*). The jurist Trebatius Testa answered in the negative and argued that these formless additions to the will should be allowed in order to mitigate the adverse circumstances faced by testators who died outside Rome. Whereas the case of Lentulus concerned a codicil that had been mentioned in the will beforehand and could therefore have been interpreted as a part of the will (Ch. 6.2.3), under the *ius novum* all formless additions were valid, even if they had not been announced or authorised by the testator in the formal will.

6.4.1 Formless Additions (Codicils)

The interplay between the requirements developed under the *ius civile* and *ius praetorium* and the imperial codicils led to a mixed collection of formal wills and formless codicils to the will:

> *Paulus, liber singularis de iure codicillorum: Conficiuntur codicilli quattuor modis: Aut enim in futurum confirmantur aut in praeteritum aut per fideicommissum testamento facto aut sine testamento. (D.29.7.8pr.)*
>
> Paul, Codicils, sole book: Codicils are drawn up in four ways: They can be confirmed [in the will] in advance; or they can been confirmed [in the will] afterwards; or they are made as a *fideicommissum*, either after a will has been made or without a will. (D.29.7.8pr.)

Paul (third century AD) distinguishes between different types of codicils. Some retain their validity as part of the will; others can only be valid as *fideicommissa*: In the first case, the requirements of the testamentary appointment according to *ius civile* and/or *ius praetorium* apply. Moreover, the addition contained in the codicil must be either announced or subsequently confirmed in the formal will. In contrast, the codicil, which is valid as a *fideicommissum*, can either create an obligation on the part of the heir or other beneficiaries of the will, or it can operate entirely on its own, i.e. without a will (against the heir on intestacy). Overview 25 summarises these four categories of codicils.

Overview 25: The Four Categories of Codicils

validity under the *ius civile/ius praetorium*	validity under the *ius novum* (*fideicommissum*)
codicillary clause in the will: 'all that I add later in the form of a codicil, shall be part of this will'.	without a will: the *fideicommissum* contained in the codicil is imposed on the heirs on intestacy.
confirmation by a later will: 'all I have written in the codicil shall apply by this will'.	with a will: the *fideicommissum* contained in the codicil is imposed on the heirs (or legatees) appointed in the will.

The coexistence of the traditional codicil under *ius civile* and *ius praetorium* and the codicil as a formless *fideicommissum* of the imperial law led to a somewhat contradictory regulation, depending on the layers of law concerned. For this reason, certain rules of the traditional law of wills were transposed into the *ius novum*:

> *Iulianus, 39 digestorum: Testamento facto etiamsi codicilli in eo confirmati non essent, vires tamen ex eo capient. Denique si ex testamento hereditas adita*

non fuisset, fideicommissum ex huiusmodi codicillis nullius momenti erit. (D.29.7.3.2.)

Julian, Edict, book 39: If a will has been made, even if a codicil is not confirmed by it, the codicil will, nevertheless, obtain all its force and effect from the will. Ultimately, if the inheritance is not accepted by the heir under the will, a *fideicommissum* created by a codicil of this kind will be invalid. (D.29.7.3.2.)

If there is a will, either under the *ius praetorium* or *ius civile*, a codicil with the effect of a *fideicommissum* is only valid if the will is valid. If the testamentary heir does not accept the inheritance, the codicil that functions as *fideicommissum* also loses its effect. This dependence of a codicil on a will only applies, however, if a will has been made. If the testator did not leave a will, but only a codicil, the latter can be effective within the scope of the *ius novum*:

Iulianus, 39 digestorum: Si quis cum testamentum nullum habebat, codicillis fideicommissa hoc modo dedit: 'Quisquis mihi heres erit bonorumve possessor, eius fidei committo,' fideicommissa praestari debent, quia pater familias, qui testamenti factionem habet et codicillos faceret, perinde haberi debet, ac si omnes heredes eius essent, ad quos legitima eius hereditas vel bonorum possessio perventura esset. (D.29.7.3pr.)

Julian, Edict, book 39: If someone, without leaving a will, has ordered *fideicommissa* in a codicil, as follows: 'Whoever shall be my heir or the *bonorum possessor* of my estate, I leave to him as trustee,' the sums left under the *fideicommissa* must be paid because the *pater familias* who had the *testamenti factio* and made a codicil, is in the same position as if all those were his heirs who would receive the estate either as statutory heirs or as *bonorum possessores*. (D.29.7.3pr.)

In the case discussed by Julian, the testator did not leave a will and was therefore succeeded on intestacy. However, the *fideicommissum* left in the codicil must be observed because the codicil expresses the decedent's wish to leave heirs on intestacy. If the decedent has *testamenti factio*, the codicil will be considered to contain an appointment (of the heirs on intestacy) and a *fideicommissum* in favour of the beneficiary mentioned in the codicil. In this manner, even though the boundaries between the will with formal requirements and the formless will were nearly abolished by the *ius novum*, the jurists nevertheless maintained a distinction between the will and the codicil:

Papinianus, 15 quaestionum: Quod per manus traditum est codicillis hereditatem dari non posse rationem illam habet, ne per codicillos, qui ex testamento valerent, ipsum testamentum, quod vires per institutionem heredum accipit, confirmari videretur. (D.29.7.10.)

Papinian, Questions, book 15: What has been handed down, namely that an inheritance cannot be assigned by a codicil, is based on the consideration that codicil taking effect by virtue of the will, cannot confirm the will by itself because it receives its effectiveness by the appointment of the heirs. (D.29.7.10.)

Papinian recalls the traditional rule, according to which the codicil could not contain the appointment of an heir. For it would be contradictory for the codicil, an addition to the will, to contain the central point of the testamentary disposition, namely the appointment of the heir (*institutio heredis*), and thus to form the basis of the will. This rule should apply even if any statement made by the testator could be interpreted as a *fideicommissum*:

Papinianus, 19 quaestionum: Tractari solet de eo, qui, cum tabulas testamenti non fecisset, codicillis ita scripsit: 'Titium heredem esse volo.' Sed multum interest, utrum fideicommissariam hereditatem a legitimo per hanc scripturam, quam codicillorum instar habere voluit, reliquerit an vero testamentum facere se existimaverit: Nam hoc casu nihil a legitimo peti poterit. [...] (D.29.7.13.1.)

Papinian, Questions, book 19: It often happens that the case is discussed of one who, having drawn up no testament, wrote the following in a codicil: 'I wish Titius to be my heir.' But there is a great difference whether by this written order, which he intended as a codicil, he left a universal inheritance *fideicommissum* at the expense of the statutory heir, or whether he thought he was making a will. In this case [that he believed he was drawing up a testament], nothing can be claimed from the statutory heir. [...] (D.29.7.13.1.)

According to Papinian, a codicil can only be interpreted as a *fideicommissum* if a *fideicommissum* was actually intended, i.e. the testator himself did not assume that a (formless) will would be made. If, however, the testator had intended to make a formal will, statutory succession was excluded because, in this case, it could not be assumed that the testator had appointed his statutory heir and imposed a codicil on him. Hence, the jurist set a limit to the possibility of reinterpreting formless wills as codicils. Following Papinian, the testator had to decide from the outset, whether he wished to make a will and supplement it with a codicil, or to make a codicil without a will, which would be effective only on intestacy. However, cautelary practice developed a clause to avoid this obstacle and to protect the codicil as a *fideicommissum*, even if it had originally been intended as an addition to the will:

Ulpianus, 4 disputationum: Saepissime rescriptum et constitutum est eum, qui testamentum facere opinatus est nec voluit quasi codicillos id valere, videri nec codicillos fecisse: Ideoque quod in illo testamento scriptum est, licet quasi in codicillis poterit valere, tamen non debetur. (D.29.7.1.)

Ulpian, Disputations, book 4: It has very frequently been stated in rescripts and imperial constitutions that if a testator was under the impression that he had made a will and did not intend it to be valid as a codicil, he is held not to have made a codicil. And therefore, what is written in that will is not owed, although it may have been effective in a codicil. (D.29.7.1.)

The will contained a clause stating that in the event of its invalidity, it should at least remain in force as a codicil, i.e. as a *fideicommissum* imposed on the heirs on intestacy. By means of this clause, the testator could benefit from the different modes of interpretation of a codicil. If the will is valid, the codicil constitutes an addition, but if the will is invalid, the codicil is treated as a *fideicommissum* imposed on the heirs on intestacy. However, such an intention is not presumed; if the will does not contain such a 'salvatory clause', the codicil shares the lot of the invalid will.

Overview 26: Possibilities of Reinterpreting a Will as a Codicil

testator's general decision	
'I make a will'	'I will not make a will'
codicil as an addition to a will	codicil on intestacy
if the will is invalid (under the *ius civile/ius praetorium*), so is the codicil.	codicil is valid as a *fideicommissum*, regardless of the testamentary rules, it binds the heirs on intestacy.
combination of both solutions through a codicillary clause: 'I wish that my will functions as a codicil if the will should prove invalid.'	

The insistence of the jurists on the need for an explicit codicillary clause must be seen as an attempt to limit the effects of codicils on formal wills, since the formless dispositions contradicted all the principles established under the *ius civile* and the *ius praetorium*. The example of the cautelary abolition of this distinction shows that this attempt was largely unsuccessful in the long run. Nonetheless, the formal requirements of the two previous layers of law were never completely abandoned. Formalism is only truly abolished by the imperial rules governing the wills of a specific category of persons, namely soldiers and their equals; hence, the soldier's will (*testamentum militis*).

6.4.2 The Soldier's Will

The rules governing a soldier's will, unlike those governing the will of a civilian (*testamentum paganorum*),[6] were developed and established by imperial instructions (*mandata*):

> *Ulpianus, 45 ad edictum: Militibus liberam testamenti factionem primus quidem divus Iulius Caesar concessit: Sed ea concessio temporalis erat. Postea vero primus divus Titus dedit: Post hoc Domitianus: Postea divus Nerva plenissimam indulgentiam in milites contulit: Eamque et Traianus secutus est et exinde mandatis inseri coepit caput tale. Caput ex mandatis: 'Cum in notitiam meam prolatum sit subinde testamenta a commilitonibus relicta proferri, quae possint in controversiam deduci, si ad diligentiam legum revocentur et observantiam: Secutus animi mei integritudinem erga optimos fidelissimosque commilitones simplicitati eorum consulendum existimavi, ut quoquomodo testati fuissent, rata esset eorum voluntas. Faciant igitur testamenta quo modo volent, faciant quo modo poterint sufficiatque ad bonorum suorum divisionem faciendam nuda voluntas testatoris'. (D.29.1.1pr.)*

Ulpian, Edict, book 45: The deified Julius Caesar was the first to grant soldiers complete testamentary freedom, but this concession was only temporary. The first after him to confer this power was the deified Titus and then Domitianus. The deified Nerva subsequently was most accommodating to soldiers in this respect. And Trajan followed his example. From that time onwards a respective chapter was inserted into the collection of imperial instructions (*mandata*). A chapter of the imperial instructions reads: 'Since I have been informed that wills left by fellow soldiers have been frequently brought forth that would be the subject of dispute if they were judged with regard to diligence and compliance with the law, I have followed the impartiality of my disposition and have formed the opinion for these excellent and most loyal fellow soldiers that their inexperience must be taken into consideration, so that their last wills – in whatever way they have been drawn up – will be effective. Therefore, let them draw up their wills in whatever form they desire; they shall do so as they are able, and for the division of his property the simple will of the testator shall suffice'. (D.29.1.1pr.)

Soldiers were already privileged regarding the making of a testament under Emperor Julius Caesar (100–44BC); i.e. towards the end of the Republic. Similar privileges were granted by Emperors Titus (AD79–81), Domitian (AD81–96) and especially Nerva (AD96–98). From the time of Emperor

---

[6] Not to be confused with *pagani* as non-Christians.

Trajan (AD98–117), a separate chapter was allocated in the imperial instructions (*mandata*) for the commanding officers. The imperial instruction allowed soldiers to make their wills in any form. As a reason for dispensing with any formal requirements of Roman law, the emperors cite the soldiers' ignorance and lack of experience for properly drawing up wills. Therefore, soldiers should be allowed to make their wills without any formalities and should not be forced to follow the strict testamentary rules of the *ius civile* and *ius praetorium*. Instead, they should be able to dispose of their estates formlessly. The emperors' fundamental decision in favour of soldiers required specification and delimitation. Both can be found in the writings of the imperial jurists who worked out the peculiarities of formless wills.

Due to the formlessness of the soldier's wills, the question may arise as to whether an oral will was also sufficient:

> *Paulus, 11 responsorum: Lucius Titius miles notario suo testamentum scribendum notis dictavit et antequam litteris perscriberetur, vita defunctus est: Quaero, an haec dictatio valere possit. Respondi militibus, quoquo modo velint et quo modo possunt, testamentum facere concessum esse, [...] (D.29.1.40pr.)*

> Paul, Replies, book 11: Lucius Titius, a soldier, dictated his will to his scribe from notes and died before it was fully written up. I ask whether this dictation can be valid [as a will]. I have answered that it is permitted to soldiers to make their wills in whatever way they desire and in whatever way they can, [...] (D.29.1.40pr.)

A soldier had dictated his will and died before it could be written up. There was no *mancipatio*, and thus no will under the *ius civile*. Moreover, since there was no sealed document, the requirements for granting a *bonorum possessio secundum tabulas* under the *ius praetorium* were not met. Paul (third century AD), referring to the imperial instruction, considers the dictated draft of the will to be valid, since in the case of a soldier's will the testator's intention is the only requirement.

The formlessness applicable to the making of a will also applied to its revocation:

> *Ulpianus, 45 ad edictum: Sicut autem hereditatem miles nuda voluntate dare potest, ita et adimere potest. Denique si cancellaverit testamentum suum vel inciderit, nullius erit momenti: Si tamen testamentum cancellaverit et mox valere voluerit, valebit ex suprema voluntate. [...] (D.29.1.15.1.)*

> Ulpian, Edict, book 45: So, just as a soldier can dispose of his estate by a formless declaration of will, he can also take it away. Then, if he cancels or cuts his will, it will not be valid. But if he has cancelled his will and soon after wished it to be valid, it will be valid owing to the last declaration of will. [...] (D.29.1.15.1.)

A soldier's will could be revoked as formless as it had been made. As Ulpian (third century AD) demonstrated, the effect of this rule was that any interference by the testator with the testamentary document could be regarded as a revocation. Moreover, the revocation of a revocation would lead to a valid will. What mattered was which intention could be proved to have been the last. Consequently, two wills could be valid side by side:

> *Ulpianus, 4 disputationum: Quaerebatur, si miles, qui habebat iam factum testamentum, aliud fecisset et in eo comprehendisset se fidei heredis committere, ut priores tabulae valerent, quid iuris esset. Dicebam: Militi licet plura testamenta facere, sed sive simul fecerit sive separatim, utique valebunt, si hoc specialiter expresserit, nec superius per inferius rumpetur, cum et ex parte heredem instituere possit, hoc est ex parte testato, ex parte intestato decedere. [...] (D.29.1.19pr.)*

> Ulpian, Disputations, book 4: It was asked what law applied if a soldier who had already made a will made another one and in it declared that he was entrusting it to his heir that the earlier will was valid. I said: a soldier is permitted to draw up several wills, but they will, whether he made them all at the same time, or whether he made them separately, all be valid if he expressly stated that he desired this to be the case. Nor is the first will annulled by the later one, because he [as a soldier] can also appoint an heir for only a part of his estate; that is to say that he can die partly with a will and partly without a will. [...] (D.29.1.19pr.)

Several wills drawn up by a soldier were valid if the soldier intended them to be in force at the same time. Therefore, a soldier could make additions to an existing will without revoking the one already made. Ulpian explained that this option resulted from the fact that the rule *nemo pro parte testatus, pro parte intestatus decedere potest* did not apply to soldiers (Ch. 4.1), so that a soldier's will could only be made for a part of the estate.

As a result of the relaxation of the formal requirements, other rules of the *ius civile* relating to a soldier's will were also suspended. This applied first of all to the prohibition of the *institutio ex certa re* (Ch. 6.2.2):

> *Ulpianus, 5 ad Sabinum: Si miles unum ex fundo heredem scripserit, creditum quantum ad residuum patrimonium intestatus decessisset: Miles enim pro parte testatus potest decedere, pro parte intestatus.* (D.29.1.6.)

> Ulpian, Sabinus, book 5: Where a soldier appoints a single heir to a property, he is considered to have died intestate with regard to the rest of his estate. For a soldier can die partly testate and partly intestate. (D.29.1.6.)

According to Ulpian, when a soldier appoints an heir to a certain item, the estate is divided. Accordingly, the heir receives only what he is appointed for;

the rest passes on intestacy. Contrary to the *ius civile* (the Rule of Sabinus, Ch. 6.1.3), a singular succession is not interpreted as a universal succession. Instead, the appointment to specific items is considered valid.

In addition, soldiers' wills could contain temporary or resolutory conditions:

> *Ulpianus, ad edictum 45: Miles et ad tempus heredem facere potest et alium post tempus vel ex condicione vel in condicionem. (D.29.1.15.4.)*
>
> Ulpian, Edict, book 45: A soldier can appoint an heir for a certain time, and another after that time. He can also appoint an heir upon fulfilment of a certain condition, or another after the condition was met. (D.29.1.15.4.)

Ulpian stressed that a soldier could appoint pre- and post-heirs and distribute the estate temporarily or conditionally between them. The *ius civile* did not allow this kind of division because it violated the principle of *semel heres, semper heres* (Ch. 6.1.3).

The examples show that the privileges of a soldier's will did not only refer to its external form, i.e. the proper *mancipatio* or sealing of the documents, but also to the internal form, i.e. its allowed content. The main consequences of this formlessness of the soldier's wills in relation to the traditional requirements are listed in Overview 27:

Overview 27: Consequences of the Formlessness of the Soldier's Will

	making a will	rules of appointment	revocation
ius civile/ius praetorium	• *mancipatio* • seven witnesses	• distinguishing between intestacy and testamentary succession • prohibition of *institutio ex certa re*; *semel heres, semper heres*	• drawing up a new will • eliminating the document
ius novum for soldiers	• also verbally (by dictation)	• application of intestacy rules next to the will • *institutio ex certa re* allowed; pre- and post-heirs allowed	• only through the expression of the intention • also partially possible

Because of the substantial differences between drawing up a will as a soldier or a civilian, it was problematic to ascertain what rules applied to persons who shifted from civilian to military status. This brings us to the personal scope of this privilege.

6.4.3 The Personal Scope of the Soldier's Will

A soldier's will could only be drawn up by a soldier. This commenced as soon as the soldier's name was on the military payroll:

> *Ulpianus, 45 ad edictum: Ex eo tempore quis iure militari incipit posse testari, ex quo in numeros relatus est, ante non: Proinde qui nondum in numeris sunt, licet etiam lecti tirones sint et publicis expensis iter faciunt, nondum milites sunt: [...] (D.29.1.42.)*

> Ulpian, Edict book 45: A person begins to be able to make a will according to military law from the time he has been entered on the military payroll, not before. Therefore, those who are not yet on the military payroll, although they have been recruited and march at public expense, are not yet soldiers [...] (D.29.1.42.)

The privilege of formless drawing up a will was only granted once the testator was enrolled on the military payroll, i.e. listed as a soldier in the imperial army. This conscription (*in numeros referre*) took place only after basic military training. Therefore, the recruit (*tiro*), who had already sworn the oath of allegiance but was not formally listed, could not leave a will as a soldier. When the recruit attained the status of a soldier, military law could, under certain circumstances, apply to the will he had made as a civilian:

> *Iulianus, 27 digestorum: Cum aliquis facto testamento militare coeperit, id quoque testamentum, quod ante quam militare coeperit fecerat, aliquo casu intellegitur militiae tempore factum, veluti si tabulas inciderit et legerit testamentum ac rursus suo signo signaverit, amplius si et aliquid interleverit perduxerit adiecerit emendaverit: Quod si nihil horum inciderit, testamentum eius ad privilegia militum non pertinebit. (D.29.1.20.1.)*

> Julian, Digest, book 27: If someone began his military service after drawing up a will, even this will, which he had made before beginning his military service, will in some cases be treated as having been made during the period of [military] service. For instance, if he opened the will, read it and resealed it with his seal. Even more so if he cancelled a part of it, defaced it or made any additions or corrections. If, however, none of these events occurred, his will is not entitled to any of the privileges granted to the will of a soldier. (D.29.1.20.1.)

Julian (under Emperor Hadrian, around AD130) determined that military law applied only if the testator had reappropriated the will as a soldier by altering the document. But a will made by a civilian could not be considered a soldier's will if the testator had left his will established before his military service unchanged. In this case, Julian maintained the requirements for civilian wills. Subsequent imperial legislation was more generous in this respect, as Ulpian tells us:

> *Ulpianus, 45 ad edictum: Testamentum ante militiam factum a milite, si in militia decesserit, iure militari valere, si militis voluntas contraria non sit, divus Pius rescripsit. (D.29.1.15.2.)*
>
> Ulpian, Edict, book 45: The deified Pius stated in a rescript that a will made by a soldier before entering active service was valid under military law if he died during service and there was no intention to the contrary. (D.29.1.15.2.)

Following a rescript by Emperor Antoninus Pius (AD138–161), it was possible to consider a will by a civilian as a valid soldier's will if the testator had not changed his mind as a soldier. Thus, unlike Julian, Antoninus Pius no longer required the incorporation of the civilian will into the military will, but presumed a corresponding will that could only be disproved by conduct to the contrary. The result of this rescript was that wills, which were initially invalid, could become valid as soon as the testator became a soldier in the Roman army.

This privilege is linked to the status of soldier from beginning to end: it therefore ceased when the soldier was discharged from the army. In the case of an honourable discharge, a transitional period of one year applied:

> *Macer, 2 militarium: Testamenta eorum, qui ignominiae causa missi sunt, statim desinunt militari iure valere, quod anni spatium testamentis eorum, qui honestam vel causariam missionem meruerunt, tribuitur. [...]* (D.29.1.26pr.)
>
> Macer, Military Law, book 2: The wills of soldiers who have been dishonourably discharged immediately cease to be valid by military law, because the period of one year [after leaving military service] is granted to the wills of those who have earned an honourable discharge or a discharge due to illness. [...] (D.29.1.26pr.)

According to Macer (beginning of the third century AD), the wills of honourably discharged soldiers remained valid for one year after their release from active service. Former soldiers thus had time to replace the formless will with a valid one in accordance with the *ius civile* or *ius praetorium*. If the soldier was dishonourably discharged, however, his will would be invalid from the day of his discharge. He would therefore have to make a will that was valid under either the *ius civile* or *ius praetorium* if he did not wish to die intestate.

A soldier was considered to be dishonourably discharged if, for example, he committed suicide to avoid service. In exceptional cases, Emperor Hadrian (AD117–138) allowed the reason for the suicide to be investigated:

> *Papinianus, 14 quaestionum: Eius militis, qui doloris inpatientia vel taedio vitae mori maluit, testamentum valere [...] divus Hadrianus rescripsit. (D.29.1.34pr.)*

> Papinian, Questions, book 14: The deified Hadrian declared in a rescript [...] that the will of a soldier who preferred to die rather than suffer the pains or annoyances of life was valid. (D.29.1.34pr.)

Emperor Hadrian, in the rescript quoted by Papinian, declared the will of a soldier who had committed suicide valid because the suicide was not committed to avoid military service but because of general dissatisfaction with life (depression). The Emperor's decision in this particular case, which made him appear benevolent, did not change the fact that, in principle, only honourably discharged soldiers could benefit from the privilege of leaving formless wills.

The temporal limitation of the privilege of leaving a will as a soldier shows the determination of the jurists to defend the traditional rules against imperial leniency. They are all the more trying to prevent a spillover of the formless making of a testament from the *ius novum* into the testamentary rules of the *ius civile* and the *ius praetorium*. Their qualification of the codicils and the soldier's will as '*ius singulare*' ('special law') is evidence of this endeavour.

6.4.4 Ius singulare

The term *ius singulare* is used to preserve the distinction between the two new imperial legal creations and the existing traditional testamentary form:

> *Iulianus, 37 digestorum: Codicillorum ius singulare est, ut quaecumque in his scribentur perinde haberentur, ac si in testamento scripta essent. [...] (D.29.7.2.2.)*

> Iulian, Digest, book 37: The rules of codicils form a 'special law' (*ius singulare*), so that anything that will be written in them must be considered to have the same effect as if it had been included in the will. [...] (D.29.7.2.2.)

> *Gaius, 15 ad edictum provinciale: De militis testamento ideo separatim proconsul edicit, quod optime novit ex constitutionibus principalibus propria atque singularia iura in testamenta eorum observari. (D.29.1.2.)*

> Gaius, Provincial Edict, book 15: The proconsul issued a separate edict concerning the wills of soldiers because he was well aware that, following the constitutions of the emperors, special and extraordinary rights had been established concerning wills. (D.29.1.2.)

The codicil is considered as a *ius singulare* because it allows additions to the will without adhering to the forms of the will; the soldier's will also deviates from the traditional tenets of testamentary forms, so that the *bonorum possessio* following a soldier's will could only be granted on the basis of a specific edict.

The above passages show that the Roman jurists did not dispute the validity of the legal institutions introduced by the *cognitio extra ordinem*. On the contrary, they recognised the legislative authority of the *princeps* (Ch. 2.1.2). This recognition, however, did not exclude criticism of the changes that were alien to the existing system:

> *Paulus, liber singularis de iure singulari: Ius singulare est, quod contra tenorem rationis propter aliquam utilitatem auctoritate constituentium introductum est. (D.1.3.16.)*
>
> Paul, Special Law, Sole book 1: Special law is what has been introduced by the authority of those establishing it on account of some particular advantage, against the sense of reason. (D.1.3.16.)

Paul defines *ius singulare* as a law which is contrary to legal reason, which was introduced for political purposes and which cannot therefore be understood as a development of existing law (Ch. 1.3.2). This definition conditions the juristic approach to the *ius singulare*:

> *Paulus, 54 ad edictum: Quod vero contra rationem iuris receptum est, non est producendum ad consequentias. (D.1.3.14.)*
>
> Paul, Edict, book 54: What has been established contrary to the rationale of law, cannot be applied to subsequent [legal cases]. (D.1.3.14.)
>
> *Iulianus, 27 digestorum: In his, quae contra rationem iuris constituta sunt, non possumus sequi regulam iuris. (D.1.3.15.)*
>
> Iulian, Digest, book 27: In those instances where something has been established contrary to the principles of the law, we cannot follow this rule of law. (D.1.3.15.)

Since the *ius singulare* was added to the existing law 'from outside', i.e. without any internal justification, it remained an alien element. Hence, the evaluation and consequences of the *ius singulare* could not be extended to the existing law. Moreover, the *ius singulare* could not form the basis of (new) law. Both statements indicate that the imperial developments could not repeal the existing rules on the making of a testament. A harmonisation of the existing rules in the sense of *ius novum* was therefore out of the question. Unlike the case of the *hereditatis petitio*, which was modified and extended by the *senatusconsultum Iuventianum* (Ch. 5.4.2), the imperial legislation regarding the codicil and the soldier's will did not allow for a revision of the existing rules on the institution of heirs.

6.5 Concluding Considerations on the Testamentary Order of Succession

1. If we consider the various layers of Roman testamentary law, we can see a development from strict formalism to freedom of form. While the will under the *ius civile* – whether as a public or as a mancipatory will – could only be conceived of as a formal act, the *ius praetorium* already dispensed with the ritual of appointment and replaced it with a written declaration sealed by seven witnesses. The development of the *ius novum* for wills, initiated by Emperor Augustus (27BC–AD14), allowed for formless additions, which were either included in the will or acted as *fideicommissa*. Later emperors even allowed formless wills for limited groups of people.
2. This gradual loosening of the form can be explained for the *ius praetorium* against the background of the procedural situation in the granting of the *bonorum possessio secundum tabulas* to the heirs appointed according to the *ius civile*. The *mancipatio* of *ius civile* had to be proved by documents as well; over time, these types of documents replaced the formal ritual, because of practical needs. This shift in perspective is accounted for by an improvement in the protection of the deed. However, the complete abandonment of the form, as promoted by the *ius novum*, served motives foreign to hereditary law, which the Roman jurists already rejected as alien to the system of the law of inheritance.
3. The jurists deal with three different layers of law in accordance with their diverging purposes: A conflict between *ius civile* and *ius praetorium* can only arise if the *ius praetorium* appoints other persons as testamentary heirs than the *ius civile*. This is the case if the evidence of the making of the will is admitted under *ius praetorium* but fails under *ius civile*, for example because non-compliance with the *mancipatio* could be proved. Also, grounds for the invalidity of the will are sanctioned more strictly under *ius civile* than under *ius praetorium*, so that in some cases the order of intestacy under *ius civile* can clash with the *bonorum possessio secundum tabulas*. The fact that the praetor gives priority to the testamentary heir in these cases follows the principle, also recognised under the *ius civile*, that intestate succession only applies if there is no (operative) will. With regard to these fundamental principles, there is therefore a parallel between the two layers of law. Conversely, the *ius novum* allowing formless additions to the will, as well as the possibility introduced for soldiers to make a formless will, contradicted the principles of the existing layers of law, with

no possibility of reconciliation. Since formless additions and formless wills were guaranteed by imperial authority, they could not be challenged. This is why jurists distinguish the *ius novum* from the other layers of law. Only in this way could conflicting rules on the making of wills continue to coexist.

7

Protecting Inheritance Expectations and the Rules of Disinheritance

The system of intestate succession (Ch. 3) and the freedom of testation (Ch. 6) are in a state of tension: while the hierarchical structure of the *familias* regarded children under the paternal power as the natural heirs, the testator was free to favour some of his children over others, or even to appoint non-members of the *familias* as heirs. The *ius civile* resolved this tension between the direct heirs' expectation of inheritance and the testator's testamentary freedom through rules on disinheritance: direct heirs could be disinherited, but their disinheritance (*exheredatio*) had to follow the relevant rules. The extension of the scope of intestate succession under the *ius praetorium* to include *emancipati* (Ch. 3.2.2) and *cognati* (Ch. 3.2.2) entailed the extension of the rules on disinheritance in order to strike a balance between the testamentary freedom and the protection of the different heirs' expectation of inheritance under the *ius praetorium*. Imperial law took a different approach to safeguarding the intestate succession. Originating from precursors from the time of the Republic, a complaint to challenge an unjust will was established during the imperial period: the *querela inofficiosi testamenti* ('complaint about undutiful will'). With this complaint, descendants and parents could challenge a will on the grounds that they had been unjustly disregarded in the will.

We will now focus first on the rules of disinheritance of the *ius civile* and on how they were shaped by the praetor in accordance to the *ius praetorium*. We will then outline the imperial development of the *querela* and its consequences for the pre-existing layers of law.

7.1 The Rules of Disinheritance under *ius civile*

The disinheritance rules of the *ius civile*, like other rules governing wills (Ch. 6.1.1), derive from the cautelary practice of the republican jurists. The requirement that a particular member of the *familias* must be disinherited before others are appointed is primarily a rule of reason. The testator must be clear about the consequences of his last will for the members of his *familias*. The *ius civile* distinguished between the disinheritance of a *filius familias* and that of other children under the paternal power. Since the *filius familias* continued the line of the father (Ch. 3.1.1), the reduction of his inheritance expectation from his *pater familias* had to be subject to strict rules. This was done by prohibiting the passing over of the son (*praeterire*):

> Inst.Gai.2.123.: *Item qui filium in potestate habet, curare debet, ut eum vel heredem instituat vel nominatim exheredet; alioquin si eum silentio praeterierit, inutiliter testabitur: [...]*

> Inst.Gai.2.123.: Again, anyone who has a son under his power must either appoint him as his heir or disinherit him by name but, if he passes him over in silence, the will becomes invalid [...]

The *pater familias* who made a will had to either appoint his *filii familias* or disinherit them by name. For each new newborn *filius familias* the will had to be adapted, so that the *mancipatio* had to be performed again or the will had to be redrafted. A *praeterire* occurred not only when the son's name was completely omitted in his father's will, but also when the son's appointment as heir or his disinheritance did not follow the established rules.

7.1.1 The Disinheritance of the filius familias

The disinheritance (*exheredatio*) of the *filius familias* could only be made by name (*nominatim*):

> Inst.Gai.2.127: *[...] Nominatim autem exheredari videtur, sive ita exheredetur: 'Titius filius meus exheres esto,' sive ita: 'Filius meus exheres esto,' non adiecto proprio nomine.*

> Inst.Gai.2.127.: A son, however, must be disinherited by name, otherwise, he is not considered to have been disinherited. A son is considered to be disinherited by name when the following expressions are used: 'Let my son Titius be disinherited' or: 'Let my son be disinherited,' without mentioning his name.

A disinheritance has been done 'by name' if it was mentioned that the disinherited was a son. If the son was not disinherited by name, the disinheritance was invalid and the son was considered to have been passed over. Consequently, the entire will was permanently invalid.

If the son had been passed over but died after the will had been made, the question arose as to whether the will could exceptionally become valid:

> Inst.Gai.2.123.: *[...] adeo quidem, ut nostri praeceptores existiment, etiam si vivo patre filius defunctus sit, neminem heredem ex eo testamento existere posse, scilicet quia statim ab initio non constiterit institutio; sed diversae scholae auctores, si quidem filius mortis patris tempore vivat, sane impedimento eum esse*

scriptis heredibus et illum ab intestato heredem fieri confitentur; si vero ante mortem patris interceptus sit, posse ex testamento hereditatem adiri putant, nullo iam filio impedimento; quia scilicet existimant non statim ab initio inutiliter fieri testamentum filio praeterito.

Inst.Gai.2.123.: [...] which goes so far that our teachers think that even if the son died during the father's lifetime, nobody can be heir under this will, because the appointment of the heir was invalid from the very beginning. But the representatives of the other school concede that if the son is still alive at the time of his father's death, he is in any case an obstacle to the heirs' appointed by the will, and that this son becomes heir without there being a will. If, however, he died before his father, they believe that the inheritance can be accepted on the basis of the will without the son now standing in the way, because they naturally think that a will that passes over a son was not automatically invalid from the beginning.

This question was disputed between the two schools of jurists of the first century AD, both called after their respective founders, the Sabinians (*Sabinus*) and the Proculians (*Proculus*). While the Sabinians argued that the initial invalidity of the will by reason of the *praeterire* of the son continued even if the son died before his father, the Proculians maintained that the initial invalidity had been cured by the death of the son. Although the Proculian view allowed a genuinely pragmatic balance between protecting the son from disinheritance and preserving the testamentary freedom, it did not prevail during the Empire. The rigid approach of the Sabinians, in line with their conservative approach to testamentary rules in general (Ch. 6.2), prevailed, namely that a will which was void at the time it was made remained void, even if the reason for its invalidity ceased to exist.

It was not until the praetorian law that this strict rule was relaxed (Ch. 6.3.1). A certain degree of flexibility also existed under the *ius civile* when the testator appointed substitute heirs (Ch. 6.1.5), i.e. when there were heirs of varying degrees:

Ulpianus, 1 ad Sabinum: Si ita testatus sit pater familias, ut a primo quidem gradu filium praeteriret, a secundo solo exheredaret, Sabinus et Cassius et Iulianus putant perempto primo gradu testamentum ab eo gradu exordium capere, unde filius exheredatus est: Quae sententia comprobata est. (D.28.2.3.6.)

Ulpian, Sabinus, book 1: If a *pater familias* makes a will in such a way that he passed over his son in the first degree and disinherited him only in the second degree, Sabinus, Cassius, and Julian believe that the will, after the lapse of the first degree, only becomes valid from the degree at which the son was disinherited. This opinion is generally accepted. (D.28.2.3.6.)

If a *pater familias* appointed an heir in the first degree without formally disinheriting the *filius familias* and at the same time appointed a substitute heir to whom the disinheritance of the son was formally declared, then the will was partially valid. The appointment of the first degree heir was void on account of the incorrect or missing disinheritance of the son. However, the appointment of a substitute heir remained valid because of the formal disinheritance of the son. The substitute heir therefore became a testamentary heir.

The usual practice of appointing a substitute heir, i.e. an heir in the second degree, thus functioned as a safeguard against the incorrect or missing disinheritance of the *filius familias* in the first degree. As we have seen, when a substitute heir was appointed, it was usually on a (suspensive) condition (Ch. 6.1.5). Since the conditional appointment of an heir makes his position as heir dependent on circumstances which are usually beyond his control and which he cannot foresee, his appointment is characterised by some uncertainty. This uncertainty was to be avoided in the case of the *filius familias*, since it was considered a '*praeterire*'. Therefore, the conditional appointment of a *filius familias* as heir is only possible within strict limits.

7.1.2 The Conditional Appointment of the filius familias

From the point of view of cautelary practice, the simplest way to avoid a passing over (*praeterire*) by a conditional appointment of the *filius familias* was for the testator to combine the conditional appointment with a conditional disinheritance:

> *Iulianus, 29 digestorum: Si quis testamento hoc modo scripserit: 'Filius meus si Titium adoptaverit, heres esto: Si non adoptaverit, exheres esto'. [...] (D.28.7.11.)*
>
> Julian, Digest, book 29: When someone writes in his will as follows: 'Let my son be my heir if he adopts Titius; if he does not adopt him, let him be disinherited'. [...] (D.28.7.11.)

In the example given by Julian, the testator made his son his heir if the latter adopted Titius. In the same will, he disinherited his son on the opposite condition, i.e. if he did not to adopt Titius. In all cases, the son's position as heir was clearly defined by the combination of the two opposing conditions: if the son adopted Titius, he would become heir. If he did not adopt him, he would be effectively disinherited. The risk of *praeterire* in the will of the *pater familias* is thus eliminated.

The prohibited uncertainty as to the position of the *filius familias* as heir could also be avoided if the testator appointed the son on a potestative condition:

> *Ulpianus, 4 ad Sabinum: Suus quoque heres sub condicione heres potest institui: Sed excipiendus est filius, quia non sub omni condicione institui potest. Et quidem sub ea condicione, quae est in potestate ipsius, potest: De hoc enim inter omnes constat. [...] (D.28.5.4pr.)*

> Ulpian, Sabinus, book 4: A direct heir can also be appointed on a condition. However, the testator's son is excluded from this, because he cannot be appointed under any [kind of] condition. He can be [appointed] on a condition which is within his power. For there is agreement among all [jurists] in this regard. [...] (D.28.5.4pr.)

All other persons under the paternal power could be appointed under any condition, but the appointment of a *filius familias* was only permissible under a potestative condition. This is understood to mean a condition whose fulfilment is within the son's power. Here the uncertainty created by the passing over is removed by the intention of the *filius familias* himself. It is up to him to fulfil the condition or not. Thus, the conditional appointment is not considered as the *pater familias* passing him over.

This approach, however, only works if the fulfilment of the condition is truly at the discretion of the son. This will depend on the circumstances of the case:

> *Ulpianus, 4 ad Sabinum: Puto recte generaliter definiri: Utrum in potestate fuerit condicio an non fuerit, facti potestas est: Potest enim et haec 'si Alexandriam pervenerit' non esse in arbitrio per hiemis condicionem: Potest et esse, si ei, qui a primo miliario Alexandriae agit, fuit imposita: Potest et haec 'si decem Titio dederit' esse in difficili, si Titius peregrinetur longinquo itinere: Propter quae ad generalem definitionem recurrendum est. (D.28.5.4.1.)*

> Ulpian, Sabinus, book 4: I think that this is how the term [potestative condition] is generally defined, and rightly so: Whether the fulfilment of the condition was in the power [of the son] or not, depends on the factual situation. For even the fulfilment of this condition 'when he arrived in Alexandria' cannot depend on the son's will, because the winter is severe. Yet it can depend on the will of someone who is a mile away from Alexandria. Similarly, the condition 'when he pays ten aurei to Titius' may be difficult to fulfil if Titius is on a long journey. Hence, one must return to the general definition. (D.28.5.4.1.)

The potestative nature of the condition must be determined on the basis of the particular circumstances of the case. It is therefore a question of fact. Whether the condition can actually be fulfilled will be determined in each individual case. If the condition proves impossible to fulfil, the will is invalid:

Paulus, 12 responsorum: Lucius Titius ita testamentum fecit: 'Aurelius Claudius natus ex illa muliere, si filium meum se esse iudici probaverit, heres mihi esto.' Paulus respondit filium de quo quaereretur non sub ea condicione institutum videri, quae in potestate eius est, et ideo testamentum nullius esse momenti. (D.35.1.83.)

Paul, Replies, book 12: Lucius Titius made his will as follows: 'Let Aurelius Claudius, the son of such and such a woman, be my heir, if he can prove before a judge that he is my son.' Paulus held that the son in question was not to be regarded as having been appointed on such a condition that was in his power to fulfil, and that the will was therefore null. (D.35.1.83.)

The testator appointed one Aurelius Claudius on the condition that the latter could prove that he was the testator's son. This condition could be understood as a potestative condition, since it is at the discretion of the son to provide the judge with evidence or not. The opinion of Paul (third century AD) demonstrates that the jurist focuses instead on the fulfilment of the condition, i.e. the actual existence of the son's status, which is not at the discretion of the appointed heir. In this case, the resulting nullity of the will leads to a paradoxical decision: as soon as Aurelius Claudius has proved that he is in fact the son of the testator, the condition is fulfilled; at the same time, the condition is inadmissible and the will null, because the identity as *filius familias* has been proved and therefore only an appointment on a potestative condition would be admissible – and this was not the case with the condition in the example given.

The nullity resulting from the appointment of a son under a non-potestative condition was remarkable, since impossible conditions for the appointment of heirs were in principle deleted and did not affect the validity of the will:

Ulpianus, 5 ad Sabinum: Sub impossibili condicione vel alio mendo factam institutionem placet non vitiari. (D.28.7.1.)

Ulpian, Sabinus, book 5: It is established that an appointment made under an impossible condition or because of another error, is not void. (D.28.7.1.)

In the case of persons other than the *filius familias*, an appointment subject to an impossible condition, i.e. a condition which the designated heir could not fulfil, resulted in an unconditional appointment. Conversely, the inheritance expectation of the *filus familias* was considered so important that the invalid condition could not merely be deleted but that the validity of the will as a whole was challenged.

The provisions of the *ius civile* to prevent a son from being passed over in the will of the *pater familias* are summarised in Overview 28:

Overview 28: The Prohibition to Pass Over the *filius familias* under the *ius civile*

filius familias must either be disinherited by name or appointed as heir		
upon a son's birth, the will must be adjusted/made anew	proper, i.e. explicit, disinheritance	proper appointment; conditional appointment only under a potestative condition
testator omits the adjustment	testator does not disinherit (by name)	testator appoints his son under a void condition
the son is passed over (*praeterire*); **the will is void.**		

As privileged heirs upon intestacy, the other children under the paternal power also have their inheritance expectancy protected under the *ius civile*. Therefore, they also had to be disinherited if the testator wanted to avoid impediments to his testamentary dispositions.

7.1.3 The Disinheritance of Other Children under the Paternal Power

A different rule of disinheritance applies to the other children under the paternal power, i.e. the daughters under the paternal power and the grandchildren of the testator's by a son. It is not as strict as the rule applicable to the *filius familias*:

> Inst.Gai.2.128.: *Ceterae vero liberorum personae vel feminini sexus vel masculini satis inter ceteros exheredantur, id est his verbis: 'Ceteri omnes exheredes sunto,' quae verba statim post institutionem heredum adici solent. Sed hoc ita est iure civili [...]*

> Inst.Gai.2.128.: Other children of both sexes may be properly disinherited by, among others, using the following words: 'let all the others be disinherited.' These words are usually added immediately after the appointment of the heirs. This, however, is only required by the *ius civile* [...]

Children who are not *filii familias* can be validly disinherited thus: 'let all the others be disinherited'. Hence, a disinheritance by a general clause is sufficient to exclude their inheritance expectations. Consequently, an omitted (or invalid) disinheritance of this group of persons does not jeopardise the validity of the will of the *pater familias*:

> Inst.Gai.2.124.: *Ceteras vero liberorum personas si praeterierit testator, valet testamentum: Sed praeteritae istae personae scriptis heredibus in partem adcrescunt, si sui heredes sint, in virilem, si extranei, in dimidiam. [...]*

Inst.Gai.2.124.: If, however, the testator passes over the other children, the will is valid, but the persons who have been passed over are entitled, together with the heirs mentioned in the will, to equal shares of the estate if they are direct heirs, and to half if they are heirs from outside the family.

If children under the paternal power who are not *filii familias* have not been duly disinherited in the will, the will still remains valid. At the same time, their intestate rights are not considered to have been extinguished, so that they participate in the inheritance regardless of the will. The division of the estate between the testamentary heirs and the participating direct heirs follows a hypothetical assessment of the intestacy rules: if the testamentary heir is also a direct heir, the inheritance is divided *per capita*. If the testamentary heir is an outside heir (*extraneus*), the children passed over receive half of the estate. Therefore, while the *ius civile* requires that the *pater familias* amends his will when a *filius familias* joins the *familias*, it does not necessarily require an amendment when other children under the paternal power are born. For their disinheritance, it is sufficient for the testator to have made a general disinheritance when drawing up his will.

Given the different criteria for the disinheritance of a *filius familias* and a *filia familias*, it was evident that a special rule had to be applied in cases where the *pater familias* did not know the gender of his child. This problem arose in the case of children under the paternal power who were born after the death of the *pater familias*, the *postumi* (posthumous children).

*7.1.4 Posthumously Born Children under the Paternal Power (*postumi*)*

Since posthumous children would be under their *pater familias*' power if he were alive at their birth, they were considered direct heirs:

Inst.Gai.2.130.: Postumi quoque liberi nominatim vel heredes institui debent vel exheredari.

Inst.Gai.2.130.: Posthumous children must be either appointed as heirs or disinherited.

Therefore, the *postumi* could not be passed over but had to be disinherited. However, disinheritance by a general clause was not enough. The *pater familias* had to disinherit these children as 'posthumous' if he wanted to avoid the nullification of his will:

Inst.Gai.2.131.: Et in eo par omnium condicio est, quod et in filio postumo et in quolibet ex ceteris liberis sive feminini sexus sive masculini praeterito valet quidem testamentum, sed postea adgnatione postumi sive postumae rumpitur, et ea ratione totum infirmatur. [...]

Inst.Gai.2.131.: In this respect, the same condition applies to all, so that if a posthumous son or any other posthumous child of either sex is passed over, the will is indeed valid; but after the additional birth of a posthumous child it [the will] is overturned, and for this reason becomes completely void. [...]

A will which does not take into account the *postumus* or *postumi* is void if a child is born to the testator after his death. This legal consequence applies regardless of the child's gender, so it also counts for a posthumous daughter. The stricter rule of disinheritance, compared with that applicable to a living *filia familias*, takes into consideration the uncertainly as to the gender and life expectancy of the child: since the testator does not know whether a son or daughter will be born to him, he is held to the highest standards of care; hence the explicit disinheritance, which otherwise applies only to the *filius familias*. At the same time, the consequences of the stricter rules applicable to the disinheritance of a *filius familias* are modified in that the will becomes invalid only if the posthumous child is actually born viable.

The term *postumi* referred not only to children born after the death of the *pater familias*, but also to those who succeeded during his lifetime. Primarily, this term referred to grandchildren born after the death of the *filius familias*, since they would take their father's position as direct heirs and can thus be characterised as *postumi* in a broader sense:

> *Scaevola, 6 quaestionum: Gallus sic posse institui postumos nepotes induxit: 'Si filius meus vivo me morietur, tunc si quis mihi ex eo nepos sive quae neptis post mortem meam in decem mensibus proximis, quibus filius meus moreretur, natus nata erit, heredes sunto'. (D.28.2.29pr.)*

> Scaevola, Questions, book 6: Gallus stated that posthumous grandchildren could be appointed as heirs as follows: 'If my son predeceases me, and grandchildren, either male or female, are born within ten months of his death, they shall be my heirs'. (D.28.2.29pr.)

According to Scaevola (second century AD), the cautelary practice of the Republic, epitomised by the jurist Aquilius Gallus (116–44BC), advised the testator to provide for the succeeding of one or more *postumi*. In the case under consideration, a grandchild was born after the testator's death and was entitled under the rules of intestacy, since the grandchild took his father's place in the order of intestacy after the latter's death (Ch. 3.1.2). The unfortunate combination of the son's death and the posthumous birth of a grandchild would have rendered the grandfather's will void. To avoid this undesirable outcome, the testator was allowed to appoint the posthumously born grandchild or grandchildren on condition that their father had predeceased them.

However, the grandchild does not only succeed the *filius familias* in the case of a posthumous birth, but also when the son leaves the *patria potestas* for other reasons, while the (already living) grandchildren remain under the power of his *pater familias*:

> *Inst.Gai.2.133.: Postumorum autem loco sunt et hi, qui in sui heredis locum succedendo quasi adgnascendo fiunt parentibus sui heredes: Ut ecce si filium et ex eo nepotem neptemve in potestate habeam, quia filius gradu praecedit, is solus iura sui heredis habet, quamvis nepos quoque et neptis ex eo in eadem potestate sint; sed si filius meus me vivo moriatur aut qualibet ratione exeat de potestate mea, incipit nepos neptisve in eius locum succedere, et eo modo iura suorum heredum quasi adgnatione nanciscuntur.*

> Inst.Gai.2.133.: But also those are considered posthumous children, who, by succeeding to the place of direct heirs, become direct heirs as it were by additional birth to their fathers. For example, if I have a son, and by him a grandson or a granddaughter who are under my power, because the son precedes them by one degree, he alone enjoys the rights of an heir, although the grandson and granddaughter by him are also under the same power as he. But if my son predeceases me, or for any other reason ceases to be under my power, then the grandson and granddaughter will succeed, and in this way acquire the rights of direct heirs, as if they had been born posthumously.

Suppose grandchildren succeed as direct heirs because the son has died or has left the *patria potestas* (*emancipatio*). In this case, they are only called posthumous (*postumi*) because they came after the will was drawn up (*postumi* in the broadest sense). Their passing over also nullified the will because of their new position as direct heirs. The *pater familias* therefore had to draw up a new will or amend the existing one if he wanted to prevent his disposition becoming inoperative when the grandchildren succeeded. Since a *filius familias* did not leave the *potestas* of the father only at death, but also by *emancipatio* (Ch. 3.1.2), so that the grandchildren would move further up the line, the testator would have to constantly amend the will if he did not want to run the risk of having his last disposition nullified by the passing over of *postumi*.

The *lex Iunia Vellaea*, dating from AD26 or 28, allowed the testator to appoint the *postumi* as conditional heirs in order to avoid these difficulties:[1]

> *Scaevola, 6 quaestionum: Et videtur primum caput eos spectare, qui, cum nascerentur, sui heredes futuri essent [...] etsi ita verba sunt: 'Qui testamentum faciet, is omnis virilis sexus, qui ei suus heres futurus erit,' et cetera. (D.28.2.29.12.)*

---

[1] For the textual reconstruction, see Peter Stein, 'Lex Iunia Vellaea' in Michael H. Crawford (ed) *Roman Statutes II* (Institute of Classical Studies 1996) 811.

> Scaevola, Questions, book 6: And it seems that the first chapter [of the *lex Iulia Vellaea*] refers to those who, after they are born, will become future direct heirs [...] even though the wording is the following: 'if someone makes a will, he can appoint as heirs all male persons who will be his direct heirs in the future,' and the like. (D.28.2.29.12.)

In its first chapter, the *lex Iunia Vellaea* gave the *pater familias* the option to appoint the grandchild as heir as a precautionary measure. This preventive appointment did not only apply if the grandchild was born after the death of its grandfather and father. But it included instances where the grandchild was born during the testator's lifetime but after the will had been made. Following the *lex Iunia Vellaea*, the testator did not have to alter or make his will anew every time a grandchild succeeded his father in the line of succession. At the same time, the law allowed the testator to appoint a future *filius familias* under a non-potestative condition. As we saw above, this kind of appointment would normally be considered a passing over and, hence, void (Ch. 7.1.2). The *lex Iunia Vellaea*, however, lifted the invalidity entailed in the passing over on account of a conditional appointment of the *filius familias* for relatives further removed:

> *Scaevola, 6 quaestionum: Etiam si vovente parente vivo nacantur, sequenti parte succedentes in locum liberorum non vult rumpere testamentum: Et ita interpretandum est, ut, si et filium et nepotem et pronepotem habeas, mortuis utrisque pronepos institutus succedens in sui heredis locum non rumpat. [...] nec solum, si nepos vivo patre decedat, nec succedens pronepos avo mortuo rumpat, sed et si supervixit patri ac decedat, dummodo heres institutus sit aut exheredatus. (D.28.2.29.13.)*

> Scaevola, Questions, book 6: In the next section, [the law] wants to avoid that those who succeed to the place of the children-in-power can break the will, even if they are born during their father's life and according to his wish. And this must be interpreted in such a way that if you have a son, a grandson and a great-grandson, and after the death of the first two, your great-grandson, having been appointed and succeeded the direct heir, will not break the will. [...] and this applies not only when a grandson predeceases his father, and the great-grandson succeeding his deceased grandfather does not break the will, but also where the grandson survives his father and then dies, provided he has either been appointed heir or disinherited. (D.28.2.29.13.)

The second chapter of the *lex Iunia Vellaea* allows the great-grandfather to preventively appoint more removed descendants, like great-grandchildren, who are set to succeed in the line of succession because of the death of a son or grandchild, to forestall the invalidity caused by passing over the *postumi*.

Here too, the testator is granted, as an exception, the right to appoint a direct heir under a condition that is not potestative. Moreover, the testator is even allowed to disinherit his *postumus* preventively:

> *Gaius, 2 institutionum: [...] Ne ergo eo modo rumpat mihi testamentum, sicut ipsum filium vel heredem instituere vel exheredare nominatim debeo, ne non iure faciam testamentum, ita et nepotem neptemve ex eo necesse est mihi vel heredem instituere vel exheredare, ne forte me vivo filio mortuo succedendo in locum eius nepos neptisve quasi adgnatione rumpat testamentum: Idque lege Iunia Vellaea provisum est. (D.28.3.13.)*

> Gaius, Institutes, book 2: '[...]' Therefore, so that he does not break my will in this way, it is necessary that, just as I have to appoint my son as heir or disinherit him by name to avoid making my will unlawfully, I must also either appoint my grandson or granddaughter through him, as heirs or disinherit them. [And this has to be done,] so that the grandson or granddaughter does not accidentally break the will, if during my lifetime after my son's death, they succeed to his place, as it were by subsequent birth. And this is provided by the *lex Iunia Vellea'* (D.28.3.13.)

The *pater familias* must appoint or disinherit both the *filii familias* and his grandchildren, stemming from the latter, to avoid a passing over of the male line that would make the will void. Since the term *postumi* includes not only those born after the death of the *pater familias* but also all those who succeeded as direct heir after the will was written, the testator must consider future direct heirs as well. Under the provisions of the *lex Iunia Vellaea*, he can appoint or disinherit them in his will under the condition that those entitled first will predecease them.

In Overview 29, we find a summary of the rules for appointing and disinheriting of different categories of posthumously born children.

Overview 29: Rules for the Disinheritance of Posthumously Born Children (*postumi*)

children born posthumously (*postumi*) must either be appointed or disinherited		
postumi (literally): legitimate children born after the death of testator	*postumi* (in a broader sense): children of predeceased children that are born after the death of *pater familias*	*postumi* (by analogy): descendants who become direct heirs due to their father's release from *patria potestas*
testator must disinherit by name or appoint them	testator can appoint them in the original will or disinherit them by name	testator can appoint or disinherit descendants in case they become direct heirs

The very fastidious rules of disinheritance of descendants belonging to different categories show the impact of the family structure on the law of inheritance of the *ius civile*. As long as the descendants (children under the paternal power, grandchildren, great-grandchildren etc.) cannot themselves hold property, *extranei* can only inherit from the family estate, guarded by the *pater familias*, under strict rules.

7.2 The Modifications of Praetorian Law

On the one hand, the *ius praetorium* helped to enforce the rules of disinheritance of the *ius civile*; on the other hand, the praetor developed new rules to protect praetorian heirs on intestacy from being disinherited.

Following the *ius civile*, the praetorian law granted the testamentary heir the *bonorum possessio secundum tabulas* (Ch. 6.3) if the will was valid. If the will was void because a *filius familias* or a *postumus* was passed over, the praetor allowed the latter to claim the *bonorum possessio ab intestato* (Ch. 3.2).

The conditional appointment of a *filius familias* creates an essential modification of the rules of the *ius civile* by the *ius praetorium*:

> *Ulpianus, 41 ad edictum: Si sub condicione heres institutus filius sit, Iulianus peraeque putavit secundum tabulas competere ei quasi scripto bonorum possessionem, qualisqualis condicio sit, etiam si haec 'si navis ex Asia venerit': Et quamvis defecerit condicio, praetor tamen filium, qui admiserit secundum tabulas, tueri debebit [...] (D.37.11.2.1.)*

> Ulpian, Edict, book 41: If a son is appointed heir under a condition, Julian believes that he can equally demand *bonorum possessio secundum tabulas* as an appointed heir, whatever kind the condition is. And even if it were as follows: 'if a ship arrived from Asia'. And although the condition has failed, the praetor must, nevertheless, protect the son whom he permitted to have *bonorum possessio secundum tabulas* [...] (D.37.11.2.1.)

While the appointment of a *filius familias* under a non-potestative condition following the *ius civile* invalidates the will (Ch. 7.1.2), the latter will receive the *bonorum possessio secundum tabulas* from the praetor. Even though the appointment under the *ius civile* is invalid, the will remains in force under praetorian law. According to the jurist Julian, the son is to receive the *bonorum possessio* if the condition lapses, while under the *ius civile* the order of intestacy would apply. The reasons behind the different approach between the two layers of law are to be found in the already observed tendency of the praetorian law to require for the *bonorum possessio secundum tabulas* only the existence of a valid written will (Ch. 6.3.1). Hence, if the son were named and appointed as heir, then *bonorum possessio secundum tabulas* would be granted. In contrast, the condition's invalidity was not pertinent under the *ius praetorium*. This case already reveals that *ius civile* and *ius praetorium* set different standards to establish the passing over of a son.

Special rules applied for disinheriting heirs on intestacy under praetorian law, mainly concerning emancipated children.

7.2.1 The bonorum possessio contra tabulas

The rules about disinheritance protected the inheritance expectancies of the heirs on intestacy, and, therefore, the variations we saw in the order of succession by intestacy under the *ius praetorium* also affected the rules on disinheritance. The rules of intestacy strengthened the position of descendants against relatives further removed and, at the same time, introduced the principle of equal treatment of all descendants, regardless of whether they were under the power of their *pater familias* or emancipated (Ch. 3.2). Both tendencies of the *ius praetorium* manifest themselves in the praetorian law of disinheritance. Consequently, the praetor set a duty to disinherit *emancipati*:

> *Inst.Gai.2.135.: Emancipatos liberos iure civili neque heredes instituere neque exheredare necesse est, quia non sunt sui heredes: Sed praetor omnes tam feminini quam masculini sexus, si heredes non instituantur, exheredari iubet, virilis sexus nominatim, feminini vel nominatim vel inter ceteros: Quod si neque heredes instituti fuerint neque ita, ut supra diximus, exheredati, praetor promittit eis contra tabulas bonorum possessionem.*

> Inst.Gai.2.135.: Emancipated children need, under the *ius civile* neither be appointed as heirs nor disinherited because they are not direct heirs under the *ius civile*. The praetor, however, orders all children of both sexes to be disinherited if they are not appointed as heirs; males must be disinherited by name, and females can be disinherited by name or by a general clause. And if they are neither appointed heirs nor disinherited, the praetor, as we have stated above, promises to grant them *bonorum possessio contra tabulas*.

Under the *ius praetorium*, children who have left the *patria potestas* through *emancipatio* had to be disinherited. At the same time, the differentiation between a *filius familias* and other children under the paternal power known from the *ius civile* also applied to the *ius praetorium*. Hence, the emancipated son had to be disinherited by name, whereas the other children could be disinherited by a general clause. If an emancipated child was passed over following these rules, it had no consequences under the *ius civile*. However, the *ius civile* will was invalidated on the level of praetorian law because the praetor granted the child that had been passed over the *bonorum possessio contra tabulas* (literally, 'against the tablets', i.e. 'against the provisions of the will'). So, even though the will was valid according to *ius civile*, it was not the testamentary heir but the emancipated children that had been passed over that were granted the *bonorum possessio contra tabulas*.

We can also discern a praetorian adjustment of the rules of *ius civile* in the *bonorum possessio contra tabulas* for the sake of the children under the paternal power who have been passed over, and whose passing over did not, as was the case of the son, invalidate the will, but led to their participation in the estate by accrual:

> Inst.Gai.2.125.: [...] *licet hae secundum ea, quae diximus, scriptis heredibus dimidiam partem modo detrahant, tamen praetor eis contra tabulas bonorum possessionem promittit, qua ratione extranei heredes a tota hereditate repelluntur [...]*

> Inst.Gai.2.125.: [...] Although according to what we have said, the heirs named in the will are only deprived of half the estate by these persons [children of the testator]; still, as the praetor promises to give the latter *bonorum possessio contra tabulas*, and following this principle, outside heirs are entirely excluded from the entire estate [...]

As we saw, the passing over of descendants of the *pater familias* – other than sons – namely, daughters under the paternal power or grandchildren, did not invalidate the will but caused accrual of the share of persons passed over, at the expense of the appointed heir (Ch. 7.1.3). Through the *bonorum possessio contra tabulas*, the praetor went beyond what the *ius civile* permitted. He granted the direct heirs, to the extent that they competed with the *extranei*, not half, as they would have been entitled to under the *ius civile*, but the entire estate. However, regarding other children under the paternal power, who were appointed as heirs, the *per capita* rules of intestacy remained in place. Later, a rescript by Emperor Antoninus Pius (AD138–161) restricted the broadened scope of the protection for daughters under the paternal power:

> Inst.Gai. 2.126.: [...] *sed nuper imperator Antoninus significavit rescripto suo non plus nancisci feminas per bonorum possessionem, quam quod iure adcrescendi consequerentur. Quod in emancipatarum quoque persona observandum est, ut hae quoque, quod adcrescendi iure habiturae essent, si in potestate fuissent, id ipsum etiam per bonorum possessionem habeant.*

> Inst.Gai.2.126.: [...] but the Emperor Antoninus recently stated in a rescript that women could not obtain more by *bonorum possessio* than they would by the right of accrual. This rule should also be observed in the case of emancipated women; that is, they will obtain exactly the same share through *bonorum possessio* as they would have obtained by the right of accrual, if they had remained under the *potestas* of their father.

The rescript by Antoninus Pius provided that women granted the *bonorum possessio contra tabulas* under the ius *praetorium* would get no more than they would have received as an accrual under the *ius civile*. As Gaius stressed, this restriction applied both to women under the paternal power and those emancipated. The latter were not entitled under the *ius civile* to accrual but were treated as *filiae familias* under the *ius praetorium* following the principle of equal treatment of all descendants.

In general, the praetor aimed at extending the protection of inheritance expectations to the *emancipati*. But he also wanted to exclude the *extranei* from the estate of the father if the latter did not declare a disinheritance of his children under his paternal power by a general clause. Hence, praetorian law, too, with its rules of disinheritance, evidently adheres to the principle of family succession, even though it defines *familias*, as we saw in the rules of intestacy (Ch. 3.2.2), differently from the *ius civile*. The most essential praetorian creation in this context is the *bonorum possessio contra tabulas*:

> *Ulpianus, 39 ad edictum: In contra tabulas bonorum possessione liberos accipere debemus sive naturales sive adoptivos, si neque instituti neque exheredati sunt. (D.37.4.1pr.)*

> Ulpian, Edict, book 39: Regarding the *bonorum possessio contra tabulas*, we must understand 'children' as both natural and adopted children if they have neither been appointed heirs nor disinherited. (D.37.4.1pr.)

The *bonorum possessio contra tabulas* was granted to every child of the decedent, provided the child–parent relationship existed, either through birth or adoption. Under the praetorian law, the protection of the inheritance expectancy depended decisively on kinship between father and child. Therefore, the emancipated children of both genders and the descendants under the paternal power, who hoped to better themselves under the praetorian law compared to the *ius civile*, were entitled to claim *bonorum possessio contra tabulas*. Only the (passed-over) *filius familias* was exempt from praetorian protection because he was already comprehensively protected under the *ius civile*. Moreover, since his passing-over annulled the father's will, he could also claim the *bonorum possessio ab intestato*.

The essential requirement for the *bonorum possessio contra tabulas* was the *praeterire* of a descendant. Hence, a descendant appointed by will could not claim the *bonorum possessio contra tabulas*:

> *Ulpianus, 39 ad edictum: Si quis ex liberis heres scriptus sit, ad contra tabulas bonorum possessionem vocari non debet: Cum enim possit secundum tabulas habere possessionem, quo bonum est ei contra tabulas dari? [...] (D.37.4.3.11.)*

> Ulpian, Edict, book 39: If one of the children is appointed heir, he must not be permitted to receive *bonorum possessio contra tabulas*. For when he is entitled to *bonorum possessio secundum tabulas*, how would it benefit to give him *bonorum possessio contra tabulas*? [...] (D.37.4.3.11.)

The child appointed as heir, is entitled to the *bonorum possessio secundum tabulas*, so there is no reason to allow it to claim *contra tabulas*.

The descendant thus appointed, however, can, in exceptional cases benefit from an alien *bonorum possessio contra tabulas*, i.e. demand to be considered for a share in a *bonorum possessio contra tabulas* of another descendant.

7.2.2 Entitlement to an Alien bonorum possessio contra tabulas

Entitlement to an alien *bonorum possessio* (*bonorum possessio commisso per alium edicto*) is recognised when direct heirs who have been appointed as heirs in the will compete with direct heirs who have been passed over in the same will:

> *Ulpianus, 39 ad edictum: [...] plane si alius committat edictum, et ipse ad contra tabulas bonorum possessionem admittetur. (D.37.4.3.11.)*

> Ulpian, Edict, book 39: [...], however, if somebody else is entitled under the edict, he [the child appointed as heir] will also be admitted to the *bonorum possessio contra tabulas*. (D.37.4.3.11.)

If a descendant who was passed over is entitled to claim the *bonorum possessio contra tabulas*, the praetor grants his *bonorum possessio* also to the descendants who were appointed as heirs in the same will. Their entitlement to an alien *bonorum possessio* can be explained by the equal treatment of all descendants that characterises the praetorian order on intestacy. Since the child that was passed over would not have received the entire estate on intestacy, it must share the *bonorum possessio contra tabulas* with all other descendants. Since both descendants were equally entitled to inherit on intestacy under praetorian law, they were allowed to equal shares if the will had become inoperative through the praetorian *bonorum possessio contra tabulas*.

Only the decedent's descendants who had been effectively disinherited were excluded from a share in the *bonorum possessio*:

> *Ulpianus, 40 ad edictum: Non putavit praetor exheredatione notatos et remotos ad contra tabulas bonorum possessionem admittendos, sicuti nec iure civili testamenta parentium turbant: [...] (D.37.4.8pr.)*

> Ulpian, Edict, book 40: The praetor believed that children who had been disgraced and excluded [from the succession] by disinheritance, should not be permitted to obtain *bonorum possessio contra tabulas* and, just as they could not disturb the wills of their *pater familias* under the *ius civile* [...] (D.37.4.8pr.)

A disinheritance valid under the *ius civile* (or *ius praetorium*) also prevents the praetorian succession against the will (*bonorum possessio contra tabulas*). Logically, it also impedes the participation in an alien *bonorum possessio contra tabulas*. This consequence can be explained by the fact that the rules of disinheritance only offered protection against the passing over of (emancipated) descendants, but did not guarantee a share in the estate.

The equal treatment of the *emancipatus* with the child under the paternal power provided for by the *bonorum possessio contra tabulas* entails that the *emancipatus* not only partakes in the paternal estate, but is also obliged to contribute his own property to the *bonorum possessio* against the will (*collatio bonorum*, 'contribution to the estate').

7.2.3 The collatio bonorum

The obligation of the *emancipatus* to contribute his property to the estate finds its justification in the situation of the children under the paternal power as direct heirs compared to the emancipated child. In fact, partaking in the estate of the *pater familias* provided a form of compensation for the children who had remained under the paternal power due to their incapacity to own property during the lifetime of the *pater familias*. In contrast, the *emancipatus* had already obtained the legal capacity to acquire property for himself. Thus, the *emancipatus* had to contribute his property if he wanted his share of the family estate through the *bonorum possessio contra tabulas*:

> *Ulpianus, 40 ad edictum: pr. Hic titulus manifestam habet aequitatem: Cum enim praetor ad bonorum possessionem contra tabulas emancipatos admittat participesque faciat cum his, qui sunt in potestate, bonorum paternorum: Consequens esse credit, ut sua quoque bona in medium conferant, qui appetant paterna.*
> *(1) Inter eos dabitur collatio, quibus possessio data est. (D.37.6.1pr.–1.)*
>
> Ulpian, Edict, book 40: pr. This section [of the edict] is certainly inspired by equity: since the praetor allows emancipated children to obtain the *bonorum possessio contra tabulas* and makes them partake in the paternal estate together with those who are under the paternal power of the decedent, he [the praetor] holds that it is logical that those who seek the paternal estate should also contribute their own estate into the total mass.
> 1. The *collatio bonorum* will take place between those to whom *possessio bonorum* is given. (D.37.6.1pr.–1.)

Therefore, according to the edict on the contribution to the estate (*collatio bonorum*), the *emancipatus* could not unilaterally benefit from the father's estate through the *bonorum possessio contra tabulas*, but had to share the property he had acquired as an *emancipatus* with the children under the paternal power who had a share in the estate. It follows from the idea of compensation that the obligation of the emancipated child to contribute to the estate only favours the children under the paternal power, but not other *emancipati*:

> *Iulianus, 23 digestorum: [...] Quotiens contra tabulas bonorum possessio datur, emancipati bona sua conferre debent his solis, qui in potestate patris fuerint. [...]. Ponamus patrem quadringenta reliquisse et duos in potestate filios, duos emancipatos, ex quibus alterum centum, alterum sexaginta in bonis habere: Is qui centum habebit centum triginta tria et trientem feret, is vero qui sexaginta contulerit centum viginti, atque ita eveniet, ut collationis emolumentum ad solos, qui in potestate remanserint, perveniat. (D.37.6.3.2.)*

> Julian, Digest, book 23: [...] Whenever *bonorum possessio contra tabulas* is given, the emancipated sons must contribute their property only in favour of those who remained under the power of their father. [...]. Suppose a father leaves four hundred sesterces, two sons are under his paternal power, and two have been emancipated. Of the latter, one will have one hundred and the other sixty sesterces in his estate. So the one who is entitled to a hundred will receive one hundred and thirty-three and a third in total. The one who contributed sixty will receive a hundred and twenty, so that the result will be that merely those who remained under their father's power will benefit from the contributions to the father's estate. (D.37.6.3.2.)

Julian explained the rule according to which the *collatio bonorum* applied only to the children who had remained under the paternal power, and used this example to illustrate the consequences of this rule for the *emancipatus*. In the case in question, the decedent had left four sons, two of whom were under the paternal power and two of whom were emancipated. The decedent's estate was four hundred, that of the first *emancipatus* (A) one hundred, and that of the second *emancipatus* (B) sixty. According to the rules of *collatio bonorum*, the property of the *emancipati* must be shared only with the children under the paternal power, but not among the emancipati themselves. The *emancipatus* A therefore shares one hundred with the two sons under the paternal power, so that each of them takes 33 1/3. Similarly, the *emancipatus* B shares his property with the two sons under the paternal power, so that each of them receives 20. The inheritance shares are therefore as follows: A gets 133 1/3, B one 120, whereas the two sons under the paternal power each obtain the amount of 153 1/3 (100 + 33 1/3 + 20). Thus, only the sons under the paternal power benefit from the *collatio bonorum*, while the *emancipati* are unlikely to have any interest in participating in the inheritance because of the obligation to contribute their own property to the father's estate.

Overview 30: Julian's Example of *collatio bonorum*

the *pater familias* leaves an estate of 400 due to a *praeterire* of one or two *emancipati* the *bonorum possessio contra tabulas* applies; hence, the *collatio bonorum*			
emancipatus A: 100	*emancipatus* B: 60	*filius familias* 1	*filius familias* 2
100	100	100	100
+33 1/3		+33 1/3	+33 1/3
	+20	+20	+20
133 1/3	120	153 1/3	153 1/3

Whether the *bonorum possessio contra tabulas* is economically advantageous for an *emancipatus* depends mainly on the value of his property in relation to the paternal estate and the number of direct heirs. The figures shown in Overview 31 illustrate this link:

Overview 31: Economical Reasons for the Claim of *bonorum possessio contra tabulas* by an *emancipatus*

property		eligibility to inherit/ share of the estate	claim of *bonorum possessio contra tabulas*
of the *pater familias*	*emancipatus*		
100 / 200	100	4 (+ *emancipatus*): 40	no
50 / 150	100	4 (+ *emancipatus*): 30	no
100 / 150	50	4 (+*emancipatus*): 30	no
100 / 140	40	4 (+*emancipatus*): 28	no
100 / 110	10	4 (+*emancipatus*): 22	yes
100 / 200	100	1 (+*emancipatus*): 100	no
100 / 150	50	1 (+*emancipatus*): 75	yes

Overview 31 shows that the *emancipatus'* claim to the *bonorum possessio contra tabulas* is only economically advantageous to him if his assets are few compared to the inheritance of the *pater familias*. Also, the *emancipatus* is more likely to benefit from his father's estate if there are few direct heirs with whom he must share his property by *collatio bonorum*. Therefore, both the size of the estate of the *pater familias* compared to that of the *emancipatus* and the expected number of co-heirs are the decisive factors.

As we have seen, both statutory and testamentary heirs can participate in the alien *bonorum possessio contra tabulas* as co-heirs of the *emancipatus* and the other children under the paternal power. Their respective shares are calculated according to the rules of intestacy. The children of the *pater familias* inherit in equal shares under the *bonorum possessio contra tabulas*.

Specific rules apply when direct heirs succeed in the line, e.g. *postumi* instead of the emancipated *filius familias* (Ch. 7.1.4).

7.2.4 The Succeeding of Children under the Paternal Power under the Praetor's Edict

The emancipation of *filii* (pl. *of filius*) *familias* from the *patria potestas* has the consequence under the *ius civile*, that children (grandchildren of the testator) succeed in their place and must either be appointed as *postumi* or be disinherited. The principle of stirpital representation of *ius civile* also applies to the *ius praetorium*:

> *Ulpianus, 39 ad edictum: Vocantur autem ad contra tabulas bonorum possessionem liberi eo iure eoque ordine, quo vocantur ad successionem ex iure civili. (D.37.4.1.1.)*
>
> Ulpian, Edict, book 39: However, children are called to the *bonorum possessio contra tabulas* by the same right and in the same order as they are called to the succession under the *ius civile*. (D.37.4.1.1.)

The application of the stirpital principle also to praetorian law meant that the *emancipates*, who had been passed over in his father's will, barred his own children, i.e. the testator's grandchildren, from the claim of *bonorum possessio contra tabulas*, even if they had also been passed over. It is only when the *emancipatus* died that his children or grandchildren took his place and, if they had been passed over in their grandfather's will, could claim the *bonorum possessio contra tabulas*.

The principle of representation could not help to decide cases, where direct heirs who descended from the emancipated son and who had taken his place under the *ius civile*, competed over their (grand-)father's inheritance. Indeed, under *ius civile*, the direct heirs enjoyed priority over the emancipated son, whereas under *ius praetorium*, he barred his descendants. However, a direct conflict could easily occur, when an *emancipatus* had been passed over and claimed *bonorum possessio contra tabulas*. As we saw, as direct heirs his children could profit from his claim (Ch. 7.2.2) and would thus directly compete regarding the (grand-)father's estate. The *edictum perpetuum* promulgated in AD130 by Emperor Hadrian (AD117–138) provides an innovative solution for these cases, called '*nova clausula Iuliani*' ('Julian's new clause') (Ch. 3.3.2). The name suggests that the rule is of imperial provenance and has been created by the jurist Julian who is known to have been the drafter of Hadrian's edict:

Ulpianus, 40 ad edictum: Si quis ex his, quibus bonorum possessionem praetor pollicetur, in potestate parentis, cum is moritur, non fuerit, ei liberisque quos in eiusdem familia habuit, si ad eos hereditas suo nomine pertinebit neque notam exheredationis meruerunt, bonorum possessio eius partis datur, quae ad eum pertineret, si in potestate permansisset, ita ut ex ea parte dimidiam, reliquam liberi eius hisque dumtaxat bona sua conferat. (D.37.8.1pr.)

Ulpian, Edict, book 40: If one of those to whom the praetor promises *bonorum possessio* was not under the *patria potestas* at the time of the death of the *pater familias*, then he [the emancipated son] and the children he had in the [decedent's] *familias*, if they were entitled to the inheritance and if they have not deserved the disgrace of disinheritance, shall be granted *bonorum possessio* for the share that would have been his if he had remained under the *potestas*. [This is done] in such a way that he [receives] half of this share and his children the other half, and that he only contributes his property to them (*collatio bonorum*). (D.37.8.1pr.)

The clause provided that the emancipated son and the grandchildren who descended from him, but had been under the power of their grandfather, were to be counted as one *stirps* (stem). Thus, the (fictitious) share that the son would have received under the *ius civile* if he had remained in the *potestas* of his father was divided between him and his children under the scope of the *bonorum possessio contra tabulas*. At the same time, the obligation of *collatio bonorum* of the *emancipatus* was limited to his descendants, i.e. it did not extend beyond his own stem. This collective consideration of both the grandchildren and the *emancipatus* required that neither of them had been duly disinherited and that all of them were therefore eligible for the *bonorum possessio contra tabulas*.

In sum, the *nova clausula Iuliani* struck a balance between the requirements of the two layers of law that could not have been achieved by the principle of stirpital representation alone:

Ulpianus, 40 ad edictum: Hoc edictum aequissimum est, ut neque emancipatus solus veniat et excludat nepotes in potestate manentes, neque nepotes iure potestatis obiciantur patri suo. (D.37.8.1.1.)

Ulpian, Edict, book 40: This edict is of the utmost equity, so that neither the emancipated son is admitted [to the estate] alone and excludes the grandsons who remain under the *patria potestas*, nor that the grandsons are opposed to their father on the ground that they were under the power of the decedent. (D.37.8.1.1.)

Ulpian (third century AD) perceived the *nova clausula Iuliani* as a precept of *aequitas*, because the regulation protected the *emancipatus* against a *praeterire* and preserved the grandchildren's status as direct heirs. In addition, the *emancipatus*' siblings are protected against a reduction of their share, as the *stirps* of the *emancipatus* does not benefit twice.

Overview 32: The Effects of the *nova clausula Iuliani*

pater familias (the will passes over the *emancipatus*)				
emancipatus (son 1)	grandchild 1	grandchild 2	son 2	son 3
bonorum possessio contra tabulas	direct heirs (*sui heredes*)			
nova clausula Iuliani	son 1 (*emancipatus*) grandchild 1 and 2		son 2	son 3
	1/3 and *collatio bonorum* through the *emancipatus*		1/3	1/3

The *nova clausula Iuliani* shows the effort to find a balance between the eligibility to inherit according to *ius civile* and the eligibility to take the estate according to *ius praetorium*. This effort is not only apparent in the Empire, but can be traced back to the praetorian rules of *bonorum possessio contra tabulas*. Thus, edicts annexed to the *bonorum possessio contra tabulas* recognised certain legal effects of a will that was valid under *ius civile* but inoperative under *ius praetorium*.

7.3 The Partial Validity of the Will under the *ius praetorium*

The *bonorum possessio contra tabulas* implied the praetor's disregard of the will valid under the *ius civile*. In fact, the praetor invalidated the will in the interest of the *emancipatus* who had been passed over (Ch. 7.2.1). This abrogation of the *ius civile*, however, was reversed when other interests worthy of protection demanded a restriction of the *bonorum possessio contra tabulas*. As we have seen above (Ch. 7.2.4), the inheritance expectations of the children who have succeeded in their father's position and of the siblings of the *emancipatus* are considered to be worthy of protection. In the same way, the praetor protected the inheritance expectations created by the will itself by imposing on the *bonorum possessor contra tabulas* the obligation to fulfil the legacies set out in the testament. This requirement was based on a special edict titled: 'on the fulfilment of legacies' (*de legatis praestandis*).

7.3.1 The Edict de legatis praestandis

The requirement on the part of the *bonorum possessor* to fulfil a legacy from an inoperative will only applied in favour of certain persons who were close to the testator:

> *Ulpianus, 40 ad edictum: Hic titulus aequitatem quandam habet naturalem et ad aliquid novam, ut, qui iudicia patris rescindunt per contra tabulas bonorum possessionem, ex iudicio eius quibusdam personis legata et fideicommissa praestarent, hoc est liberis et parentibus, uxori nuruique dotis nomine legatum. (D.37.5.1pr.)*

> Ulpian, Edict, book 40: This section [of the edict] displays a certain natural equity and, in some matters, a new equity, so that those who annul the will of the father by the *bonorum possessio contra tabulas* [nevertheless] fulfil the legacies and *fideicommissa* towards certain persons according to the father's wishes. This is for the benefit of the children, the parents, the wife and the daughters-in-law with regard to what is left to them as dowry. (D.37.5.1pr.)

The obligation of the *bonorum possessor contra tabulas* to fulfil the legacies and *fideicommissa* of the will was seen as a precept of natural equity (*aequitas naturalis*) and of a new equity (*aequitas nova*). Both were concerned with reconciling the interests of those named in the will with the *emancipatus* who had been passed over. Only the general inheritance expectations of the testator and the parents of the testator as well as the expectation of a dowry by the testator's wife or daughter-in-law were considered worthy of protection. If the testator had left bequests in favour of the aforementioned persons, they were exempted from the consequences of the *bonorum possessio contra tabulas*, and their bequests were therefore considered valid:

> *Ulpianus, 40 ad edictum: Generaliter parentes et liberos praetor excepit nec gradus liberorum parentiumve enumeravit: in infinitum igitur eis praestabitur. Sed nec personas prosecutus est, utrum ex virili sexu an ex feminino descendent. Quisquis igitur ex liberis parentibusque fuerit, ad legati petitionem admittetur, sed ita demum, si iura cognationis sunt inter eos. (D.37.5.1.1.)*

> Ulpian, Edict, book 40: The praetor has made a general exception for ancestors and descendants, without taking into account the degrees of relationship of children or parents; thus [the fulfilment of legacies] will be granted to them by unlimited degrees. But he has also made no distinction as to whether the persons descended from the male or female line. Therefore, whoever comes from the line of children and parents will be allowed to claim the legacy only if there were ties of cognatic kinship between them [the testator and the legatee]. (D.37.5.1.1.)

All those who are directly related to the descendant are spared (*personae exceptae*, 'persons exempt') from the sanction of the will by the *bonorum possessio contra tabulas*. There is no restriction according to degrees of kinship and no distinction is made between agnatic and cognatic kinship. The only prerequisite is that the person is related in a direct line and has received a legacy from the testator. The related legatee's expectation, concretised by the will, can be held against the *bonorum possessor contra tabulas*.

It should be noted that only the *emancipatus* is obliged to fulfil the legacies. This is important, e.g., if the testator has passed over both a *filius familias* and an *emancipatus*:

> *Paulus, 41 ad edictum: Is qui in potestate est praeteritus legata non debebit praestare, etsi contra tabulas bonorum possessionem petierit, quia et non petita bonorum possessione intestati hereditatem optineret: [...] (D.37.5.15pr.)*

> Paul, Edict, book 41: Someone who was under the paternal power and was passed over will not be obligated to fulfil legacies, even if he has demanded the *bonorum possessio contra tabulas*, because he would also obtain the inheritance, even if he had not demanded the *bonorum possessio intestati* [...] (D.37.5.15pr.)

The *praeterire* of a *filius familias* invalidated the will according to *ius civile*, so that the *filius familias* could apply for the *bonorum possessio intestati* (Ch. 7.2) and also become the direct owner of the estate as direct heir. In contrast, the *emancipatus* could demand the *bonorum possessio contra tabulas*, since his *praeterire* was only relevant according to the *ius praetorium* and a testamentary document was nonetheless available. The structure of the praetorian edict, which primarily promises the *bonorum possessio* when a will is available and only secondarily regulates the *bonorum possessio* in the absence of a will (Ch. 4.2.1), has the consequence that the *bonorum possessio contra tabulas* of the *emancipatus* takes precedence over the *bonorum possessio intestati* of the *filius familias*. As we have seen, however, the *filius familias* who has not been effectively disinherited can participate in the alien *bonorum possessio contra tabulas*; both sons therefore share the *bonorum possessio contra tabulas*. However, the obligation of the *bonorum possessor contra tabulas* to fulfil legacies did not apply to the *filius familias*, who would have been entitled to apply for the *bonorum possessio* on the basis of intestacy. If both an *emancipatus* who had been passed over and a direct heir who had been passed over applied for the *bonorum possessio contra tabulas*, the estate had to be divided:

> *Tryphoninus, 19 disputationum: Legata tamen ex parte sua iste emancipatus liberis et parentibus praestare cogetur non solida, sed deminuta in dimidium, quod relinquitur manenti in potestate. Sed nec adversus eum constituendae actionis legatorum ratio est, qui mero iure intestato heres exstitit. (D.37.4.20.2.)*

> Tryphoninus, Disputations, book 19: The *emancipatus*, however, will be compelled to fulfil the legacies from his share to the children and parents, though not in full, but reduced by half, which he has left to the *filius familias*. But there is also no reason to allow a claim against him [the *filius familias*] for the legacies, since he has rightfully become the heir on intestacy. (D.37.4.20.2.)

As Tryphoninus (third century AD) points out, the emancipated son, who has been admitted to the *bonorum possessio contra tabulas*, must fulfil the legacies according to this share, i.e. half. In contrast, the son under the paternal power, who shares the *bonorum possessio* with him as a direct heir, is not obliged to fulfil.

The coexistence of intestate succession (*filius familias*) and testamentary succession (*emancipatus*) thus achieved shows that the strict separation between intestate and testamentary succession, which initially dominated the *ius civile* (*nemo pro parte testatus, pro parte intestatus decedere potest* Ch. 4), could not be maintained in the *ius praetorium* of the Empire. Moreover, juristic interpretation from Julian onwards (second century AD) even advocated treating the testamentary appointments as valid alongside the *bonorum possessio contra tabulas*.

7.3.2 Preserving a Share of the Inheritance

The functional equivalence of bequests and shares of the inheritance when it comes to providing for close relatives was cited as justification for this development in the law:

> *Ulpianus, 40 ad edictum: Sed et si portio hereditatis fuerit adscripta ei, qui ex liberis parentibusve est, an ei conservanda sit, ut solent legata? Et Iulianus saepissime scripsit in portione quoque hereditatis idem quod in legato probandum [...] (D.37.5.5.6.)*

Ulpian, Edict, book 40: But even if a share of the inheritance has been ascribed to a descendant or ascendant, does it have to be preserved for him, as is customary for legacies? And Julian has repeatedly stated that one must also approve with regard to the share of the inheritance the same that applies with regard to the legacy [...] (D.37.5.5.6.)

The edict *de legatis praestandis* was also applicable if the exempted persons did not receive a legacy but were appointed as heirs. Since the purpose of both the appointment of an heir and the bequest of a legacy was to ensure the livelihood of close relatives and to provide for them in the future, the Roman jurists applied the legal consequences of the edict *de legatis praestandis* mutatis mutandis also to the appointment of an heir. This extension of the edict *de legatis praestandis* to the appointment of heirs was laid down in imperial law:

Ulpianus, 40 ad edictum: [...] cuius sententia rescripto divi Pii comprobata est, cum hereditates non modo honestiore titulo, sed et pleniore onere tribuantur. (D.37.5.5.6.)

Ulpian, Edict, book 40: [...] whose opinion [of Julian] was confirmed by a rescript of the deified Pius, since inheritances are assigned [to someone] not only as an honourable title, but also as a more significant burden [compared to legacies]. (D.37.5.5.6.)

The rescript of Emperor Antoninus Pius (AD138–161) addresses the technical difference between the appointment of an heir and a legacy, but declares it to be of secondary importance. It states that the title of 'heir' is not only honorific (*honor institutionis*), but also serves to benefit the person appointed. In this respect, there was no difference between a legacy and an appointment. Rather, the appointment as heir was more solidly beneficial, and should therefore also be taken into account when applying the edict *de legatis praestandis*. As a result, the *bonorum possessor* had to share his estate with the appointed heirs if the latter belonged to the circle of the *personae exceptae*.

In this way, both the *emancipatus* challenging the will (*bonorum possessio contra tabulas*) and the testamentary heir have a share in the estate. One could therefore speak of a 'partial invalidity' of the will. Such invalidity is characterised by the fact that the praetorian annulment of the civil will does not affect all beneficiaries of the will. Insofar as the testator has appointed descendants or parents as heirs or has made them beneficiaries of legacies, these orders remain in force even after the passed over *emancipatus* has been granted the *bonorum possessio contra tabulas*. This seemingly paradoxical outcome manifests the complexity of the praetorian rules of disinheritance. In fact, the praetorian edict had created a nuanced system to protect the various inheritance expectations under the title of the *bonorum possessio contra tabulas*.

Overview 33: The System of *bonorum possessio contra tabulas*

protection of the *emancipatus* from being passed over (*praeterire*) = edict on the *bonorum possessio contra tabulas*			
equal treatment of all descendants on intestacy	protection of direct heirs as 'natural' heirs	principle of stirpital representation and protection of the direct heirs	preservation of the testator's will
option to participate in an alien *bonorum possessio contra tabulas*	duty of the *emancipatus* to *collatio bonorum*	*nova clausula Iuliani*: joining of *emancipatus* and grandchildren in the son's ficticious share	duty of the *bonorum possessor* to fulfil a legacy (expansion on inheritances)

While the *ius praetorium* already tended to weigh up the conflicting interests in the individual case and to treat wills as partially valid, depending on the persons involved, the imperial law established a genuine control of the content of the will. Based on this, the claim against a will was no longer limited to objecting that the disinheritance was formally incorrect or had been omitted. Rather, it could also be claimed that the disinheritance was unjustified and that the allocated inheritance share or the bequested amount was unjustly inadequate.

7.4 The Complaint about Undutiful Will

The 'complaint about undutiful will' (*querela inofficiosi testamenti*) was a specific action under the imperial jurisdiction. It had its roots in the Republic and was probably originally a complaint of a moral nature. It went, in fact, against the sense of duty towards the family (*pietas*) not to sufficiently consider parents and descendants in a will or even to disinherit them. Compliance with this duty was probably initially monitored by the censors. The *cognitio extra ordinem* of the Empire turned it into an actionable obligation.

7.4.1 The Undutiful Will

The complaint is raised with the claim that the will has been made undutifully:

> Marcellus, 3 digestorum: *Inofficiosum testamentum dicere hoc est allegare, quare exheredari vel praeteriri non debuerit: Quod plerumque accidit, cum falso parentes instimulati liberos suos vel exheredant vel praetereunt.* (D.5.2.3.)
>
> Marcellus, Digest, book 3: To say that a will is undutiful is to claim why one should not have been disinherited or passed over. This mainly happens

because parents are influenced to disinherit or pass over their children by a false suspicion. (D.5.2.3.)

A will is considered 'undutiful' if it contains a disinheritance or passing over without justification. Parents disinheriting their children on account of a false suspicion is an example of this. The testamentary disregard for a child without reasonable cause cannot be justified. A testator who nonetheless has passed over, or did not sufficiently consider a child or parent cannot not have truly wanted this:

> *Marcianus, 4 institutionum: Hoc colore inofficioso testamento agitur, quasi non sanae mentis fuerunt, ut testamentum ordinarent. Et hoc dicitur non quasi vere furiosus vel demens testatus sit, sed recte quidem fecit testamentum, sed non ex officio pietatis: [...] (D.5.2.2.)*

> Marcian, Institutes, book 4: A complaint about undutiful will is usually made colourful with the assertion that the testators had not been of sound mind, when they made their will. This is not meant to say that he was actually insane or demented when he made his will, but that he made it according to law, yet not in the way familial duty dictates [...] (D.5.2.2.)

Thus, the complaint is based on the premise that the testator has committed an error in judgement when drawing up his will and has, therefore, wrongly disinherited or has not sufficiently considered the offspring or parent by mistake. Marcian (third century AD) stressed that the complaint about undutiful will was not aimed at declaring the testator insane or legally incapable of making a will. Instead, it purported to emendate the manifest intention in the will because it was mistaken or disregarded family obligation:

> *Paulus, 2 quaestionum: Cum contra testamentum ut inofficiosum iudicatur, testamenti factionem habuisse defunctus non creditur. [...] (D.5.2.17.1.)*

> Paul, Questions, book 2: When judgment is rendered against a testament as being undutiful, the decedent is held to have been lacking the *testamenti factio*. [...] (D.5.2.17.1.)

The aim of the *querela inofficiosi testamenti* was thus to declare the testator incapable of making a will. If the complaint was successful, the will became inoperative:

> *Ulpianus, 14 ad edictum: Si quis ex his personis, quae ad successionem ab intestato non admittuntur, de inofficioso egerit (nemo enim eum repellit) et casu optinuerit, non ei prosit victoria, sed his qui habent ab intestato successionem: Nam intestatum patrem familias facit. (D.5.2.6.1.)*

> Ulpian, Edictum, book 14: If someone with no right to succession by intestacy brings forth a complaint about undutiful will (and nobody contests his right to do so) and by chance succeeds, his victory will not benefit him, but only those who are entitled to the succession on intestacy because he makes the *pater familias* intestate. (D.5.2.6.1.)

The will was even considered invalid if persons who were not heirs on intestacy challenged the will as undutiful. Though the latter did not stand to profit from the annulment of the will, the complaint was effective, i.e. it led to intestate succession. Hence, the heirs on intestacy, both under the *ius civile* and *ius praetorium* were called upon (Ch. 3):

> *Ulpianus, 14 ad edictum: Si ex causa de inofficiosi cognoverit iudex et pronuntiaverit contra testamentum nec fuerit provocatum, ipso iure rescissum est: Et suus heres erit secundum quem iudicatum est et bonorum possessor, si hoc se contendit: [...] (D.5.2.8.16.)*

> Ulpian, Edict, book 14: If a judge has examined a case of an undutiful will and delivered a judgment against the will, and no appeal was brought forth, the will is automatically nullified. The party who succeeds will become the decedent's direct heir and *bonorum possessor* [of the estate] if he claims it [...] (D.5.2.8.16.)

Once the judge declared the will inoperative, the order of succession on intestacy set in. If the claimant was a statutory heir, he could claim the *bonorum possessio ab intestato*.

However, the will would not always become completely invalid. Notably, if several persons were instituted as heirs, it could occur that the estate had to be split after individual complaints against each of them had resulted in different outcomes.

7.4.2 A Complaint against Several Heirs

Contradictory decisions against various testamentary heirs were probable because the competency of the court depended on the place of residence of the appointed heir:

> *Ulpianus, 5 opinionum: In ea provincia de inofficioso testamento agi oportet, in qua scripti heredes domicilium habent. (D.5.2.29.4.)*

> Ulpian, Opinions, book 5: A complaint about undutiful will must be brought in the province where the testamentary heirs reside. (D.5.2.29.4.)

Since the competency of the court depended on the place of residence of the appointed heir, it could happen that if several heirs were appointed, the claim had to be split among several jurisdictions, which carried with it an elevated risk of contradictory decisions:

> *Ulpianus, 48 ad Sabinum: Circa inofficiosi querellam evenire plerumque adsolet, ut in una atque eadem causa diversae sententiae proferantur. Quid enim si fratre agente heredes scripti diversi iuris fuerunt? Quod si fuerit, pro parte testatus, pro parte intestatus decessisse videbitur. (D.5.2.24.)*
>
> Ulpian, Sabinus, book 48: Concerning the complaint about undutiful will, two different judgments are often delivered for the same case. What, e.g., if the brother started proceedings and the appointed heirs had different legal standing [with regard to the claim]? In this case, the decedent will be held to have died partly testate and partly intestate. (D.5.2.24.)

According to Ulpian, it could even happen that the various courts where the complaint had been brought forth decided differently; hence, one court could grant the complaint while the other dismissed the case. In the example above, the testator's brother had filed a complaint against individual co-heirs at various courts and was successful only in some cases. As a consequence, the will was only partially invalid, and the testamentary heir succeeded the testator for the part it had not been declared undutiful. As far as the complaint had been successful, the claimant, i.e. the testator's brother, succeeded on intestacy. This split of the estate also applied to the creditors of the estate:

> *Papinianus, 14 quaestionum: Filius, qui de inofficiosi actione adversus duos heredes expertus diversas sententias iudicum tulit et unum vicit, ab altero superatus est, et debitores convenire et ipse a creditoribus conveniri pro parte potest et corpora vindicare et hereditatem dividere: [...] (D.5.2.15.2.)*
>
> Papinian, Questions, book 14: A son brought a complaint against two heirs about undutiful will and has obtained different decisions from the judges, defeating one heir and being defeated by the other. He can sue the debtors of the estate, and the creditors may sue him to the extent of his share. He can, moreover, claim property and divide the estate [...]. (D.5.2.15.2.)

A son had lodged a complaint against two of the appointed heirs about undutiful will. The complaint was successful against one of the heirs but not against the other. As far as the son received the estate on intestacy, he could also be held liable by the estate's creditors because he was seen as an heir only to the extent that the complaint had been successful.

Despite the risk of contradictory decisions, the *querela inofficiosi testamenti* was a powerful remedy in the hands of a relative who believed he had been disinherited without justification or had not been adequately considered. The main reason for this is that the *querela*, like other imperial legal developments, directly altered the *ius civile*. Unlike the praetorian *bonorum possessio contra tabulas*, which could lead to the (partial) disrespect of a will, the *querela* automatically nullified the will insofar as it proved to be undutiful.

Because their consequences differ, questions of demarcation between the imperial complaint and the protection of inheritance expectancies under the *ius civile* and *ius praetorium* are frequent and difficult to resolve.

7.4.3 Conflict of Actions and Questions of Demarcation

At first sight, no conflict exists between the protection against disinheritance under the *ius civile* and *ius praetorium* on the one hand, and the *querela* on the other, because the former requested a formally valid disinheritance, while the *querela inofficiosi testamenti* examined whether a disinheritance could be justified in term of content. The following fragment is an example of this demarcation:

> *Paulus, liber singularis de inofficioso testamento: Si ponas filium emancipatum praeteritum et ex eo nepotem in potestate retentum heredem institutum esse: Filius potest contra filium suum, testatoris nepotem petere bonorum possessionem, queri autem de inofficioso testamento non poterit. Quod si exheredatus sit filius emancipatus, poterit queri et ita iungetur filio suo et simul cum eo hereditatem optinebit. (D.5.2.23pr.)*

> Paul, On Undutiful Wills, sole book: Consider the case of an emancipated son who has been passed over and a grandson by him, in the power of the testator, is appointed heir. The son can claim *bonorum possessio contra tabulas* against his own son, the testator's grandson, but cannot bring a complaint about undutiful will. But, if the emancipated son has been disinherited, he will be able to bring forth the complaint and, will thus, be joined with his son; therefore, he will obtain the estate along with him. (D.5.2.23pr.)

An *emancipatus* was passed over, while the grandson, who remained under the *patria potestas* of his grandfather was instituted as heir. As the grandfather had passed over his son, the *emancipatus* could claim the *bonorum possessio contra tabulas*. He would only be able to raise the complaint about undutiful will if he had been disinherited. This would open the order of intestacy, hence, would allow a claim for the *bonorum possessio ab intestato*. Following the *nova clausula Iuliani* applying to the rules of intestacy, the son and the grandson would jointly receive the son's (fictional) share (Ch. 3.3.2).

However, as an exception, the *querela* could be raised instead of the *bonorum possessio contra tabulas*. This applied mostly to women, for whom neither disinheritance rules of *ius civile* nor of *ius praetorium* existed:

> *Paulus, liber singularis de septemviralibus iudiciis: Cum mater militem filium falso audisset decessisse et testamento heredes alios instituisset, divus Hadrianus decrevit hereditatem ad filium pertinere ita, ut libertates et legata praestentur. Hic illud adnotandum quod de libertatibus et legatis adicitur: Nam cum inofficiosum testamentum arguitur, nihil ex eo testamento valet. (D.5.2.28.)*
>
> Paul, Jurisdiction of the Septemvirs, sole book: Where a mother heard a false report that her son, a soldier, had died, and thus appointed other heirs, the deified Hadrian decided that her inheritance should belong to the son with the condition that testamentary manumissions and legacies should be kept. What was added about manumissions and legacies should carefully be noted, for where a will is decided to be undutiful, nothing in it is valid. (D.5.2.28.)

A mother has passed over her son because she heard he had fallen in war. Emperor Hadrian (AD117–138) granted the son who brought forth the *querela* the position of heir, whereas he ordered him to fulfil the legacies and manumissions (of slaves). Paul (third century AD) highlights this decision (*decretum*) because it preserved some of the dispositions of an inoperative will. It is in fact notable that Hadrian's *decretum* tallied with that of the edict on legacies for the benefit of certain persons, which applied to the *bonorum possessio contra tabulas* (Ch. 7.3.1). Pursuant to this edict, legacies left to a certain group of persons remained intact even though the praetor invalidated the will. In principle, neither the rules for the *bonorum possessio contra tabulas* nor the edict *de legatis praestandis* were applicable to women's wills. The imperial interpretation of the *querela*, however, served as a substitute to apply the praetorian legal tenets to women that had existed only for men.

The sweeping nature of the complaint facilitated this extended application: a will was undutiful if the testator violated his moral obligations. But what these obligations were and what they entailed were questions of fact that the judge had to decide in any given case. This allowed additional moral obligations to be stated depending on the circumstances, hence, enabling adaptation to societal change. The downside of this malleability of the complaint was the lack of legal certainty. A similar observation applies to the persons protected by the *querela*:

> *Ulpianus, 14 ad edictum: Meminisse autem oportebit eum, qui testamentum inofficiosum improbe dixit et non optinuit, id quod in testamento accepit perdere et id fisco vindicari quasi indigno ablatum. [...](D.5.2.8.14.)*
>
> Ulpian, Edict, book 14: It must be remembered that where a party improperly alleges that a will is undutiful and loses his case, he will also lose what was

left him by the will, and it will be claimed by the imperial treasury as if he had been deprived of the inheritance as an unworthy heir. [...] (D.5.2.8.14.)

If somebody instituted as heir in a will considered the initial benefit inadequate and undutiful, he could challenge the will with the *querela inofficiosi testamenti*. But if he lost the lawsuit because the judge had dismissed the undutifulness, the claimant would lose any entitlement to the estate. The reason for this is that he had wrongly accused the testator of being undutiful and would hence be considered unworthy (*indignus*) to take. The legacy or the share escheated to the treasury as *bona caduca* (Ch. 4.4.3), which can be seen as a punishment of the designated heir. In fact, he should have been more cautious when alleging the undutifulness of the will.

Similar to other legal developments of the Empire, the *querela* is proof of a moralisation of the law of inheritance as well as of the importance of fiscal interests for the growing imperial interventions into last wills and testaments.

Overview 34 puts together the various stages of development of the rules of disinheritance from the ancient *ius civile* to the imperial law.

Overview 34: Stages in the Development of the Rules on Disinheritance

ius civile:	*ius praetorium:*	*imperial law:*
duty to disinherit the *filii familias* by name; other children-in-power by a general clause	duty to disinherit all descendants (including *emancipati*) by name or by a general clause	duty of pietas disinheritance or diminished inheritance only upon justification
consequences:	consequences:	consequences:
nullity of the will, order of intestacy	*bonorum possessio ab intestato* (if void under the *ius civile*) *bonorum possessio contra tabulas* (if void under the *ius praetorium*)	nullity of the will against the instituted heir, against whom the *querela* is raised
problems:	problems:	problems:
conditional appointment of the *filius familias*; disinheritance and appointment of *postumi*	relations of *bonorum possessio contra tabulas* to the *ius civile* (*collatio bonorum, de legatis praestandis*, share to an alien *bonorum possessio*); consideration of postumi (*nova clausula Iuliani*)	imprecisely defined complaint; frequent inconsistent adjudication and split of the estate

7.5 Concluding Considerations on the Rules of Disinheritance

If we comprehensively assess the array of the rules of disinheritance against the background of the three main questions asked at the outset (Ch. 1.3.3), we must highlight, first of all, the parallel development of the layers of law between rules of disinheritance and rules on intestacy.

1. The rules on disinheritance of the *ius civile* protected the direct heirs by prescribing a formal disinheritance for the *pater familias*. In contrast to this, the *ius praetorium* expanded the scope of the protection against disinheritance, especially by regulating the disinherison for *emancipati*. Finally, the law of the Empire, which made the cognatic family equal to the agnatic with respect to intestacy, protected the heir from undutiful treatment by the testator. Thus, it was no longer the form of disinheritance that mattered, but the reason for it. Now the heir could also raise the complaint on the ground that he had not been adequately considered in the will.
2. The principles that apply for the protection against wills in the respective layer of law correspond to the trends already observed with regard to rules on intestacy: for one, in the *ius civile*, the protection of the direct heirs as shareholders of the family property is paramount. At the same time, the freedom of testation, as a freedom to decide about the content of the will, is hailed. The rules addressing the testator pre-eminently concern the form of appointment and disinheritance. The *ius praetorium*, which also clings to formalism as a prerequisite of valid disinheritance, assumes a different notion of familial ties, by emphasising more decidedly the cognatic relations, especially those of the emancipated children to their birth families. At the same time, the *ius praetorium* displays a tendency to settle the differing interests of the heirs under the *ius civile* and *ius praetorium*. These efforts also condition the imperial interventions into the *ius praetorium*. They tend to fuse existing institutions, e.g. the testamentary rule with those of intestacy, and shift to a perspective that was based on the moral outlook of the testator, especially in the *querela inofficiosi testamenti*. Even though this complaint originated in the Republic, the legal control of the testator's motives in the imperial adjudication corresponds to the public interventions in the law of inheritance that set in with the Augustan marital laws. The imperial control invaded the private legal prerogatives of last will and testament.
3. The Roman jurists seem to have been seminal in shaping the rules of inheritance in its various stages. The jurists of the Republic, through their cautelary practice, had a share in the development of testamentary rules of the *ius civile* and, hence, also in the articulation of rules of disinheritance.

The *ius praetorium* too was an area where the jurists were called upon to even out the conflicting interests between testamentary heirs and descendants who had been passed over. Hence, it does not surprise us that the Digest preserves a rich variety of case law for the *bonorum possessio contra tabulas*, including a plethora of juristic controversies. The scope of application of the *querela* during the time of the Empire is preserved in less detail. This might be due to the fact that the gist of this remedy lies in examining questions of fact, namely, assessing whether the will is undutiful. For this moral question, guidelines and examples could be cited that admitted various solutions. But they were limited to particular cases. The legal questions, however, raised by contradictory decisions and the conflict of actions between *bonorum possessio contra tabulas* and *querela inofficiosi testamenti* commanded a broader interest and, therefore, were given priority when the compilers had to decide what to include in the Digest.

8

The Law of Legacies

The legacy (*legatum*) already existed in the law of the twelve tables (*ca.* 450BC), where we find the sentence: '*uti legassit super familia pecuniave tutelave sua, ita ius esto*' (V.3). It is said to have originally regulated a 'will of legacies' (German: 'Legatentestament', Ch. 6.1), i.e., a will consisting merely of a series of bequests to different persons. In the law of the late Republic and the Empire, legacies form the counterpart of the appointment of an heir:

> *Florentinus, 11 institutionum: Legatum est delibatio hereditatis, qua testator ex eo, quod universum heredis foret, alicui quid collatum velit. (D.30.116pr.)*
>
> Florentinus, Institutes, book 11: A legacy is a deduction from an estate whereby a testator wishes that something is given to a person from what would have in its entirety belonged to the heir. (D.30.116pr.)

The legacy reduced the estate that devolved to the heir as the universal successor to the decedent. While the appointment of an heir created a universal succession, the legatee (*legatarius*) received only a single object or a defined number of objects from the estate. The content usually left by legacy is listed in the titles of books 33–34 of the Digest. The titles are: 'annual legacies', 'right of use', 'usufruct', 'income', 'right of habitation and services given by legacies', 'legacies of servitute', '*praelegatum* of dowry', 'legacies of wheat, wine or oil', 'legacy of *instructum* or *instrumentum*', 'the legacy of a *peculium*', 'the legacy of stores' (*penus legata*), 'legacy of furniture', 'aliment or legacies of provisions', 'legacies of gold, silver, toiletries, jewellery, ointments, clothing or garments and statutes', and 'release by will'. All of the aforementioned could be the subject of legacies, whereby this non-exhaustive catalogue already shows that legacies primarily provided for persons who were close to the testator or who were vulnerable and who were to be cared for even after the testator's death.

The variety of objects to a legacy warranted a broad differentiation of rules and consequences. This applied not only to the various layers of law, but also to the *ius civile*. We will therefore examine the rules of *ius civile* applicable to legacies, including the statutory limitations on legacies, before turning to the praetorian protection of a legatee and the imperial developments of the legal rules governing legacies.

8.1 Legacies under the *ius civile*

The *ius civile* recognised four different types of bequest that differed in their justification and consequences:

> Inst.Gai.2.192.: *Legatorum itaque genera sunt quattuor: Aut enim per vindicationem legamus aut per damnationem aut sinendi modo aut per praeceptionem.*

> Inst.Gai.2.192.: Hence, there are four types of legacies: for we make legacies per *vindicationem,* per *damnationem,* by *sinendi modo,* or *per praeceptionem.*

The four categories of legacies of the *ius civile* are the legacy *per vindicationem* that gave a real action, the legacy *per damnationem* that entailed an *actio in personam*, and the two special categories, the legacy *sinendi modo* ('in the manner of allowing') and the legacy *per praeceptionem* ('to take first'). These categories of legacies differ in their requirements and consequences.

8.1.1 Legacy per vindicationem *and* per damnationem

The beneficiary of the legacy *per vindicationem* obtained the most far reaching legal position:

> Inst.Gai.2.194.: *Ideo autem per vindicationem legatum appellatur, quia post aditam hereditatem statim ex iure Quiritium res legatarii fit; et si eam rem legatarius vel ab herede vel ab alio quocumque, qui eam possidet, petat, vindicare debet, id est intendere suam rem ex iure Quiritium esse.*

> Inst.Gai.2.194.: A legacy left *per vindicationem* is so called because after the estate has been accepted, the legatee receives the property of the bequeathed object straightaway under the law of the *Quirites*. And if the legatee claims the bequeathed object from the heir or from anyone else who possesses it, he must bring a *rei vindicatio* to recover it, that is to say, claim that the property is his by the law of the *Quirites*.

The legatee of a legacy *per vindicationem* received ownership of the bequeathed item as soon as the testamentary heir accepted the estate. Therefore, the legatee could claim the item from the heir by an action of *rei vindicatio*. This form of legacy required the use of a particular formula:

> Inst.Gai.2.193.: *Per vindicationem hoc modo legamus: 'Titio' verbi gratia 'hominem Stichum do lego'; sed et si alterutrum verbum positum sit, veluti 'do' aut 'lego,' aeque per vindicationem legatum est: [...]*

Inst.Gai.2.193.: We bequeath legacies *per vindicationem* e.g. in this way: 'I give and legate my slave Stichus to Lucius Titius'. But if only one of the expressions, 'I give' or 'I legate' is used, the legacy is duly made *per vindicationem*.

The legacy *per vindicationem* was usually made using a duplicated synonym: 'I give, I legate' (*do lego*). By the time of Gaius (second century AD), however, one of the two words was sufficient. Both verbs denoted that the legatee received ownership directly from the testator; hence, the legacy had a real effect and could only be made for objects owned by the testator:

> Inst.Gai.2.196.: *Hae autem solae res per vindicationem legantur recte, quae ex iure Quiritium ipsius testatoris sunt. [...]*

> Inst.Gai.2.196.: Only those objects can be duly bequeathed *per vindicationem*, which belonged to the testator himself by the law of the *Quirites*. [...]

The legacy *per vindicationem* over the property of a third party was invalid. However, the imperial law (*senatusconsultum Neronianum*) at the time of Gaius (second century AD), permitted the interpretation of an invalid legacy *per vindicationem* as a legacy *per damnationem* (Ch. 8.4.1). In contrast, the legacy *per damnationem* is merely obligational:

> Inst.Gai.2.201.: *Per damnationem hoc modo legamus: 'Heres meus Stichum servum meum dare damnas esto;' sed et si 'dato' scriptum fuerit, per damnationem legatum est.*

> Inst.Gai.2.201.: We leave a legacy *per damnationem*, as follows: 'let my heir be bound to give my slave Stichus' or if it is only written, 'let him give my slave Stichus', this is a legacy *per damnationem*.

It is usually made using the phrase: '*heres damnas esto*' ('let the heir be bound'). Similar expressions such as, 'let him give' *(dato)* were permissible in the second century AD. Thus, the legatee was not the owner until the heir had transferred ownership to him. The legatee could sue the heir if the latter refused to fulfil the legacy *per damnationem*. He could do this through the action on the grounds of a will (*actio ex testamento*):[1]

> *Iudex esto. Si paret Numerium Negidium Aulo Agerio sestertium X milia ex testamento dare oportere, qua de re agitur, tantam pecuniam et alteram tantam iudex Numerium Negidium Aulo Agerio condemnato; si non paret absolvito.*

---

[1] The reconstruction adheres to Otto Lenel, *Das Edictum Perpetuum* (3rd edn, Tauchnitz 1927) 367–368.

You shall be appointed judge. If it is proved that Numerius Negidius (the defendant) must give Aulus Agerius (the plaintiff) ten thousand sesterces from the will, the object of dispute, you shall condemn Numerius Negidius (the defendant) to pay Aulus Agerius (the plaintiff) twice the said amount. If it is not proved, you shall release him.

Following this formula, the legatee had to prove that the will granted him a right to claim a certain sum or an object of the estate. If he succeeded, the heir was ordered to pay a sum of money (*condemnatio pecuniaria*, Ch. 5.2) equivalent to the bequeathed item's value.[2] The defendant was ordered to pay an amount of money not only if, as in the said formula, the legatee was bequeathed money, but could be ordered to do so, instead of restitution in kind, if the heir was obliged to transfer ownership by the bequest. The legatee received the item itself only if the heir was willing to transfer it. During the procedure, the legatee could only claim the payment of the monetary equivalent, as the judge had only limited power to condemn the defendant.

As opposed to a legacy *per vindicationem*, the legacy *per damnationem* merely contained an obligation of the heir to transfer the property of a certain object and could thus be made for items that did not belong to the testator:

> Inst.Gai.2.202.: *Eoque genere legati etiam aliena res legari potest, ita ut heres redimere et praestare aut aestimationem eius dare debeat.*

> Inst.Gai.2.202.: Through this type of legacy, property belonging to another can also be bequeathed, so that the heir will either be obliged to buy the property and deliver it or pay for its value.

The legacy *per damnationem* could not only oblige the heir to transfer the property of an object belonging to the estate. Rather, the testator could also charge the heir with the duty to acquire the bequeathed object, that was not part of the estate, in order to give it to the legatee. If the owner refused to sell it to the heir, or if the heir was unwilling to buy it, then the legatee could use the *actio ex testamento* to claim the monetary value of the object left in the legacy.

Apart from the *legata per vindicationem* and *per damnationem*, there are two sub-categories of legacies, called *legatum sinendi modo* and the legacy *per praeceptionem*, that serve particular purposes.

---

[2] The formula mentions the doubling of the disputed amount; however, it needs to be clarified what the requirements were, and, therefore, it will not be elaborated upon here.

8.1.2 *Legacy* sinendi modo *and* per praeceptionem

The legacy *sinendi modo* allowed the legatee to take assets from the estate for himself and keep them:

> Inst.Gai.2.209.: *Sinendi modo ita legamus: 'Heres meus [dare] damnas esto sinere Lucium Titium hominem Stichum sumere sibique habere'.*

> Inst.Gai.2.209.: We leave a legacy *sinendi modo* thus: 'Let my heir be condemned to permit Lucius Titius to take and to have my slave Stichus as his own.'

The legacy *sinendi modo* compelled the heir to tolerate the legatee's taking of assets. Gaius perceives this 'duty to tolerate' as a middle way between the legacies *per vindicationem* and *per damnationem*:

> Inst.Gai.2.210.: *Quod genus legati plus quidem habet quam per vindicationem legatum, minus autem quam per damnationem: nam eo modo non solum suam rem testator utiliter legare potest, sed etiam heredis sui, cum alioquin per vindicationem nisi suam rem legare non potest, per damnationem autem cuiuslibet extranei rem legare potest.*

> Inst.Gai.2.210.: This kind of a legacy has a broader scope than one left *per vindicationem*, but narrower than a legacy *per damnationem*, for in this way a testator can legally bequeath not only his property, but also that of his heirs; while *per vindicationem* he can only bequeath his property, and *per damnationem* he can bequeath any property belonging to anyone.

Since the *legatum sinendi modo* compelled the heir to tolerate that the legatee helped himself to take what had been left to him, this legacy could not be validly made for objects belonging to a third party. But it allowed the bequest of items belonging to the heir. Hence, it was more flexible than the legacy *per vindicationem* that only allowed bequests of items owned by the testator. Still, it did not reach as far as the legacy *per damnationem*, which imposed a duty upon the heir to provide the bequeathed object. The following text is an example of a legacy *sinendi modo*:

> Paulus, 9 ad Plautium: *Ei cui fundum in quinquennium locaveram legavi quidquid eum mihi dare facere oportet oportebitve ut sineret heres sibi habere. Nerva Atilicinus, si heres prohiberet eum frui, ex conducto, si iure locationis quid retineret, ex testamento fore obligatum aiunt, quia nihil interesset, peteretur an retineret: Totam enim locationem legatam videri.* (D.34.3.16.)

Paul, Plautius, book 9: I leased a farm for five years and left the tenant everything that he was obliged to give or provide for me, and the heir must allow him to have it. Both Nerva and Atilicinus say that if the heir prevents him [the tenant and legatee] from enjoying this, he will be liable for an action on the lease. If he were to retain anything arising from the contract of hiring, he would be liable under the will because it makes no difference whether he demands something from the tenant or retains possession of it, as the entire lease is considered bequeathed. (D.34.3.16.)

A testator who has leased a parcel of land for five years bequeathed to the tenant all obligations arising from the lease, allowing the tenant to keep everything that he would have had to hand over to the heir as the legal successor of the lessor. Thus, as the jurists Nerva and Atilicinus (both first century AD) argued, the lease was not terminated because the legatee could claim his rights as a tenant against the lessor's heirs. Instead, the testator merely transferred his rights as a lease giver to the tenant; therefore, the heir could not claim the rights of the lease giver against the legatee.

The legacy *per praeceptionem* (*legatum per praeceptionem*, from *praecipere*, literally 'to take in advance') entailed a particular legal consequence:

Inst.Gai.2.216.: Per praeceptionem hoc modo legamus: 'Lucius Titius hominem Stichum praecipito'.

Inst.Gai.2.216.: We bequeath property by a legacy *per praeceptionem* thus: 'let Lucius Titius have my slave Stichus taken in advance.'

A legacy *per praeceptionem* allowed a person to take something from a shared property in advance. The item was therefore exempted from the joint estate and did not form part of the division of the inheritance (Ch. 4.1.1). Instead, the bequeathed object was granted in advance to one of the heirs and did not fall to the joinder of heirs. Consequently, the value of this object was not added to the beneficiary's share, but was granted to him in addition. Since the 'taking in advance' presupposed that the legatee was also an heir, it was disputed whether the legacy *per praeceptionem* could be made for a non-heir:

Inst.Gai.2.217.: Sed nostri quidem praeceptores nulli alii eo modo legari posse putant nisi ei, qui aliqua ex parte heres scriptus esset. Praecipere enim esse praecipuum sumere; quod tantum in eius persona procedit, qui aliqua ex parte heres institutus est, quod is extra portionem hereditatis praecipuum legatum habiturus sit.

Inst.Gai.2.217.: Our teachers, however, believe that such a bequest can only be made to a person appointed heir to a certain share of an estate. For to take by a legacy *per praeceptionem* means to receive more than what one is entitled to as heir, and he only can do so who has been appointed heir to a certain part of the estate, and is entitled to it as a legacy *per praeceptionem* over and above his share of the said estate.

Again, we encounter a dispute between the two schools of jurists of the first century AD. Whereas the Sabinians ('our teachers') only considered a legacy *per praeceptionem* as valid if made for an heir, the Proculians favoured a reinterpretation:

> Inst.Gai.2.221.: *Sed diversae scholae auctores putant etiam extraneo per praeceptionem legari posse, proinde ac si ita scribatur: 'Titius hominem Stichum praecapito,' supervacuo adiecta praesyllaba 'prae'; ideoque per vindicationem eam rem legatam videri: [...]*

> Inst.Gai.2.221.: But the teachers of the other school believe that a legacy *per praeceptionem* can be left even to a non-heir, just as if it were written in the will as follows: 'let Titius take my slave Stichus,' and that the prefix '*prae*' has been added superfluously; and, therefore, that the legacy appears to be left *per vindicationem* [...]

According to the Proculians, a legacy *per praeceptionem* made for a non-heir could not be valid as such, but had to be interpreted as a legacy *per vindicationem*, because the permission to take something in advance (*praecipere*) contained in the *legatum per praeceptionem* entailed a real effect for the bequest.

The four types of legacies under the *ius civile* offer a differentiated set of remedies that allowed the testator to specify the legal nature of the bequest by choosing a category of a legacy. In particular, the two special forms of the legacies, *modo sinendi* and *per praeceptionem*, show that the different forms of bequests corresponded to distinct purposes. While the legacy *per vindicationem* gave the legatee direct access to the object without interposition of the heir, the legacy *per damnationem* made it possible to bequeath property belonging to a third party, i.e. future property of the heir. The legacy *modo sinendi* was created for the special case of property belonging to the heir himself whereas the legacy *per praeceptionem* was appropriate when heir and legatee were partly identical. Thus, according to *ius civile*, the purpose pursued with the legacy, is recognisable and implemented in its particular form. The testator could only achieve the desired purpose if he adhered to the prescribed form of each legacy.

Overview 35: Different Types of Legacies of the *ius civile*

per vindicationem:	*per damnationem:*	*modo sinendi:*	*per praeceptionem:*
'I give, I legate' (*do lego*)	'the heir shall be obligated' (*damnas esto*)	'the heir shall be bound to allow' (*damnas esto sinere*)	'he may take in advance' (*praecipito*)
real effect: the legatee becomes owner once the heir accepts. He can claim with *rei vindicatio*	**obligational**: the legatee can claim once the heir accepts the inheritance. He can bring the *actio ex testamento*	**obligational**: the heir must tolerate the legatee's taking by himself	**real effect**: disputed whether valid only for heirs (Sabinians) or if also *per vindicationem* for non-heirs (Proculians)
only for property belonging to the testator	also for property belonging to a third party (heir's obligation to acquire)	also for property belonging to the heir (obligation to permit)	only for property belonging to the testator

In addition to choosing a specific type of legacy, the testator could modify it by attaching ancillary provisions, thus linking the bequest to certain external circumstances or to certain behaviour on the part of the bequest's beneficiary.

8.1.3 Ancillary Provisions to a Legacy

Republican jurists already systematised ancillary provisions according to their prerequisites and effects, by distinguishing between a (suspensive) time limit (*dies*), a condition (*condicio*), and a modality (*modus*). A legacy under a modality was unconditional; hence, the modality did not alter the legacy's validity:

> *Valens, 5 fideicommissorum: Si tibi legatum est [...] relictum, uti quid facias, etiamsi non interest heredis id fieri, negandam tibi actionem, si non caveas heredi futurum, quod defunctus voluit, Nerva et Atilicinus recte putaverunt. (D.32.19.)*

> Valens, Fideicommissa, book 5: Nerva and Atilicinus correctly held that where a legacy was left to you so that you do something specific [...], even if it was not to the interest of the heir for this to be done, the right to bring an action should be denied to you if you did not give a security (*cautio*) to ensure that the wishes of the decedent will be fulfilled. (D.32.19.)

Fulfilment of a modality was secured because the heir could refuse to fulfil the bequest until the legatee fulfilled the modality or gave surety for it. If the legatee sued for the legacy, the heir's condemnation would depend on whether the legatee had promised (*cautio*) to perform (*facere*) what was required in the modality. Since a formal promise guarantees the creditor a swift compensation in the event of an infringement by the debtor, the legatee's *cautio* for his conduct was considered equivalent to the actual fulfilment of the modality. The case decided by Nerva and Atilicinus (both first century AD) was particular because the heir had no interest in the legatee fulfilling the modality. In this case, it was up to the praetor to compel the legatee to give surety to protect the testator's intention, once a lawsuit was filed.

If the legacy was limited in time or conditional, differentiations were appropriate:

> *Pomponius, 3 ad Quintum Mucium: (1) Cum dies certus adscriptus est, quamvis dies nondum venerit, solvi tamen possunt, quia certum est ea debitu iri.*
> *(2) Dies autem incertus est, cum ita scribitur 'heres meus cum morietur, decem dato': Nam diem incertum mors habet eius. Et ideo si legatarius ante decesserit, ad heredem eius legatum non transit, quia non cessit dies vivo eo, quamvis certum fuerit moriturum heredem.*
> *(3) Inest autem condicio legati, veluti cum ita legamus: 'Quod ex Arescusa natum fuerit, heres dato' aut 'fructus, qui ex eo fundo percepti fuerint, heres dato' aut 'servum, quem alii non legavero, Seio dato'. (D.35.1.1.1–3.)*

> Pomponius, Quintus Mucius, book 3: (1) Where a specific date is prescribed [for the performance of a legacy], even though the time has not yet arrived, it can still be performed because it is inevitable that it will be due.
> (2) The date is uncertain when it is formulated thus: 'let my heir pay ten when he dies,' because the heir's death is uncertain. Hence, if the legatee dies before him, the legacy will not pass to his heir because the time set did not arrive during his lifetime, although it is certain that the heir will eventually die.
> (3) A legacy contains a condition, for example, if we make a bequest as follows, 'let my heir give what is born of [the slave] Arescusa' or 'let my heir give the crops that will be collected from this field', or 'let my heir give the slave, whom I will not have bequeathed to anyone else, to Seius'. (D.35.1.1.1–3.)

Pomponius (second century AD) differentiated between a specific date (*dies certus*) from an uncertain date (*dies incertus*) and the condition (*condicio*). While there was no doubt that the actionable obligation from the legacy with a specific date would come into existence and could thus be fulfilled immediately, it could not be enforced in court until the time limit set by the definite date had elapsed. In contrast, the uncertain date or the condition made it unclear whether the legacy would ever become valid. The legacy would not pass to the latter's heir if the legatee died before the occurrence of an uncertain date or of a condition. However, a legacy with a specific date would pass to the legatee's heir even before the deadline. These differentiations lead to the various conditions required for the acquisition of legacies.

8.1.4 The Acquisition of a Legacy

As seen, the validity of a legacy required not only the fulfilment of a specific formality, but its effectiveness also depended on the valid appointment of an heir in the same will:

> *Inst.Gai.2.229.: Ante heredis institutionem inutiliter legatur, scilicet quia testamenta vim ex institutione heredis accipiunt, et ob id velut caput et fundamentum intellegitur totius testamenti heredis institutio.*
>
> Inst.Gai.2.229.: A legacy made before the appointment of an heir is invalid because wills derive their force from the appointment of an heir, and on this account, the appointment of the heir is considered to be the beginning and foundation of the entire will.

The dependence of a legacy on the appointment of an heir was clearly expressed in the requirement that legacies had to be written after the appointment of the heir, since the appointment was the main object and foundation of the entire will (*caput et fundamentum totius testamenti*). Furthermore, legacies were only valid if the appointed heir accepted the estate. The legatee was therefore dependent either on the direct heirs not renouncing the inheritance or on the *extraneus* accepting it (Ch. 4.1.3).

This linking of the effects of the legacy with the *institutio heredis*, created an important distinction between two crucial deadlines regarding the effect of the legacy. These were the *dies cedens* (literally 'the day that is falling') and the *dies veniens* (literally 'the day coming'). The *dies cedens* or date of occurrence, i.e. the date on which the legacy took effect, was the date of the testator's death. The *dies veniens* or day of acquisition was the day the legacy could be enforced in court. It occurred when the heir accepted the inheritance.

As the legacy was already considered to have 'vested' at the moment of the testator's death (*dies cedens*), the legatee was protected against the heir's wilful delay. If the legatee died while waiting for the heir to accept the inheritance, the bequest did not become part of the estate but went to the heir of the legatee. The heir who speculated on avoiding the enforceability of the legacy by delaying acceptance of the inheritance would thus be disappointed:

Ulpianus, 20 ad Sabinum: Si post diem legati cedentem legatarius decesserit, ad heredem suum transfert legatum. (D.36.2.5pr.)

Ulpian, Sabinus, book 20: If a legatee dies after the *dies cedens* of the legacy, the legacy is transferred to his heir.' (D.36.2.5pr.)

In principle, the *dies cedens* is the date of the testator's death; in other words the legacy vests with the inheritance, unless the testator has not postponed the legacy to vest to another date. Adding ancillary provisions to the legacy could have a bearing on the *dies cedens*:

*Ulpianus, 20 ad Sabinum: (1) Itaque si purum legatum sit, ex die mortis dies eius cedit: si vero post diem sint legata relicta, simili modo atque in puris dies cedit, nisi forte id fuit legatum, quod ad heredem non transit: [...]
(2) Sed si sub condicione sit legatum relictum, non prius dies legati cedit quam condicio fuerit impleta, ne quidem si ea sit condicio, quae in potestate sit legatarii. (D.36.2.5.1–2.)*

Ulpian, Sabinus, book 20: (1) Therefore, if a legacy is left unconditionally, it takes effect from the day of [the testator's] death. If legacies are left to take effect at a future date, they vest like other unconditional legacies [at the date of the testator's death]; unless something has been bequeathed that cannot pass to the heir [...].
(2) But where a legacy is left under a condition, it does not begin to take effect before the condition is complied with, not even if it is a condition that lies in the power of the legatee to fulfil it. (D.36.2.5.1–2.)

Not every ancillary condition attached to a legacy had a bearing on the *dies cedens*. The attachment of a fixed date (*dies*) and of a modality (*modus*) did not change the *dies cedens*. It remained the date of the testator's death. The *dies cedens* could, however, be displaced by the addition of a (suspensive) condition (*condicio*). Since, in the latter case, the validity of the legacy depended on the fulfilment of the condition, the legacy could only take effect after both the fulfilment of the condition and death of the testator. The *dies cedens* was the date on which the last of the two events occurred; therefore, the *dies cedens* was suspended until the entry of the *dies veniens*.

If, however, the condition was impossible and therefore inoperative, an exception applied:

Ulpianus, 20 ad Sabinum: Idemque et in impossibili condicione, quia pro puro hoc legatum habetur. (D.36.2.5.4.)

Ulpian, Sabinus, book 20: The same applies in case of an impossible condition since a legacy of this kind is considered unconditional. (D.36.2.5.4.)

If the condition was impossible, it was considered not to have been written (Ch. 6.1.3), so the legacy was treated as unconditional and the day of the testator's death was the *dies cedens*.

A further exception concerned cases where the fulfilment of the condition of a legacy was prevented by the heir or a person in the power of the heir:

> *Iulianus, 55 digestorum: Iure civili receptum est, quotiens per eum, cuius interest condicionem impleri, fit, quo minus impleatur, ut perinde habeatur, ac si impleta condicio fuisset: Quod plerique et ad legata et ad heredum institutiones perduxerunt. [...] (D.35.1.24.)*

> Julian, Digest, book 55: The *ius civile* holds that a condition is always considered fulfilled if the party interested in its fulfilment prevents it from being fulfilled. Many authorities have extended the application to legacies and the appointment of heirs. [...] (D.35.1.24.)

Under the *ius civile*, a condition was assumed to have been fulfilled if someone with an interest in its fulfilment or non-fulfilment had prevented it. This principle applied not only to an heir, or co-heir, whose benefit would be reduced by the legacy, but to any person with an interest in the estate remaining intact, such as a creditor of the estate. The rationale for this fiction was to prevent persons with an interest in the estate from benefiting at the heir's or legatee's expense, which is why this rule applied both to conditional appointments of heirs and conditional legacies.

The effect of this fiction can be seen in cases where the legatee was burdened with a condition to give something to the heir or a third party in order to receive the bequest:

> *Ulpianus, 20 ad Sabinum: Item si qua condicio sit, quae per legatarium non stat quo minus impleatur, sed aut per heredem aut per eius personam, in cuius persona iussus est parere condicioni, dies legati cedit, quoniam pro impleta habetur: Ut puta si iussus sim heredi decem dare et ille accipere nolit. [...] (D.36.2.5.5.)*

> Ulpian, Sabinus, book 20: Equally, if the condition is such that the legatee is not responsible for non-compliance with it, but the heir or a person ordered to comply with the condition, then the legacy will take effect because the condition is considered to have been fulfilled. For example, if I was ordered to pay the heir ten, but he refused to accept. [...] (D.36.2.5.5.)

Ulpian discussed a case where a legacy was given on the condition that the legatee gave the heir a certain amount of money. The *dies cedens* was therefore the day on which the condition was fulfilled. However, if the heir prevented the fulfilment of the said condition by refusing to accept the payment, the condition was still assumed to have been fulfilled nonetheless. Thus, the legacy became effective at the moment of the heir's refusal.

A final peculiarity of the (suspensive) conditional legacy was formed by a legacy under a negative potestative condition. In this case, all that was certain was that the forbidden conduct had not been performed at the time of the legatee's death. The republican jurist Quintus Mucius Scaevola (consul in 95BC) developed a cautelary solution to allow the legatee to enjoy the legacy during his lifetime. The jurist's solution was for the legatee to give a *cautio* (from *cavere*, 'to provide'), through which he promised to return the legacy or its value if he infringed the negative potestative condition. Later jurists called this surety '*cautio Muciana*', after its creator:

> *Ulpianus, 18 ad Sabinum: Mucianae cautionis utilitas consistit in condicionibus, quae in non faciendo sunt conceptae, ut puta 'si in Capitolium non ascenderit,' 'si Stichum non manumiserit' et in similibus: Et ita Aristoni et Neratio et Iuliano visum est. [...] (D.35.1.7pr.)*

> Ulpian, Sabinus, book 18: The *cautio Muciana* is beneficial regarding conditions entailing that something is not to be done. For example: 'if he has not climbed the Capitol', 'if he has not manumitted Stichus,' and similar conditions. This was also the view of Aristo, Neratius, and Julian. [...] (D.35.1.7pr.)

The *cautio Muciana* made it possible to treat a condition as fulfilled in which the legatee had been requested to abstain from doing something, i.e. if the testator had asked the legatee not to climb the Capitol. The legatee's formal promise (*cautio*) to return the legacy if he violated the negative potestative condition, allowed him to profit from the conditional legacy during his lifetime. Once the legatee had performed the *cautio Muciana*, the negative potestative condition was treated as fulfilled, so that the legacy was considered both effective (*dies cedens*) and enforceable (*dies veniens*) from that point on.

Overview 36 summarises the consequences of the various ancillary conditions on the legacy. The very detailed rules bear testament to the deep practical relevance of the law of legacies and show that the testator had to balance the interests of the legatee and the heir and to choose the appropriate ancillary conditions to harmonise them.

Overview 36: The Acquisition of a Legacy with Various Ancillary Provisions Attached

	unconditional legacy and legacy with a modality (*modus*)	legacy appointed for a specific date (*dies certus*)	legacy appointed for an uncertain date (*dies incertus*)	a conditional legacy (*condicio*)
dies cedens (vesting)	death of the testator: the legacy can be passed to the legatee's heir straightaway		the legacy takes effect only after both the condition/uncertain date and the testator's death. If the condition/uncertain date is not fulfilled upon the testator's death, the legacy will not vest	
dies veniens (enforceability)	the acceptance of the inheritance by the *extraneus*; the passing of the time limit for renunciation by direct heirs	the occurrence of the (specific) date or heir's acceptance of the estate (both must be fulfilled)	like *dies cedens* exceptions apply to both, if the condition is impossible or the fulfilment of the condition is impeded (fiction of the fulfilment of the condition)	

The rules governing the form and acquisition of a legacy under the *ius civile* are supplemented by the equally detailed provisions concerning the invalidity of legacies.

8.2 The Invalidity and Limitations of the Legacy under the *ius civile*

The dependence of the legacy on a valid appointment of an heir (Ch. 8.1.4) entailed that the legacy would become void if the will was invalid, hence, if it was defective in form or content (Ch. 6.2, Ch. 7.1). Furthermore, the differentiation between four different types of legacy under the *ius civile* meant that the testator had to choose the appropriate type of legacy for his bequest and then use the prescribed formal words to express it (Ch. 8.1.1, Ch. 8.1.2). In addition, the testator had to respect all substantive restrictions regarding each type of legacy. In addition to all these requirements, there were general guidelines for the design and content applicable to all different types of bequest.

8.2.1 Flaws of Content

The first general rule was that the testator was prohibited from leaving a legacy solely for punitive purposes:

> *Inst.Gai.2.235.: Poenae quoque nomine inutiliter legatur. Poenae autem nomine legari videtur, quod coercendi heredis causa relinquitur, quo magis heres aliquid faciat aut non faciat, veluti quod ita legatur: 'Si heres meus filiam suam Titio in matrimonium collocaverit, X milia Seio dato', vel ita: 'Si filiam Titio in matrimonium non collocaveris, X milia Titio dato'; [...].*

> Inst.Gai.2.235.: Punitive legacies are void. A legacy is considered punitive if left for the purpose of compelling the heir either to do something, or to refrain him from doing so. As, e.g., if the legacy is made: 'if my heir gives his daughter in marriage to Titius let him pay ten thousand sesterces to Seius'; or as follows: 'if you do not give your daughter in marriage to Titius, you shall pay him ten thousand sesterces' [...]

Gaius (second century AD) drew the line between a legacy that legitimately controlled the behaviour of a legatee and a penal legacy by identifying the testator's aim. Legacies left under a potestative condition, which is within the power of the legatee to fulfil, give the latter the opportunity to receive the bequest if the legatee acts in accordance with the condition. A penal legacy, on the contrary, aimed solely at controlling the behaviour of the heir. Hence, the bequest to the legatee was merely a means of forcing the heir to a certain conduct. In fact, the testator expected that the heir did not want to fulfil the legacy and would try to prevent it from coming into effect by following the specifications of the condition. In this case, the testator's aim was not to benefit the legatee but to chastise the heir, which was an obvious abuse of the law of legacies. A penal legacy was thus illegitimate and void.

As a second general rule for the law of legacies, the testator was not allowed to leave a legacy to an unspecified group of persons rather than to a specific person:

> *Inst.Gai.2.238.: Incertae personae legatum inutiliter relinquitur. Incerta autem videtur persona, quam per incertam opinionem animo suo testator subicit, velut cum ita legatum sit: 'Qui primus ad funus meum venerit, ei heres meus X milia dato'; [...]. Sub certa vero demonstratione incertae personae recte legatur, velut: 'Ex cognatis meis, qui nunc sunt, qui primus ad funus meum venerit, ei X milia heres meus dato.'*

> Inst.Gai.2.238.: A legacy left to an uncertain person is void. An uncertain person also is considered to be one about whom the testator has only a vague notion in his mind. As for example, where a bequest is made thus: 'let my heir pay ten thousand sesterces to the first person who comes to my funeral'; [...]. The legacy is valid where the designation of the group to which the person belongs is described with certainty, but the individual

to whom it is left is uncertain; as, for instance: 'let my heir pay ten thousand sesterces to that one of my surviving blood relatives who comes first to my funeral.'

The testator had to have a clear idea of the person he wanted to benefit through a legacy. It was not permitted to leave a legacy by chance. Therefore, a legacy for the benefit of 'the one who will come first to my funeral' was void. However, a legacy left to 'the one from the surviving blood relatives who will come first to my funeral' was valid because the testator had specified a clearly identifiable group of persons from which one person was chosen by means of the condition. The testator was otherwise free to choose his legatees. The only requirement was that the person mentioned needed the (passive) ability to receive a legacy under the *ius civile*. This requirement was the *testamenti factio*, which was also necessary to become a testamentary heir under a Roman will (Ch. 4.3).

The legacy, such as the appointment of an heir (Ch. 6.1.3), had to be valid from the moment the will was made until it was opened. This condition of the law of legacies is called *regula Catoniana* and goes back to Cato Licinianus, the son of Cato the Elder, who died around 152BC:

> *Celsus, 35 digestorum: Catoniana regula sic definit, quod, si testamenti facti tempore decessisset testator, inutile foret, id legatum quandocumque decesserit, non valere. Quae definitio in quibusdam falsa est. (D.34.7.1pr.)*
>
> Celsus, Digest, book 35: The rule of Cato provides, that any legacy which would have been invalid if the testator had died at the time the will was made, is invalid whenever he [the testator] died. This statement of the rule is misleading in certain cases. (D.34.7.1pr.)

According to Celsus (second century AD), Cato's rule that a legacy was only valid if it had been valid at the time the will was made was not universally applicable.

> *Celsus, 35 digestorum: Quid enim, si quis ita legaverit: 'Si post kalendas mortuus fuero, Titio dato? An cavillamur?' Nam hoc modo si statim mortuus fuerit, non esse datum legatum verius est quam inutiliter datum. (D.34.7.1.1.)*
>
> Celsus, Digest, book 35: But what if anyone leaves a legacy thus: 'let it be given to Titius if I die after the Kalends. Are we splitting hairs?' If the testator dies immediately, it is better [to hold] that the legacy does not take effect rather than that is has been made invalidly. (D.34.7.1.1.)

Exceptions applied for conditional bequests, which, as we saw (Ch. 8.1.3), could become valid afterwards, since they did not take effect at the moment the will was made, but once the condition was fulfilled. A typical example of such a modified application of the *regula Catoniana* can be found here:

> *Ulpianus, libro 21 ad Sabinum: (1) Sed ea quae aedibus iuncta sunt legari non possunt, quia haec legari non posse senatus censuit Aviola et Pansa consulibus. (2) Tractari tamen poterit, si quando marmora vel columnae fuerint separatae ab aedibus, an legatum convalescat. Et si quidem ab initio non constitit legatum, ex post facto non convalescet, [...]. Sed si sub condicione legetur, poterit legatum valere, si exsistentis condicionis tempore [...] aedibus iuncta non sit, [...]. Purum igitur legatum Catoniana regula impedit, condicionale non, quia ad condicionalia Catoniana non pertinet. (D.30.41.1–2.)*

> Ulpian, Sabinus, book 21: (1) But ornaments joined to buildings cannot be bequeathed because the Senate during the consulship of Aviola and Pansa decided that they could not be left through a legacy.
> (2) It can be discussed whether the legacy becomes valid once pieces of marble or columns are separated from the building. And, indeed, if it was not valid from the beginning, it cannot become so subsequently [...] Still, if the something is bequeathed under a condition, the legacy can become valid if, when the condition was fulfilled, [...] the object is not fastened to the building [...]. Hence, Cato's rule stands in the way of a legacy left unconditionally but is not opposed to a conditional one because it does not apply to conditional legacies. (D.30.41.1–2.)

A *senatusconsultum* dating from AD122 prohibited the bequest of ornaments attached to a building. This was meant to prevent buildings from being destroyed against all economic sense in order to fulfil legacies. Ulpian (third century AD) asked whether a later removal of ornaments from a building could make the legacy valid, or whether, following the *regula Catoniana*, an invalid legacy remained invalid. He agreed with a strict application of the rule and denied that the legacy could afterwards become valid. However, the jurist allowed an exception for conditional legacies: if the testator left the legacy under the condition that the ornaments were separated from the building, the legacy was valid once the ornaments were no longer attached to the building at the time of the opening of the will.

These differentiations show that the *regula Catoniana*, like other rules on will-making under the *ius civile*, was intended to force the testator to examine and plan his will carefully. The *regula Catoniana* only penalised the testator who had not investigated the underlying facts, e.g. he had not checked whether the ornaments were joined to the building, and thus had not diligently planned his succession.

8.2.2 Limitations on the Number of Legacies Allowed on the Right to Set Out Legacies: The lex Falcidia

The *ius civile* initially allowed legacies without limitation as to their number and extent:

> *Inst.Gai.2.224.: Sed olim quidem licebat totum patrimonium legatis atque libertatibus erogare nec quicquam heredi relinquere praeterquam inane nomen heredis; idque lex XII tabularum permittere videbatur, qua cavetur, ut quod quisque de re sua testatus esset, id ratum haberetur, [...] quare, qui scripti heredes erant, ab hereditate se abstinebant, et idcirco plerique intestati moriebantur.*

> Inst.Gai.2.224.: Once, anyone was permitted to exhaust his entire estate by legacies and the manumission of slaves; thus leaving nothing to his heir but an empty name; and the law of the twelve tables seem to allow it, since it is provided that a person may dispose of his property by will [...] and for this reason, those who were appointed heirs rejected the inheritance and, therefore, most people died intestate.

As the law of the twelve tables (*ca.* 450BC) did not limit the number of legacies that could be left, the estate was often overburdened with legacies, so that the heir renounced the estate as it provided no benefit to him. Without the acceptance of the heir, the will was considered void and the legatee could not profit from the legacy, as the testator died intestate. The laws of the Republic sought to redress this problem. A solution, however, could only be reached after several failed attempts to curb the overburdening of the estate by law.

The *lex Furia* (after AD204) and the *lex Voconia* (169BC) are regarded as such failed attempts:

> *Inst.Gai.2.225.: Itaque lata est lex Furia, qua exceptis personis quibusdam ceteris plus mille assibus legatorum nomine mortisve causa capere permissum non est. Sed et haec lex non perfecit, quod voluit: Qui enim verbi gratia quinque milium aeris patrimonium habebat, poterat quinque hominibus singulis millenos asses legando totum patrimonium erogare.*

> Inst.Gai.2.225.: Hence the *lex Furia* was enacted, by the terms of which (except in the case of certain persons) it was not permitted to accept more than a thousand asses either as a legacy or as a gift on account of death. This law, however, did not accomplish what was intended. For example, anyone who had an estate of five thousand asses could leave to five men a thousand asses each, and, by doing so, drain the entire estate.

The *lex Furia* prohibited taking legacies above one thousand asses with an exception for blood relatives under the sixth degree. The law, however, did not invalidate legacies exceeding the prescribed amount, but foresaw a penalty four times the amount of the legacy (*poena quadrupli*). According to Gaius, the law was not successful because it did not prevent the testator from leaving countless legacies of up to one thousand asses.

Therefore, the later *lex Voconia* required the testator to keep an appropriate ratio between the value of each individual legacy and the value of the heirs' share:

> Inst.Gai.2.226.: *Ideo postea lata est lex Voconia, qua cautum est, ne cui plus legatorum nomine mortisve causa capere liceret, quam heredes caperent. Ex qua lege plane quidem aliquid utique heredes habere videbantur; sed tamen fere vitium simile nascebatur. Nam in multas legatariorum personas distributo patrimonio poterat testator adeo heredi minimum relinquere, ut non expediret heredi huius lucri gratia totius hereditatis onera sustinere.*

> Inst.Gai.2.226.: In consequence of this, the *lex Voconia* was subsequently passed, by which it was provided that no one could, as a legatee, or a beneficiary on account of death, take more than the heirs received. It is clear that by this law, the heirs appeared to receive something from the estate. However, it still contained almost the same defect, for the testator could, in distributing his estate among many legatees, manage to leave so little to the heir that it was not advantageous for the heir to shoulder the burden of the entire estate for such little a profit.

Following the *lex Voconia*, the testator was not allowed to leave more in the individual legacies than he left to his heir. But this rule was circumvented by leaving various legacies to different legatees, so that the estate was still overburdened. Eventually, the *lex Falcidia* of 40BC successfully prevented the overburdening of the inheritance with legacies:

> *Paulus, liber singularis ad legem Falcidiam: Lex Falcidia lata est, quae primo capite liberam legandi facultatem dedit usque ad dodrantem his verbis: 'Qui cives Romani sunt, qui eorum post hanc legem rogatam testamentum facere volet, ut eam pecuniam easque res quibusque dare legare volet, ius potestasque esto, ut hac lege sequenti licebit.' Secundo capite modum legatorum constituit his verbis: 'Quicumque civis Romanus post hanc legem rogatam testamentum faciet, is quantam cuique civi Romano pecuniam iure publico dare legare volet, ius potestasque esto, dum ita detur legatum, ne minus quam partem quartam hereditatis eo testamento heredes capiant, eis, quibus quid ita datum legatumve erit, eam pecuniam sine fraude sua capere liceto isque heres, qui eam pecuniam dare iussus damnatus erit, eam pecuniam debeto dare, quam damnatus est'. (D.35.2.1pr.)*

Paul, Lex Falcidia, sole book: The lex Falcidia was enacted and granted in its first chapter free power to dispose of an estate up to three-fourths as follows: 'those Roman citizens who desire to make a will after the enactment of this law shall have the right and power to give and to bequeath their money and their property to anyone whom they choose [and] as will be lawful under the subsequent provisions.' In the second chapter, the amount of the legacies that can be bequeathed is established thus: 'any Roman citizen who will make a will after the enactment of this law shall have the right and the power to give and to bequeath as large a sum of money as he wishes to any other Roman citizen, under the *ius publicum*; provided the legacy is bequeathed in such a way that the heirs receive at least one-fourth of the estate. Moreover, those to whom anything is given or bequeathed in accordance to this law, shall be entitled to receive this advantage without any detriment; and that heir who has been ordered and charged to give the advantage, has to give it exactly, as he has been obliged to do.' (D.35.2.1pr.)

The first chapter of the *lex Falcidia* recalled the freedom of testamentary disposition under the *ius civile* and emphasised that the testator was allowed to make a legacy to any person he wished. The second chapter limited this freedom to the extent that the sum of all legacies could not exceed three-fourth of the estate; one-fourth of the estate, the *quarta Falcidia*, had to remain with the heir. However, the legatee did not have to accept other limitations on the legacy, as the said *lex* highlighted conclusively. The heir had to fulfil the legacy up to three-fourths.

The *lex Falcidia* did not only furnish a directive that the testator had to observe when making a legacy with respect to the appointment of heir. The rule also provided a legal consequence if the legacy charged exceeded three-fourths of the inheritance:

> *Gaius, 18 ad edictum provinciale: Ergo optimum quidem est statim ab initio ita testatorem distribuere legata, ne ultra dodrantem relinquantur. Quod si excesserit quis dodrantem, pro rata portione per legem ipso iure minuuntur: Verbi gratia si is, qui quadringenta in bonis habuit, tota ea quadringenta erogaverit, quarta pars legatariis detrahitur: Si trecenta quinquaginta legaverit, octava. [...] (D.35.2.73.5.)*

Gaius, Provincial Edict, book 18: Therefore, it is best if the testator distributes the legacies from the start in a way they do not exceed three-fourths. But if anyone exceeds three-fourths, the legacies will, by operation of law, be reduced proportionally. For example, if a man has an estate of four hundred and bequeaths the whole of it in legacies, the fourth part of his legacy will be taken from each legatee. If he bequeaths three hundred and fifty, one-eighth will be deduced from each legacy [...] (D.35.2.73.5.)

If the testator left the four hundred he owned in legacies, the total of all the legacies had to be reduced by one hundred, so that each legacy had to be reduced by one-fourth. If the testator left only three hundred and fifty out of four hundred, then the legacies charged were in excess of only fifty; therefore, they had to be reduced by one-eighth. This reduction occurred by operation of law (*ipso iure*). The right of the legatees was immediately reduced by the amount necessary for all the legacies in order to preserve the *quarta Falcidia* for the sake of the heir. If, after the legacies had been handed over, it was found that the inheritance had been excessively overburdened, the heir could claim the amount to be deducted from the legatee on the ground of unjust enrichment.

It should be noted that the deduction applied only to legacies that did not exceed the value of the estate:

> *Gaius, 18 ad edictum provinciale:[...] Quod si quingenta legaverit habens quadringenta, initio quinta, deinde quarta pars detrahi debet: Ante enim detrahendum est, quod extra bonorum quantitatem est, deinde quod ex bonis apud heredem remanere oportet. (D.35.2.73.5.)*

> Gaius, Provincial Edict, book 18: [...] What if he bequeaths five hundred, having only four hundred? First, a fifth part and then a fourth part will be deducted. In the first place, what is not part of the estate must be deducted, then the share that must remain with the heir. (D.35.2.73.5.)

If the testator, whose estate was valued at four hundred, left legacies of five hundred, the *quarta Falcidia* would only be deducted from the real value of the estate, which was four hundred. Thus, the amount in excess of the real value of the estate had to be deducted before the *quarta Falcidia* could be calculated. This example illustrates an attempt to circumvent the provisions of the *lex Falcidia*: if one were to deduct one hundred (*quarta*) from five hundred, the heir would receive nothing, despite the law prescribing that he should receive one-fourth. Therefore, the real value of the estate had to be ascertained before the quarter could be calculated. Naturally, the *lex Falcidia* did not apply if the legacies were valued at less than three-fourths of the estate. In this respect, the testator's freedom of disposition remained intact. If the testator wanted to avoid a dispute about the *lex Falcidia*, he could limit the legacies to three-fourths of the estate or even less. For the sake of the heir, the law only set an outer limit to the legacies, but did not prescribe how the estate should be distributed.

The balance struck by the *ius civile* between the interests of the legatees and those of the testator was complemented by the provisions of the *ius praetorium*, which dealt in particular with the procedural aspects of the problem.

8.3 Praetorian Protection in the Law of Legacies

As we saw (Ch. 4.2), the praetor had to ensure that the heir appointed in a will also received access to the estate. This was achieved through the *bonorum possessio secundum tabulas* (possession of the estate following a will). However, praetorian law not only protected the testamentary heir, but also aimed at evening out the interests between the legatees and the testamentary heir. For this purpose, the edict foresaw various remedies by which the legatee could force the heir to comply with the bequest. In contrast, the praetor prohibited the legatee from taking the law into his own hands.

8.3.1 Interdictum quod legatorum

The heir was protected by an interdict (*interdictum*, from *interdicere*, to forbid) against illegitimate self-help by the legatee. The purpose of the interdict was to protect the *bonorum possessor* from illegitimate interventions by the legatees. Generally speaking, an interdict was an order issued by the praetor at the request of a claimant; it was a provisional remedy and its procedure was summary, without examination of evidence:

> *Ulpianus, 67 ad edictum: (1) Hoc interdictum volgo 'quod legatorum' appellatur.*
> *(2) Est autem et ipsum apiscendae possessionis et continet hanc causam, ut, quod quis legatorum nomine non ex voluntate heredis occupavit, id restituat heredi. Etenim aequissimum praetori visum est unumquemque non sibi ipsum ius dicere occupatis legatis, sed ab herede petere: Redigit igitur ad heredes per hoc interdictum ea, quae legatorum nomine possidentur, ut perinde legatarii possint eum convenire. (D.43.3.1.1–2.)*
>
> Ulpian, Edict, book 67: (1) this interdict is commonly called 'what of legacies'.
> (2) It is about obtaining possession, and its aim is that someone must restore whatever he has taken under the pretext of a legacy against the will of the heir, for it seemed most equitable to the praetor that nobody should resort to self-help by taking possession of the legacy, but should first claim it from the heir. Therefore, using this interdict, the praetor restored to the heir what are possessed as legacies, so that the legatees can sue the heir. (D.43.3.1.1–2.)

This interdict takes its name from the first words of the remedy, hence, *quod legatorum* ('what of legacies'). The title refers to the reason alleged by the legatee to justify the forcible removal of items from the estate. He would claim that the object had been left to him as a legacy and that the *bonorum possessor* was unlawfully withholding it from him. The praetor forbade the legatee from using illegitimate self-help, and therefore did not allow him to remove the item from the estate. Instead, the legatee was to be induced to seek judicial assistance to enforce his rights. Anything that the legatee had removed from the estate without the consent of the *bonorum possessor* was to be returned to him by order of the praetor. This interdict, along with several other measures taken by the praetor during the Republic, was intended to curb unlawful interference and prevent legatees from taking law into their own hands.

In return, the *ius praetorium* supported the legatee in enforcing his legacy against the heir if the latter delayed or denied to fulfil the bequest. For this purpose, the praetor's edict compelled the heir to provide the legatee with security for the fulfilment of the bequest.

8.3.2 Cautio legatorum servandorum causa

To give security (*satisdatio*, from *satisdare*, 'to give security', 'to stand as guarantor') meant that the debtor gave a guarantee to the creditor. Unlike a *cautio*, which in its simplest form consisted of the formal promise (*stipulatio*) of the original debtor, the *satisdatio* implied an additional personal guarantee, assumed by one or more sureties who promised to cover the debt if the debtor himself was unable or unwilling to fulfil his obligations. This mechanism was also used for legacies, as the praetor compelled the heir to give 'security for the protection of the legacy' (*cautio legatorum servandorum causa*):

> *Ulpianus, 79 ad edictum: Legatorum nomine satisdari oportere praetor putavit, ut, quibus testator dari fierive voluit, his diebus detur vel fiat dolumque malum afuturum stipulentur. (D.36.3.1pr.)*

> Ulpian, Edict, book 79: The praetor considered it fitting that security should be given for legacies, so that those to whom the testator wished something given or done, should be promised that it might be given or done within the appointed dates and that no deceit is committed. (D.36.3.1pr.)

With this *cautio*, the heir promised to fulfil the legacy according to the will and to abstain from fraud. The promise was secured by a surety. If the heir did not fulfil his promise, the legatee could sue him for payment of the value of the legacy or hold the surety liable for the same amount.

Since legacies did not take effect until the heir had accepted the inheritance (*dies veniens*), the legatees were able to secure their rights even before that date:

> *Ulpianus, 52 ad edictum: Tunc ante aditam hereditatem satisdandum de legatis est, cum adhuc dubium est, an hereditas adeatur. Ceterum si certum sit repudiatam vel omissam hereditatem [...], frustra hoc edictum imploratur, cum certum sit legatum [...] non deberi. (D.36.4.1.4.)*

> Ulpian, Edict, book 52: Security must be given for legacies before acceptance of the inheritance if it is still doubtful whether it will be accepted. Moreover, if it is certain that it will be rejected or relinquished, [...] the protection of this edict will be sought in vain, as it is clear that the legacy [...] will not be owed. (D.36.4.1.4.)

The *cautio legatorum servandorum causa* was admissible if the heir had not renounced the inheritance, so that the validity of the will and the legacies were still pending. If, however, the heir renounced the inheritance in the meantime, the legatee could no longer request security for the fulfilment of his legacy, since the legacy had become obsolete (or would now burden another heir, i.e. a substitute heir). As long as the heir had not decided whether or not to accept the inheritance, the *ius praetorium* strengthened the protection of the legatee, introduced by the *ius civile*, against the heir who speculated in order to delay or to avoid the enforceability of the legacy. The legatee's application for a *cautio* required only proof that the legacy had vested, i.e. the arrival of the *dies cedens*, which was the day of the testator's death.

The sole purpose of the *cautio* was to ensure the enforcement of the legacy. Hence, the application for a *cautio* became inadmissible if the legatee claimed the fulfilment of the legacy in court or if the legacy turned out to be invalid:

> *Ulpianus, 79 ad edictum: Si quis sub condicione legatum stipulatus pendente condicione decesserit, stipulatio evanescit, quia nec legatum transmittitur. [...]. (D.36.3.1.14.)*

> Ulpian, Edict, book 79: Where anyone has stipulated for a legacy under a condition, and, while the condition is pending, the stipulation lapses because the legacy is not transmitted [...] (D.36.3.1.14.)

As we saw above (Ch. 8.1.4), a legacy left subject to a suspensive condition vests (*dies cedens*) when the condition is fulfilled. Since the *cautio* given by the heir for the legacy, was intended to secure the enforcement of the legacy, its purpose became obsolete as soon as the legacy became ineffective because the condition failed.

If the heir could not or did not want to give security, the legatee was granted participation in the *bonorum possessio* of the heir:

> *Ulpianus, 79 ad edictum: Nec sine ratione hoc praetori visum est, sicuti heres incumbit possessioni bonorum, ita legatarios quoque carere non debere bonis defuncti: Sed aut satisdabitur eis aut, si satis non datur, in possessionem bonorum venire praetor voluit. (D.36.3.1.2.)*

> Ulpian, Edict, book 79: The praetor has good reason for the view that as the heir gains possession of the estate, so the legatees shall not be deprived of

the goods of the decedent. But they are either granted security or, if not, the praetor wishes that they acquire possession. (D.36.3.1.2.)

If the heir had brought forth the document proving his entitlement (Ch. 6.3) and requested *bonorum possessio* on the basis of the will, the praetor would ask him to provide security for the legatees, i.e. to pledge the fulfilment of their legacies. If the heir refused to provide security by promising the *cautio legatorum servandorum causa* the praetor would grant *bonorum possessio* jointly to the heir and the legatee.

This order, like the *cautio* it replaced, was provisional:

Ulpianus, 52 ad edictum: Is cui legatorum [...] nomine non cavetur missus in possessionem nunquam pro domino esse incipit. Nec tam possessio rerum ei quam custodia datur: Neque enim expellendi heredem ius habet, sed simul cum eo possidere iubetur, ut saltem taedio perpetuae custodiae extorqueat heredi cautionem. (D.36.4.5pr.)

Ulpian, Edict, book 52: A person who has not been given *cautio* for the fulfilment of a legacy [...] will never become owner [of the estate], although he has acquired possession. Since it is not so much the possession of the estate as the custody given to him, he has no right to expel the heir. Still, he is ordered to possess with him, so that he may compel the heir to provide security by the tedium of perpetual custody. (D.36.4.5pr.)

The grant of possession with the heir did not enable the legatee to acquire ownership through prescriptive acquisition of the estate (Ch. 4.1.4). The sole purpose of the joint possession was to give the legatee control over the administration of the estate. In this way, the legatee would be protected from dispositions by the heir. At the same time, the heir was induced to fulfil the legacy in order to get rid of the burdensome participation of the legatee in the administration of the estate.

Of course, the legatee was not granted possession of the estate if there was nothing left of it:

Paulus, 3 sententiarum: Si nullae sint res hereditariae, in quas legatarii [...] mittantur, in rem quidem heredis mitti non possunt, sed per praetorem denegatas heredi actiones ipsi persequuntur. (D.36.4.10.)

Paul, Sentences, book 3: Where there is nothing belonging to an estate of which the legatees [...] can be placed in possession, they cannot be given possession of the estate belonging to the heir. They can, however, bring any actions concerning the estate which the praetor has denied to the heir. (D.36.4.10.)

Even if the legatee could not be given possession of the estate or of items belonging to it, e.g. because they had been sold by the heir, the praetor still wished the legatee to participate in the estate. The praetor achieved this by denying the heir the right to claim the actions in favour of the inheritance and, exceptionally, granting it to the legatee. Thus, by pursuing the estate's claims, the legatee could obtain the value of the legacy from the estate's debtors.

The *ius praetorium* ensured that the legatee had a stake in the estate to the extent of his legacy through this graduation of remedies, i.e. compulsory *cautio* for the heir, the legatee's participation in the heir's *bonorum possessio* and the granting of the estate's claims to the legatee. The different levels of praetorian protection of the legatee are summarised in Overview 37:

Overview 37: The graduated Praetorian Protection of the Legatee

granting of security (*cautio*) by the heir		granting *bonorum possessio*	granting of the estate's claims
upon legatee's request	upon request of the heir for *bonorum possessio secundum tabulas*	instead of security (*cautio*)	instead of granting *bonorum possessio*
evidence (from the document of the will): • for the legacy • for *dies cedens*		+ heir refuses to provide security; security does not fail because of the legatee	+ absence of items of the estate, which could be granted to the legatee

Leaving aside the peculiarities of the praetorian will (Ch. 6.3), the overview shows that the praetor did not depart from the law of legacies under the *ius civile*, but that he reinforced the position of the legatee defined by this layer of law. Only imperial law changed the formal and substantive requirements for legacies, modifying the rules of the *ius civile* and making formless legacies binding according to *ius novum*.

8.4 Imperial Interventions into the Law of Legacies of the *ius civile*

Like other imperial interventions, the imperial modification of the law of legacies created *ius civile* with immediate effect.

8.4.1 The senatusconsultum Neronianum

The first reform aimed at levelling the four different types of legacies of *ius civile*. The *senatusconsultum Neronianum de legatis*, a *senatusconsultum* under Emperor Nero (AD54–68), provided that a legacy that was invalid because it did not fulfil the formal criteria could still be valid if it fulfilled the requirements of another legally recognised type of legacy. This legal adjustment was conducive for legacies *per vindicationem* about alien property:

> Inst.Gai.2.197.: [...] Postea vero auctore Nerone Caesare senatusconsultum factum est, quo cautum est, ut si eam rem quisque legaverit, quae eius numquam fuerit, proinde utile sit legatum, atque si optimo iure relictum esset. Optumum autem ius est per damnationem legati, quo genere etiam aliena res legari potest, [...]

> Inst.Gai.2.197.: [...] Later, a *senatusconsultum* was enacted by Emperor Nero, which foresaw that if a testator bequeathed anything which had never belonged to him, the legacy would be valid just as if it had been left in the most favourable form. 'The most favourable form' means that it is left *per damnationem*, by which property belonging to another can be bequeathed, [...]

The *senatusconsultum Neronianum de legatis* allowed casting the invalid legacy into a valid type of legacy. Since the legacy *per vindicationem* would have been invalid for property belonging to a third party (Ch. 8.1.1), it could still be valid as a legacy *per damnationem*.

It was disputed whether the *senatusconsultum Neronianum de legatis* could also provide remedy in the case of a legacy *per praeceptionem* left to a non-heir (Ch. 8.1.2):

> Inst.Gai.2.218.: Ideoque si extraneo legatum fuerit, inutile est legatum, adeo ut Sabinus existimaverit ne quidem ex senatusconsulto Neroniano posse convalescere: 'Nam eo,' inquit, 'senatusconsulto ea tantum confirmantur, quae verborum vitio iure civili non valent, non quae propter ipsam personam legatarii non deberentur.' Sed Iuliano et Sexto placuit etiam hoc casu ex senatusconsulto confirmari legatum; nam ex verbis etiam hoc casu accidere, ut iure civili inutile sit legatum, inde manifestum esse, quod eidem aliis verbis recte legatur, veluti per vindicationem, per damnationem, sinendi modo; [...]

> Inst.Gai.2.218.: Therefore, if a legacy of this kind is bequeathed to a non-heir, it will be void, and to such an extent is this true that Sabinus held that the *senatusconsultum Neronianum* could not even remedy the flaw. He says: 'indeed, it [the *senatusconsultum Neronianum*] only cures those faults which render invalidate a legacy under the *ius civile* on account of their wording, and not with regard to the person of the legatee.' It was, however, held by Julian and Sextus that, even in this instance, the legacy was rendered valid by the *senatus consultum*, for it might happen, in a case of this kind, that by the words employed a legacy would be void at civil law; and hence it is clear that a proper bequest could be made to the same person by other words, for example, *per vindicationem, per damnationem*, or *sinendi modo*; [...]

As we saw (Ch. 8.1.2), there was no agreement between the two schools of jurists of the first century AD as to whether the legacy *per praeceptionem* could also be left to a non-heir. This controversy continued even after the *senatusconsultum Neronianum de legatis* had been issued, with the Sabinians claiming that the question did not concern the form but the nature of the legacy *per praeceptionem*. The Proculians, on the contrary, saw this *senatus consultum* as confirming their view that a legacy *per praeceptionem* in favour of a non-heir could be turned into a legacy *per vindicationem*. The matter was settled by the time of Gaius (second century AD) by the opinions of Julian and Africanus (both second century AD). They stressed that the appropriate choice of words, which had been settled by the *senatusconsultum Neronianum*, could not be separated from the question of the legacy's legal nature. Consequently, they stated that the imperial provision also applied to the legacy *per praeceptionem* to a non-heir, which could be turned into a legacy *per vindicationem*.

As a result, the *senatus consultum* had lifted the strict type-casting of legacies under the *ius civile* and relaxed the requirement to adhere to the chosen type. After this repeal, it was sufficient for the legacy to follow any form that was somehow valid under the *ius civile*. The Senate's minimisation of the formalities for legacies of *ius civile* was in keeping with the general trend during the Empire to reduce the formal requirements of wills under the *ius civile* (Ch. 6.4). In this respect it should also be noted that the rules of *caducum* per *lex Iulia et Papia* applied to legacies as much as they restricted the appointment of heirs (Ch. 4.4.1).

8.4.2 Lex Iulia et Papia

The lack of capacity to obtain of the unmarried and childless under the *lex Iulia et Papia* (Ch. 4.4.1) also applied to legacies. Following the *lex Iulia*, the unmarried (*caelibes*) could not take upon will and the childless (*orbi*) could only receive half of what was left to them. The remainder accrued initially to the legatees who had the capacity to obtain, but later escheated to the imperial treasury. As in the case of testamentary appointments, there were exceptions for the benefit of descendants and parents up to the third degree. Hence, as far as the testator left legacies to close relatives in the direct line, the latter had the capacity to obtain, regardless of their marital status and number of children.

In addition to the general rules on the capacity to obtain legacies, Augustan marital laws also affected the content of legacies. We have seen (Ch. 4.4) that since the law on marriage within the orders (*lex Iulia de maritandis ordinibus* from 18BC) introduced the obligation to marry and also the obligation to remarry after divorce or the death of a spouse, previously valid conditions imposed on a legacy given by a husband to his wife were now considered invalid. This applied pre-eminently for the condition not to remarry:

> *Terentius Clemens, 4 ad legem Iuliam et Papiam: Cum vir uxori 'si a liberis ne nupserit' in annos singulos aliquid legavit, quid iuris sit? Iulianus respondit posse mulierem nubere et legatum capere. Quod si ita scriptum esset 'si a liberis impuberibus ne nupserit,' legem locum non habere, quia magis cura liberorum quam viduitas iniungeretur (D.35.1.62.2.)*

> Terentius Clemens, Lex Iulia et Papia, book 4: What is the law if a man leaves an annual bequest to his wife under the condition that 'she shall not marry away from the children?' Julian answers that the woman can marry and take the legacy. If, however, it said, 'if she does not marry away from her children as long as they are under the age of puberty,' then the rule does not apply because [the condition] imposes a duty [on the woman] to care for the children rather than the status of an unmarried woman. (D.35.1.62.2.)

The testator had left his wife an annual legacy on the condition that she would not abandon their children if she remarried. Since the legacy asked this woman not to remarry, this condition violated the duty of the *lex Iulia* to be married. Therefore, Julian (second century AD) decided to cancel that condition so that the woman could remarry and still receive her annual pension. According to Julian, the *lex Iulia* was not violated if the condition only concerned the care of children who were still minors. In this case, the condition was valid, so that a new marriage of the woman resulted in the loss of the legacy.

Even more important than the individual imperial interventions in the *ius civile* regarding legacies was the imperial enforcement of formless bequests, i.e. the legal revolution linked to the *fideicommissa* (sing. *fideicommissum*, 'given in trust').

8.5 Formless Bequests under the *ius novum* (*fideicommissa*)

A *fideicommissum*, i.e. a request to give something to a person without *testamenti factio passiva*, was initially only morally binding. It was therefore at the discretion of the person charged by the deceased to fulfil the wish. However, from the time of Emperor Augustus (27BC–AD14), these moral obligations became binding and their fulfilment could be claimed in court (Ch. 6.4):

> *Inst.2.23.1: Sciendum itaque est, omnia fideicommissa primis temporibus infirma esse quia nemo invitus cogebatur praestare id de quo rogatus erat: Quibus enim non poterant hereditates vel legata relinquere, si relinquebant, fidei committebant eorum qui capere ex testamento poterant: Et ideo fideicommissa appellata sunt, quia nullo vinculo iuris, sed tantum pudore eorum qui rogabantur, continebantur. Postea primus divus Augustus semel iterumque gratia personarum motus, vel quia per ipsius salutem rogatus quis diceretur, aut ob insignem quorundam perfidiam iussit consulibus auctoritatem suam*

interponere. Quod, quia iustum videbatur et populare erat, paulatim conversum est in adsiduam iurisdictionem: Tantusque favor eorum factus est, ut paulatim etiam praetor proprius crearetur, qui fideicommissis ius diceret, quem fideicommissarium appellabant.

Inst.2.23.1.: It is therefore important to realise that all *fideicommissa* were originally unenforceable, since no one could be coerced against his will to fulfil a request that was merely asked of him. Since there were certain categories of persons to whom testators could not leave inheritances or legacies, they charged those who had the *testamenti factio passiva* with a *fideicommissum* if they wished to leave them something. This is why they were called '*fideicommissa*', because the constraints of the law did not enforce them, but only by the fideicommissary's decency. Afterwards, the deified Emperor Augustus was the first to order the consuls once and repeated, either out of favour towards certain persons or because the request was said to be made in the name of his welfare or because he was moved to it by individual and flagrant cases of duplicity to enforce the duty by their authority. And as this was considered just and approved by the people, a new and permanent jurisdiction was gradually developed. The *fideicommissa* became so popular that soon a special praetor was appointed to deal with the complaints concerning them and he was called the *praetor fideicommissarius*.

Fideicommissary requests became legally binding when Emperor Augustus instructed the consuls to enforce the *fideicommissa*. Initially, consuls were mandated to use their authority to ensure the fulfilment of moral duty in cases where non-compliance was perceived as a blatant disregard for the moral order. Subsequently, the level of protection granted to fideicommissaries rose to such an extent that it became necessary to appoint a separate praetor. This *praetor fideicommissarius* would decide claims of non-compliance with the *fideicommissa* through a *cognitio extra ordinem*.

Augustus' reforms did not repeal the existing law of legacies, but added the legal protection of the new type of bequest to the existing types of legacies under the *ius civile*. However, this coexistence led to an unequal competition between the bequests of the *ius civile*, which were subject to a rigorous formalism, and the formless *fideicommissa*, which were measured only by moral standards.

We will now trace the consequences of the formlessness of *fideicommissa* for testamentary practice. Then we will examine the imperial legal enactments which sought to bring the law of *fideicommissa* (*ius novum*) into line with the existing law of legacies (*ius civile*).

8.5.1 *The Formlessness of the* fideicommissa

The main characteristic of *fideicommissa* is their formlessness. Hence, their legal consequences can initially be circumscribed negatively, i.e. by the absence of all customary formal requirements of the law of legacies:

> Inst.Gai.2.249.: *Verba autem utilia fideicommissorum haec [recte] maxime in usu esse videntur: 'Peto, rogo, volo, fidei committo,' quae proinde firma singula sunt, atque si omnia in unum congesta sint.*
>
> Inst.Gai.2.249.: The words that are most appropriate and most in use for leaving a *fideicommissum* are: 'I beg; I ask; I wish; I entrust'; and these are just as binding if used on their own as they are if connected in a single phrase.

Gaius (second century AD) mentioned words regularly used in *fideicommissa* like 'to ask', 'to wish for', and 'to entrust.' However, unlike appointing heirs and leaving legacies under the *ius civile*, using specific words was unnecessary for *fideicommissa*. It was sufficient that the intention of the testator was unambiguously expressed:

> Inst.Gai.2.281.: *Item legata Graece scripta non valent; fideicommissa vero valent.*
>
> Inst.Gai.2.281.: Legacies left in Greek are not valid, but *fideicommissa* are.

Consequently, *fideicommissa* were also valid even if they were not written in Latin but in Greek, whereas Latin was mandatory for the validity of a will under the *ius civile*.

The leniency with regard to the formal requirements for *fideicommissa* also implied freedom of content, even though imperial legislation later tried to assimilate the conditions for valid *fideicommissa* with the requirements for legacies (Ch. 8.6). Despite the freedom of form, the testator's capacity to draw up a will had also always been indispensable for the *fideicommissa*.

> Ulpianus, 1 fideicommissorum: *Sed si filius familias vel servus fideicommissum reliquerit, non valet. [...] (D.32.1.1.)*
>
> Ulpian, Fideicommissa, book 1: But, if a *filius familias*, or a slave, leaves a *fideicommissum*, it will not be valid. [...] (D.32.1.1.)

Therefore, slaves and children under the paternal power were as incapable of leaving *fideicommissa* (Ch. 6.1.2) as they were of leaving wills. Initially, if the fideicommissary lacked the legal capacity to inherit, this did not invalidate the *fideicommissum*:

Inst.Gai.2.285.: Ut ecce peregrini poterant fideicommissa capere, et fere haec fuit origo fideicommissorum [...]

Inst.Gai.2.285.: For instance, non-Romans could act as beneficiaries of the *fideicommissa*, and this was probably how *fideicommissa* originated [...]

Whereas the appointment of heirs and the leaving of legacies under the *ius civile* required that the beneficiary was a Roman citizen and thus possessed the capacity to be considered an heir, *fideicommissa* could initially also be granted to non-Romans who lacked the passive *testamenti factio*.

Moreover, the introduced lack of capacity to obtain (*incapacitas*) under the *lex Iulia et Papia* for childless and unmarried persons did not at first affect the ability to acquire by *fideicommissa*.

Inst.Gai.2.286–286a (286): Caelibes quoque, qui per legem Iuliam hereditates legataque capere prohibentur, olim fideicommissa videbantur capere posse.
(286a) Item orbi, qui per legem Papiam ob id, quod liberos non habent, dimidias partes hereditatum legatorumque perdunt, olim solida fideicommissa videbantur capere posse. [...]

Inst.Gai.2.286–286a.: (286) Persons who are unmarried are, under the *lex Iulia* prohibited from taking estates and legacies, were once considered capable of being the beneficiaries of a *fideicommissum*.
(286a) In the same way, the childless, who under the terms of the *lex Papia* loose half of their inheritances and legacies because they have no children, were formerly considered capable of taking the full benefit of *fideicommissa*. [...]

Naturally, a *fideicommissum* made it possible to circumvent the limitations of the *ius civile* by making somebody a fideicommissary who lacked capacity to obtain under a will because of the *lex Iulia et Papia*.

Also, the requirement for the legacy of the *ius civile* to leave legacies only to certain persons did not initially apply to *fideicommissa*:

Inst.Gai.2.287.: Item olim incertae personae [...] per fideicommissum relinqui poterat, quamvis <is> neque heres institui neque legari ei posset. [...]

Inst.Gai.2.287.: Again, in former times, something could be left by a *fideicommissum* to an unspecified group of persons, [...] although an uncertain person could neither be appointed an heir nor a legatee. [...]

Unlike a legacy, the testator did not have to specify the beneficiary in advance, but could leave it to chance. Similarly, the prohibition of penal legacies imperial provisions only later extended (Ch. 8.2.1) to *fideicommissa*:

> *Inst.Gai.2.288.: Item poenae nomine iam non dubitatur nec per fideicommissum quidem relinqui posse.*

> Inst.Gai.2.288.: Similarly, nowadays it is uncontested that property cannot be left under a *fideicommissum* as a means of punishment.

By the time of Gaius (second century AD), the interpretation of the jurists and the imperial legislation had already reached such an extent of assimilation between *fideicommissa* and legacies that the former could no longer be left with the sole intention of punishing the heir.

However, legacies and *fideicommissa* were not assimilated because of their different dependence on the appointment of an heir and the necessary integration in the will. Whereas legacies could only be charged to an heir, *fideicommissa* could burden anyone who stood to benefit from the estate. A first example of beneficiaries of the estate are the legatees:

> *Ulpianus, 8 disputationum: Fideicommissum, quod a legatario relinquitur, ita demum ab eo debetur, si ad legatarium legatum pervenerit. (D.30.78.)*

> Ulpian, Disputations, book 8: Where a legatee is charged with a *fideicommissum*, he is only obligated to deliver it if he has actually received the legacy. (D.30.78.)

It turns out that a legatee himself could be charged with a *fideicommissum*. However, he was only obligated to fulfil the *fideicommissum* if he had actually benefited from the legacy. In addition, the amount to be given because of the *fideicommissum* was limited by the size of the legacy, which implied that the legatee would only be obliged to return what he had received.

However, *fideicommissa* were valid even without a will:

> *Inst.Gai.2.270.: Item intestatus moriturus potest ab eo, ad quem bona eius pertinent, fideicommissum alicui relinquere; cum alioquin ab eo legari non possit.*

> Inst.Gai.2.270.: In the same way, a person who is about to die intestate can charge his heir to transfer his estate to a third party under the terms of a *fideicommissum*, but he cannot charge him with a legacy.

As we saw (Ch. 8.1.4), under the *ius civile*, a valid legacy required a valid will, i.e. a duly appointed heir and the latter's acceptance of the estate. If the heir disclaimed the estate, the order of intestacy applied, and the legacy became invalid. The reverse was true for *fideicommissa*, which could also be charged to an heir by intestacy.

However, for a *fideicommissum* to be validly charged on an heir by intestacy, it was a requirement that the testator had wanted or at least considered succession by intestacy:

Paulus, liber singularis de iure codicillorum: Sed ideo fideicommissa dari possunt ab intestato succedentibus, quoniam creditur pater familias sponte sua his relinquere legitimam hereditatem. (D.29.7.8.1.)

Paul, Codicils, sole book: But the reason why *fideicommissa* can be charged on those succeeding on intestacy is that the *pater familias* is considered to have left them his estate as statutory heirs out of his free will. (D.29.7.8.1.)

If the testator had planned the succession by intestacy, and thus deliberately left no will, he could charge the heirs by intestacy with *fideicommissa*. However, if the testator's will was invalid, the heir by intestacy could not be charged with a *fideicommissum*:

Gaius, 1 fideicommissorum: Ex filio praeterito, licet suus heres erit, fideicommissum relinqui non potest. (D.32.2.)

Gaius, Fideicommissa, book 1: A *fideicommissum* cannot be charged to a son who has been passed over in a will, even though he should be a direct heir. (D.32.2.)

If a father's will was invalid because the *filius familias* had been passed over (Ch. 7.1.1), the latter would become an heir on intestacy. However, as Gaius (second century AD) explained he could not be charged with a *fideicommissum* because the *fideicommissum* had not been left for the case of intestacy. This means that the *fideicommissa* left in the will could not be upheld once the order of intestacy came into force:

Paulus, 9 quaestionum: Si quis testamento facto a filiis suis, quos heredes instituisset, fideicommissa reliquisset non ut a legitimis heredibus, sed ut a scriptis, et testamentum aliquo casu irritum factum sit, filii ab intestato venientes fideicommissa ex testamento praestare compelli non possunt. (D.31.81.)

Paul, Questions, book 9: If anyone makes a will, appointing his children as heirs and charges them with *fideicommissa*, on the assumptions that they are appointed heirs and not statutory heirs, and if the will becomes void for some reason, and his children become heirs on intestacy, they cannot be compelled to deliver the *fideicommissa*. (D.31.81.)

In the case discussed by Paul, the order of intestacy set in because the will was incorrect. Even though the heir appointed in the will was identical with the heir by intestacy, i.e. the children of the decedent were called upon in both cases, the *fideicommissum* did not burden the heir by intestacy. A *fideicommissum* on the heir by intestacy would only be valid if the testator had refrained from appointing an heir by will.

The expressed wish of the testator to die intestate was decisive for the validity of the *fideicommissum* imposed on the heir by intestacy. The testator could therefore provide for intestacy on his death:

> *Marcianus, 8 institutionum: Qui intestato decedit et scit bona sua ad fiscum perventura vacantia, fidei fisci committere potest. (D.30.114.2.)*
>
> Marcian, Institutes, book 8: A person who dies intestate and knows that his property will fall to the imperial treasury can charge it with a *fideicommissum*. (D.30.114.2.)

In this way, even the imperial treasury (*fiscus*) could be charged with a *fideicommissum* as heir by intestacy, provided that the testator was aware that the estate would escheat to the *fiscus* as vacant (*bona vacantia*, Ch. 6.2.1). In this case, the testator anticipated his intestate death and the treasury's acquisition of his estate.

This separation of *fideicommissa* from testamentary appointments ultimately made it possible to leave formless legacies not only on the death of the benefactor but also in the event of the death of the beneficiary:

> *Inst.Gai.2.277.: Item quamvis non possimus post mortem eius, qui nobis heres extiterit, alium in locum eius heredem instituere, tamen possumus eum rogare, ut, cum morietur, alii eam hereditatem totam vel ex parte restituat; et quia post mortem quoque heredis fideicommissum dari potest, idem efficere possumus et si ita scripserimus: 'Cum Titius heres meus mortuus erit, volo hereditatem meam ad Publium Maevium pertinere'. [...]*
>
> Inst.Gai.2.277.: In like manner, although we cannot, after the death of a person who was our heir, appoint another in his place. Still, we can request him to transfer the entire estate, or a share of the same, to another party when he dies. For the reason that a *fideicommmissum* of inheritance may be created to take effect after the death of an heir, we may bring about the same result by inserting in the will: 'When my heir Titius dies, I want my estate to belong to Publius Mævius'. [...]

While the principle *semel heres, semper heres*, prevented the appointment of another heir on the death of the first heir (Ch. 6.1.3), a *fideicommissum* could be made for the death of the heir. In this case, at the time of his death, the burdened heir had to transfer the estate to the fideicommissary.

The divergences between the law of testamentary succession under the *ius civile* and the initial freedom of the *fideicommissa* in form, content and scope show that their judicial enforcement, introduced by Emperor Augustus (27BC–AD14), had brought about a fundamental change in the law of legacies.

Overview 38: Initial Differences between Legacies and *fideicommissa*

	drawing up:	beneficiary:	chargee:	effect:
legacies:	special wording; only if the will itself is valid; only to certain persons; not only for the punishment of the heir	Romans with capacity to obtain	only a testamentary heir (who has accepted the inheritance)	only for one's own death
fideicommissa:	formless; also without a (valid) will; also to unspecified groups; also for the punishment of the heir	- also *peregrini* - also persons without the capacity to obtain	- testamentary heir - legatee - heir on intestacy - imperial treasury (vacant estate)	also in the event of the heir's death

From the point of view of the testator, the differences and points of divergence between the *fideicommissa* and the law of legacies and wills of the *ius civile* (Overview 38) offered new possibilities for organising his succession. We will now focus on two typical applications of the *fideicommissa*, namely the *fideicommissum* of inheritance and the family *fideicommissum*.

8.5.2 The Universal fideicommissum

Since a *fideicommissum* could be imposed on anyone who might benefit from an inheritance, it was particularly suitable for obliging an heir, a legatee or even a fideicommissary to transfer the received benefit to a third party. This mechanism was frequently used in the *fideicommissum* of inheritance, i.e. the obligation of an heir to transfer all or part of the inheritance received to a third party (universal *fideicommissum*).

> Inst.Gai.2.250.: *Cum igitur scripserimus: 'Lucius Titius heres esto,' possumus adicere: 'Rogo te, Luci Titi, petoque a te, ut cum primum possis hereditatem meam adire, Gaio Seio reddas restituas.' Possumus autem et de parte restituenda rogare; et liberum est vel sub condicione vel pure relinquere fideicommissa vel ex die certa.*
>
> Inst.Gai.2.250.: Therefore, when we have written: 'let Lucius Titius be my heir,' we can add: 'I ask you, Lucius Titius, and I beg you, that as soon as

you can accept my inheritance, to deliver and transfer it to Gaius Seius'; and we can also ask him to return a part of it. It is also permitted to leave the *fideicommissum* under a condition, unconditionally, or for a specific date.

While the *ius civile* did not allow for a time limit on the appointment of an heir, the *fideicommissum* of inheritance allowed for the appointment of two heirs in succession. For this purpose, the first heir had to be appointed as heir, while the second heir was appointed as fideicommissary and could claim the estate from the former on a specific date or after the fulfilment of a condition. As in the case of legacies, the validity of the *fideicommissum* was, in these instances, subject to a condition or a limitation. However, the obvious difference between legacies and *fideicommissum* of inheritance is that the fideicommissary did not merely receive a legacy, but the proprietary position of an heir.

This universal *fideicommissum* could be included directly in the will or mentioned in a formless addition to a will (codicil; Ch. 6.4.1):

> *Paulus, 14 responsorum: Paulus respondit his verbis: 'Semproni, heredem te non scripsi festinans per infirmitatem: Ideoque ei dari volo tantum, quantum pro uncia hereditatis competeret', videri quidem magis quantitatem, quam portionem hereditatis relictam, sed sic accipiendum, uti videatur de uncia etiam restituenda sensisse. (D.36.1.63.)*
>
> Paul, Replies, book 14: Paul replied thus, 'Sempronius, I have not appointed you as my heir because I rushed on account of my weakness. Therefore, I want him to receive the amount equal to a twelfth of my estate.' This seems to be rather an amount than a share of the estate. But it must rather be taken to mean that the testator intended to leave him the restitution of one-twelfth of his estate. (D.36.1.63.)

A testator had appointed several heirs. Due to the heir's old age or illness, the name of Sempronius was not added in the list of heirs. Since an actual appointment was no longer possible, the heirs appointed in the will were obliged by a codicil to let Sempronius have a determined share of the estate. Even though this appointment for a specific amount would have been invalid under the *ius civile* as an *institutio ex certa re* (Ch. 6.2.2), it was valid as a *fideicommissum*. Therefore, the heirs mentioned in the will had to transfer the equivalent of 1/12 of the estate to the beneficiary Sempronius.

A *fideicommissum* of inheritance could also be used to leave something to a person who had no capacity to own property, or lacked capacity to obtain at the time of succession taking the perspective that the person would later have the capability to profit from the estate. Accordingly, children were often made the beneficiaries with the provision that the estate should only be transferred in total or partially once they had reached a certain age:

Papinianus, 20 quaestionum: Cum Pollidius a propinqua sua heres institutus rogatus fuisset filiae mulieris 'quidquid ex bonis eius ad se pervenisset, cum certam aetatem puella complesset, restituere,' idque sibi mater ideo placuisse testamento comprehendisset, ne filiae tutoribus, sed potius necessitudini res committerentur, [...]. (D. 22.1.3.3.)

Papinian, Questions, book 20: Pollidius was appointed heir by a female relative and asked by her 'to deliver to her daughter any property belonging to her estate that might come into his hands once she had reached a certain age'. And the mother stated in her will that she had decided thus to place her daughter's affairs in the hands of a relative rather than her daughter's guardians, [...] (D. 22.1.3.3.)

Papinian discusses a case where Pollidius, a relative of the testator, was charged with a *fideicommissum* to prevent the daughter's guardians from accessing the estate. Instead of appointing her daughter as heir and allowing the estate to be controlled by the daughter's guardians until the daughter came of age (*pubertas*), the mother appointed Pollidius as sole heir and charged him with a *fideicommissum* to give everything he would acquire from the estate to the daughter as soon as she had reached maturity.

Moreover, the *fideicommissum* of inheritance was used to divide the estate among the heirs even before the partition of the estate. A case in point is the following:

Scaevola, 21 digestorum: Maevia filium heredem instituit ex quincunce, Titiam filiam ex quadrante, Septicium filium ex triente, cuius fidei commisit in haec verba: 'Te rogo, fili Septici, si intra vicensimum annum sine liberis morieris, quidquid ex hereditate mea ad te pervenerit, hoc fratribus tuis restituas.' Quaesitum est, an Septicio filio defuncto intra vicensimum annum sine liberis hoc fideicommissum utrum pro portionibus hereditariis ad fratrem et sororem eius pertineat an vero aequaliter. Respondit pro parte hereditaria. (D.36.1.80.5.)

Scaevola, Digest, book 21: Maevia appointed her son heir to five-twelfths of her estate, her daughter, Titia, to one-fourth, and her other son, Septicius, to one-third. The latter she charged with a *fideicommissum* thus, 'My son, Septicius, I ask you to return to your siblings whatever you might receive from my inheritance, should you die childless before the age of twenty.' Since Septicius died without offspring before his twentieth year, the question is whether the *fideicommissum* belongs to his brother and sister in proportion to their shares in the inheritance or equally. He replied that it would belong to them in proportion to their respective shares. (D.36.1.80.5.)

In the case discussed by Scaevola, a mother has appointed her children to different parts of the estate (first son: 5/12, daughter: 1/4 = 3/12, second son: 1/3 = 4/12). At the same time, she charged her second son with a *fideicommissum* in favour of his siblings if he died without offspring before or at the age of twenty. Hence, if the son died childless before his twentieth year, his siblings could request his mother's inheritance from his heirs. It thus turns out that the mother has used the *fideicommissum* of inheritance to distribute her estate even after the death of one of her sons, thus ensuring that her estate remained in the hands of her children. The case needed juristic interpretation because the mother had not specified to which parts the estate should be distributed among the remaining siblings. Scaevola decided that the proportion arranged for in the will should be used to determine the siblings' shares; accordingly, the sister would get 37.5 per cent of the estate of the second son, the second brother 62.5 per cent.

The family entail (*fideicommissum familiae relictum*) aimed at an even stronger attachment of the estate or items from the estate to the family and its members.

8.5.3 The Family Entail

A family entail (*fideicommissum familiae relictum*) was a *fideicommissum* obligating future generations of a family to pass a certain object, usually a farmstead or a parcel of land, only to members of the said family:

> *Marcianus, 8 institutionum: Cum pater filio herede instituto, ex quo tres habuerat nepotes, fideicommisit, ne fundum alienaret et ut in familia relinqueret, et filius decedens duos heredes instituit, tertium exheredavit, eum fundum extraneo legavit, divi Severus et Antoninus rescripserunt verum esse non paruisse voluntati defuncti filium. (D.30.114.15.)*
>
> Marcianus, book 8: When a father appointed his son by whom he had three grandsons as his heir and charged him by *fideicommissum* not to sell the farm but to keep it in the family; and the son, upon his death, appointed two of his children as heirs, disinheriting a third, and bequeathed the said farm to a stranger, the deified Severus and Antoninus stated in a rescript that it was true that the son had not complied with the wish of the decedent. (D.30.114.15.)

A father charged his son with a *fideicommissum* to keep the farmstead beyond the latter's death in the family. Since the son had bequeathed the farmstead to a non-family member, he had violated the family entail. The question was whether this *fideicommissum* invalidated the acquisition of the non-member, hence if the family entail had a 'real' effect. If this were so, subsequent generations could claim the restitution of the land from the third parties on the basis of the initial *fideicommissum*:

Marcianus, 8 institutionum: Divi Severus et Antoninus rescripserunt eos, qui testamento vetant quid alienari nec causam exprimunt, propter quam id fieri velint, nisi invenitur persona, cuius respectu hoc a testatore dispositum est, nullius esse momenti scripturam, quasi nudum praeceptum reliquerint, quia talem legem testamento non possunt dicere: Quod si liberis aut posteris [...] aut heredibus aut aliis quibusdam personis consulentes eiusmodi voluntatem significarent, eam servandam esse, sed haec neque creditoribus neque fisco fraudi esse: [...] (D.30.114.14.)

Marcian, Institutes, book 8: The deified Severus and Antoninus have stated in a rescript that if a testator forbids by will that anything from his estate should be sold, but does not explain his motivation, and no one is found in whose favour this disposition was inserted, the disposal ban is invalid, just as if they [the testators] had left a bare request because such a disposition is not binding in a will. But this [the ban] is valid, if he expressed such a wish in favour of his children, [other] descendants, [...] heirs, or specified other persons. However, this [ban] will not work to the detriment of creditors or the imperial treasury [...] (D.30.114.14.)

According to the rescript of the Emperors Septimius Severus (AD193–211) and Caracalla (AD211–217), mentioned by Marcian, the family entail could only be brought against third parties if, in addition to the general prohibition on transferring the item of the estate outside the family, it also mentioned the beneficiaries as well as the testator's motivation for the disposal ban. The testator's statement that he acted out of care for the descendants or heirs was considered a sufficient reason. This statement also explicitly named the beneficiaries of the ban. However, the thus valid family entail only hindered the transfer of ownership to a third party if it resulted from a sale or an inheritance. In contrast, it could not forestall escheatment to the imperial treasury or administration of an estate, effected by its creditors through *venditio bonorum*.

Whether a particular claimant belonged to the circle of beneficiaries was decided by means of interpretation:

Modestinus, 9 regularum: In fideicommisso quod familiae relinquitur hi ad petitionem eius admitti possunt, qui nominati sunt, aut post omnes eos exstinctos qui ex nomine defuncti fuerint eo tempore, quo testator moreretur, et qui ex his primo gradu procreati sint, nisi specialiter defunctus ad ulteriores voluntatem suam extenderit. (D.31.32.6.)

Modestinus, Rules, book 8: Where a *fideicommissum* is left to the family, those are allowed to claim it who have been expressly mentioned, or, if all of them are dead, those who had the name of the decedent at the time of the testator's death, as well as their descendants in the first degree;

unless the decedent included especially those further removed in his will. (D.31.32.6.)

The testator left a *fideicommissum* in which he mentioned the beneficiaries, but the they all died. Whether other descendants could also claim the *fideicommissum* if the heir acted against the testator's wishes was debated among Roman jurists. Modestinus (third century AD) argued that the *fideicommissum* was valid even after the death of the named beneficiaries. After the beneficiaries' deaths, their direct descendants were to be seen as beneficiaries. The beneficiary's heir on intestacy was thus protected from subsequent dispositions by the heir.

Both the *fideicommissum* of inheritance and the family entail demonstrate the flexibility and the freedom of disposition granted to the testator by the newly created institution. This explains the popularity and the frequency of *fideicommissa*, and the emperors' efforts to further regulate them.

8.6 The Further Configuration of the Law on *fideicommissa*

The need to further regulate the *fideicommissa* arose initially in relation to the universal *fideicommissa* which resulted in the separation of a legal heir and an actual beneficiary of the estate after the transfer of the inheritance:

> Inst.Gai.2.251.: *Restituta autem hereditate is, qui restituit, nihilo minus heres permanet; [...]*

> Inst.Gai.2.251.: After the inheritance has been transferred, the one who transferred it will continue to be the heir [...]

The heir charged with a *fideicommissum* remained the statutory heir, even after having transferred the estate in total or partially to the beneficiary. The fideicommissary who was in possession of the estate could therefore not take action against the debtors of the estate. Conversely, the legal heir was fully liable for the debts of the estate, albeit he obtained little or no financial gain from the inheritance. This discrepancy between the status of the inheritance and the benefits of the inheritance was a well-known problem in the sale of an inheritance (*venditio hereditatis*). The legal mechanisms developed for such a sale were therefore also used to deal with the *fideicommissum* of inheritance:

> Gai.2.252.: *[...] Et quae stipulationes inter venditorem hereditatis et emptorem interponi solent, eaedem interponebantur inter heredem et eum, cui restituebatur hereditas, id est hoc modo: Heres quidem stipulabatur ab eo, cui restituebatur hereditas, ut quidquid hereditario nomine condemnatus fuisset sive quid alias bona fide dedisset, eo nomine indemnis esset, et omnino si quis cum eo hereditario nomine ageret, ut recte defenderetur; ille vero, qui*

recipiebat hereditatem, invicem stipulabatur, ut si quid ex hereditate ad heredem pervenisset, id sibi restitueretur, ut etiam pateretur eum hereditarias actiones procuratorio aut cognitorio nomine exequi.

Inst.Gai.2.252.: [...] and the same stipulations which are usually entered into between the vendor and the purchaser of an estate were accustomed to take place between the heir and the party to whom the estate was conveyed. This was done in the following manner: The heir made the party to whom the estate was transferred promise by stipulation that he would be indemnified on account of whatever he might have been convicted to pay because of the inheritance, or might have paid in good faith. And if anyone were to bring an action against him [the heir] because of the inheritance, that he would be properly defended. In turn, the party who received the estate [fideicommissary] made the heir promise by stipulation that if anything came into the heir's hands which belonged to the estate it would be restored to him [the fideicommissary] and also that he [the fideicommissary] would be permitted, either as formless (*procurator*) or as formal representative (*cognitor*) of the heir, to bring any actions which the latter was entitled to bring in his own name.

By using the *stipulatio* of the buyer and seller of the estate (*stipulationes emptae et venditae hereditatis*), the fideicommissary and the heir promised each other that they would act as if the position of an heir had been transferred with the estate. The fideicommissary promised to indemnify the heir against any action that might be brought against the estate, and thus against the heir. In return, the heir promised the fideicommissary to hand over or reimburse all benefits from the estate. In addition, the heir permitted the fideicommissary to claim payment from the debtors of the estate on the heir's behalf. Thus, the stipulations did not actually transfer the position of heir to the fideicommissary, but the mutual promises put the parties in a position as if not only the inheritance but also the position of heir had been transferred.

The *senatusconsultum Trebellianum* of 25 August AD55 simplified this procedure.

8.6.1 Senatusconsultum Trebellianum

Ulpian renders the text of the *senatus consultum* thus:

Ulpianus, 3 fideicommissorum: (1) Factum est enim senatus consultum temporibus Neronis octavo calendas septembres Annaeo Seneca et Trebellio Maximo consulibus, cuius verba haec sunt:
(2) 'Cum esset aequissimum in omnibus fideicommissariis hereditatibus, si qua de his bonis iudicia penderent, ex his eos subire, in quos ius fructusque

transferretur, potius quam cuique periculosam esse fidem suam: Placet, ut actiones, quae in heredem heredibusque dari solent, eas neque in eos neque his dari, qui fidei suae commissum sic, uti rogati essent, restituissent, sed his et in eos, quibus ex testamento fideicommissum restitutum fuisset, quo magis in reliquum confirmentur supremae defunctorum voluntates.' (D.36.1.1.1–2.)

Ulpian, Fideicommissa, book 3: (1) This *senatusconsultum* was made in the time of Nero, on the eighth day before the Kalends of September, during the consulate of Annaeus Seneca and Trebellius Maximus, it reads thus:

(2) 'Since it was most equitable for most fideicommissary inheritances if any actions were pending concerning the estate, that they lied against those to whom the right and use are transferred, rather than that anybody should be put in danger by his faithful [fulfilment of the *fideicommissum*]. It is thus decided that actions usually granted against the heir [as defendant], or in favour of heirs [as claimants], will be granted neither against them nor against those to who have surrendered the *fideicommissum* as requested. Rather, the actions shall be granted to these and against those to whom the the *fideicommissum* has been conveyed by the will so that the last expressions of the decedent's will may be all the more respected in the future.' (D.36.1.1.1–2.)

The *senatusconsultum*, enacted during the reign of Emperor Nero (AD54–68), foresaw that once the inheritance had been transferred to the fideicommissary, the latter was to be treated as the heir even without carrying out the aforementioned *stipulationes*. As a result, all actions on behalf of the estate were to be granted to the fideicommissary and the latter was to be held liable for all debts of the estate. In return, the heir was released from all liabilities arising from the inheritance, but could not claim any rights from the estate. The *senatusconsultum Trebellianum* based this rule on equity (*aequitas*) and the consideration of the decedent's last wishes. It would be unfair to hold the heir liable even after he had transferred the estate since he had not actually benefited from it. In addition, it would be contrary to the testator's wishes if the fideicommissary was not treated as an heir.

The aim of the *senatusconsultum* was carried out by the praetor. In the same way that the magistrate had granted the *bonorum possessor* the claims of the heir and enabled inheritance claims against the praetorian heir (Ch. 4.2.2), he now assigned the active and the passive legitimation of claims for and against the estate to the fideicommissary by allowing the creditors of the estate to sue him and by appointing him as claimant against the debtors of the estate. This remedy is called a 'transfer of actions.' The law was simplified not only to get rid of cumbersome stipulations, but also to encourage heirs to accept the inheritance despite a fideicommissum of inheritance:

Ulpianus, 3 fideicommissorum: Sublata est hoc senatus consulto dubitatio eorum, qui adire hereditatem recusare seu metu litium seu praetextu metus censuerunt. (D.36.1.1.3.)

Ulpian, Fideicommissa, book 3: This *senatus consultum* puts an end to the doubts of those who decided to renounce inheritances, either because of a fear of litigation or under the pretext of such a fear. (D.36.1.1.3.)

The purpose of the *senatusconsultum Trebellianum* was to encourage the heir to accept the inheritance, even if he had to convey it to the fideicommissary with immediate effect. Indeed, accepting an inheritance that would only bring liabilities and debts was not attractive. But if the heir refused to accept the inheritance, the *fideicommissum* of inheritance would become ineffective. By making the fideicommissary liable for the debts of the estate after its restitution, the *senatusconsultum* eased the position of the heir and thus incited him to accept the inheritance and to fulfil the *fideicommissum* of inheritance.

However, there was still a risk that the *fideicommissum* would become ineffective if the heir refused to accept the inheritance:

Ulpianus, 3 fideicommissorum: Hoc autem senatus consultum locum habet, sive ex testamento quis heres esset sive ab intesto rogatusque sit restituere hereditatem. (D.36.1.1.5.)

Ulpian, Fideicommissa, book 3: This *senatus consultum* applies whether the heir charged with the estate transfer is a testamentary heir or an heir on intestacy. (D.36.1.1.5.)

Since an heir on intestacy could also be burdened with a *fideicommissum*, the testator risked not only becoming intestate but also dying without heirs if the heir on intestacy renounced the inheritance because of the *fideicommissum* of inheritance. The estate could then be claimed as vacant by the imperial treasury. As we saw (Ch. 8.5.1), it was even possible to charge the imperial treasury with a *fideicommissum*, but this presupposed that the deceased had considered the possibility of the treasury taking the estate beforehand. If the estate came to the treasury only after the inheritance had been renounced, the testator could not charge the *fiscus* with a *fideicommissum* for the same reason that he could not charge the heirs on intestacy after the testamentary order of succession had failed.

A *senatusconsultum Pegasianum*, enacted during the reign of Emperor Vespasian (AD69–79), revealed that the *senatusconsultum Trebellianum* did not effectively address the uncertainties the testator was facing when leaving *fideicommissa*, especially *fideicommissa* of inheritances.

8.6.2 *The* Senatusconsultum Pegasianum

The *senatusconsultum Pegasianum* contained various regulations to promote the acceptance of an inheritance, albeit the latter was burdened with a *fideicommissum*. Just as the *senatusconsultum Trebellianum*, its first rule concerned an heir who was charged with a *fideicommissum* of inheritance:

> *Gai.2.254: Sed rursus quia heredes scripti, cum aut totam hereditatem aut paene totam plerumque restituere rogabantur, adire hereditatem ob nullum aut minimum lucrum recusabant atque ob id extinguebantur fideicommissa, postea Pegaso et Pusione consulibus senatus censuit, ut ei, qui rogatus est hereditatem restituere, proinde liceret quartam partem retinere, atque e lege Falcidia in legatis retinenda conceditur: [...]*
>
> Inst.Gai.2.254.: But again, because the appointed heirs, when requested to convey either all the estate, or nearly all of it, renounced to accept it on account of the little or no advantage received, and hence the *fideicommissa* became inoperative, it was afterwards in the consulate of Pegasus and Pusio, that the Senate decided that the heir who had been requested to convey an estate should be permitted to retain one-fourth of the estate, just as he is permitted to do under the *Lex Falcidia* in the case of legacies; [...]

Following the *senatusconsultum Pegasianum*, the heir who had to convey the inheritance in part or as a whole because of a *fideicommissum* of inheritance was encouraged to accept the inheritance by being allowed to retain one-fourth of the estate. Like an heir charged with a legacy, who could keep one-fourth under the *lex Falcidia* (Ch. 8.2.2), the heir charged with a *fideicommissum* of inheritance should be able to keep one-fourth of the estate. The provisions of the *senatusconsultum Pegasianum* partially repealed those of the *senatusconsultum Trebellianum*:

> *Inst.Gai.2.255–256: (255) Ergo si quidem non plus quam dodrantem hereditatis scriptus heres rogatus sit restituere, tum ex Trebelliano senatus consulto restituitur hereditas, et in utrumque actiones hereditariae pro rata parte dantur, in heredem quidem iure civili, in eum vero, qui recipit hereditatem, ex senatus consulto Trebelliano; quamquam heres etiam pro ea parte, quam restituit, heres permanet eique et in eum solidae actiones competunt; sed non ulterius oneratur, nec ulterius illi dantur actiones, quam apud eum commodum hereditatis remanet.*
> *(256) At si quis plus quam dodrantem vel etiam totam hereditatem restituere rogatus sit, locus est Pegasiano senatus consulto.*
>
> Inst.Gai.2.255–256.: (255) Therefore, if the appointed heir is asked to transfer no more than three-fourths of the estate, it will then be transferred under

the *senatusconsultum Trebellianum* and the actions will be granted pro rata on both sides against the heir according to the *ius civile*, and against the beneficiary of the *fideicommissum* in application of the *senatusconsultum Trebellianum*. For, although the heir continues to be such even concerning that part of the estate which he has conveyed to the fideicommissary, and actions for and against the estate can be brought by and against him; still, he cannot be made liable for anything more, nor can actions be granted against him for any further claims beyond the amount of gain which he has obtained from the estate.

(256) If someone is requested to transfer more than three-fourths of the estate or all of it, there is ground for applying the *senatusconsultum Pegasianum*.

Both *senatusconsulta* applied in proportion to the size of the share that the heir had to convey to the fideicommissary. If the testator had charged the heir with the restitution of less than three-fourths of the estate, leaving him one quarter from the outset, only the *senatusconsultum Trebellianum* applied. The transfer of actions foreseen by this *senatusconsultum* was conditioned by the percentage allotted to the heir and the fideicommissary, respectively. Thus, the heir was liable for the estate's debt only to the extent that he benefited from it; the fideicommissary, on the contrary, received the estate's actions only in proportion to his share in the estate.

However, if the testator had charged the heir with the restitution of the entire estate or more than three-fourths to the fideicommissary, so that the heir did not retain a quarter, the new *senatusconsultum Pegasianum* applied. It ordered that, against the testator's instructions, the heir should keep one-fourth of the estate, which meant that the fideicommissary received only three-fourths of the estate. The distribution of actions for and against the estate depended on whether the heir had accepted the inheritance voluntarily or had been forced to accept it in view of the *fideicommissum* of inheritance:

> Inst.Gai.2.257.: *Sed is, qui semel adierit hereditatem, si modo sua voluntate adierit, sive retinuerit quartam partem sive noluerit retinere, ipse universa onera hereditaria sustinet; sed quarta quidem retenta quasi partis et pro parte stipulationes interponi debent tamquam inter partiarium legatarium et heredem; si vero totam hereditatem restituerit, ad exemplum emptae et venditae hereditatis stipulationes interponendae sunt.*

Inst.Gai.2.257.: But if he has once accepted the inheritance, if only by his free will, shall personally bear all burdens of the inheritance, whether he keeps one-fourth of the estate or has not wished to retain it. But if he keeps one-fourth, the stipulations *partis et pro parte* must be concluded as if between partiary legatee (*legatarius partitiarius*) and an heir. But if he has conveyed the entire estate, the stipulations between a buyer and a seller of the inheritance must be interposed.

If the heir, who had been charged by the testator with the restitution of more than three-fourths of the estate, accepted the inheritance, the *senatusconsultum Trebellianum* would not apply regardless of whether the heir decided to retain one-fourth of the inheritance or not. Since no transfer or actions took place, the heir was fully liable to the estate's creditors. In order to obtain relief, the heir would have to enter stipulations that transferred liability to the fideicommissary and would, in turn, allow the fideicommissary to bring forth all actions of the estate, just as it had been the legal practice before the enactment of the *senatusconsultum Trebellianum*. The nature and scope of the applicable stipulations depended on whether the heir had retained one-fourth of the estate or had conveyed the entire estate to the fideicommissary. If the heir restored the estate in its entirety, the stipulations on the sale of the estate would apply (Ch. 8.6.1). If the heir had retained one-fourth, the fideicommissary would be treated as a partiary legatee (*legatarius partiarius*) in the event of a *partitio legata*. As result of such a legacy, the heir was obliged to share the estate with the legatee in the defined proportion, but without the latter becoming an heir. Also in the case of a *partitio legata*, it was customary to use stipulations to divide responsibilities and liabilities between the heir and the partiary legatee in consideration of their respective shares. These stipulations were similar to those used for the sale of an inheritance, except that the former did not apply to the entire estate but only to the share of the estate left to the legatee. Following the *senatusconsultum Pegasianum*, the shares were fixed at one-fourth and three-fourths. Thus, the fideicommissary promised the heir to shield him from liabilities of the estate for up to three-fourths, and the heir allowed the fideicommissary to pursue the debtors of the estate up to the same amount.

This rule of the *senatusconsultum Pegasianum*, i.e. the application of stipulations for partiary legacies, also applied to *fideicommissa* of individual objects (singular *fideicommissum*):

Inst.Gai.2.254.: [...] ex singulis quoque rebus, quae per fideicommissum relincuntur, eadem retentio permissa est. per quod senatus consultum ipse onera hereditaria sustinet; ille autem, qui ex fideicommisso reliquam partem hereditatis recipit, legatarii partiarii loco est, id est eius legatarii, cui pars bonorum legatur; quae species legati partitio vocatur, quia cum herede legatarius partitur hereditatem. [...]

Inst.Gai.2.254.: [...] the same retention [of one-fourth] is permitted when the *fideicommissum* concerns single items. Under this *senatusconsultum*, he [the heir] carries the burden of inheritance himself. But he who receives the remaining part of the estate is treated like a *legatarius partiarius*, that kind of legatee who has been left a part of the estate. This legacy is called *legati partitio* because the legatee shares the estate with the heir. [...]

If the heir had restored the item out of his free will to the fideicommissary following the *fideicommissum*, he remained heir, but he could share the advantages and detriments of the estate with the fideicommissary. The fideicommisary's involvement in the claims and liabilities of the estate was again effected through mutual stipulations and only for the percentage corresponding to the value of the item in question.

The *senatusconsultum Pegasianum*, by subjecting the *fideicommissum* of inheritance and the singular *fideicommissum* to one regulation, avoided the inconsistencies that could occur following the *senatusconsultum Trebellianum* when the estate consisted mainly of one piece of property of value, i.e. a parcel of land.

However, the legal situation discussed here under the *senatusconsultum Pegasianum*, which left the heir in his position and reverted to the cautelary solution of the *senatusconsultum Trebellianum* only applied if the heir accepted the inheritance voluntarily. If the heir was forced to accept it, a different rule would apply:

> Inst.Gai.2.258.: *Sed si recuset scriptus heres adire hereditatem ob id, quod dicat eam sibi suspectam esse quasi damnosam, cavetur Pegasiano senatus consulto, ut desiderante eo, cui restituere rogatus est, iussu praetoris adeat et restituat, proindeque ei et in eum, qui receperit, actiones dentur, ac iuris esset ex senatus consulto Trebelliano.* [...]

> Inst.Gai.2.258.: But if the appointed heir refuses to accept [the inheritance] because he claims it to be suspicious that its liabilities exceed its assets, it is provided by the *senatusconsultum Pegasianum*, that on application of the fideicommissary he may be ordered by the praetor to accept [the inheritance] and to transfer it [to the beneficiary]. Whereupon the actions of the estate will be for and against the fideicommissary as it would be the law under the *senatusconsultum Trebellianum*. [...]

This coercion to accept the inheritance, i.e. taking an estate upon the praetor's orders, occurred upon application by the fideicommissary. If the fideicommissary became aware that the heir would not accept the estate, thereby jeopardising his rights, he could ask the praetor to compel the heir to accept the estate and convey it to him. The *senatusconsultum Pegasianum* held that the heir who had been compelled to accept the estate could not be considered to be an heir in the proper sense, since he was unwilling to comply with the testator's wishes. He therefore forfeited his right to claim his quarter but was also not considered an heir to third parties. Rather, the *senatusconsultum Trebellianum* treated the fideicommissary, who had coerced the heir in accepting the inheritance and to convey it as heir. The compulsory acceptance of an inheritance occurred mainly in the case of an over-indebted estates. This situation of a suspicious inheritance could result from a burdening of the estate with *fideicommissa*. It could also occur because the testator had been insolvent.

Overview 39 summarises the rules of the *senatusconsultum Pegasianum* for different situations of *fideicommissa*.

Overview 39: The Rules of the senatusconsultum Pegasianum Creating a Balance between the Heir and the Fideicommissary

the testator leaves the heir less than 1/4:		the testator leaves the heir 1/4 or more:	the heir renounces on account of the estate's over-indebtedness:
senatusconsultum Pegasianum: heir remains heir; stipulations between the parties to distribute responsibilities		*senatusconsultum Trebellianum*: transfer of actions; fideicommissary is treated as heir	*senatusconsultum Trebellianum*: transfer of actions; fideicommissary is treated as heir
the heir accepts and claims the 1/4 per *senatusconsultum Pegasianum*	the heir accepts and waives claim of 1/4 per *senatusconsultum Pegasianum*	the heir takes the estate; fideicommissary takes the rest	*senatusconsultum Pegasianum*: forced acceptance and restitution by the heir
stipulations of the *partitio legata*	stipulations for the sale of inheritance		the heir gets nothing; the fideicommissary receives the estate

Next to the rules on the legal succession between the heir and the fideicommissary, the *senatusconsultum Pegasianum* also regulated the application of the *lex Iulia et Papia* on *fideicommissa*:

> Inst.Gai.2.286a.: [...] Sed postea senatus consulto Pegasiano proinde fideicommissa quoque ac legata hereditatesque capere posse prohibiti sunt; eaque translata sunt ad eos, qui in eo testamento liberos habent, aut si nullus liberos habebit, ad populum, sicuti iuris est in legatis et in hereditatibus, quae eadem aut simili ex causa vel tota vel ex parte caduca fiunt.
>
> Inst.Gai.2.286a.: [...] But, afterwards, the *senatusconsultum Pegasianum* barred them [those incapable of acquiring under the *lex Iulia et Papia*]

from taking *fideicommissa*, as they had been prevented from taking legacies, and inheritances. And these *fideicommissa* were transferred to those named in the will who have children, and if nobody has children, to the Roman people. And the law is the same as it is for legacies and inheritances that are forfeited for the same, or similar reason.

After the *senatusconsultum Pegasianum* had been enacted, *fideicommissa* could therefore no longer circumvent the *caducum* rules of the *lex Iulia et Papia*. *Fideicommisssa* for the benefit of unmarried (*caelibes*) and childless (*orbi*) were as invalid as legacies left to them. The share that lapsed due to the failure of the unmarried to take, or the reduction of the share for the childless would accrue to those mentioned in the will who had the capacity to obtain, and if there was no eligible person, the *bona caduca* escheated to the public coffers or the imperial treasury (Ch. 4.4.1). The fact that the *senatusconsultum Pegasianum* settled the question about the capacity to obtain, in addition to the heir's compulsory acceptance of the inheritance, the matters of the *quarta Falcidia*, and the transfer of actions, shows that the *senatusconsultum* in question aimed at a comprehensive settlement of the issues raised by the frequent use of *fideicommissa*. At the same time, it sought to eliminate inconsistencies between the *fideicommissa* and the legacies. The same rationale underpins the various individual rulings that are preeminently documented under the reign of Emperor Hadrian (AD117–138). The first harmonisation concerned the application of the *fideicomissa* to non-Romans (*peregrini*):

> Inst.Gai.2.285.: [...] *Sed postea id prohibitum est, et nunc ex oratione divi sacratissimi Hadriani senatusconsultum factum est, ut ea fideicommissa fisco vindicarentur.*

> Inst.Gai.2.285.: [...] But afterwards, this was forbidden. And now, following an *oratio* by the deified and holiest Hadrian, a *senatusconsultum* was passed to the effect that the *fiscus* may claim those *fideicommissa*.

A *senatus consultum* passed during the reign of Emperor Hadrian determined that *fideicommissa* left for *peregrini* were as invalid as legacies left to them, and that these bequests escheated to the imperial treasury.

In addition, *fideicommissa* for unspecified groups of people were declared void by Hadrian:

> Inst.Gai.2.287.: [...] *Sed senatus consulto, quod auctore divo Hadriano factum est, idem in fideicommissis, quod in legatis hereditatibusque constitutum est.*

> Inst.Gai.2.287.: [...] but by a *senatus consultum*, passed by the motion of the deified Hadrian, it was decided that *fideicommissa* were treated like legacies and inheritances.

Hadrian extended the interdiction to leave legacies to uncertain persons also to *fideicommissa*. In the same vein, the prohibition on leaving legacies with the sole purpose of punishing the heir (Ch. 8.2.1), was extended to *fideicommissa* (Ch. 8.5.1).

All these rulings show that in the course of the Empire, *fideicommissa* were assimilated to legacies in order to preserve the core of the mandatory requirements applicable to legacies of *ius civile* and to avoid their circumvention through *fideicommissa*. Nevertheless, fundamental differences persisted between the two types of bequests. Legacies could only be left in a valid will, and only at the charge of a testamentary heir. In contrast to this, *fideicommissa* could be left at the charge of the heirs on intestacy and also upon the heir's death. Overview 40 illustrates the repealed and the persisting differences between the law of *fideicommissa* (*ius novum*) and the law of legacies under the *ius civile*:

Overview 40: Persisting Differences Between *Fideicommissa* and Legacies

	drawing up:	beneficiary:	chargee:	effect:
legacies:	specific wording; formalities of a will; only to certain persons; not for punishment	Roman citizens with the capacity to obtain under the *lex Iulia et Papia*	only a testamentary heir	only for one's own death
fideicommissa, initially:	no specific wording; no formal will; also to unspecified persons; also to punish an heir	also to non-Romans (*peregrini*); also to persons without the capacity to obtain under the *lex Iulia et Papia*	- also the legatee - also an heir on intestacy - also the imperial treasury (vacant inheritance)	also for the heir's death
fideicommissa:	no specific wording; no formal will; only to certain persons; not for punishment	only Roman citizens with the capacity to obtain under the *lex Iulia et Papia*	unchanged	unchanged

The differences between the law of the *fideicommissa* and that of the legacies, which persisted in the third century, were the direct consequence of the formless character of the *fideicommissum*. Because of their few legal requirements, *fideicommissa* were constantly used to sideline prohibitions to acquire, especially those contained in the *lex Iulia et Papia* and the *senatusconsultum Pegasianum* intended to extend the statutory prohibitions also to *fideicommissa*.

8.6.3 Clandestine fideicommissa

The formlessness of *fideicommissa* made it possible to leave them to circumvent laws (*tacitum fideicommissum*, 'tacit, secret *fideicommissum*'):

> *Iulianus, 83 digestorum: In tacitis fideicommissis fraus legi fieri videtur, quotiens quis neque testamento neque codicillis rogaretur, sed domestica cautione vel chirographo obligaret se ad praestandum fideicommissum ei qui capere non potest. (D.30.103.)*

> Julian, Digest, book 83: Secret *fideicommissa* constitute a fraud against the law whenever somebody is asked neither by a will nor by codicil, but merely binds himself by a private deed of debt, or by a confidential document to hand out the *fideicommissum* to a person who is incapable to obtain. (D.30.103.)

Secret *fideicommissa* were a means of circumventing the laws because they were not included in the primary testamentary documents, but in additional hidden agreements between the parties. Therefore, these documents had to be brought before the praetor when the heir requested *bonorum possessio* or for the procedure of the opening of the will (Ch. 6.3.3). Such agreements aimed to hide bequests for persons who had no (full) capacity to obtain under the *lex Iulia et Papia* because they were either unmarried or childless and to prevent it from escheatment by the imperial treasury.

When this attempted sideline became known, the *fideicommmissum* fell to the treasury, while the *senatusconsultum Plancianum*, probably under the reign of Emperor Hadrian (AD117–138), punished an heir who had fulfilled a secret *fideicommissum*:

> *Modestinus, 9 pandectarum: Praeterea qui non capienti rogatus est restituere hereditatem, senatus consulto Planciano non conceditur quartam retinere: Sed ea quarta, quam non retinuit, ad fiscum pertinet ex rescripto divi Pii. (D.35.2.59.1.)*

> Modestinus, Pandects, book 9: Moreover, when an heir is requested to transfer the estate to someone lacking capacity to keep what he had obtained

under the *lex Iulia et Papia*, he is not allowed to retain one-quarter of the said estate under the *senatusconsultum Plancianum*. Instead, the said quarter will belong to the treasury following a rescript of the deified Pius. (35.2.59.1.)

The *senatusconsultum Plancianum* withdrew from the heir the benefits granted to him by the *lex Falcidia*. This withdrawal was justified on the grounds of his participation in the circumvention of the law. Even though the heir himself did not profit from the secret *fideicommissum*, he should loose his share of the estate if he had pledged restitution to a person who lacked the capacity to keep what they had obtained. For as long as all the parties involved, especially the beneficiary, honoured their forbidden agreements, the state had only limited access to the secret *fideicommissa* and the inheritances linked to them. In truth, by using a secret *fideicommissum*, which could not be claimed in court, the testator reverted to the legal situation that applied before Emperor Augustus (27BC–AD14) decided to enforce *fideicommissa* in the *cognitio extra ordinem*. Like the testator from the time before the Augustan reform, the testator of a secret *fideicommissum* trusted that the heir or any other person charged with a secret *fideicommissum* would fulfil it so that the beneficiary would not need to resort to legal action.

8.7 Concluding Considerations on the Law of Legacies

1. The various stages in the development of the law of legacies can be distinguished in parallel with the three layers of law, *ius civile*, *ius praetorium* and the overarching *ius novum*. The cesura that marks the beginning of the Principate is more visible in the law of legacies than in other areas of the Roman law of inheritance. The introduction of the enforceability of the *fideicommissa* changed testamentary practice, allowing arrangements that were not possible or even prohibited under the *ius civile* and its dependent *ius praetorium*. However, the defunct forms were not formally repealed. Gaius, in his textbook from the second century, still describes in great detail the various types of legacies and their differing ramifications under the *ius civile*. However, the distinctions between the four different types of legacies had already become obsolete by the *senatusconsultum Neronianum* issued during the first century AD.
2. Among the principles that shape the different layers of law, the legacy's strict formality and its dependence on the will must be mentioned for the *ius civile*. For the *ius praetorium*, in dependency to the *ius civile*, the protection of the legatee from delays or the refusal to accept the estate by the heir as well as the protection of the heir against self-help by the legatee must be highlighted. The *ius novum*, eventually, invoked the principle of equity (*aequitas*) and the testator's intentions, which were to be preserved at all

cost. In contrast, formal requirements or requirements about the content were of secondary importance, although imperial legislation extended some of them to the *fideicommissa*.

3. It seems that the jurists were more concerned with the precise identification of the interests of the legatee and the testator than with the harmonisation of the three layers of law. It is possible, however, that the imperial quest for harmonisation between the *ius civile* and the *ius novum* was based on the advice given to the *princeps* by the jurists of the Empire. We do not find open debate among the jurists on the inconsistencies between the legacies and the *fideicommissa*, apart from the summary of these divergences found in Gaius' *Institutes*. The state of documentation could also be the result of the textual transmission. The differences between legacies and *fideicommissa* had vanished by the time of the Emperor Justinian (AD527–565), so the Emperor's compilers had no reason to include juristic controversies relating to them in the Digest.

9

The Interpretation of Wills

A significant part of the jurists' opinions on the law of inheritance preserved in the Digest deals with the interpretation of wills in order to determine their content and validity. The interpretation of a will is crucial in any succession case, as it defines the (testamentary) heirs and legatees. Moreover, the outcome of the interpretation will decide whether the will is valid or whether the order of intestacy is reinstated due to its invalidity (Ch. 3.2 and 6.2). The changes that the law of wills, like the law of *legacies*, underwent from *ius civile* and *ius praetorium* to *ius novum* are thus especially visible in the jurists' opinions on the interpretation of wills. A historical analysis of the Roman law of inheritance makes it possible to identify the peculiarities of the interpretation of wills in each layer of law and to delineate their different functions. Moreover, the interpretation shows how the different layers of law are used in parallel and how their sometimes conflicting rules can be reconciled when applied to one and the same case.

9.1 Interpretative Maxims of *ius civile*

The will under the *ius civile* is, as we have seen (Ch. 6.1), a formal act. To be valid, it requires the performance of a ritual, the *mancipatio*, and the use of specific formulas. At the same time, the combination of written documentation and solemn verbal announcement (*nuncupatio*) forms the first point of reference for the interpretation:

> *Ulpianus, 1 ad Sabinum: Institutum autem heredem eum quoque dicimus, qui scriptus non est, sed solummodo nuncupatus. (D.28.5.1.1.)*
>
> Ulpian, Sabinus, book 1: We also say that an heir has been appointed where the testator did not write but only solemnly declared his name. (D.28.5.1.1.)

The fact that an heir can be appointed not only by a written will but also by *nuncupatio* shows that the *ius civile* considers not only the testator's written instructions as a 'will', but also the verbal declarations made by *mancipatio*.

Therefore, if the witnesses who were present at the act of *mancipatio* state that the person who claimed to be a testamentary heir was appointed heir in a *nuncupatio*, then the written document that did not mention that person is amended. Roman jurists describe this kind of supplementary interpretation of the written will with the words 'rather the solemnly declared than the written' (*plus nuncupatum quam scriptum*).

9.1.1 Plus nuncupatum quam scriptum

The principle of *plus nuncupatum quam scriptum* makes it possible, first of all, to correct obvious omissions by the testator in a written will:

> *Ulpianus, 1 ad Sabinum: Si autem sic scribat: 'Lucius heres', licet non adiecerit 'esto', credimus plus nuncupatum, minus scriptum: Et si ita: 'Lucius esto', tantundem dicimus: [...] (D.28.5.1.5.)*

> Ulpian, Sabinus, book 1: If someone wrote 'Lucius heir', but did not add 'let him be', we maintain that more was declared than was written. And if he wrote 'let Lucius be', we hold that it would amount to the same [...] (D.28.5.1.5.)

The expression 'Lucius heir' is not formally a valid appointment because the instruction 'is to be' is missing (Ch. 6.1.3). This glaring omission is corrected by the principle *plus nuncupatum quam scriptum*. Since the testator named Lucius as heir in front of all the witnesses, he has validly appointed him despite leaving out the relevant words.

However, where a legacy depends on the valid appointment of an heir, there is a limit to such interpretations:

> *Paulus, 5 ad legem Iuliam et Papiam: Si palam heres nuncupatus sit, legata autem in tabulis collata fuerint, Iulianus ait tabulas testamenti non intellegi, quibus heres scriptus non est, et magis codicilli quam testamentum existimandae sint: Et hoc puto rectius dici. (D.29.7.20.)*

> Paul, Lex Iulia et Papia, book 5: If an heir has been solemnly declared, but the legacies are written on tablets, Julian says that these tablets should not be considered a will, but rather as a codicil, and I believe this is the better view. (D.29.7.20.)

The testator made the legacies in writing, but appointed the heir orally. Since the appointment is omitted in the written will, we might ask whether the tablets, which contain only the legacies, can be regarded as a valid will. Julian (second century AD) denies this; as the appointment of the heir is missing, the document cannot be a will. Therefore, the legacies can at best be seen as codicils, i.e. additions to the will (Ch. 6.4.1). These additions are only valid under the *ius civile* if they are announced in a formally valid will with the appointment of the heir or are confirmed by a subsequent will. Without the appointment of an heir, they could still be valid as *fideicommissa* under the *ius novum* (Ch. 6.4.1).

The principle of *plus nuncupatum quam scriptum* was not only applied to supplement a document with the declarations of the testator during the act of *mancipatio*. It could also be used to reconcile discrepancies between the document and the testator's wishes:

> *Ulpianus, 5 ad Sabinum: Sed si non in corpore erravit, sed in parte, puta si, cum dictasset ex semisse aliquem scribi, ex quadrante sit scriptus, Celsus [...] posse defendi ait ex semisse heredem fore, quasi plus nuncupatum sit, minus scriptum: [...] (D.28.5.9.2.)*

> Ulpian, Sabinus, book 5: If, however, he did not make a mistake as to the identity of the beneficiary, but as to the share, e.g., if he had dictated that someone should be appointed heir to half, whereas it was written down 'to a quarter', Celsus says, [...] that it can be argued that the heir will inherit half of the estate, as the larger amount was declared, the smaller one was written [...] (D.28.5.9.2.)

The testator dictated that the heir should be appointed 'for half', whereas the scribe wrote, 'for a quarter'. Celsus (first century AD) held that also in this case the testator declared something different ('half') from what was written ('a quarter'). Obviously, this application of the principle of interpretation cannot be justified by the duality between the testamentary document and the *nuncupatio*. Rather, *nuncupare* refers to the drawing up of the written will, i.e. the oral declaration of the testator during the dictation of the testamentary tablets. As omissions and mistakes can also occur here, Celsus applies the principle *plus nuncupatum quam scriptum* also to these declarations of the testator, even though they are not solemn. Thus, the principle is no longer a consequence of the two formal elements of the will by *mancipatio* (written document and *nuncupatio*). Instead, it refers to the testator's wishes beyond the inadequately expressed document.

However, if the testator's intentions are not clear from the testamentary document, or if the written declaration is unclear or ambiguous, it is necessary to ascertain what the testator actually or probably intended.

9.1.2 Voluntatis quaestio

Determining the testator's intentions is an essential part of the interpretation of wills. Jurists call this a 'question of intention' (*voluntatis quaestio*). As the deceased testator is no longer available, the answer to this question is complicated. Therefore, it cannot be a matter of determining the actual will.

Rather, it is a question of determining what the testator would most probably have wanted, given the circumstances. The first and most important point of reference for this assessment is the testamentary document, i.e. the text of the will (*scriptum*). If the wording is ambiguous (*ambiguitas*, 'ambiguity'), or if there is a discrepancy between the wishes of the testator and the wording of the document, as alleged by the heir or legatee, further arguments are needed to assess the testator's probable intentions.

The factual nature of the determination of the testator's intentions in the interpretation of wills can best be understood by analysing the most famous lawsuit concerning the interpretation of a will, the 'case of Curius' (*causa Curiana*). The affair, which dates from 93BC, is not recorded in legal writings, but is recalled by Cicero. The dispute concerned the will of Coponius, who had appointed his unborn children as heirs: 'if a child, or more, are born to me, they shall be my heirs' (*si mihi filius genitur unus pluresve, is mihi heres esto*).[1] He also provided that 'in case the child dies before reaching puberty, [...]' (*si filius ante moritur, quam in tutelam suam venerit* [...]),[2] Manius Curius would be the substitute heir. Both the appointment of a posthumous child (*postumus*) and the appointment of a substitute for the child who had not reached puberty (*substitutio pupillaris*) were recognised options in a will under *ius civile* (Ch. 6.1.5; Ch. 7.1.4).

The dispute arose because no child had been born to Coponius; a situation for which there was no contingency. The parties to the dispute were the appointed substitute heir, Manius Curius, and the closest agnate (*proximus agnatus*) entitled to inherit by intestacy. The heir on intestacy claimed that the testamentary heir had never been born, so that the will was void and the order of intestacy reinstated (Ch. 3). Curius, however, claimed that he had been appointed not only in the event of the child's death, but also as a substitute heir if the inheritance lapsed for any other reason.

The wording of the will was open to both interpretations. However, since the testator had expressly made the appointment of a substitute heir (*substitutio pupillaris*) conditional on the death of the child, the *scriptum* supported the interpretation favouring the heir on intestacy. The jurist Quintus Mucius Scaevola (140–82BC), who represented the *agnatus proximus* in court, therefore emphasised this:

> Cic. Brut. 196: [...] *quam captiosum esse populo quod scriptum esset neglegi et opinione quaeri voluntates et interpretatione disertorum scripta simplicium hominum pervertere?*

---

[1] Cicero, *De inventione*, 2. 122.
[2] Ibid.

> Cic. Brut. 196: [...] How deceptive would it be for the common people if what has been written were neglected, and [alleged] declarations were sought by conjecture, and if written declarations of the common people were perverted by the art of interpretation of eloquent men?

Thus, the jurist defended his client by cautioning against assuming an intention of the testator that he did not have, simply in order to achieve the desired goal and to 'improve' the testator's intention.

Against this, the orator Lucius Licinius Crassus, who defended the substitute heir Manius Curius, argued that the pupillary substitution must also have been intended in the event that no *postumus* was born:

> Cic. Brut. 197: [...] *deinde hoc voluisse eum qui testamentum fecisset, hoc sensisse, quoquo modo filius non esset qui in suam tutelam veniret, sive non natus sive ante mortuus, Curius heres ut esset; ita scribere plerosque et id valere et valuisse semper.* [...]

> Cic. Brut. 197: [...] Hence [he claimed] that the testator truly intended that if no son of his, who was of age, survived, whether such a son was never born or died before he came of age, Curius was to be heir; that most people wrote their wills in this way, and that it was a valid procedure and had always been valid. [...]

According to this argument, the wording of the condition for the appointment of Curius is not binding. Rather, Crassus' interpretation is based on the intended purpose of the appointment, namely to provide a contingency for the lapse of the son's inheritance. In support of this interpretation, Crassus pointed out that this very intention was reflected in common testamentary practice, and therefore had to be ascribed to Coponius' will.

Ultimately, Crassus won the lawsuit and Manius Curius was found to be testamentary heir. But, according to Cicero, the argument that won the day – the differentiating between the death of a minor and the failure of his birth – was an unnecessary subtlety that only jurists could fall for.

Contrary to popular belief, the *causa Curiana* was not intended to establish a general principle of testamentary interpretation. Instead, the case illustrates a typical conflict over the interpretation of wills, in which one party relies on the testator's implied intention and the other on the wording of the document. Interestingly, both parties claim to have the testator's (probable) wishes on their side. In order to prove their conflicting interpretations, they both rely on the wording and on the testator's intent as revealed by other evidence.

Similar contradictions can be found in the Roman jurists' controversies on the interpretation of wills collected in the Digest. The discussed cases show that the circumstantial evidence used to determine the testator's intention is often manifold and contradictory. In fact, the interpretation of the indicia depends on the individual context and can therefore lead to conflicting results as to the testator's probable intention when considered in the light of different circumstances. Some examples are given in the following.

Two typical argumentative topoi for inferring an intention inadequately expressed in the written will are the benevolent (*benigna*) and the more humane interpretation (*humanior interpretatio*). These two arguments are used to supplement an elliptically expressed intention:

> *Ulpianus, 6 regularum: Nominatim exheredatus filius et ita videtur 'filius meus exheres esto', si nec nomen eius expressum sit, si modo unicus sit: Nam si plures sunt filii, benigna interpretatione potius a plerisque respondetur nullum exheredatum esse. (D.28.2.2.)*

> Ulpian, Rules, book 6: A son is also considered disinherited by name in this way: 'let my son be disinherited'. This applies even if his name was not expressly mentioned, provided he is the only son. For, if there are several sons, most jurists will interpret rather favourably that none of the sons is disinherited. (D.28.2.2.)

A testator with several sons has disinherited 'his son' in his will. Since the son's name is missing, the disinheritance is ambiguous and cannot be attributed to a particular son. In principle, therefore, it would be possible to consider all the father's sons as disinherited. On the contrary, Ulpian (third century AD) argues for a benevolent interpretation in favour of the sons, which leads him to consider that no son is validly disinherited, but that all of them are passed over (*praeterire*). In his interpretation, the jurist uses the concept of *benignitas* to argue for the testator's mindset towards his sons. Ulpian assumes that the father wanted the best for his sons and therefore could not have wished to disinherit all of them, which implies that no son is considered disinherited. The interpretatory principle of benevolence is thus applied to the testator's intention, even if the result of his presumed wishes is not beneficial to him. In fact, his will is deemed void because it passes over (*praeterire*) the testator's sons-in-power (Ch. 7.1).

Similarly, humane indulgence (*humanitas*) could be used to interpret a will:

> *Pomponius, 12 epistularum: De illo quoque quaeritur: Fundus quibusdam legatus est, si pecuniam certam in funus impensamque perferendi corporis in aliam regionem dedissent. Nam nisi uterque dederit, neutri est legatum, quoniam condicio nisi per utrumque expleri non potest. Sed haec humanius interpretari solemus, ut, cum duobus fundus legatus sit, si decem dedissent, et alteri dando partem legatum quoque debeatur. (D.35.1.112.2.)*

Pomponius, Letters, book 12: The following question was raised. A plot of land has been bequeathed to two or more legatees under the condition that they pay a specified sum for the burial and for the expenses of transporting the body to another region. If neither of them paid, the property was not bequeathed to either of them, because the condition can only be fulfilled by both of them. But usually we interpret this [condition] more humanely, so that if a property has been bequeathed to two legatees, if they have given ten, and one of them pays his share, his proportion of the bequest is due to him. (D.35.1.112.2.)

A plot of land is bequeathed to two or more people on the condition that they pay a specific sum towards the testator's funeral expenses. If all the legatees refuse to pay, the condition is not fulfilled and the legacy fails. The testator did not expressly consider the possibility that only one or a few of them might fulfil the condition. A humanely lenient interpretation requires that the individual legatee who fulfils the testator's condition should receive his share, whether or not the others pay. Hence, the principle of *humanitas* leads to the conclusion that the testator had the intention of conferring separate shares of the legacy to the individual beneficiaries. *Humanitas* is therefore not a normative principle, but a guideline for determining the probable intention of the testator, who is presumed to have wished to favour each of his legatees.

On another level, there is the common argument that the heir should be favoured if the content of the will is unclear:

> *Proculus, 6 epistularum: Sempronius Proculus Nepoti suo salutem. Binae tabulae testamenti eodem tempore exemplarii causa scriptae (ut volgo fieri solet) eiusdem patris familias proferuntur: In alteris centum, in alteris quinquaginta aurei legati sunt Titio: Quaeris, utrum centum et quinquaginta aureos an centum dumtaxat habiturus sit. Proculus respondit: In hoc casu magis heredi parcendum est ideoque utrumque legatum nullo modo debetur, sed tantummodo quinquaginta aurei. (D.31.47.)*

Proculus, Letters, book 6: Sempronius Proculus greets Nepos. Two wills, written at the same time to make a copy (as is customary), by one and the same *pater familias*, are presented. In one will, he left one hundred *aurei* to Titius; in the other, he left him fifty. You ask whether he [Titius] will receive one hundred and fifty or only fifty *aurei*. Proculus answered that in this matter, one must rather spare the heir and therefore in no way are both legacies due, but only fifty. (D.31.47.)

Proculus (first century AD) tells of a case in which two copies of a will diverged as to the amount set aside for a legacy to Titius. According to one copy, he should receive a hundred; according to the other, fifty gold coins. While one jurist (Nepos) even considered adding the two sums together to reach one hundred and fifty, Proculus only grants a legacy of fifty. He bases this interpretation on the need to favour the heir (*favor heredis*). The principle of favouring the heir does not mean being partial or favouring his interests excessively. Instead, the argument refers to the uncertainty of the evidence: since both copies of the will were established at the same time and are equally reliable, there is no basis for giving preference to one document over the other. Hence, the question ariscs as to who should bear the burden of proof. According to Proculus, it is the legatee because he claims to have been granted a benefit from the testator. This rule is in line with the general principle that, when in doubt, the burden of proof lies with the party claiming a benefit. If the legatee cannot provide evidence of the higher amount, only the lower amount is due, since only the latter is clearly documented.

9.1.3 The Law of Legacies: falsa demonstratio non nocet

Identifying the testator's intention raises particular issues when applied to legacies. Generally speaking, the heir must specify the object of the legacy in order to avoid disputes between the legatee and the heir and to ensure that the legacy is fulfilled quickly. However, even a meticulous testator cannot always avoid doubts as to the identity of the bequeathed object:

> *Pomponius, 6 ad Sabinum:* 'Titiae textores meos omnes, praeterquam quos hoc testamento alii legavi, lego. Plotiae vernas meos omnes, praeterquam quos alii legavi, lego.' Cum essent quidam et vernae idem et textores, Labeo ait, quoniam nec quos Titiae textores non legaverit, aliter apparere possit, quam si cognitum fuerit, quos eorum Plotiae legaverit, nec quos Plotiae vernas non legaverit, possit, neutrius legato exceptos esse eos de quibus quaeritur et ideo communes ambobus esse: Hoc enim iuris est et si neutrius legati nomine quicquam esset exceptum. (D.30.36pr.)*

> Pomponius, Sabinus, book 6: 'I bequeath to Titia all my slaves who are weavers, except those I have bequeathed to another by this will. I bequeath to Plotia all my slaves born in my house, except those I have bequeathed to another.' Since some slaves born in his house were also weavers, Labeo says that it cannot be ascertained which weavers the testator did not bequeath to Titia unless it is known which ones he bequeathed to Plotia. And as it cannot be established which homeborn slaves he has not bequeathed to Plotia [unless it is known which of the latter he has bequeathed to Titia], the slaves in question are excluded from neither legacy and are therefore common to both legatees; for this is the rule when something has not been expressly excluded from either of the legacies. (D.30.36pr.)

In a will, all slaves who work as weavers are bequeathed to Titia, while all slaves who are 'homeborn' (*vernae*)[3] are bequeathed to Plotia. The bequeathed slaves are thus identified by their specific attributes. At the same time, these legacies are distinguished from other legacies by excluding from Titia's legacy (weaver slaves) and from Plotia's legacy (homeborn slaves) all slaves 'who are bequeathed to somebody else in this will'.

The ambiguity of the instructions requires an interpretation of the testator's intention, as some slaves are both weavers and homeborn. Moreover, the testator did not give priority to one of the legacies, but merely placed them both behind other legacies which are not further explained in Pomponius' fragment. Because of this uncertainty, Labeo decided that the slaves, who were both weavers and homeborn, belonged jointly to the two legatees. As a result, three separate legacies must be distinguished: the weaver slaves belong to Titia; the homeborn slaves belong to Plotia; the homeborn weaver slaves belong to both women jointly. If the testator had wanted to avoid a joint legacy, he should have separated the two legacies more clearly and identified the bequeathed objects more precisely.

The overt need to accurately identify the bequeathed objects carries the risk of attributing characteristics to an object that it does not possess. If the words of the heir were taken literally in such cases, it would not be possible to identify the bequeathed object and the legacy would thus be void. In order to prevent the invalidity of legacies, the jurists from the time of the Republic coined the principle 'a false description does not harm' (*falsa demonstratio non nocet*).

This principle applies first of all to an incorrect description of the bequeathed object:

> *Gaius, 2 de legatis ad edictum praetoris: Demonstratio falsa est, veluti si ita scriptum sit: 'Servum Stichum, quem de Titio emi' fundum Tusculanum, qui mihi a Seio donatus est.' Nam si constat, de quo homine, de quo fundo senserit testator, ad rem non pertinet, si is, quem emisse significavit, donatus esset, aut quem donatum sibi esse significaverat, emerit. (D.35.1.17pr.)*

> Gaius, Praetor's Edict, Legacies, book 2: A description is false if it is made, e.g., in this way: 'I legate the slave Stichus, who I have bought from Titius', or 'the Tusculan estate that Seius gave me as a gift', for if it is certain which slave or which estate the testator had in mind, it is irrelevant whether the one whom he described as having bought it from him, had actually given it to

---

[3] The word *vernae* is not a legal term: cf. Elisabeth Hermann-Otto, *Ex ancilla natus. Untersuchungen zu den 'hausgeborenen' Sklaven und Slavinnen im Westen des römischen Kaiserreiches* (Franz Steiner Verlag 1994).

him as a present, or whether the one whom he described as having received it as a present had actually sold it to him. (D.35.1.17pr.)

The testator used the wrong place of origin to describe the bequeathed slave or plot of land. As long as the slave or the plot of land can be clearly identified from other features, the legacy is valid and applies to the slave or plot of land the testator intended.

The option to disregard a wrong description is especially important if the testator has given the wrong attributes to the bequeathed object:

> *Gaius, 2 de legatis ad edictum praetoris: Igitur et si ita servus legatus sit: 'Stichum cocum', 'Stichum sutorem Titio lego,' licet neque cocus neque sutor sit, ad legatarium pertinebit, si de eo sensisse testatorem conveniat: Nam et si in persona legatarii designanda aliquid erratum fuerit, constat autem, cui legare voluerit, perinde valet legatum ac si nullus error interveniret. (D.35.1.17.1.)*
>
> Gaius, Praetor's Edict, Legacies, book 2: Therefore, where a slave is bequeathed thus: 'I legate to Titius my cook, Stichus, or my cobbler, Stichus', although the slave may be neither, he will belong to the legatee if it is certain that the testator thought of him. For even if a mistake has occurred in the designation of the person of the legatee, but it is ascertained to whom the testator wished to bequeath, the bequest will be as valid as if no error had occurred. (D.35.1.17.1.)

Suppose the testator writes 'Stichus, the cook' or 'Stichus, the cobbler' to describe the bequeathed slave more precisely, even though the slave in question does not practice any of the professions mentioned. In this case, the attribution of the occupation to the slave is incorrect. However, as long as the slave Stichus can be identified with certainty, the legacy is valid. Gaius (second century AD) justifies this by stating that the beneficiary of the legacy is also not identified by the description, but by whom the testator intended. As a rule, false descriptions do not affect the validity of the legacy, provided that the bequeathed objects and the recipient legatee can be identified with certainty.

Finally, the principle of *falsa demonstratio non nocet* applies if the testator has given a false reason (*causa*, 'reason') for the legacy:

> *Gaius, 2 de legatis ad edictum praetoris: Quod autem iuris est in falsa demonstratione, hoc vel magis est in falsa causa, veluti ita 'Titio fundum do, quia negotia mea curavit', item 'fundum Titius filius meus praecipito, quia frater eius ipse ex arca tot aureos sumpsit': Licet enim frater huius pecuniam ex arca non sumpsit, utile legatum est. (D.35.1.17.2.)*

Gaius, Praetor's Edict, Legacies, book 2: This rule concerning a false designation is all the more true when the reason is incorrect, as, e.g.: 'I give this plot of land to Titius because he took care of my business'; likewise: 'let Titius, my son, have, as a legacy *per praeceptionem*, this parcel of land because his brother took so many *aurei* from my cash box', even if the brother did not take the money from the cash box, the legacy will be valid. (D.35.1.17.2.)

Suppose the testator has left a legacy *per praeceptionem* to his son Titius to settle certain payments received by the son's brother during the testator's lifetime. In this case, the legacy is valid even though the son never received any money. If it is certain that the testator left the legacy to Titius, the reason for which it was left is irrelevant. Therefore, a legacy is not void if the testator is mistaken about the facts that motivate his gift and mentions this *falsa causa* in the legacy. If the testator wanted the legacy to depend on the other son having already received money, he could have achieved this by leaving a conditional legacy. The legacy *per praeceptionem* in favour of Titius, as a conditional legacy, would only be valid if the brother had benefited from the payments from his father's purse (Ch. 8.1.2). If the legacy was unconditional, then the testator's motive for making the bequest was irrelevant, even if it was explicitly mentioned. This line of argument and the generous interpretation of false descriptions and erroneous reasons show that the Roman jurists held the testator responsible for the correct expression of his intention. If the testator wants his motive to be decisive for the validity of the bequest, he must state it as a condition, so that its non-fulfilment invalidates the legacy. If he chooses not to do so, the incorrect *causa* has no effect on the validity of the bequest (Ch. 8.1).

The rules for interpretation of a will under the *ius civile* are summarised in Overview 41:

Overview 41: Rules for the Interpretation of Wills under the *ius civile*

interpreting a will to determine its content		
plus nuncupatum quam scriptum	establishing the testator's probable intention behind the testamentary document	a special rule for legacies: *falsa demonstration non nocet*
the wording of the written will is supplemented and corrected with the elements contained in the solemn declaration (*nuncupatio*) or the testator's intentions while dictating the will	the testator's intention is the point in issue; the aim is to prove the probability of a certain intention that has been (perhaps incompletely) expressed in the written will	the bequeathed object must be specified, so it can be clearly identified
supplementary interpretation of obvious omissions	wording (*scriptum/verba*) vs. intention (*voluntas*): two contradictory positions in a specific case	correction of wrong descriptions and wrongly ascribed features
correcting errors	further possible arguments: rationale of the will, testamentary practice, *benignior interpretatio*, *humanior interpretatio*, *favor heredis* (decision about the burden of proof)	deleting erroneous motives for the legacy

The strict formalism and the cautelary nature of the Roman will of the *ius civile* explain the existence of well-defined rules of interpretation (*plus nuncupatum quam scriptum* and *falsa demonstratio non nocet*) for this layer of law. In fact, in the same way that certain words were prescribed for the appointment of an heir or a legatee, traditional rules governed the way in which wills were to be understood and evaluated in practice.

9.2 The Minor Importance of Interpretative Issues under the *ius praetorium*

Whereas the *ius civile* and the *ius novum* contain a series of jurists' opinions on the interpretation of wills, the *ius praetorium* limits the interpretatory decisions to the edict and its application. Hence, under the *ius praetorium*, the focus is not on ascertaining the testator's intention. Rather, the main focus of the jurists under praetorian law lies on determining the appropriate praetorian remedies with regard to the testamentary dispositions and on defining the best procedural options for the parties and the valid proceedings.

Examples of this have already been discussed in the analysis of the invalidity of wills under praetorian law. Thus, it has been shown that, unlike the *ius civile*, the praetor required the testator's *testamenti factio* only when the will was drawn up and opened. As a result, a temporary loss of the *testamenti factio* did not invalidate the praetorian will (Ch. 6.3). Similarly, the praetor granted the *bonorum possessio secundum tabulas* even if the son was appointed under a condition that was not potestative (Ch. 7.1.2). These examples show that the praetor dealt with wills according to rules different from those of the *ius civile*. These criteria, however, were not the result of a different method of determining the intention, but were due to the fact that the praetor, in developing his legal protection, the *bonorum possessio*, partly departed from the rules of *ius civile*.

In contrast, the interpretation of testamentary dispositions following the *ius novum* is particularly significant.

9.3 Interpretation of Wills under the *ius novum*

Testamentary dispositions under the *ius novum* are the additions to the will that are valid as *fideicommissa* (codicils, Ch. 6.4.2), the formless wills of soldiers (soldiers' wills, Ch. 6.4.2) and the formless legacies (*fideicommissa*, Ch. 8.5), which may be either universal or singular. These dispositions share a lack of formality, which means that the testator's intention determines both the content and the scope of the disposition. Accordingly, as long as the rules of interpretation of the *ius civile* give priority to the testator's intention, they will also apply in the *ius novum*. This is true of the principles of *plus nuncupatum quam scriptum* and *falsa demonstratio non nocet*, both of which give precedence to the testator's intention over an erroneous or incomplete declaration in the written document:

> *Papinianus, 19 quaestionum: Si omissa fideicommissi verba sint et cetera quae leguntur cum his, quae scribi debuerunt, congruant, recte datum et minus scriptum exemplo institutionis legatorumque intellegetur: [...] (D.31.67.9.)*

> Papinian, Questions, book 19: If words of a *fideicommissum* are omitted, but the rest of the read [words] correspond to what should have been written, then it [the *fideicommissum*] is valid, and the missing text is understood according to the example of the appointment of heirs and legatees [...] (D.31.67.9.)

As in the case of the will under the *ius civile*, the wording of the *fideicommissum* may be supplemented with the words which, having regard to all the circumstances, appear to be lacking. Hence, the principle *plus nuncupatum quam scriptum* for determining the testator's intention also applies to the *fideicommissa*.

However, since the *fideicommissum* has no formal requirements, the application of said principle may also lead to the creation of a *fideicommissum* by interpretation:

> *Papinianus, 19 quaestionum: Item Marcus imperator rescripsit verba, quibus testator ita caverat: 'Non dubitare se, quodcumque uxor eius cepisset, liberis suis reddituram', pro fideicommisso accipienda. Quod rescriptum summam habet utilitatem, ne scilicet honor bene transacti matrimonii, fides etiam communium liberorum decipiat patrem, qui melius de matre praesumpserat: Et ideo princeps providentissimus et iuris religiosissimus cum fideicommissi verba cessare animadverteret, eum sermonem pro fideicommisso rescripsit accipiendum. (D.31.67.10.)*

> Papinian, Questions, book 19: Similarly, Emperor Marcus stated in a rescript that where a testator phrased his provision thus 'that he did not doubt that his wife would return to her children everything she had received from him', it should be considered a *fideicommissum*. This rescript is most valuable, to ensure that the honourable consideration of a well-managed marriage, and also the trust in the joint children, do not deceive a father who expected better of the mother. Therefore, when the emperor, being both precautionary and meticulous in legal matters to the utmost, realised that the necessary words for a *fideicommissum* were missing, he decided that the [father's] statement should be accepted as sufficient for a *fideicommissum*. (D.31.67.10.)

The testator left behind his wife and children. Instead of explicitly asking his wife to leave the estate or legacy to the (joint) children when they reach puberty, or in the event of her death, the testator declared that he assumed that his wife would act accordingly. In this case, the testator formulated his expectations but did not issue an order. Rather, he deliberately refrained from doing so because he considered it unnecessary.

If the mother does not do as expected, the question is whether the children can claim the transfer of their father's estate by virtue of the father's will. Papinian (third century AD) grants the claim, citing a rescript of Emperor Marcus Aurelius (AD161–180), which he considers to be an application of the principle of *plus nuncupatum quam scriptum*. This case shows that the aforementioned principle, derived from the *ius civile*, is used in the *ius novum* not only to overcome the defects of the declaration, but also to substantially modify the testator's intention, which was not declared but should have been.

The formlessness in the imperial law of wills leads to a high degree of flexibility in testamentary dispositions. Dispositions can be made orally, they can be limited in time and they can be imposed on an heir by intestacy

(Ch. 6.4; Ch. 8.5). All these modifications lead to an accumulation of possible interpretations of the testator's intentions. Whereas the *ius civile* (Ch. 9.1) was primarily concerned with deducing the testator's probable intention from the declaration contained in the will, the *ius novum* requires a comprehensive examination of all the circumstances. The uncertainty resulting from this approach explains why considerations of social and moral value are increasingly included in the interpretation of wills. Thus, the validity and content of the will are no longer determined by the formal testamentary requirements, but by the underlying individual and collective motives of the testators in order to decide on the 'true' intentions of the testator.

9.3.1 Interpretation in Accordance to Terms of Value

Under *ius civile*, concepts of value such as *benignitas* and *humanitas* serve to reveal the testator's intention when the wording of the will is unclear (Ch. 9.1.2). Contrary to this, the *ius novum* relies on these concepts to confer validity on an ambiguous or uncertain testamentary intention:

> *Marcellus, 11 digestorum: Cum in testamento ambigue aut etiam perperam scriptum est, benigne interpretandum et secundum id, quod credibile est cogitatum, credendum est. (D.34.5.24.)*
>
> Marcellus, Digest, book 11: When a testamentary statement is ambiguous or even incorrectly written, it should be interpreted benevolently, and any credible intention on the testator's part should be credited. (D.34.5.24.)

Starting from the premise that ambiguous or erroneous dispositions are to be interpreted favourably, Marcellus invokes the principle of interpretation in favour of the will *(favor testamenti)*. This principle means that, when in doubt, the intention that would make the testamentary disposition valid is to be chosen. Hence, in the absence of indications to the contrary, the testator's intention is assumed to be that which allows the validity of the will to be upheld:

> *Scaevola, 19 digestorum: Scaevola respondit, si pater filium suum impuberem ex asse scripserit heredem eique codicillis substituerit, deinde filius impubes decesserit, licet substitutio inutilis sit, quia codicillis hereditas neque dari neque adimi potest, tamen benigna interpretatione placet, ut mater, quae ab intestato pupillo successit, substitutis fideicommisso obligetur: [...] (D.36.1.78.)*
>
> Scaevola, Digest, book 19: Scaevola replied that if a father had appointed his son, who had not reached the age of puberty, as his sole heir, and had appointed a substitute heir for him by a codicil, and if the son had died before reaching the age of puberty, the substitution would be invalid, because an estate cannot be bequeathed or taken away by a codicil. However,

by a favourable interpretation, it should be held that the mother, who succeeded the *pupillus* on intestacy, is liable to the substitute under the terms of the *fideicommissum* [...] (D.36.1.78.)

A father had appointed his son, who had not yet reached the age of puberty (*pupillus*), as his sole heir and had appointed a substitute heir in a codicil in the event of the son's death before he reached the age of puberty. The appointment of a substitute for the *pupillus* through a codicil is invalid because a mere addition to the will cannot contain the appointment of an heir or a disinheritance (Ch 6.4.1). Hence, the death of a son who was below the age of puberty opens the order of intestacy, which leads to the mother inheriting from her child (*senatusconsultum Tertullianum*, Ch. 3.4.1). Scaevola (second century AD) argues that, according to a favourable interpretation, the mother must transfer the estate to the substitute heir appointed in the codicil, since the substitution can be regarded as a valid universal *fideicommissum*. As we have seen above (Ch. 6.4.1), it is only possible to convert an invalid codicil into a *fideicommissum* if the testator has expressly provided for this reinterpretation by means of a salvatory clause in his will. In contrast to this, Scaevola uses the *benigna interpretation* to reinterpret the invalid appointment of a substitute heir as a valid *fideicommissum* of inheritance. In the absence of an explicit provision to save the invalid disposition, the benign assumption is that if the testator had known of the invalidity of the appointment, he would have added a salvatory clause. It is thus the testator's optimal intention that is relevant for this reinterpretation, not an assessment of the testator's probable wishes.

Similarly, in the *ius novum* an interpretation in accordance with the principle of *humanitas* is used to compensate for deficiencies in testamentary dispositions:

> *Paulus, 8 quaestionum: Miles testamentum fecerat, deinde non ignominiae causa missus rursum cinctus est in alia militia: Quaerebatur, an testamentum eius, quod in militia fecerat, valeret. Quaesivi, utrum iure militari an communi iure testatus est. Et si quidem communi iure testatus est, nulla dubitatio est, quin valeat. Sed si ut miles fecisset testamentum, agitare coepi, quando adsumptus fuisset, postquam desiit in numeris esse, utrum intra annum an post annum: Cognovi intra annum eum adsumptum. Ergo si, cum adhuc iure militari valeret, rursus eodem iure posset testari, numquid etiam post annum eo mortuo valeat testamentum? Me movebat, quod alia militia est posterior: Sed humanius est dicere valere testamentum, quasi coniuncto munere militiae. [...] (D.29.1.38.1.)*

Paul, Questions, book 8: A soldier had made a will and then, having not been dishonourably discharged, enlisted again for another mission. The question was whether the will he had made during his [first] service was valid. I asked whether he had made the will in accordance with military law or general law. And if indeed he had made it following the general law, there is no doubt that it is valid. But, if he had made the will as a soldier, I began to inquire when he had been enlisted (again) after his discharge, whether within a year or after a year. I found out that he had enlisted within a year. Therefore, as his will was still valid under military law, and he could make another will under the same law, would his will be valid if he died after one year? I was concerned because the later period of service was separate. It is, however, more humane to state that the will is valid as if the periods of military service had been combined. [...] (D.29.1.38.1.)

A soldier who had made a soldier's will enlisted again within a year and participated in another military campaign without drawing up a second will. Paul (third century AD) decided that human leniency required that the will made during the first campaign should be valid for the second. As we have seen (Ch. 6.4.3), a soldier's will remained valid for one year after his (honourable) discharge. After that, it had to be replaced by a regular will. However, there was no regulation for cases in which a former soldier re-enlisted without making a second will. Here, it is helpful to argue with *humanitas* and to establish an intention capable of overcoming the absence of a second will. This interpretation of the testator's conduct is more lenient because it helps to correct human weakness – be it the lack of diligence in drawing up a new will or the lack of knowledge of the will's time limit – and accommodates the testator in his misjudgement.

A proper revision of the testator's will can, exceptionally, be carried out with reference to the sense of familial duty, the *pietas*:

> *Papinianus, 9 responsorum: Cum avus filium ac nepotem ex altero filio heredes instituisset, a nepote petit, ut, si intra annum trigesimum moreretur, hereditatem patruo suo restitueret: Nepos liberis relictis intra aetatem supra scriptam vita decessit. Fideicommissi condicionem coniectura pietatis respondi defecisse, quod minus scriptum, quam dictum fuerat, inveniretur. (D.35.1.102.)*

Papinianus, Replies, book 9: After a grandfather had appointed his son and a grandson of another son as his heirs, he asked his grandson to transfer the estate to his uncle if he should die before the age of thirty. The grandson died before the age of thirty, leaving children. I replied that considering the familial duty, the condition of the *fideicommissum* failed because it had to be considered that less had been written than had been said. (D.35.1.102.)

The testator appointed his son and his grandson by another son as his heirs. He requested the grandson, by means of a *fideicommissum*, to transfer his share to his uncle, the son of the testator and co-heir, should he die before the age of thirty. Conditions on the heir's death are valid for *fideicommissa* (Ch. 8.5.1), they aim to keep the estate in the family in case of the heir's early death. In the case under discussion here, Papinian (third century AD) denies the son the claim from the *fideicommissum* by considering the condition 'dying before the age of thirty' to be obsolete, since the grandson himself has left children who should inherit their father's estate. If the grandfather had known that the grandson had children of his own, he would have included this in the condition. In fact, the sense of familial duty *(pietas)* required that the grandson not be burdened at the expense of the next generation, which led to an interpretation of the condition in the sense that it could not apply once the grandson had become a father himself. As a result, the interpretation of the grandfather's will does not follow the actual testator's intentions, but what the testator should have wanted according to his sense of familial duty. In this interpretation, the condition reads 'if he dies before reaching the age of thirty without leaving any children'. Despite its clear wording, the moral obligation of the testator not to request the transfer of the inheritance if the heir has to provide for his own descendants leads to doubt about the condition and to rewrite it in accordance with social values.

The two examples of the benevolent and humane interpretation of wills under the *ius novum* show a shift in emphasis compared with their respective application under the *ius civile*. As we have seen (Ch. 9.1.2), in *ius civile* the concepts of *benignitas* and *humanitas* serve to identify the testator's intention and to uncover his motives. The *ius novum*, in contrast, relies on both concepts in order to prevent the invalidation of the will. Thus, the concepts of *benignitas* and *humanitas* in the *ius novum* are not arguments for determining the testator's intentions. Rather, they define the jurists' attitude in applying the law. This shift in interpretative objective is particularly evident when comparing the case of *ius civile*, where the *benignior interpretatio* serves to protect the disinherited sons (Ch 9.1.2), with the case of *ius novum*, where leniency is shown towards the testator in order to obtain a valid will.

This noticeable tendency of the *ius novum* to uphold the testamentary dispositions of the heir through the presumption of a 'correct' intention is also manifested in cases where a will invalid under the *ius civile* is converted into a valid legal disposition of the *ius novum*.

9.3.2 Reinterpreting invalid ius civile into ius novum

The testator's intention serves as a justification for maintaining an invalid will as a *fideicommissum*. Based on the assumption that the testator wanted his invalid will to be upheld as a *fideicommissum*, the grounds for the will's invalidity under *ius civile* could be avoided under *ius novum*.

A first application of this interpretation is the *institutio ex certa re* (Ch. 6.2.2):

> *Marcianus, 4 institutionum: Si quis priore facto testamento posterius fecerit testamentum, etiamsi ex certis rebus in posteriores tabulas heredes instituit, superius tamen testamentum sublatum est, ut divi quoque Severus et Antoninus rescripserunt, cuius constitutionis verba rettuli, cum alia quoque praeterea in constitutione expressa sunt: 'Imperatores Severus et Antoninus Cocceio Campano. Testamentum secundo loco factum, licet in eo certarum rerum heres scriptus sit, iure valere, perinde ac si rerum mentio facta non esset, sed teneri heredem scriptum, ut contentus rebus sibi datis aut suppleta quarta ex lege Falcidia hereditatem restituat his, qui priore testamento scripti fuerant, propter inserta fideicommissaria verba, quibus ut valeret prius testamentum expressum est, dubitari non oportet.' Et hoc ita intellegendum est, si non aliquid specialiter contrarium in secundo testamento fuerit scriptum. (D.36.1.30.)*

Marcianus, Institutes, book 4: If someone who had made a previous will made a subsequent one, even though the later will appointed heirs to a specific property, the former will was still annulled, as the deified Emperors Severus and Antoninus stated in a rescript. I have quoted the constitution because other matters are mentioned there too. 'The Emperors Severus and Antoninus (Caracalla) to Cocceius Campanus. There is no doubt that a second will is valid, even though the heir may have been appointed to receive a specific property, as if the specific property had not been mentioned. But that the appointed heir must either be satisfied with whatever is left to him, or, after the completion up to the *quarta Falcidia*, restore the estate to those appointed in the previous will, on account of the words of a *fideicommissum* which were inserted to state what should have been stated in order to make the first will valid.' However, this only applies if the second will does not expressly state otherwise. (D.36.1.30.)

The testator has left two wills. One was duly made; the other contained the appointment of an heir to a specific property. As we have seen above (Ch. 6.2.2), the *institutio ex certa re*, which was invalid under the *ius civile*, could be preserved as an appointment of heirs by cancelling the specific property and retaining the institution, following Sabinus (first century AD). Marcianus (third century AD) quotes Emperors Septimius Severus (AD193–211) and Caracalla (AD211–217), who initially followed this opinion, stating that the first will was annulled by the second one. However, the emperors differed from Sabinus in that they also attached legal value to the appointment of an heir to a specific property, treating the addition as a *fideicommissum*. As a consequence, those appointed in the second will are considered to be the testamentary heirs; as the testator wishes to give them only the specific property, the *institutio ex certa re* is interpreted as meaning that they should be content with it. This means that they can keep the specific property, but the rest of the estate must be left to the heirs named in the first will. In conclusion, even though the first will was annulled by the second under the *ius civile*, it remained in force under the *ius novum* to the extent that the persons appointed therein as heirs became beneficiaries. This combination of two wills, which was excluded under the *ius civile*, is justified by the testator's intention. Since the testator appointed the heirs in the second will in respect of a specific item, he obviously intended to annul the appointment contained in his first will. Moreover, it can be assumed that he did not wish the second heirs to be beneficiaries of the entire estate, but that he implicitly requested them to hand over the estate to the extent it exceeded the specific property left to them.

We can explain a judgment of Emperor Marcus Aurelius (AD161–180), in which he applies the law of *fideicommissa* to remedy defects in a will under the *ius civile* and *ius praetorium*, with similar considerations. In this respect, the rules of *fideicommissa* seem to serve as a secondary order to implement the testator's intention in the best possible way:

> *Marcellus, 29 digestorum: Proxime in cognitione principis cum quidam heredum nomina induxisset et bona eius ut caduca a fisco vindicarentur, diu de legatis dubitatum est et maxime de his legatis, quae adscripta erant his, quorum institutio fuerat inducta. Plerique etiam legatarios excludendos existimabant. Quod sane sequendum aiebam, si omnem scripturam testamenti cancellasset: Nonnullos opinari id iure ipso peremi quod inductum sit, cetera omnia valitura. Quid ergo? Non et illud interdum credi potest eum, qui heredum nomina induxerat, satis se consecuturum putasse, ut intestati exitum faceret? Sed in re dubia benigniorem interpretationem sequi non minus iustius est quam tutius. [...] (D.28.4.3.)*

> Marcellus, Digest, book 29: Recently, the emperor heard a case where someone had erased the names of the heirs, and his estate was claimed by the imperial treasury as forfeited. A long discussion ensued about legacies, and especially about those bequeathed to those whose appointment as heirs had been erased. Most [of the legal counsellors] thought that they should also be excluded as legatees. Which, indeed, should follow, I said, if [the testator] had cancelled the entire text of the will. Some [of them] held that what had been erased would automatically be annulled, while the rest would be valid. What now? Could it not sometimes be argued that a testator who had deleted the names of his heirs believed that he had done enough to make himself intestate heir? But when in doubt, a more favourable interpretation is not only fairer, but also safer. [...] (D.28.4.3.)

This case concerns the partial invalidity of a will. When the will was opened, it was found that the testator had crossed out the names of the appointed heirs. Since the deleted heirs were considered unworthy (*indignus*), the estate passed to the imperial treasury (Ch. 4.4.3). The legatees, however, brought an action against the imperial treasury to fulfil the bequests that the testator had not crossed out. Marcellus (second century AD) argued for a more lenient interpretation (*benignior interpretatio*) to the effect that the legatees would succeed against the treasury.

After the jurist mentions different opinions on the matter, we find a record of the judicial proceedings in the presence of Emperor Marcus Aurelius, in which the arguments presented are repeated:

> *Marcellus, 29 digestorum: [...] Sententia imperatoris Antonini Augusti Pudente et Pollione consulibus. 'Cum Valerius Nepos mutata voluntate et inciderit testamentum suum et heredum nomina induxerit, hereditas eius secundum divi patris mei constitutionem ad eos qui scripti fuerint pertinere non videtur.' Et advocatis fisci dixit: 'Vos habetis iudices vestros.' Vibius Zeno dixit: 'Rogo, domine imperator, audias me patienter: De legatis quid statues?' Antoninus Caesar dixit: 'Videtur tibi voluisse testamentum valere, qui nomina heredum induxit?' Cornelius Priscianus advocatus Leonis dixit: 'Nomina heredum tantum induxit'. Calpurnius Longinus advocatus fisci dixit: 'Non potest ullum testamentum valere, quod heredem non habet'. [...] Antoninus Caesar remotis omnibus cum deliberasset et admitti rursus eodem iussisset, dixit: 'Causa praesens admittere videtur humaniorem interpretationem, ut ea dumtaxat existimemus Nepotem irrita esse voluisse, quae induxit'. [...] (D.28.4.3.)*

> Marcellus, Digest, book 29: [...] The judgement of the Emperor Antoninus Augustus [Marcus Aurelius] in the consulship of Pudens and Pollio (AD166): 'since Valerius Nepos, having changed his mind, cut open his will and crossed out the names of his heirs, his estate does not belong to those appointed in said will, in accordance with the constitution of my deified father.' And he said to the advocates of the imperial treasury: 'you will have your own judges'. Vibius Zeno said, 'I ask, my Lord and Emperor, that you hear me patiently. What do you decide regarding the legacies?' The Emperor Antoninus Caesar [Marcus Aurelius] replied: 'does it seem to you that someone who has crossed out the names of his heirs still wants his will to stand?' Cornelius Priscianus, advocate of Leo, said: 'he has merely crossed out the names of his heirs'. Calpernius Longinus, advocate of the imperial treasury, answered: 'a will with no heir cannot be valid'. [...] The Emperor Antoninus [Marcus Aurelius] sent them all away while he considered the matter, then called them back again, and spoke thus: 'the matter at hand

seems to deserve a more humane interpretation, so that we hold the opinion that Nepos intended to annul only that part of his will that he had crossed out'. [...] (D.28.4.3.)

First, Marcellus mentions the emperor's judgement, which resulted in the estate's escheat to the imperial treasury. The decision was that the testator's erasure of the heirs led to the invalidity of the appointment of the heirs, which in turn would also affect the validity of the legacies under *ius civile* (Ch. 6.2). The emperor's judgement is unambiguous, but the emperor's advisors discuss whether there are ways of upholding the legacies nonetheless. The advocate of the imperial treasury takes the floor first, stating that he does not want the emperor to make a decision, but rather a referral to the court of the imperial treasury, which would rule against the legatees according to the current regulations. It seems plausible to interpret the statement 'you will have your own judges' in this way. Then, a certain Vibius Zeno argues in the opposite direction. He represents the legatees and demands that the imperial treasury fulfil them. Obviously, he wanted to avoid the emperor, from whom an equitable decision could be expected, delegating the matter to a civil servant. For this reason, Vibius Zeno asks for imperial leniency. 'I beg of you, my Master and Emperor, listen carefully. How do you decide regarding the legacies?' The emperor's response highlights the unusual nature of the request. 'Does it seem to you that someone [Nepos] who has crossed out the names of the heirs still wants his will to stand?' At the same time, the emperor examined the substance of the case. In the course of the examination, a certain Calpurnius Longinus reminded him of the principle that the legacies presupposed the validity of the appointment. Finally, the more lenient (*benignior*) interpretation that Marcellus already referred to in his introduction prevailed. In his judgement, Emperor Marcus Aurelius (AD161–180) merely uses a different wording, describing his decision as 'more humane' (*humanior*). Following this interpretation, only the appointment of heirs is invalid while the other parts of the will, i.e. the legacies, remain valid. The emperor's leniency consists in exempting both the testator and the legatees from the archaic rules of the *ius civile*, which required a valid appointment of heirs for legacies. Instead, the emperor accepts the argument that only what is crossed out is invalid, while all the other provisions of the will remain intact. The validity of an independent singular bequest without the appointment of an heir is only conceivable as a *fideicommissum*. Hence, the *benignior interpretatio* does nothing other than transform the testator's testamentary dispositions into *fideicommissa:* the appointment of heirs is considered a universal *fideicommissa*, invalidated by the testator; however, the legacies, now singular *fideicommissa*, remain valid and burden the imperial treasury as the successor of the deceased. In sum, the inevitable invalidity of legacies under the *ius civile* is overcome by their transformation into *fideicommissa* under the *ius novum*, which results in the obligation of the imperial treasury to fulfil them.

A similar approach can be found in a case decided by Emperors Septimius Severus (AD193–211) and Caracalla (AD211–217):

> *Paulus, 1 imperialium sententiarum in cognitionibus prolatarum seu 2 decretorum: Pactumeius Androsthenes Pactumeiam Magnam filiam Pactumeii Magni ex asse heredem instituerat, eique patrem eius substituerat. Pactumeio Magno occiso et rumore perlato, quasi filia quoque eius mortua, mutavit testamentum Noviumque Rufum heredem instituit hac praefatione: 'Quia heredes, quos volui habere mihi contingere non potui, Novius Rufus heres esto.' Pactumeia Magna supplicavit imperatores nostros et cognitione suscepta, licet modus institutioni contineretur, quia falsus non solet obesse, tamen ex voluntate testantis putavit imperator ei subveniendum. Igitur pronuntiavit hereditatem ad Magnam pertinere, sed legata ex posteriore testamento eam praestare debere, proinde atque si in posterioribus tabulis ipsa fuisset heres scripta. (D.28.5.93.1.)*

> Paul, imperial decisions pronounced in judicial examinations, book 1 or decrees, book 2: Pactumeius Androsthenes had appointed Pactumeia Magna, the daughter of Pactumeius Magnus, as his sole heir, and appointed her father as her substitute. Since Pactumeius Magnus was killed, and the rumour spread that his daughter had also died, Androsthenes changed his will. He appointed Novius Rufus as his heir, prefacing the appointment thus, 'let Novius Rufus be my heir since I have not been able to keep those heirs whom I wished.' Pactumeia Magna petitioned our emperors, and having held a *cognitio*, the emperor decided that she should be helped in accordance with the testator's wishes, although a modality was placed on the appointment of an heir which, as a rule, constitutes no impediment [to the appointment], even if it was false. Therefore, the emperor decided that the estate belonged to Pactumeia Magna, but that she was obliged to pay the legacies bequeathed by the second will, just as if she had been appointed heir in the subsequent will. (D.28.5.93.1.)

The testator Androsthenes has left two wills. In the first, he appointed Pactumeia Magna as his heir and her father as substitute heir. In the second will, which he drew up after the death of Pactumeia's father and after hearing rumours of her death, he appointed another heir, called Novius Rufus. In an introductory note, the testator clarified that he had only changed his will because he could not have those he had originally wanted as heirs. After the death of Androsthenes, it was discovered that Pactumeia Magna was still alive and she asked the Emperors Septimius Severus (AD193–211) and Antoninus Caracalla (AD211–217) for help. The emperors accommodated her by taking into account the preface Androsthenes had attached to the will. Since the heir, whom Androsthenes had presumed dead, was alive, the testator erred about a circumstance relevant to his will. Without this error, he would never have made the second will, which appointed Novius Rufus. In consideration of this, the emperors grant the estate to Pactumeia Magna. She must, however, fulfil the bequests that were left in the second will, even though, as the emperors point out, she was not appointed heir in the second will.

The legal construction chosen by the emperors is not explained, since Paul (third century AD) simply states that 'Pactumeia Magna is entitled to the estate' (*hereditatem ad Magnam pertinere*). This could refer either to an heir under the *ius civile* or to a *fideicommissum*. In the first case, the emperors would have combined the two wills, thus preserving the appointment of Pactumeia from the first will, but burdening her with the legacies of the second. In the second case, if we take '*hereditatem pertinere*' to refer to a *universal fideicommissum*, this would mean that the decision was based on the *ius novum*. In this case, the preface to Androsthenes' will would have been seen as establishing a *fideicommissum* in benefit of Pactumeia Magna. However, this universal succession was charged with singular *fideicommissa* in favour of the legatees of the second will. The fact that Paul underlines that the introduction must be regarded as a *falsa causa* without legal consequences, leaving the second will valid, supports the view that the emperors assumed *fideicommissa* for all the dispositions they intended to maintain. Since Pactumeia Magna was granted a remedy by reference to the testator's intention, the imperial decision was not based on *ius civile* but on the *ius novum*. This shift to a different jural layer also explains the preservation of the legacies that burdened the heir. Since the universal fideicommissary had to bear all the burdens of the heir, Pactumeia Magna had to assume the obligation of administering the legacies as soon as she accepted the inheritance. The shift to the law of the *fideicommissa* therefore allowed a fairer solution based on the testator's intention, whereas the *ius civile* would not have allowed the problem to be resolved.

The transformation of an invalid disposition under *ius civile* into *fideicommissa* under *ius novum* is summarised in Overview 42:

Overview 42: Reinterpreting the *ius civile* into *ius novum*

the case of Cocceius Campanus (D.36.1.30) two consecutive wills; will 2 contains an *institutio ex certa re*	
ius civile	*ius novum*
under the *ius civile* will 1 is invalidated by will 2; the appointment to one specific item must be erased (rule of Sabinus); however, will 1 contains a provision following which it must be preserved as a *fideicommissum*	both wills apply together and are interpreted as *fideicommissa*: will 2: appointment of the heir mentioned by leaving a *fideicommissum* for the heir from will 1; the heir mentioned in will 2 may keep the item left to him
the case of Valerius Nepos (D.28.4.3) the testator crossed out the names of the designated heirs	
ius civile	*ius novum*
under the *ius civile* the will is inoperative because the names of the heirs are crossed out (unworthiness); escheat to the imperial treasury; the legacies are invalid because of the invalid appointment	the will is treated as a *fideicommissum* of inheritance charged to the imperial treasury; hence, only the *fideicommissum* of inheritance is 'invalid'; the legacies can be maintained as singular *fideicommissa*
the case of Pactumeia Magna (D.28.5.93.1) preface to the will mentions an impediment to the appointment of the heir actually intended	
ius civile	*ius novum*
Novius Rufus is appointed as heir in the will; the preface, in which the testator states that he would have preferred to appoint Pactumeia Magna, is irrelevant	preface that shows that Pactumeia Magna shall be appointed heir is seen as a universal *fideicommissum* for the benefit of the latter. She can claim the estate; as a quasi-heir, she must fulfil the remaining legacies as *fideicommissa*

9.4 Concluding Considerations on the Interpretation of Wills

1. The distinction between the three layers of law is also crucial for the interpretation of wills and allows a more nuanced understanding of the means of interpretation available to Roman jurists. In contrast to the *ius civile* and the *ius novum*, questions of interpretation are of secondary importance under the *ius praetorium*. This is mainly due to the procedural nature of praetorian law. In particular, it regulates the conditions of praetorian remedies and the rules for court proceedings. In this respect, the *ius praetorium* either implements or complements the objectives of other layers of law.
2. The *ius civile* and the *ius novum* converge in their interpretative objectives: the content of the will must be determined on the basis of the

testator's intention. However, their respective methodology follows different rules, corresponding to the differences observed between the strict formalities of *ius civile* and the formless testamentary dispositions of the *ius novum*. Whereas interpretation under the *ius civile* is conditioned both by its formalism and by the dispositive powers granted to the testator, the *ius novum* is characterised by its orientation towards the intention of the testator, which is not tied to a specific form. At the same time, the imperial interpretation aimed to achieve the testator's best possible intention, which could prevent the testamentary disposition from becoming invalid.

3. The tendency of the *ius novum* to attribute an ideal will to the testator by means of a benevolent and humane interpretation is also used to avoid the consequences of invalidity under the *ius civile*. To this end, the jurist or emperor who interprets a will shifts to another layer of law by interpreting a will that would be invalid under the *ius civile* into a *fideicommissum*. Hence, the different layers of law are used to allow greater flexibility in the application of the law. This shift finally breaks through the barrier created by jurists, at least for soldiers' wills and the law of codicils, under the concept of *ius singulare* (Ch. 6.4.4). To the extent that it can be justified by the testator's intention, seemingly inevitable consequences of the *ius civile* can be overcome by reference to the *ius novum*.

10

Final Conclusions

In this book, we have examined the evolution of the Roman law of inheritance from its first palpable traces in the law of the twelve tables (approx. 450BC) to the third century AD. In this examination, the basic dogmatic structures of each institute of the law of inheritance have first been presented, before analysing the contradictory legal development of different aspects of the law. The interest in the evolution of law also explains, why the often neglected imperial law, especially the *senatus consulta* and the imperial adjudication, which seminally shaped private law, has been considered in detail. Indeed, the imperial measures, like the Augustan marital laws, despite their controversy already at the time of their enactment, formed a reality with which the Roman jurists had to deal, either in restraint (*ius singulare*) or in assenting (*senatusconsultum Iuventianum*).

Furthermore, the focus on the law of inheritance as a multifaceted, well-documented area of law is suitable for understanding more accurately the various layers of Roman private law, and thus a peculiar feature of the Roman legal culture. At the same time, fragments from the Digest were used to illustrate how Roman jurists decided cases and developed innovative solutions when confronted with new legal problems.

The following conclusions will comprise the answers to the three main questions posed at the beginning of this book (Ch. 1.3.3).

10.1 The Layers of the Roman Law of Inheritance

The *ius civile*, as enshrined in the law of the twelve tables forms the oldest layer of law of the Roman law of inheritance. With the words: 'as he disposed over his household, property and guardianship, so shall it be lawful' (*uti legassit super familia pecuniave tutelave sua, ita ius esto*), the law of the twelve tables (V. 3., approx. 450BC) foresaw the option of making a will. At the same time, the said law determined graduated rules for intestate succession and contained rules on co-heirs. The jurists of the late Republic refined these precepts by creating, first of all, rules for making wills. It is notable that subsequent generations of jurists perceived these rules, developed through cautelary practice, as much as *ius civile* as the law of the twelve tables itself.

The *ius civile* did not contain rules for probate proceedings. Therefore, those entitled to the inheritance, relied on the protection of the praetor's edict. Since the greatest danger for the heir was the deprivation of the estate, the praetor offered protection by granting possession of the estate (*bonorum possessio*). As a *bonorum possessor*, the person entitled could obtain factual control over the estate and, if he was not the heir, could acquire the estate through prescriptive acquisition. These peculiarities of *bonorum possessio* reveal the procedural nature of praetorian law. Indeed, the praetor could not create an heir of *ius civile* but merely granted the appointed heirs the option to have their lawful rights effectively protected. Furthermore, as a court magistrate, the praetor could ensure that the *bonorum possessor*, who was not an *ius civile* heir, was nevertheless treated like one. In fact, the praetor granted the *bonorum possessor* all actions for and against the estate, as if he had become a civil heir. Moreover, the praetor used his jurisdiction to adapt the provisions of *ius civile* in individual cases which as a result led to a new order of succession.

Lastly, the imperial law created new *ius civile* through *senatus consulta* and, more importantly, it established new regulations for many specific cases, putting the existing legal formulas and actions under pressure to adjust. At the same time, imperial law did not repeal the traditional types of wills under the *ius civile*. However, since it recognised formless wills and legacies as actionable, formal appointments and legacies became gradually obsolete. Moreover, the formless character of the imperial types of hereditary dispositions permitted new forms of testamentary content that would have been impossible under the *ius civile* or the *ius praetorium*. The jurists, nonetheless, clung to the testamentary types of the *ius civile* and *ius praetorium* and defended both against the imperial practice, even calling the latter '*ius singulare*'. However, the coexistence of the *ius antiquum* and *ius novum* facilitated the interpretation of the testamentary disposition if the preservation of the testator's recognisable intention could ultimately be achieved through a shift to another layer of law, namely to the *ius novum*. As a consequence, the imperial law had the tendency to gradually replace the *ius civile*, especially when it came to the interpretation of a testamentary disposition.

10.2 The Lines of Development of Roman Private Law

In perusing the various topics of the law of inheritance, namely, the rules of intestacy, the position of the heir, the will, legacies, rules of disinheritance and the interpretation of wills, we repeatedly observed similar turning points in the development of the law. The law of the twelve tables (approx. 450BC) always forms the starting point for any legal evolution, as it remained authoritative also for the jurists of the third century AD. The rules of intestacy and the will were, at least according to their reading, enshrined in the law of the twelve tables and developed from its interpretation. The latter, i.e. the juristic interpretation, was crucial for the traditional *ius civile*. From its experience in cautelary jurisprudence, the juristic interpretation had developed binding guidelines on the ideal way in which the testator should make his will. The time frame for this interpretative work is likely to be between the passing of the law of the twelve tables and the last century of the Republic. In this period we also find a series of pieces of legislation, some of which supported the juristic interpretation of wills, but some of which also attempted to restrict them, e.g. by limiting the freedom of testamentary disposition (*lex Falcidia*). Parallel to this, the praetor, as a new player in this field, created his own system of inheritance law when stating edictal rules on *bonorum possessio*. Firstly, this newly created inheritance law served to enforce and rationalise the application of the *ius civile*; later, the *ius praetorium* partly supplemented and corrected the *ius civile*, e.g., by allowing persons to inherit who under the *ius civile* were not entitled as heirs.

The beginning of the Principate under Emperor Augustus (AD27) marks a watershed in the history of the Roman inheritance law. Various pieces of legislation concerned the law of inheritance. They affected the capacity to obtain (*lex Iulia et Papia*), the inheritance tax and the probate process (*lex Iulia de vicesima hereditatum*). Most importantly, however, Augustus made *fideicommissa* and codicils enforceable, thus enabling formless dispositions upon death. Likewise, the inheritance legislation of the later emperors proved seminal and should not be underestimated when discussing Roman private law. The *senatusconsulta Tertullianum, Orfitianum, Iuventianum, Neronianum, Trebellianum* and *Pegasianum* changed the law of inheritance significantly by accepting new types of heirs on intestacy, by establishing requisites for the actions on inheritance, by relaxing formal requirements for legacies and by stating binding rules for *fideicommissa*. At the same time, the imperial reforms regularly had an impact not only on the specific area for which they were enacted, but on the whole legal system, as they were perceived as paradigmatic and generalisable. The jurists of the Empire were responsible for this development because, on the one hand, they respected the imperial law and sought to underpin it dogmatically, but on the other hand they adhered to the unity of the law of inheritance by incorporating the imperial reforms into the existing system as much as possible. This uninterrupted development of the established rules is also linguistically recognizable, e.g., in the naming of the praetorian edict newly promulgated by Emperor Hadrian (AD130). Rather than being cited as 'imperial law', it was referred to as '*ius praetorium*'. This nomenclature is even upheld for rules that were clearly inserted in the course of the drafting of the imperial *edictum perpetuum*, e.g. for the *nova clausula Iuliani* that stemmed from an imperial rather than a praetorian initiative.

The lines of development elucidated here, allow us to draw conclusions regarding the legal reasoning of the Roman jurists.

10.3 The Roman Legal Reasoning

The Roman legal order has been described as an accumulation of layers of law, proceeding gradually through casuistic judicial findings by the jurists and the emperor. Indeed, the concept of layers of law has proven meaningful also for the evolution of the Roman law of inheritance. Most matters of the law of inheritance pertain to the three layers of law of which it is composed, namely, the *ius civile*, *ius praetorium* and *ius novum,* while their peculiarities and interactions become apparent. It has been found that jurists of the Empire not only perceived the individual layers of law as merely sequential, but also as parallel accretions that could be applied next to, and against, each other. This coordination of differing legal sources, however, is not the result of a general hierarchy of norms, but was, instead, negotiated on a case-by-case basis. By studying the various texts of the Roman legal tradition, which have been presented and treated in this book, this casuistic approach to law, i.e. focusing on the individual case while arguing from similar cases and precepts, can be substantiated.

In addition, the importance of republican and imperial legislation must not be underestimated. Although it only selectively altered the rules and seldom repeals them, its mere existence conditions a shift in the application of the law in individual cases and thus changes the legal order. The analogous application of *senatusconsultum Iuventianum*, e.g., shows the jurists' inclination to broaden the scope of imperial law, as far as it was not seen as *ius singulare*, and to apply it on similar cases. Conversely, the fact that imperial jurists challenged the *regula Catoniana* shows that the imperial prerequisites for a valid legacy also affected the existing *ius civile* and called for an adjustment of the traditional testamentary rules.

The jurists, however, did not merely obediently apply the various layers of law, but they consciously shaped them, as shown by the differentiation between the *ius novum* and *ius antiquum* in the application of *senatusconsultum Tertullianum* and *Orfitianum*. Evidence of this can also be discerned with regard to codicils and soldiers' wills, which the jurists set apart from the general law, with the help of the concept of the *ius singulare*. This conceptuality shows, in turn, that the judicial findings of Roman jurists, despite their case-law nature, were 'systematic' in as far as they took as their directive the existing sources in their comprehensive review, which needed to be evened out for individual cases.

10.4 On the Complexity of the Roman Law of Inheritance

The opinion expressed in the past that the Roman law of inheritance was opaque or an underdeveloped part of private law (Ch. 1.3.1), pre-eminently revealed the beholder's expectations. It is common knowledge that the historical interpreter cannot shake off his or her time-conditioned bias when looking at Roman sources, thus, despite all efforts to contextualise and to remain objective, he or she ultimately acts self-referentially. This knowledge necessitates a regular review of scholarly perceptions of Roman private law and to nuance previous assumptions and prejudices.

> Each generation must find its concept of the past [...] History is always twofold, consisting of what has happened and the one who seeks to comprehend what has happened, out of his place and time [...] Every work on history tells us something about the time it treats and the time of its writing. In hindsight, it even does more of the latter than the former. The task is this: to organise knowledge, old and new; to rearrange delineations and emphases; to allow new writers to speak about an old story.[1]

The wealth of cases, arguments, questions and juristic material in the Roman legal sources gains new meaning against the background of today's legal concerns and challenges. Namely, the plurality of norms and the inconsistencies between legal precepts manifest themselves as a problem beyond Roman inheritance law. Given this historical example, the reader can profit from the study of the Roman legal evolution for the present. This does not mean that Roman examples should serve as a paradigm for the situation today. Instead, the historical experience can sharpen our perception and enable us to reflect critically on current questions while maintaining an analytical distance.

---

[1] Golo Mann, *Propyläen Weltgeschichte. Eine Universalgeschichte, Band 8: Das Neunzehnte Jahrhundert* (Propyläen 1960) 13.

Bibliography

1 Introduction
1.1 A Roman Will Dating from AD142:

Octave Guéraud and Pierre Jouguet, 'Un testament latin per aes et libram de 142 après J.-C. (Tablettes L. Keimer)' (1940) 6 Études de papyrologie 1–20; Vincenzo Arangio-Ruiz (ed), *Fontes iuris romani anteiustiniani III* (No. 47, 2nd edn, Barbèra 1943) 129–132; Jean Macquéron, 'Le Testament d'Antonius Silvanus (Tablettes Keimer)' (1945) 23 RHD 123–170; Vincenzo Arangio-Ruiz 'Il testamento di Antonio Silvano e il senatoconsulto di Nerone' in Vincenzo Arangio-Ruiz and Giuseppe Lavaggi (eds), *Studi Emilio Albertario I* (Giuffrè 1953) 203–212; Detlef Liebs, 'Das Testament des Antonius Silvanus, römischer Kavallerist in Alexandria bei Ägypten, aus dem Jahre 142 n. Chr.' in Klaus Märke and Christian Otto (eds), *Festschrift Weddig Fricke* (Alber 2000) 113–128; Livia Migliardi Zingale, '*Testamentum Antonii Silvani equitis* (Alexandria, 27 marzo 142 d. C.)' in Giovanni Purpura (ed), *Revisione ed integrazione dei Fontes Iuris Romani Anteiustiniani (FIRA). Studi preparatori II. Auctores – Negotia* (Giappichelli 2012) 147–151; Benedikt Strobel, *Römische Testamentsurkunden aus Ägypten vor und nach der Constitutio Antoniniana* (C.H. Beck 2014); Elizabeth Anne Meyer, 'Practice, Emperors, and the Mechanics of Testaments' in Werner Eck, Federico Satangelo and Konrad Vössing (eds), *Emperor, Army, and Society. Studies in Roman Imperial History for Anthony R. Birley* (Habelt 2022); Michel Humbert, '§ 1 Faktoren der Rechtsbildung' in Ulrike Babusiaux, Christian Baldus, Wolfgang Ernst, Franz-Stefan Meissel, Johannes Platschek, Thomas Rüfner (eds), *Handbuch des Römischen Privatrechts* (Mohr Siebeck 2023) 3–32.

Corpus iuris civilis: Tammo Wallinga, *Tanta-Dedoken. Two Introductory Constitutions to Justinian's Digest* (E. Forsten 1989); Mario Bretone, *Geschichte des römischen Rechts. Von den Anfängen bis Justinian* (C.H. Beck 1992); Detlef Liebs, *Römisches Recht. Ein Studienbuch* (6th edn, UTB 2004); Franz Wieacker, *Römische Rechtsgeschichte. Zweiter Abschnitt. Ein Fragment, aus dem Nachlaß hrsg. v. Joseph Georg Wolf* (C.H. Beck 2006); Tony Honoré, *Justinian's Digest.*

Character and Compilation (OUP 2010); Wolfgang Kaiser, 'Justinian and the *Corpus Iuris civilis*' in David Johnston (ed), *The Cambridge Companion to Roman Law* (CUP 2015) 119-148.

Interpolation Criticism: Fridolin Eisele, 'Zur Diagnostik der Interpolationen in den Digesten und im Codex' (1886) 7 ZRG rom. 15-31, (1889) 10 ZRG rom. 296-322; Otto Gradenwitz, *Interpolationen in den Pandekten. Kritische Studien* (Weidmannsche Buchhandlung 1887); Otto Lenel, 'Interpolationenjagd' (1925) 45 ZRG rom. 17-38; Paul Kretschmar, 'Kritik der Interpolationenkritik' (1939) 59 ZRG rom. 102-218; Max Kaser, 'Zur Glaubwürdigkeit der römischen Rechtsquellen. (Über die Grenzen der Interpolationenkritik)' in Pietro Paradisi (ed), *La critica del testo – Atti del secondo Congresso internazionale della Società italiana di Storia del Diritto I* (Olschki 1971) 291-370; Franz Wieacker, 'Zur gegenwärtigen Lage der romanistischen Textkritik)' in Pietro Paradisi (ed), *La critica del testo – Atti del secondo Congresso internazionale della Società italiana di Storia del Diritto II* (Olschki 1971) 1099-1122; Max Kaser, 'Ein Jahrhundert Interpolationenforschung an den römischen Rechtsquellen', originally in (1979) 116 Anzeiger der phil. hist. Klasse der Österreichischen Akademie der Wiss. 83-113, now in Max Kaser (ed), *Römische Rechtsquellen und angewandte Juristenmethode* (Böhlau 1986) 112-154; Franz Wieacker, 'Textkritik und Sachforschung' (1974) 91 ZRG rom. 1-40; Franz Wieacker, *Textstufen klassischer Juristen* (Vandenhoeck & Ruprecht 1960, 2nd edn 1975); J. H. A Lokin, 'The End of an Epoch: Epilegomena to a Century of Interpolation Criticism' in Robert Feenstra (ed), *Collatio iuris romani: etudes dediees a Hans Ankum, I* (J.C. Gieben 1995) 261-273; Ralph Backhaus, 'Interpolationsforschung' (1999) 14 DNP 617-619; Martin Avenarius et al. (eds), *Gradenwitz, Riccobono und die Entwicklung der Interpolationenkritik. Gradenwitz, Riccobono e gli sviluppi della critica interpolazionistica. Methodentransfer unter europäischen Juristen im späten 19. Jahrhundert. Circolazione di modelli e metodi fra giuristi europei nel tardo Ottocento* (Mohr Siebeck 2018).

The Institutes of Gaius: Peter Stein, 'The Development of the Institutional System' in Peter Stein and A. D. E. Lewis (eds), *Studies in Justinian's Institutes in memory of J. A. C. Thomas* (Sweet A. Maxwell 1983) 151-163; Tomasz Giaro, 'Gaius' 4 (1998) DNP 736-738; Ulrich Manthe, *Gaius Institutiones. Die Institutionen des Gaius* (2nd edn, WBG 2010); Cristina Vano, *Der Gaius der Historischen Rechtsschule. Eine Geschichte der Wissenschaft vom Römischen Recht* (Vittorio Klostermann 2008); Mario Varvaro, *Le istituzioni di Gaio e il Glücksstern di Niebuhr* (Giappichelli 2012); Ulrike Babusiaux and Dario Mantovani (eds), *Le Istituzioni di Gaio. Avventure di un bestseller. Trasmissione, uso e trasformazione del testo* (Pavia University Press 2020).

1.2 The Sources of the Roman Law of Inheritance

1.3 De testamentis et de legatis:

Roman Law of Inheritance: Fritz Schulz, *Classical Roman Law* (Clarendon Press 1951); Pasquale Voci, *Diritto ereditario romano I: Introduzione, Parte generale, Mailand 1960, II: Successione ab intestato, successione testamentaria* (2nd edn, Giuffrè 1963); Max Kaser, *Das römische Privatrecht. 1. Abschnitt: Das altrömische, das vorklassische und klassische Recht* (2nd edn, Giuffrè 1971); Alan Watson, *The Law of Succession in the Later Roman Republic* (Clarendon Press 1971); Alfonso Castro Saénz, *Herencia y mundo antiguo. Estudio de derecho sucesorio romano* (Editorial Universidad de Sevilla 2002); Franciszek Longchamps de Bérier, *Law of Succession. Roman Legal Framework and Comparative Law Perspective* (Wolters Kluwer 2011); Ulrich Manthe, *Geschichte des römischen Rechts* (4th edn, C.H. Beck 2011); Giovanna Coppola Bisazza, 'I patti successori dispositivi' (2021) 11 Quaderni Lupiensi di Storia e Diritto 552–562; Patrizia Giunti et al., *Il diritto nell'esperienza di Roma antica* (Giappichelli 2021); Riccardo Cardilli, *Fondamento romano dei diritti odierni* (Giappichelli 2021).

Legal Reasoning of Roman Jurists: Fritz Schulz, *Geschichte der römischen Rechtswissenschaft* (H. Böhlaus Nachfolge 1961); Max Kaser, 'Zur Methode der römischen Rechtsfindung', originally in Max Kaser (ed), *Zur Methode der römischen Rechtsfindung I* (Vandenhoeck & Ruprecht 1962) 47–78; Elmar Bund, 'Zur Argumentation der Römischen Juristen' in *Studi Edoardo Volterra I* (Giuffrè 1971) 571–587; Alan Watson, *Law Making in the Later Roman Republic* (Clarendon Press 1974); Franz Horak, *Rationes decidendi. Entscheidungsbegründungen bei den älteren römischen Juristen bis Labeo I* (Scientia 1969); Franz Wieacker, 'Zur Rolle des Arguments in der römischen Jurisprudenz' in Dieter Medicus and Hans Hermann Seiler (eds), *Festschrift Max Kaser* (C.H. Beck 1976) 3–27; Heinrich Honsell, 'Das Gesetzesverständnis in der römischen Antike' in Walter Wilhelm (ed), *Festschrift Helmut Coing I* (C.H. Beck 1982) 129–148; Mario Bretone, *Tecniche e ideologie dei giuristi romani* (2nd edn, E.S.I. 1982); Max Kaser, *Römische Rechtsquellen und angewandte Juristenmethode* (Vandenhoeck & Ruprecht and Böhlau 1986); Letizia Vacca, *Contributo allo studio del metodo casistico nel diritto romano* (reprinted Giuffrè 1982); Tomasz Giaro, 'Über methodologische Werkmittel der Romanistik' (1988) 105 ZRG rom. 180–262; Mihaly Maczonkai, 'Pragmatic Legal Reasoning and its Antecedents in Roman Law' in Gábor Hamza (ed), *Iura antiqua – iura moderna Festschrift für Ferenc Benedek zum 75. Geburtstag* (Dialóg Campus Kiadó 2001) 169–186; George Sheets, 'Distinguishing Cases and Conditions in Roman Legislation' (2005) 52 RIDA 359–373; Letizia Vacca, *Metodo casistico e sistema prudenziale* (CEDAM 2006); Mario Bretone, *Ius controversum nella giurisprudenza classica* (Accademia Nazionale dei Lincei 2008); Dieter Nörr, '*exempla nihil per se valent*. Bemerkungen zu Paul. 15 *quaest.*, D. 46,3,98,8; 72 ad ed. D. 45,1,83,5' (2009) 126 ZRG rom. 1–54; Ulrike Babusiaux, 'Coordination of different Layers of Law in the Roman Empire and in the European Union' in Ulrike Babusiaux and Mariko Igimi (eds), *Messages from Antiquity. Roman Law and Current Legal Debates* (Böhlau 2019) 131–167.

2 The General Historical and Legal framework
2.1 The General Historical Framework

In General: Klaus Bringmann, *Römische Geschichte. Von den Anfängen bis zur Spätantike* (C.H. Beck 2008); Wolfgang Schuller, *Das römische Weltreich. Von der Entstehung der Republik bis zum Ausgang der Antike* (2nd edn, Theiss 2003); Géza Alföldy, *Römische Sozialgeschichte* (4th edn, F. Steiner 2011); Michael Sommer, *Römische Geschichte. Von den Anfängen bis zum Untergang* (Alfred Kröner 2013); Matthew Dillon and Lynda Garland, *The Ancient Romans: History and Society from the Early Republic to the Death of Augustus* (Routledge 2021).

The Roman Republic: Corey Brennan, *The Praetorship in the Roman Republic* (OUP 2000); Jochen Bleicken, *Die Verfassung der Römischen Republik* (8th edn, Schöningh 2008); Martin Jehne, *Die römische Republik. Von der Gründung bis Caesar* (2nd edn, C.H. Beck 2008); Karl-Joachim Hölkeskamp and Henry Heitmann-Gordon, *Reconstructing the Roman Republic. An Ancient Political Culture and Modern Research* (Princeton University Press 2010); Jan Valgaeren, *The Jurisdiction of the Pontiff in the Roman Republic: A Third Dimension* (Wolf Legal Publishers 2012); Pierangelo Buongiorno, '§ 2 Republik' in Ulrike Babusiaux and others (eds), *Handbuch des Römischen Privatrechts* (Mohr Siebeck 2023) 32–54.

The Principate: Heinz Bellen, *Die Kaiserzeit von Augustus bis Diocletian. Grundzüge der römischen Geschichte* (2nd edn, WBG 2010); Werner Dalheim, *Die römische Kaiserzeit* (R. Oldenbourg 2013); Accademia Nazionale dei Lincei (ed), *Augusto. La costruzione del principato* (Bardi 2017); Emanuele Stolfi, '§ 3 Prinzipat' in Ulrike Babusiaux and others (eds), *Handbuch des Römischen Privatrechts* (Mohr Siebeck 2023) 54–73.

Late Antiquity: Christopher Kelly, *Ruling the Later Roman Empire* (Harvard University Press 2004); Alexander Demandt, *Die Spätantike. Römische Geschichte von Diocletian bis Justinian (284–565 n. Chr.)* (2nd edn, C.H. Beck 2007); Jens-Uwe Krause, 'Die Spätantike (284 bis 565 n. Chr.)' in Hans-Joachim Gehrke and Helmuth Schneider (eds), *Geschichte der Antike. Ein Studienbuch*, (4th edn, J.B. Metzler 2013) 429–499; Stephen Mitchell, *A History of the Later Roman Empire. AD 284–641* (2nd edn, Wiley-Blackwell 2015); Rita Lizzi Testa (ed), *Late Antiquity in Contemporary Debates* (Cambridge Scholars Publishing 2019); Adriaan Sirks, 'Could after the division of administration in 364 an emperor issue a law for the entire empire?' (2021) 138 ZRG rom. 555–567; Lorena Atzeri, '§ 4

Vom Prinzipat zur Spätantike' in Ulrike Babusiaux and others (eds), *Handbuch des Römischen Privatrechts* (Mohr Siebeck 2023) 75–100.

Roman Jurists: Wolfgang Kunkel, *Herkunft und soziale Stellung der römischen Juristen* (2nd edn, Böhlau 1967, reprinted in 2001); Franz Wieacker, 'Juristen und Jurisprudenz im Prinzipat' (1977) 94 ZRG rom. 319–358; Franz Wieacker, '*Respondere ex auctoritate principis*' in Hans Ankum, Johannes Spruit and Felix Wubbe (eds), *Robert Feenstra* (Universitätsverlag Freiburg 1985) 71–94; Mario Talamanca, 'Développements socio-économiques et jurisprudence romaine à la fin de la République' in *Studi Cesare Sanfilippo VII* (Giuffrè 1987) 774–791; Detlef Liebs, *Hofjuristen der römischen Kaiser bis Justinian* (C.H. Beck 2010); Kaius Tuori, 'The *ius respondendi* and the Freedom of Roman Jurisprudence' (2004) 51 RIDA 295–337; Anna Plisecka, 'The Roman Jurists' Law during the passage from the Republic to the Empire' in Szabolcs Hornyák and others (eds), *Turning Points and Breaklines* (Martin Meidenbauer 2009) 372–392; Ulrike Babusiaux, 'Legal Writing and legal Reasoning' in Paul J. Du Plessis, Clifford Ando and Kaius Tuori (eds), *The Oxford Handbook of Roman Law and Society* (OUP 2016) 176–187; Michele Ducos, 'Tours et détours de la parole: les juristes romains' in Christine Hunzinger, Guillemette Mérot and Georgios Vassiliadès (eds), *Tours et détours de la parole dans la littérature antique* (Ausonius 2017) 215–226; Dario Mantovani, *Les juristes écrivains de la Rome antique. Les œuvres des juristes comme littérature* (Les Belles Lettres 2018); Fara Nasti and Aldo Schiavone, *Jurists and Legal Science in the History of Roman Law* (Routledge 2022).

2.2 The Different Layers of Roman Private Law:

Layers of Law: Moriz Wlassak, *Kritische Studien zur Theorie der Rechtsquellen im Zeitalter der klassischen Juristen* (Leuschner & Lubensky 1884), see Alfred Pernice (1885) 6 ZRG rom. 287–299; Alexander Beck, 'Gedanken zum rechtsstaatlichen Aufbau vornehmlich des ausgehenden Prinzipats' in *Mélanges Philippe Meylan* (Imprimerie centrale de Lausanne 1963) 19–42; Max Kaser, *Römische Rechtsgeschichte* (2nd edn, Vandenhoeck & Ruprecht 1967) 128–155; Antonio Guarino, *Storia del diritto romano* (5th edn, Jovene 1975); Ludwig Schnorr von Carolsfeld, 'Methodische Bemerkungen zu allgemeinen Entwicklungstendenzen in der Rechtsgeschichte' in Heinz Hübner, Ernst Klingmüller and Andreas Wacke (eds), *Festschrift Erwin Seidl* (P. Hanstein 1975) 130–142; Theo Mayer-Maly, 'Der Gedanke der Rechtsordnung und das römische Recht' (1982) 99 ZRG rom. 300–302; Theo Mayer-Maly, 'Das Verhältnis zwischen Gesetz und Verordnung in der Rechtsgeschichte' (1955/1956) 41 Archiv des öffentlichen Rechts 157–173; Jean Gaudemet, 'Tentatives de systématisation du droit à Rome' originally in (1986) 31 Archives de philosophie du droit 11–28, now in Jean Gaudemet (ed), *Droit et Société aux derniers siècles de l'Empire romain* (Jovene 1992) 333–350; Theo Mayer-Maly 'Nachdenkliches über *ius*' in Alfred Dufour and others (eds), *Mélanges Bruno Schmidlin* (Helbing Lichtenhahn 1998) 481–500; Gianni Santucci 'Das Gesetz im römischen Recht. Ein Überblick' in *Studi Giovanni Nicosia VII* (Giuffrè 2007) 283–305; Dario Mantovani '*Legum multitudo* e diritto privato. Revisione critica della tesi di Giovanni Rotondi' in Jean-Louis Ferrary (ed), *Leges publicae. La legge nell'esperienza giuridica romana* (IUSS 2012) 707–767; Patrizia Giunti, '*Iudex* e *iurisperitus*. Alcune considerazioni sul diritto giurisprudenziale romano e la sua narrazione' (2013) 61 Iura 47–85; Matthijs Wibier, 'Cicero's Reception in the Juristic Tradition of the Early Empire' in Paul du Plessis (ed), *Cicero's Law: Rethinking Roman Law of the Late Republic* (Edinburgh University Press 2016) 100–122; Dario Mantovani and Ulrike Babusiaux, *Die Bedeutung der Gesetze im römischen Privatrecht* (Duncker & Humblot 2018); Luigi Sandirocco and Andrea Lattocco, *Introduzione alla nostra storia del diritto romano. Mos ius lex* (Carabba 2021); Ulrike Babusiaux, '§ 6 Römische Rechtsschichten' in Ulrike Babusiaux and others (eds), *Handbuch des Römischen Privatrechts* (Mohr Siebeck 2023) 114–193.

ius naturale: Max Salomon, 'Der Begriff des Naturrechts bei den Sophisten' (1911) 32 ZRG rom. 129–167; Jean Gaudemet, 'Quelques remarques sur le droit naturel à Rome' (1952) 1 RIDA 445–467; Otfried Höffe, 'Grundaussagen über den Menschen bei Aristoteles' (1976) 30 Zeitschrift für philosophische Forschung 227–245; Philippe Didier, 'Les diverses conceptions du droit naturel à l'oeuvre dans la jurisprudence romaine des IIe et IIIe siècles' (1981) 47 SDHI 195–262; Wolfgang Waldstein, 'Bemerkungen zum *ius naturale* bei den klassischen Juristen' (1988) 105 ZRG rom. 702–711; Laurens Winkel, 'Deux conceptions du droit naturel dans l'Antiquité' (2015) 93 RHD 341–350; Benedikt Forschner, 'Law's Nature: Philosophy as a Legal Argument in Cicero's Writings' in Paul du Plessis (ed), *Cicero's Law: Rethinking Roman Law of the Late Republic* (EUP 2016) 50–67; Laurens Winkel, 'Remarks on the Uniformity of Natural Law Concepts in the History of Legal Philosophy' (2018) 24 Fundamina 161–173.

ius gentium: Theo Mayer-Maly, 'Das *ius gentium* bei den späteren Klassikern' (1983) 34 Iura 91–102; Max Kaser, *Ius gentium* (Böhlau 1993); Laurens Winkel, 'Einige Bemerkungen über *ius naturale* und *ius gentium*' in Martin J. Schermaier and Zoltán Végh (eds), *Festschrift für Wolfgang Waldstein* (F. Steiner 1993) 443–449; Mario Talamanca, '*Ius gentium* da Adriano ai Severi' in *La codificazione del diritto dall'antico al moderno. Incontri di studio* (Jovene 1998) 191–227; Wolfgang Waldstein, '*Natura debere, ius gentium* und *natura aequum* im klassischen römischen Recht' (2007/2008) 52 AUPA 429–460; Christian Baldus, 'Interkulturalität und ius gentium: Erbrecht in den Juristentexten?' in Christan Baldus (ed), *Espacios particulares, espacios de juristas Estudios dogmáticos de derecho privado romano, 2006–2016* (Pons 2017) 289–319; Dietmar Schanbacher, 'Zum Phänomen der Rechtsrezeption in der Antike' (2020) 137 ZRG rom. 1–38.

ius civile: Max Kaser, '*Mores maiorum* und Gewohnheitsrecht' (1939) 59 ZRG rom. 52–101; Franz Wieacker, 'Solon und die XII Tafeln' in *Studi Edoardo Volterra III* (Giuffrè 1971) 757–784; Max Kaser, '*'Ius honorarium'* und *'ius civile"* (1984) 101 ZRG rom. 1–114; Oliviero Diliberto, *Materiali per la palingenesi delle XII Tavole I* (Edizioni AV 1992); Dieter Flach and Andreas Flach, *Das Zwölftafelgesetz. Leges XII tabularum* (WBG 2004); Michel Humbert (ed), *Le Dodici Tavole. Dai Decemviri agli Umanisti* (IUSS Press 2005); Detlef Liebs, 'Die Zwölf Tafeln im Vergleich mit griechischen und israelitischen Kodifikationen' in Leonhard Burckhardt (ed), *Gesetzgebung in antiken Gesellschaften Israel* (de Gruyter 2007) 87–102; Michel Humbert, Andrew D. E. Lewis and Michael H. Crawford, '*Lex duodecim tabularum*' in Michael H. Crawford (ed), *Roman Statutes II* (Institute of Classical Studies 1996) 555–721; Jean-Louis Ferrary (ed), *Leges publicae. La legge nell'esperienza giuridica romana* (Pavia 2012); Thibaud Lanfranchi, 'Edicts and Decrees during the Republic: A Reappraisal' (2019) 136 ZRG rom. 47–83.

ius praetorium: Otto Lenel, *Edictum perpetuum. Ein Versuch zu seiner Wiederherstellung* (3rd edn, B. Tauchnitz 1927, reprint Scientia 1985); Max Kaser, 'Zum *ius honorarium*' originally in *Estudios jurídicos en homenaje al prof. Ursicino Alvarez Suárez* (Universidad Complutense de Madrid 1978) 231–249, now in Max Kaser (ed), *Römische Rechtsquellen und angewandte Juristenmethode* (Vandenhoeck & Ruprecht 1986) 84–111; Walter Selb, 'Das prätorische Edikt: Vom rechtspolitischen Programm zur Norm' in Hans-Peter Benöhr and others (eds), *Festschrift Max Kaser* (C.H. Beck 1986) 259–272; Dario Mantovani, 'L'édit comme code' in Edmond Lévy (ed), *La codification des lois dans l'Antiquité. Actes du Colloque de Strasbourg 27–29 novembre 1997* (Diffusion de Boccard 2000) 257–272; Kaius Tuori, 'Hadrian's Perpetual Edict: Ancient Sources and Modern Ideals in the Making of a Historical Tradition' (2006) 27 Journal of Legal History 219–237; John Briscoe, 'Notes on the Functions of the Peregrine Praetor in the Republic' (2012) 71 Latomus 996–999; Franciszek Longchamps de Bérier, 'The praetor as a promoter of *bonum commune*' (2014) 3 Legal Roots 217–231; Cristina Rosillo-López, 'The Consilium as Advisory Board of the Magistrates at Rome during the Republic' (2021) 70 Historia 396–436.

Imperial law: Jean Gaudemet, 'L'empereur-l'interprète du droit' in Wolfgang Kunkel and Hans Julius Wolff (eds), *Festschrift Ernst Rabel II* (Mohr Siebeck 1954) 170–203; Wolfgang Kunkel, 'Über das Wesen des augusteischen Prinzipats' (1961) 68 Gymnasium 353–370; Dieter Nörr, 'Zur Reskriptenpraxis in der hohen Prinzipatszeit' originally in (1981) 98 ZRG rom. 1–46, now in *HIA* II 1323–1368; Karl Christ, 'Die Dialektik des Augusteischen Principats' in Karl Christ (ed), *Römische Geschichte und Wissenschaftsgeschichte I* (WBG 1982) 253–263; Dieter Nörr, 'Zu einem fast vergessenen Konstitutionentyp: *Interloqui de plano*' originally in *Studi Cesare Sanfilippo III* (Giuffrè 1983) 519–543, now in *HIA* III 1501–1534; Frédéric Hurlet, 'La *Lex de imperio Vespasiani* et la légitimité augustéenne' (1993) 52 Latomus 261–280; Tony Honoré, *Emperors and Lawyers* (2nd edn, Clarendon Press 1994); Jean-Pierre Coriat, *Le prince législateur. La technique législative des Sévères et les méthodes de création du droit impérial à la fin du Principat* (Ecole française de Rome, 1997); William Turpin, 'Formula, cognitio, and proceedings *extra ordinem*' (1999) 46 RIDA 499–574; Detlef Liebs, 'Reichskummerkasten. Die Arbeit der kaiserlichen Libellkanzlei' in Anne Kolb (ed), *Herrschaftsstrukturen und Herrschaftspraxis* (Akademie Verlag 2006) 137–152; Dario Mantovani, 'La *lex regia de imperio* Vespasiani. Il *vagum imperium* e la legge costante' in Luigi Capogrossi Colognesi and Elena Tassi Scandone (eds), *La Lex de imperio Vespasiani e la Roma dei Flavi* (L'Erma 2009) 125–156; Detlef Liebs, *Hofjuristen der römischen Kaiser bis Justinian* (C.H. Beck 2010); Kaius Tuori, *The Emperor of Law. The Emergence of Roman Imperial Adjudication* (OUP 2016); Fara Nasti, 'I senatus consulta nella Historia Augusta. Provvedimenti senatori e opere giurisprudenziali' in Andrea Balbo, Pierangelo Buongiorno and Ermanno Malaspina (eds), *Rappresentazione e uso dei 'senatus consulta' nelle fonti letterarie del principato* (F. Steiner 2019) 245–275; Francesco Bono, 'The Value of the Stability of the Law: A Perspective on the Role of the Emperor in Political Crises' in Oliver Hekster and Koenraad Verboven (eds), *The Impact of Justice on the Roman Empire, Proceedings of the Thirteenth Workshop of the International Network Impact of Empire* (Brill 2019) 68–85; Luigi Capogrossi-Colognesi, 'Le costituzioni imperiali e la genesi di una nuova idea dell'ordinamento giuridico' in Emmanuelle Chevreau, Carla Masi Doria and Johannes Michael Rainer (eds), *Liber amicorum: mélanges en l'honneur de Jean-Pierre Coriat* (Éditions Panthéon-Assas 2019) 91–102; Matthijs Wibier, 'Legal Education, Realpolitik, and the Propagation of the Emperor's Justice' in Oliver Hekster and Koenraad Verboven (eds), *The Impact of Justice on the Roman Empire, Proceedings of the Thirteenth Workshop of the International Network Impact of Empire* (Brill 2019) 86–102; Philippe Cocatre-Zilgien, 'L'ultime captation des sources du droit par le pouvoir impérial: la constitution *Si imperialis maiestas* de Justinien du 30 octobre 529' in Emmanuelle Chevreau, Carla Masi Doria and Johannes Michael Rainer (eds), *Liber amicorum: mélanges en l'honneur de Jean-Pierre Coriat* (Éditions Panthéon-Assas 2019) 125–155.

3 The Rules of Intestacy

3.1 *The Hierarchical Structure of Family*

Law on Intestacy: Giovanni Finazzi, 'La successione ab intestato' in Maria Floriana Cursi (ed), *XII Tabulae Testo e commento I* (Edizioni Scientifiche Italiane 2018) 231–296; Markus Wimmer, '§ 54 Gesetzliche Erbfolge' in Ulrike Babusiaux and others (eds), *Handbuch des Römischen Privatrechts* (Mohr Siebeck 2023) 1329–1373.

The Structure of the Roman Family: Rudolf Leonhard *'Familia'* (1909) 2 RE VI 1980–1984; Egon Weiss 'Kindesaussetzung' (1921) 1 RE XI 468–471; Leopold Wenger, 'Hausgewalt und Staatsgewalt im römischen Altertum' in *Miscellanea Francesco Ehrle. Scritti di Storia e Paleografia II. Per la Storia di Roma* (Biblioteca apostolica Vaticana 1924) 1–55; Walter Selb, 'Vom *ius vitae necisque* zum beschränkten Züchtigungsrecht und zur magistratischen Züchtigungshilfe' (1966) 1 The Irish Jurist 136–150; Giovanni Lobrano, *Pater et filius eadem persona. Per lo studio della ‚patria potestas' I* (Giuffrè 1984); Theo Mayer-Maly, *'Familia'* in Hans-Georg Knothe and Jürgen Kohler (eds), *Festschrift Andreas Wacke* (C.H. Beck 2001) 261–265; John Crook, *'Patria Potestas'* (1967) 17 The Classical Quarterly 113–122; Friedrich Vittinghoff, 'Soziale Struktur und politisches System der hohen römischen Kaiserzeit' (1980) 230 Historische Zeitschrift 31–55; Richard P. Saller, *'Familia, domus*, and the Roman Conception of the Family' (1984) 38 Phoenix 336–355; Richard P. Saller, *'Patria potestas* and the stereotype of the Roman Family' (1986) 1 Continuity and Change 7–22; William V. Harris, 'The Roman Father's Power of Life and Death' in Roger S. Bagnall and William V. Harris (eds), *Studies Arthur Schiller* (Brill 1986) 81–95; Christoph Paulus, 'Die Verrechtlichung der Familienbeziehungen in der Zeit der ausgehenden Republik und ihr Einfluß auf die Testierfreiheit' (1994) 111 ZRG rom. 425–435; Beryl Rawson (ed), *A Companion to Families in the Greek and Roman World* (Wiley-Blackwell 2011).

Intestate Entitlement of Children-in-Power: Ernst Rabel, 'Nachgeformte Rechtsgeschäfte' (1906) 27 ZRG rom. 290–335 and (1907) 28 ZRG rom. 311–379; Emilio Betti, 'Wesen des altrömischen Familienverbands (Hausgemeinschaft und Agnatengenossenschaft)' (1954) 71 ZRG rom. 1–24; Theo Mayer-Maly, 'Das Notverkaufsrecht des Hausvaters' (1958) 75 ZRG rom. 116–155; Andreas Wacke, 'Erbrechtliche Sukzession als Persönlichkeitsfortsetzung' (2006) 123 ZRG rom. 197–296; Martin Avenarius, *'Continuatio dominii*. Die vorklassische Mitberechtigung der künftigen Hauserben und der Vonselbsterwerb im klassischen Recht' in *Studii Luigi Labruna I* (Scientifica 2007) 231–252; Thomas Rüfner, 'Intestate Succession in Roman Law' in Kenneth Reid, Marius de Waal and Reinhard Zimmermann (eds), *Comparative Succession Law. Vol. II: Intestate Succession* (OUP 2015) 1–32.

Intestate Entitlement of Agnates and Gentiles: Otto Lenel, 'Die Rechtsstellung des *proximus adgnatus* und der *gentiles* im altrömischen Erbrecht' (1916) 37 ZRG rom. 129–135; Mario Talamanca, 'L'acquisto dell'eredità da parte dei *'gentiles'* in XII Tab. 5.5' in Michel Humbert and Yan Thomas (eds), *Mélanges André Magdelain* (Editions Panthéon-Assas 1998) 447–476; Hein L. W. Nelson and Ulrich Manthe, *Gai Institutiones III 1–87. Intestaterbfolge und sonstige Arten der Gesamtnachfolge* (Duncker & Humblot 1992); Alfonso Castro Sáenz, 'Contribución al estudio de la sucesión legítima en el sistema sucesorio romano: Fundamentos sociales y jurídicos' (1995/96) 99 BIDR 760–778.

Intestate Entitlement of Women: Bernhard Kübler, 'Das Intestaterbrecht der Frauen im alten Rom' (1920) 41 ZRG rom. 15–43; Edoardo Volterra, *La conception du mariage d'après les juristes romains* (La Garangola 1940); Jane F. Gardner, *Women in Roman Law and Society* (Croom Helm Ltd 1986); John Antony Crook, 'Women in Roman Succession' in Beryl Rawson (ed), *The Family in Ancient Rome: New Perspectives* (Cornell University Press 1986) 58–82; Ulrich Manthe, 'Das Erbrecht der römischen Frauen nach der *lex Papia Poppaea* und die *ratio Voconiana*' in Paul Nève and Chris Coppens (eds), *Vorträge gehalten auf dem 28. Deutschen Rechtshistorikertag in Nimwegen 1990* (Gerard Noodt Inst. 1992) 33–46; Gabriele Heyse, *Mulier non debet abire nuda. Das Erbrecht und die Versorgung der Witwe in Rom* (Peter Lang 1994); Isabella Piro, *'Usu' in manum convenire* (Edizioni Scientifiche Italiane 1994); Marie-Odile Charles Laforge, 'Patrimoines et héritages à Rome: l'exemple des princesses antonines' in Clément Chillet, Cyril Courrier and Laure Passet (eds), *Arcana Imperii, Mélanges d'histoire économique, sociale et politique offerts au Pr. Yves Roman* (de Boccard 2015) 233–271.

3.2 The Praetorian Rules of Intestacy

3.3 Conflicts between ius civile *and* ius praetroium*:*

Burkhard Wilhelm Leist, *Die bonorum possessio. Ihre geschichtliche Entwicklung und heutige Geltung* (Vandenhoeck & Ruprecht I 1844, II 1848); Rudolf Leonhard, '*Bonorum possessio*' in (1897) 1 RE III 708–712; Paul Moriaud, *De la simple famille paternelle en droit romain* (Librairie Georg 1910); Antonio Guarino, 'Pauli de gradibus et adfinibus et nominibus eorum liber singularis' e la compilazione di D.38.10' (1944) 10 SDHI 267–289; Bernardo Albanese, '*Capitis deminutio*' in *Studi Andrea Arena* (CEDAM 1981) 31–66; Hein L. W. Nelson and Ulrich Manthe, *Gai Institutiones III, 1–87. Intestaterbfolge und sonstige Arten der Gesamtnachfolge* (Duncker & Humblot 1992); Ulrike Babusiaux, 'The *nova clausula Iuliani* – a change of paradigm in the praetorian law of succession?' in Boudewijn Sirks (ed), *Nova Ratione – Change of paradigms in Roman Law* (Harrassowitz 2014) 9–31.

3.4 Imperial Reforms:

Friedrich von Woess, *Das römische Erbrecht und die Erbanwärter. Ein Beitrag zur Kenntnis des römischen Rechtslebens vor und nach der Constitutio Antoniniana* (Vahlen 1911); Marianne Meinhart, 'Die Datierung des *SC Tertullianum*, mit einem Beitrag zur Gaiusforschung' (1966) 83 ZRG rom. 100–141; Marianne Meinhart, *Die Senatusconsulta Tertullianum und Orfitianum in ihrer Bedeutung für das klassische römische Erbrecht* (Böhlaus 1967); Paul Jörs, Wolfgang Kunkel and Leopold Wenger, *Römisches Recht* (4th edn, Springer 1987) 62–65; Thomas

A. J. McGinn, 'The Marriage Legislation of Augustus: A Study in Reception' (2013) 2 Legal Roots 7–43; Ulrike Babusiaux, 'Römisches Erbrecht im *Gnomon des Idios Logos*' (2018) 135 ZRG rom. 108–177; Raymond Saleilles, 'Le Principe de la continuation de la personne du défunt par l'héritier en droit romain' in *Festschrift Otto Gierke* (Böhlau 1911) 1015–1034; Eduard Hölder, 'Die Stellung des römischen Erben' (1895) 16 ZRG rom. 221–229; Bruno Schmidlin, 'Sinn, Funktion und Herkunft der Testamentsregeln: *nemo pro parte testatus, pro parte intestatus decedere potest – hereditas adimi non potest*' (1975) 78 BIDR 71–91; David G. Orr, 'Roman Domestic Religion: The Evidence of the Household Shrines' in Wolfgang Haase (ed), *ANRW II.16* (De Gruyter 1978) 1557–1591; Maurici Perez Simeon, *Nemo pro parte testatus pro parte intestatus decedere potest. El principio de incompatibilidad entre la sucesion testamentaria y la intestada en derecho romano* (Marcial Pons 2001); Martin Avenarius, 'Römisches Erbrecht und Religion: Interdependenzen von Herrschafts-, Vermögens- und Kultperpetuierung in Pontifikaljurisprudenz sowie Dogmatik und Praxis des *ius civile*' in Reinhard Zimmermann (ed), *Der Einfluss religiöser Vorstellungen auf die Entwicklung des Erbrechts* (Mohr Siebeck 2012) 7–78.

4 The Position of the Heir

4.1 *The Acquisition of Inheritance under the* ius civile

Coheirs and Accrual: Ernst Rabel, 'Elterliche Teilung' in *Festschrift zur 49. Versammlung deutscher Philologen und Schulmänner* (E. Birkhäuser 1907) 521–538; Hein L. W. Nelson, 'Zur Terminologie der römischen Erbschaftsteilung: *Ercto non cito, familiae erciscunda*' (1966) 44 Glotta 41–60; Giuseppina Arico Anselmo, '„Societas inseparabilis" o dell'indissolubilità dell'antico consorzio fraterno' in *Studi Mario Talamanca I* (Jovene 2001) 149–191.

Acquisition and Acceptance of the Inheritance: Hugo Krüger, 'Erwerb und Ausschlagung der Erbschaft und der *bonorum possessio* durch das Hauskind, den *pupillus* und den *furiosus*' (1944) 64 ZRG rom. 394–416; Giovanna Coppola, *Studi sulla pro herede gestio. I. La struttura originaria del 'gerere pro herede'* (Giuffrè 1987); Thomas Rüfner, 'Antritt der Erbschaft unter unsicheren Voraussetzungen: D. 29,2,21,3 (Ulp. 7 ad Sab.)' (2010) 127 ZRG rom. 286–295; Martin Avenarius, 'L'adizione dell'eredità e la rilevanza della volontà nella prospettiva di Gaio' (2012) 55 AUPA 9–40; Benedikt Strobel, '§ 56 Anfall, Antritt und Ausschlagung' in Ulrike Babusiaux and others (eds) *Handbuch des Römischen Privatrechts* (Mohr Siebeck 2023) 1418–1437.

Hereditas Iacens and Acquisition of Inheritance through Prescription: Rudolf von Jhering, 'Die Lehre von der *„hereditas iacens"*' in *Abhandlungen aus dem römischen Recht* (Breitkopf & Härtel 1844) 147–262; Hugo Krüger, 'Die *usucapio pro herede* nach klassischem Recht' (1934) 54 ZRG rom. 80–97; Theo

Mayer-Maly, 'Studien zur Frühgeschichte der *usucapio* I' (1960) 77 ZRG rom. 16–51; Ulrich von Lübtow, 'Betrachtungen zur „*hereditas iacens*" in *Studi Giuseppe Grosso II* (Giappichelli 1968) 583–636; Ubaldo Robbe, *La „hereditas iacet" e il significato della „hereditas" in diritto romano I* (Giuffrè 1975); Riccardo Orestano, '*Hereditas nondum adita*' (1982) 33 Iura 1–24; Maxime Lemosse, '*Crimen expilatae hereditatis*' (1998) 76 RHD 255–260; Eric Pool, 'Die Erbschaftsersitzung in Gai. 2, 54 und Theo Mayer-Malys Thesen zum Ursprung der *usucapio*' (2012) 129 ZRG rom. 113–160; Johannes Platschek, 'Nochmals zur Erbschaftsersitzung in Gai. 2,54' (2013) 130 ZRG rom. 405–412.

4.2 The Acquisition of Inheritance under the ius praetorium:

The Liability of Heirs: Victor Korošec, *Die Erbenhaftung nach römischem Recht I* (T. Weicher 1927) 12–25; Heinrich Siber, 'Geschichtliches und Rechtsvergleichendes über die Haftung für Nachlassschulden' in *Acta Academiae Universalis Jurisprudentiae Comparativae I* (Hermann Sack, Marcel Rivière and Sweet & Maxwell 1928) 986–1041; Gunter Wesener, 'Zur Erbenhaftung in historischer Sicht' in Klaus Slapnicar (ed), *Festschrift Ulrich von Lübtow* (Schäuble 1991) 113–128; Gunter Wesener, 'Beschränkungen der Erbenhaftung im römischen Recht: *separatio bonorum* und *beneficium inventarii*' in Martin Josef Schermaier and Zoltán Végh (eds), *Festschrift Wolfgang Waldstein* (F. Steiner 1993) 401–416.

Venditio bonorum; Slaves as heredes necessarii: Antonio Guarino, 'Il *beneficium separationis* dell'*heres necessarius*' (1940) 60 ZRG rom. 185–225; Vincenzo Giuffrè, 'Sull'origine della „*bonorum venditio*" come esecuzione patrimoniale' (1993) 39 Labeo 317–364; Patrizia Giunti, *Ius controversum* e *separatio bonorum* (Edizioni AV 1993); Max Kaser and Karl Hackl, *Römisches Zivilprozeßrecht* (2nd edn, C.H. Beck 1996) 388–407; Thomas Finkenauer, 'Freilassung durch Nachlaßübernahme. Zur *addictio bonorum libertatis causa*' in Thomas Finkenauer (ed), *Symposium Hans Josef Wieling* (Springer 2006) 19–57.

*4.3 The Capacity to Inherit (*testamenti factio*) under the* ius civile *and* ius praetorium:

Fritz Schulz, 'Die Lehre von den drei Momenten' (1914) 35 ZRG rom. 112–128; Walter Scheidel, '*Servi alieni* als Erben: Zum gesellschaftlichen Hintergrund' (1993) 110 ZRG rom. 648–651; Eva Cantarella, 'Identità, genere e sessualità nel mondo antico' in Alessandro Corbino, Michel Humbert and Giovanni Negri (eds), *Homo, caput, persona. La costruzione giuridica dell'identità nell'esperienza romana* (IUSS Press 2010) 79–89; Lucia Monaco, *Hereditas e mulieres. Riflessioni in tema di capacità successoria della donna in Roma antica* (Jovene 2000); Generoso Melillo, 'La condizione femminile a Roma: due norme di Claudio' (2002) 68 SDHI 55–93; Olga Tellegen-Couperus, '*Tutela mulierum*, une institution rationnelle' (2006) 84 RHD 423–435; Francesca Terranova, 'Due brani a confronto in tema di testamenti factio (cum testibus): D. 28.1.20.2 (Ulp. 1 ad Sab.) e I. 2.10.9' (2018) 61 Ann. Sem. Giur. 287–314; Wolfram Buchwitz, '§ 58 Erbenhaftung' in Ulrike Babusiaux and others (eds), *Handbuch des Römischen Privatrechts* (Mohr Siebeck 2023) 1519–1537.

4.4 The Capacity to Obtain and the Worthiness to Inherit under the ius novum:

Albert Levet, 'La quotité disponible et les incapacités de recevoir entre époux d'après les lois caducaires' (1935) 14 RHD 195–238; Erwin Seidl, '*Lex Papia Poppaea*' in VI (1935) RE Suppl. 227–232; Robert Besnier, 'L'application des lois caducaires d'Auguste d'après le Gnomon de l'Idiologue' in Lucien Caes, René Dekkers and Roger Henrion (eds), *Mélanges Fernand de Visscher I* (Office International de Librairie 1949) 93–118; Peter A. Brunt, 'The «*Fiscus*» and Its Development' (1966) 56 Journal of Roman Studies 75–91; Riccardo Astolfi, 'I beni vacanti e la legislazione caducaria' (1965) 68 BIDR 323–336; Tullio Spagnuolo Vigorita, '«*Bona caduca*» e giurisdizione procuratoria agli inizi del terzo secolo d. C.' (1978) 24 Labeo 131–168; Elizabeth Clare Tilson, *Augustus and Law Making* (University of Edinburgh 1986); Riccardo Astolfi, 'Note per una valutazione storica della «lex Iulia et Papia»' (1973) 39 SDHI 187–238; Dieter Nörr, 'Planung in der Antike. Über die Ehegesetze des Augustus' originally in Horst Baier (ed), *Beiträge für Helmut Schelsky* (VS Verlag für Sozialwissenschaften 1977) 309–334, now in *HIA* II 1093–1118; Leo Ferrero Raditsa, 'Augustus' Legislation Concerning Marriage, Procreation, Love Affairs and Adultery' in Wolfgang Haase and Hildegard Temporini (eds), *ANRW II.13* (De Gruyter 1980) 278–339; Andrew Wallace-Hadrill, 'Family and Inheritance in the Roman Marriage Laws' (1981) 27 Proceedings of the Cambridge Philological Society 58–80; Klaus-Peter Müller-Eiselt, *Divus Pius constituit. Kaiserliches Erbrecht* (Duncker & Humblot 1982); Riccardo Astolfi, *La lex Iulia et Papia* (2nd edn, CEDAM 1986); Ulrich Manthe, 'Testierfreiheit und *lex Papia: Papinian* 19 *quaestionum* D. 30.11' in Okko Behrends, Malte Diesselhorst and Wulf E. Voss (eds), *Symposion Franz Wieacker* (Gremer 1991) 113–138; Angelika Mette-Dittmann, *Die Ehegesetze des Augustus. Eine Untersuchung im Rahmen der Gesellschaftspolitik des Princeps* (F. Steiner 1991); Ulrich Manthe, 'Caducum' (1997) 2 DNP 882; Ulrich Manthe, '*Lex Iulia et Papia*' (1999) 7 DNP 121; Martin Avenarius, *Der pseudo-ulpianische liber singularis regularum. Entstehung, Eigenart und Überlieferung einer hochklassischen Juristenschrift* (Wallstein 2005).

5 The Protection of the Position of Heir

5.1 The legis actiones *and* sponsio *Procedures:*

Joseph Georg Wolf, 'Zur *legis actio sacramento in rem*' in Okko Behrends, Malte Diesselhorst and Wulf E. Voss (eds), *Römisches Recht in der europäischen Tradition,*

Symposion Wieacker (Böhlau 1985) 1–39; Max Kaser, 'Zur *legis actio sacramento in rem*' (1987) 104 ZRG rom. 53–84; Karl Hackl, 'Der Sakramentsprozeß über Herrschaftsrechte und die *in iure cessio*' (1989) 106 ZRG rom. 152–179; János Zlinszky, 'Gedanken zur *legis actio sacramento in rem*' (1989) 106 ZRG rom. 106–151; Mario Varvaro, '§ 9 Die Legisaktionen' in Ulrike Babusiaux and others (eds), *Handbuch des Römischen Privatrechts* (Mohr Siebeck 2023) 322–341.

5.2 The hereditatis petitio *of the Formulary Procedure:*

Elena Sànchez Collado, 'La legitimación pasiva del possessor iuris en la acción de petición de herencia en el derecho romano y en el derecho español' in Alfonso Murillo Villar et al. (eds), *Homenaje al profesor Armando Torrent* (Dykinson, S.L. 2016) 1033–1050; Eric Pool, '*Causa* und *titulus*. Die Qualifikation von Besitzlagen und ein terminologischer Wandel in Ulp. D. 5, 3, 13, 1' (2021) 138 ZRG rom. 83–179; Francisco Javier Andrés Santos, '§ 64 Erbschaftsklage (*hereditatis petitio*)' in Ulrike Babusiaux and others (eds), *Handbuch des Römischen Privatrechts* (Mohr Siebeck 2023) 1752–1772.

5.3 The Protection of the bonorum possessor

5.4 Imperial Law: The senatusconsultum Iuventianum*:*

Friedrich Carl von Savigny, 'Ueber das Interdict *quorum bonorum*' (1825) 5 ZRG rom. 1–25 and (1828) 6 ZRG rom. 229–272; Max Kaser, 'Die Passivlegitimation zur *hereditatis petitio*' (1955) 72 ZRG rom. 90–126; Fritz Schwarz, 'Studien zur *hereditatis petitio*' (1956) 24 TR 279–323; Max Kaser, '*Pro herede vel pro possessore*' in *Studi di onore di Arnaldo Biscardi II* (Cisalpino 1982) 221–260; Martina Müller-Ehlen, *Hereditatis petitio. Studien zur Leistung auf fremde Schuld und zur Bereicherungshaftung in der römischen Erbschaftsklage* (Böhlau 1998); Yuri González Roldán, *Il senatoconsulto Q. Iulio Balbo et P. Iuventio Celso consulibus factum nella lettura di Ulpiano* (Cacucci 2008); Dieter Nörr, 'Minima prosopographica zu Celsus *filius*' in Karlheinz Muscheler (ed), *Festschrift Detlef Liebs* (Duncker & Humblot 2011) 489–504.

6 The Testamentary Order of Succession
6.1 The Will under ius civile*:*

Thomas Rüfner, '§ 53 Testamentarische Erbfolge' in Ulrike Babusiaux and others (eds), *Handbuch des Römischen Privatrechts* (Mohr Siebeck 2023) 1311–1328.

Roman Wills in Roman Society: David Daube, 'The Preponderance of Intestacy at Rome' (1965) 39 Tulane Law Review 253–262; John Crook, 'Intestacy in Roman Society' (1973) 19 The Cambridge Classical Journal 38–44; Mireille Corbier, 'Idéologie et pratique de l'héritage (Ie s. av. J.-C. – IIe s. ap. J. C.)' (1985) 13 Index 501–528; Edward Champlin, *Final Judgements. Duty and Emotion in*

Roman Wills, 200 BC–AD 250 (University of California Press 1991); Richard P. Saller, 'Roman Heirship Strategies in Principle and in Practice' in Ian Kertzer and Richard P. Saller (eds), *The Family in Italy from Antiquity to the Present* (Yale University Press 1991) 26–47; Christoph Paulus, *Die Idee der postmortalen Persönlichkeit im römischen Testamentsrecht* (Duncker & Humblot 1992); Yaakov Stern, 'The Testamentary Phenomenon in Ancient Rome' (2000) 49 Historia 413–428; Jacob Stern, *Aspects de la pratique sociale des testaments à Rome. Voluntas du testateur face aux instititutions légales et aux normes sociales et transmission des patrimoines par voie testamentaire à l'époque républicaine et du principat* (Jovene 2022); Elizabeth Anne Meyer, 'Practice, Emperors, and the Mechanics of Testaments' in Werner Eck, Federico Santangelo and Konrad Vössing (eds), *Emperor, Army, and Society. Studies in Roman Imperial History for Anthony R. Birley* (Dr. Rudolf Habelt 2022) 337–347.

Wills Before the *testamentum per aes et libram*: Franz Wieacker, 'Hausgenossenschaft und Erbeinsetzung. Über die Anfänge des römischen Testaments' in *Festschrift Heinrich Siber I* (Weicher 1940) 3–57; Sibylle von Bolla, 'Zur Geschichte der römischen Vermächtnisverfügungen' (1951) 68 ZRG rom. 502–511; Ugo Coli, 'Il testamento nella Legge delle XII Tavole' (1956) 7 Iura 24–91.

***Testamentum per aes et libram*; Institution of Heirs:** Otto Lenel, 'Zur Geschichte der *heredis institutio*' in Paul Vinogradoff (ed), *Essays in Legal History* (OUP 1913) 120–142; Egon Weiß, '*Mandatela* und *custodela*' (1921) 42 ZRG rom. 102–114; Carlo Alberto Maschi, 'La solennità della *"heredis institutio"* nel diritto romano' (1937) 17 Aegyptus 197–232; Ugo Coli, 'Il testamento nella legge delle XII tavole' (1956) 7 Iura 24–91; Mario Amelotti, *Il testamento romano attraverso la prassi documentale, I: Le forme classiche del testamento* (Le Monnier 1966); Maria Nowak, '*Titius heres esto*. The Role of the Legal Practice in the Law-Creation in Late Antiquity' (2010) 40 JJP 161–184; Maria Nowak, '*Mancipatio* and its Life in Late-Roman Law' (2011) 41 JJP 103–122; Francesca Terranova, *Ricerche sul testamentum per aes et libram. I. Il ruolo del familiae emptor* (Giappichelli 2011); Maria Floriana Cursi, 'La *mancipatio familiae*: una forma di testamento?' in Alfonso Murillo Villar and others (eds), *Homenaje al profesor Armando Torrent* (Dykinson, S.L. 2016) 185–195; Maria Floriana Cursi, 'La "mancipatio" e la "mancipatio familiae"' in Maria Floriana Cursi (ed), *XII Tabulae. Testo e commento, I* (Edizioni Scientifiche Italiane 2018) 339–380; Paolo Marra, *Fiduciae causa* (CEDAM 2018).

Cautelary Practice, *testamenti facti* and Rules for Wills: Eduard Höhler, 'Das Wesen der Erbgründe und der Erbfolge nach römischem Recht' (1909) 30 ZRG rom. 65–99; Hugo Krüger, '*Testamenti factio*' (1933) 53 ZRG rom. 505–508; Edoardo Volterra, 'Sulla capacità delle donne a far testamento' (1941) 48 BIDR 74–87; Hans Julius Wolff, 'The *Lex Cornelia de Captivis* and the Roman Law of Succession' (1941) 17 TR 136–183; Pierre Leuregans, '*Testamenti factio non privati sed publici iuris est*' (1975) 53 RHD 225–257; Olga Eveline Tellegen-Couperus, 'Livy and Gaius on the Making of Wills by Women' (1985) 88 BIDR 359–382; Martin Avenarius, 'Formularpraxis römischer Urkundenschreiber und *ordo scripturae* im Spiegel testamentsrechtlicher Dogmatik' in Martin Avenarius, Rudolf Meyer-Pritzl and Cosima Möller (eds), *Festschrift Okko Behrends* (Wallstein 2009) 13–41; Aglaia McClintock, 'The *Lex Voconia* and Cornelia's Jewels' (2013) 60 RIDA 183–200; Maria Nowak, *Wills in the Roman Empire. A Documentary Approach* (The Taubenschlag Foundation 2015); Thomas Rüfner, '§ 52 Erbfähigkeit' in Ulrike Babusiaux and others (eds), *Handbuch des Römischen Privatrechts* (Mohr Siebeck 2023) 1280–1310.

Joint Heirs and Accrual: Reinhard Zimmermann, '*Coniunctio verbis tantum*. Accrual, the methods of joinder in a will and the rule against partial intestacy in Roman-Dutch and Roman Law' (1984) 101 ZRG rom. 234–274; Sebastian Lohsse, *Ius adcrescendi. Die Anwachsung im römischen Vermächtnisrecht* (Böhlau 2008); Susanne Lösch, *Die coniunctio in testamentarischen Verfügungen des klassischen römischen Rechts* (Mohr Siebeck 2014); Patrizia Giunti, 'Il consortium ercto non cito: fraternità e solidarismo nelle pieghe della storia' (2020) 9 Legal Roots 275–299; Riccardo Astolfi, 'Sabino e il consortium ercto non cito' (2021) 69 Iura 490–491.

Substitution of Heirs; Conditional Appointment of Heirs: Pietro Delogu, *Delle condizioni nei testamenti secondo il diritto romano* (Avvenire di Sardegna 1878); Geoffrey MacCormack, 'Impossible Conditions in Wills' (1974) 21 RIDA 263–297; Giovanni Finazzi, '*Heredem esse ed in tutelam suam venire*. Riflessioni sulla struttura della sostituzione pupillare'(1991/1992) 94/95 BIDR 105–156; Giovanni Finazzi, *La sostituzione pupillare* (Jovene 1997).

6.2 The Invalidity and Revocation of the Will under the ius civile*:*

Otto Lenel, 'Das erzwungene Testament' (1889) 10 ZRG rom. 71–82; Giuseppe Gandolfi, '*Prius testamentum ruptum est*' in *Studi Emilio Betti* (Giuffrè 1962) 211–228; Hans Josef Wieling, *Testamentsauslegung im römischen Recht* (C.H. Beck 1972); Sandro Serangeli, *Studi sulla revoca del testamento in diritto romano. Contributi allo studio delle forme testamentarie I* (Giuffrè 1982); Thomas Rüfner, 'Testamentary Formalities in Roman Law' in Kenneth G. C. Reid, Marius J. De Waal and Reinhard Zimmermann (eds), *Testamentary Formalities* (OUP 2011) 1–26.

6.3 The Will under the ius praetorium*:*

The Testamentary Document: Vincenzo Arangio-Ruiz, 'Intorno alla forma scritta del "*testamentum per aes et libram*"' originally in Guiscardo Moschetti (ed), *Atti del Congresso internazionale di diritto romano e di storia del diritto III*

(Giuffrè 1953) 79–90, now in Brunella Biondo (ed), *Scritti di diritto romano IV* (Jovene 1977) 183–194; Gian Gualberto Archi, 'Oralità e scrittura nel *testamentum per aes et libram*' in *Studi Pietro De Francisci IV* (Giuffrè 1956) 287–318; Mario Amelotti, *Il testamento romano attraverso la prassi documentale. I: Le forme classiche di testamento* (Le Monnier 1966); Pasquale Voci, 'Testamento pretorio' in *Studi Giuseppe Grosso I* (Giappichelli 1968) 99–133; Mario Talamanca, 'D.29,7,20 (Paul. 5 ad l. Iui. et Pap.): Oralità e scrittura nel *testamentum per aes et libram*' in Roland Ruedin (ed), *Mélanges Carlo Augusto Cannata* (Helbing and Lichtenhahn 1999) 73–90. Lucia C. Colella, 'Copia Frammentaria di un protocollo di apertura di testamento in lingua latina' (2018) 33 Tyche 55–60 fig. 4; Nunzia Donadio, 'La constituzione delle testimonianza scritta tra precettistica retorica e prassi processuale in eta Flavia' (2019) 66 RIDA 63–95.

Protection of Wills Against Falsification: Luigi De Sarlo, 'Sulla repressione penale del falso documentale in diritto romano' (1937) 14 Rivista di diritto processuale civile 318–353; Gian Gualberto Archi, 'Problemi in tema di falso nel diritto romano' originally in *Studi nelle scienze giuridiche e sociali* (Mattei & c. 1941) 1–114, now in *Scritti di diritto romano III* (Giuffrè 1981) 1487–1587; Jean Macquéron, 'Le Sénatus-Consulte Néronien et le caractère secret du testament' (1957) 34 RHD 459–475; Eberhard E. Kocher, *Überlieferter und ursprünglicher Anwendungsbereich der lex Cornelia de falsis* (Schoen 1965); Fabio Marino, 'Il falso testamentario nel diritto romano' (1988) 105 ZRG rom. 634–663; Silvia Schiavo, *Il falso documentale tra prevenzione e repressione. Impositio fidei criminaliter agere civiliter agere* (Giuffrè 2007); Armin Eich, 'Überlegungen zur juristischen und sozialen Bewertung der Fälschung öffentlicher Urkunden während der späten Republik und der Kaiserzeit' (2008) 166 Zeitschrift für Papyrologie und Epigraphik 227–246; Eva Jakab, 'Senecas Misstrauen in Brief und Siegel' in Rena van den Bergh and others (eds), *Essays Laurens Winkel I* (Fundamina 2014) 416–426; Massimiliano Vinci, *De falsa moneta: Ricerche in tema di falso nummario tra diritto domano e numismatica* (Jovene 2021) 563–568.

***Vicesima hereditatium*:** Keith R. Bradley, 'The *vicesima hereditatis*: Its History and Significance' (1984) 66 Klio 175–182; Sven Günther, 'Die Einführung der römischen Erbschaftssteuer (*vicesima hereditatium*)' (2005) 24 Münstersche Beiträge zur Antiken Handelsgeschichte 1–30; Carmen Lopez-Rendo Rodriguez, 'De la vicesima hereditatium al impuesto sucesorio en el derecho espanol' (2015) 14 Ridrom 188–270.

6.4 The Formless Will of the Imperial Law:

Codicils: Giovanni Negri, *La clausola codicillare nel testamento inofficioso* (Giuffrè 1975); Antonio Metro, *Studi sui codicilli I* (Giuffrè 1979); Antonio Metro, 'Inst. 2.25pr. e l'origine dei codicilli' in Atti dell II Seminario Romanistico

Gardesano: 12–14 Giugno 1978 (Giuffrè 1980) 232–248; Olga Tellegen-Couperus and Jan W. Tellegen, 'Le caractère hybride du fidéicommis romain' in Roger Vigneron and others (eds), *Mélanges Fritz Sturm I* (Juridiques de l'Université de Liège 1999) 453–476; Alessia Spina, *Ricerche sulla successione testamentaria nei responsa di Cervidio Scevola* (Giuffrè 2012); Wolfang Kaiser, 'Zum Text der Epistula in D. 34, 4, 30, 1 (Scaev. 20 dig.)' (2020) 137 ZRG rom. 280–290; Eva Jakab, 'Parakatatheke und letztwillige Verfügungen: Zum Hintergrund von D. 32, 37, 5' (2021) 138 ZRG rom. 338–378.

Soldiers' Wills: Vincenzo Arangio-Ruiz, 'L'origine del „*testamentum militis*" e la sua posizione nel diritto romano classico' (1906) 18 BIDR 157–196; Sibylle von Bolla Kotek, 'Zum römischen Soldatentestament' in *Studi Vincenzo Arangio-Ruiz I* (Jovene 1953) 273–278; Eric Sander, 'Das Recht des römischen Soldaten' (1958) 101 Rheinisches Museum für Philologie 152–191; James Frank Gilliam, 'Enrollment in the Roman Imperial Army' (*Symbolae* Taubenschlag II 1956) 48 Eos 207–216; Laurent Chevallier, 'Notes sur le testament militaire dans la doctrine des juriconsultes classiques dans la législation impériale' in *Varia. Études de droit romain* (Sirey 1959) 1–54; William G. Sinnigen, '*Tirones* and *Supernumerarii*' (1967) 62 Classical Philology 108–112; Vincenzo Scarano Ussani, 'Il „*testamentum militis*" nell'età di Nerva a Traiano' in *Scritti Antonio Guarino III* (Jovene 1984) 1383–1395; Jakob F. Stagl, *Favor dotis. Die Privilegierung der Mitgift im System des römischen Privatrechts* (Böhlau 2009); Jakob F. Stagl, 'Das „*testamentum militare*" in seiner Eigenschaft als „*ius singulare*"' (2014) 36 Revista de estudios histórico-jurìdicos 129–157; Iolanda Ruggiero, 'I privilegi dei militari in tema di successioni dalle costituzioni imperiali alle leges barbarorum' (2019) 113 BIDR 237–257; Adrian C. Linden-High, 'Testamentary Manumission for Slaves of Roman Imperial Soldiers' (2020) 35 Tyche 99–125.

7 Protecting Inheritance Expectations and the Rules of Disinheritance

7.1 The Rules of Disinheritance under ius civile*:*

Children under the paternal power, especially sons-in-power: Karl-Heinz Vogel, 'Über die bedingte Erbeinsetzung von *sui heredes* nach *ius civile*' (1951) 68 ZRG rom. 490–502; Marianne Meinhart, 'Die bedingte Erbeinsetzung des Haussohnes' in Dieter Medicus and Hans Hermann Seiler (eds), *Studien Max Kaser* (Duncker & Humblot 1973) 111–136; Andrea Sanguinetti, 'Considerazioni sull'origine del principio "*sui heredes instituendi sunt vel exheredandi*"' (1993) 59 SDHI 259–278; Yan Thomas, 'L'enfant à naître et "l'héritier sien". Sujet de pouvoir et sujet de vie en droit romain' (2007) 62 Annales 29–68; Reinhard Zimmermann, 'Compulsory Heirship in Roman Law' in Kenneth G. C. Reid, Marius J. de Waal and Reinhard Zimmermann (eds), *Exploring the Law of Succession. Studies National, Historical and Comparative* (Edinburgh University Press 2007) 27–48.

Postumi: Ubaldo Robbe, *I postumi nella successione testamentaria romana* (Giuffrè 1937); Uwe Wesel, *Rhetorische Statuslehre und Gesetzesauslegung der römischen Juristen* (C. Heymann 1967); Francesca Lamberti, *Studi sui postumi nell'esperienza giuridica romana I* (Jovene 1996); Francesca Lamberti, *Studi sui postumi nell'esperienza giuridica romana II. Profili del regime classico* (Giuffrè 2001).

7.2 The Modifications of Praetorian Law:

Ulrike Babusiaux, '§ 57 Nachlassbesitz (*bonorum possesio*)' in Ulrike Babusiaux and others (eds), *Handbuch des Römischen Privatrechts* (Mohr Siebeck 2023) 1437–1518.

Collatio bonorum: Antonio Guarino, *Collatio bonorum, con una nota di lettura di Vincenzo Giuffrè* (Jovene 2014) 330; Federica Bertoldi, *Profili ricostruttivi della collazione ereditaria* (Mucchi 2020).

7.3 The Partial Validity of the Will under the ius praetorium*:*

Burkhard Wilhelm Leist, *Die bonorum possessio: ihre geschichtliche Entwicklung und heutige Geltung II* (Vandenhoeck und Ruprecht 1848); Otto Lenel, *Das 'edictum perpetuum'. Ein Versuch zu seiner Wiederherstellung* (3rd edn, B. Tauchnitz 1927); Jesus Burillo, 'Sobre la *collatio emancipati*' (1965) 31 SDHI 199–221; Letizia Vacca, 'In tema di *bonorum possessio contra tabulas*' (1977) 80 BIDR 159–193; Jane F. Gardner, *Family and Familia in Roman Law and Life* (Clarendon Press 1998) 15–20; Giovanni Finazzi, *L'exceptio doli generalis nel diritto ereditario romano* (CEDAM 2006); Andreas Staffhorst, *Die Teilnichtigkeit von Rechtsgeschäften im klassischen römischen Recht* (Duncker & Humblot 2006); Ulrike Babusiaux, 'The *nova clausula Iuliani* – A Change of Paradigm in the Praetorian Law of Succession?' in Boudewijn Sirks (ed), *Nova Ratione – Change of Paradigms in Roman Law* (Harrassowitz 2014) 9–31.

7.4 The Complaint about Undutiful Will:

Friedrich Eisele, 'Zur *Querela inofficiosi*' (1894) 15 ZRG rom. 256–306; Friedrich von Woess, *Das römische Erbrecht und die Erbanwärter. Ein Beitrag zur Kenntnis des römischen Rechtslebens vor und nach der constitutio Antoniniana* (Franz Vahlen 1911); Matteo Marrone, 'Sulla natura della „*Querela inofficiosi testamenti*"' (1955) 21 SDHI 74–122; Englebert Renier, *Etude sur l'histoire de la querela inofficiosi en droit romain* (Thèse Liège 1945); Serena Querzoli, '„*Inofficiosum testamentum dicere*". Tribunale centumvirale, potere imperiale e giuristi tra i Flavi e gli Antonini' (1999) 8 Ostraka 503–540; Serena Querzoli, *I testamenti e gli officia pietatis. Tribunale centumvirale, potere imperiale e giuristi tra Augusto e i Severi* (Loffredo 2000); Daniela Di Ottavio, *Ricerche in tema di querela inofficiosi testamenti I* (Jovene 2012); Lorenzo Gagliardi, *Studi sulla legittimazione alla querela inofficiosi testamenti in diritto romano e bizantino* (Giuffrè 2017); Maurici Perez

Simeon, 'La facultas agendi en la *querela inofficiosi testamenti* clásica' (2017) 65 Iura 239–276; Elena Köstner, 'Eine unheilvolle Allianz. Zur Kumulation von Testament und Falschmeldung bei Cicero und Valerius Maximus' (2021) 128 Gymnasium 332–354; Markus Wimmer, '§ 55 Testamentsanfechtung (*querela inofficiosi testamenti*)' in Ulrike Babusiaux and others (eds), *Handbuch des Römischen Privatrechts* (Mohr Siebeck 2023) 1373–1417.

8 The Law of Legacies

8.1 Legacies under the ius civile*:*

Different Types of Legacies: Karl Bernstein, 'Zur Lehre vom römischen Voraus' (1894) 15 ZRG rom. 26–144; Moriz Wlassak, 'Vindikation und Vindikationslegat. Studien zur Erforschung des Sachenrechts der Römer' (1910) 31 ZRG rom. 196–321; Silvio Romano, *Sull'acquisto del legato 'per vindicationem'* (CEDAM 1933); Pasquale Voci, *Teoria dell'acquisto del legato secondo il diritto romano* (Giuffrè 1936); Giuseppe Grosso, *I legati nel diritto romano. Parte generale* (2nd edn, Giappichelli 1962); Jean-François Leuba, *Origine et nature du legs per praeceptionem* (Impr. Vaudoise 1962); Riccardo Astolfi, *Studi sull'oggetto dei legati in diritto romano I* (CEDAM 1964); Riccardo Astolfi, *Studi sull'oggetto dei legati in diritto romano II* (CEDAM 1969); Nicola Palazzolo, *Dos praelegata. Contributo alla storia del prelegato romano* (Giuffrè 1968); Maria Grazia Scacchetti, 'Note sulle differenze di metodo fra Sabiniani e Proculiani' in *Studi Arnaldo Biscardi* (Cisalpino 1984) 369–404; Olivia F. Robinson, *Ancient Rome. City Planning and Administration* (Routledge 1992); Riccardo Astolfi, *Studi sull'oggetto dei legati in diritto romano I-III* (CEDAM 1964/1969/1979); Markus Wimmer, *Das Prälegat* (Böhlau 2004); Pierfranco Arces, 'La disciplina dei legati e la tecnica di scrittura nelle Istituzioni di Gaio' (2013) 8 Rivista di Diritto Romano 1–19; Lisa Isola, 'Überlegungen zur Litiskreszenz bei der *actio ex testamento*' (2020) 137 ZRG rom. 70–135; Markus Wimmer, '§ 60 Dinglich wirkendes Vermächtnis (*legtatm per vindicationem*)' in Ulrike Babusiaux and others (eds), *Handbuch des Römischen Privatrechts* (Mohr Siebeck 2023) 1632–1675; Sebastian Lohsse, '§ 97 Klage aus Testament (*actio ex testamento*)' in Ulrike Babusiaux and others (eds), *Handbuch des Römischen Privatrechts* (Mohr Siebeck 2023) 2661–2690.

Ancillary Provisions to a Legacy: Hugo Krüger, 'Cautio Muciana' in *Mélanges Paul Frédéric Girard II* (Rousseau 1912) 1–34; Ernst Levy, 'Zur Lehre von der *Muciana cautio* im klassischen römischen Recht' (1903) 24 ZRG rom. 122–151; Settimio Di Salvo, *Il legato modale in diritto romano. Elaborazioni dommatiche e realtà sociali* (Jovene 1973); Daniel Effe-Uhe, 'Wirkung der *condicio* im römischen Recht' (Nomos 2008) 72–161; Giovanni Cossa, *Regula Sabiniana. Elaborazione giurisprudenziali in materia di condizioni impossibili* (Giuffrè 2013).

8.2 The Invalidity and Limitations of the Legacy under the ius civile*:*

Werner Flume, 'Die *regula Catoniana* – ein Exempel römischer Jurisprudenz' in Erik Jayme and others (eds), *Festschrift Hubert Niederländer zum siebzigsten Geburtstag am 19. Februar 1991* (Böhlau 1991) 17–26.

Limitations of the Legacy: Fritz Schwarz, 'War die "*Lex Falcidia*" eine "*Lex perfecta*"?' (1951) 17 SDHI 225–247; Uwe Wesel, 'Über den Zusammenhang der *lex Furia, Voconia* und *Falcidia*' (1964) 81 ZRG rom. 308–316; Andreas Wacke, 'Die Rechtswirkungen der *lex Falcidia*' in Dieter Medicus and Hans Hermann Seiler (eds), *Studien Max Kaser* (Duncker & Humblot 1973) 209–251; Max Kaser, *Über Verbotsgesetze und verbotswidrige Geschäfte im römischen Recht* (Österreichische Akademie der Wissenschaften 1977); Walter Selb, 'Gedanken zur römischen "*lex imperfecta*" und zu modernen Normvorstellungen in der Rechtsgeschichte' in Gottfried Baumgärtner and others (eds), *Festschrift Heinz Hübner* (De Gruyter 1984) 253–261; Ernst Baltrusch, *Regimen morum: die Reglementierung des Privatlebens der Senatoren und Ritter in der römischen Republik und frühen Kaiserzeit* (C.H. Beck 1989); Vincenzo Mannino, *Il calcolo della "quarta hereditatis" e la volontà del testatore* (Jovene 1989); Dietmar Schanbacher, *Ratio legis Falcidiae. Die falzidische Rechnung bei Zusammentreffen mehrerer Erbschaften in einer Hand* (BRILL 1995); Peter Stein, '*Lex Falcidia*' in Michael Crawford (ed), *Roman Statutes II* (Institute of Classical Studies/University of London 1996) 779 f.; Maria Eugenia Ortuno Perez, 'A New Perspective on the Limitation of Legacies (lex Falcidia de legatis)' (2014) 80 SDHI 411–418; Dietmar Schanbacher, '§ 100 Beschränkung der Testierfähigkeit (*lex Falcidia und SC Pegasianum*)' in Ulrike Babusiaux and others (eds), *Handbuch des Römischen Privatrechts* (Mohr Siebeck 2023) 2724–2784.

8.3 Praetorian Protection in the Law of Legacies:

Philipp Lotmar, 'Zur Geschichte des *Interdictum quod legatorum*' (1910) 31 ZRG rom. 89–158; Otto Lenel, 'Das *interdictum Quod legatorum utile*' (1932) 52 ZRG rom. 282–284; Max Kaser, '*Ius publicum* und *ius privatum*' (1986) 103 ZRG rom. 1–101; Thomas Finkenauer, *Vererblichkeit und Drittwirkungen der Stipulation im klassischen römischen Recht* (Böhlau 2010).

8.4 Imperial Interventions in the law of legacies of the ius civile*:*

Robert Piaget, *Le sénatus-consulte néronien* (Impr. La Concorde 1936); on the *lex Iulia et Papia* see 4.4. The Capacity to Obtain and the Worthiness to Inherit under the *ius novum*.

8.5 Formless Bequests under the ius novum *(*fideicommissa*):*

Giambattista Impallomeni, 'L'efficacia del fedecommesso pecuniario nei confronti dei terzi. La *in rem missio*' (1967) 70 BIDR 1–104; Maria Gabriella Zoz, 'Sulla capacità a ricevere fedecommessi alimentari' (1974) 40 SDHI 303–328; Armando Torrent, *Fideicommissum familiae relictum* (Servicio de Publicaciones, Universidad de Oviedo 1975); David Johnston, 'Prohibitions and Perpetuities: Family Settlements in Roman Law' (1985) 102 ZRG rom. 220–290; David Johnston, *The Roman Law of Trusts* (Clarendon 1988); Alfonso Murillo Villar, *El fideicomiso de residuo en derecho romano* (Secretariado de Publicaciones, Universidad de Valladolid 1989); Venanzia Giodice-Sabbatelli, *La tutela giuridica dei fedecommessi fra Augusto e Vespasiano* (Cacucci 1993); Richard P. Saller, *Patriarchy, Property and Death in the Roman Familiy* (CUP 1994); Franciszek Longchamps de Bérier, *Il fedecommesso universale nel diritto romano classico* (LIBER 1997); Franciszek Longchamps de Bérier, 'Il rispetto per la volontà del *de cuius* sull'esempio dei fedecommessi romani' (1998) 45 RIDA 479–500; Lucetta Desanti, *Restitutionis post mortem onus. I fedecommessi da restituirsi dopo la morte dell'onerato* (Giuffrè 2003); Lucetta Desanti, 'Il fantasma del fedecommesso – Fedecommesso, fiducia testamentaria, sostituzione fedecommissaria' (2006) 20 Annali dell'Università Ferrara. Sc. Giur. N. S. 97–141; Thomas Rüfner, '§ 98 Fideikommisse und ihre Durchsetzung' in Ulrike Babusiaux and others (eds), *Handbuch des Römischen Privatrechts* (Mohr Siebeck 2023) 2690–2712.

8.6 The Further Configuration of the Law on fideicommissa*:*

Milan Bartošek, 'Das *Senatusconsultum Trebellianum*' in *Scritti Ferrini III* (Nakladem České Akademie Věd a Umění 1948) 308–336; David Daube, 'Sale of Inheritance and Merger of Rights', originally in (1957) 74 ZRG rom. 234–315, now in David Cohen and Dieter Simon (eds), *Collected Studies in Roman Law* (V. Klostermann 1991) 649–722; Klaus Peter Müller-Eiselt, *Divus Pius constituit. Kaiserliches Erbrecht* (Duncker & Humblot 1982); Francesco Arcaria, '"*Missio in possessionem*" e "*cognitio*" fedecommissaria' (1986) 89 BIDR 245–304; Ana Bustelo, 'Fideicomiso sub condicione y adicin ex Pegasiano' (1988) 35 RIDA 113–130; Ulrich Manthe, *Das Senatusconsultum Pegasianum* (Duncker & Humblot 1989); Federica Bertoldi, 'L'esecutore testamentario nel diritto romano' (2018) 65 RIDA 53–75; Veronika Kleňová, 'Scaevola D. 32,37,3: Fideicommissum a debitore oder a donatario relictum?' (2019) 136 ZRG rom. 345–357; Ulrike Babusiaux, 'Zum Rechtsschutz von Fideikommissen im Prinzipat' (2019) 136 ZRG rom. 140–213; Andreas Wacke, '*Quae vivus/viva praestabam*. Unterhaltsfortzahlungsvermächtnisse nach Maßgabe lebzeitiger Zuwendungen' (2021) 69 Iura 391–443.

9 The Interpretation of Wills
9.1 Interpretative Maxims of ius civile*:*

The Interpretation of Wills: Fritz Schulz, 'Der Irrtum im Beweggrund bei der testamentarischen Verfügung' in Erich Genzmer and others (eds),

Gedächtnisschrift Emil Seckel (Springer 1927) 70–144; Gerhard Dulckeit, 'Plus nuncupatum minus scriptum. Ein Beitrag zur Entwicklung des römischen Testamentsrechts' (1953) 70 ZRG rom. 179–213; Giuseppe Gandolfi, *Studi sull'interpretazione degli atti negoziali in diritto romano* (Giuffrè 1966); Hans Josef Wieling, *Testamentsauslegung im römischen Recht* (C.H. Beck 1972); Jan Dirk Harke, '*Verba* und *voluntas* – was bedeutet Testamentsauslegung für die Hochklassiker' in Jan Dirk Harke (ed), *Facetten des römischen Erbrechts* (Springer 2012) 55–77.

Interpretation of Legacies: Uwe John, *Die Auslegung des Legats von Sachgesamtheiten im römischen Recht bis Labeo* (C.F. Müller 1970); Hans Josef Wieling, 'Falsa demonstratio, condicio pro non scripta, condicio pro impleta im römischen Testament' (1970) 87 ZRG rom. 197–245; Olga Vannucchi Forzieri, *Studi sull'interpretazione giurisprudenziale romana* (Giuffrè 1973); Herbert Hausmaninger, 'Zur Legatsinterpretation des Celsus' (1984) 35 Iura 16–46; Elisabeth Herrmann-Otto, *Ex ancilla natus. Untersuchungen zu den 'hausgeborenen' Sklaven und Sklavinnen im Westen des römischen Kaiserreiches* (F. Steiner 1994); Natale Rampazzo, 'La *falsa demonstratio* e l'oggetto dei legati' (2001) 29 Index 259–299; Jan-Luca Beck, '*Fundus cum nimio instrumento*: unwirtschaftliche Destinationsakte in der Vermächtnisauslegung – Exegetische Betrachtungen zu D. 33.7.25pr' (2021) 1 Interpretatio Prudentium VI 127–165.

Causa Curiana: Johannes Stroux, '*Summum ius, summum iniuria*' in *Römische Rechtswissenschaft und Rhetorik* (Stichnote 1949) 1–66; Franz Wieacker, 'The *Causa Curiana* and Contemporary Roman Jurisprudence' (1967) 2 The Irish Jurist 151–164; Wilfried Stroh, *Taxis und Taktik: Die advokatische Dispositionskunst in Ciceros Gerichtsreden* (B.G. Teubner 1975) 85–87; Gian Luigi Falchi, 'Interpretazione „tipica" nella „causa Curiana"' (1980) 46 SDHI 388–430; Jan Willem Tellegen, '*Oratores, Iurisprudentes* and the „*Causa Curiana*"' (1983) 30 RIDA 293–311; John W. Vaughn, 'Law and Rhetoric in the *Causa Curiana*' (1985) 4 Classical Antiquity 208–222; Ulrich Manthe, 'Ein Sieg der Rhetorik über die Jurisprudenz. Der Erbschaftsstreit des Manius Curius. Eine vertane Chance der Rechtspolitik' in Ulrich Manthe and Jürgen von Ungern-Sternberg (ed), *Große Prozesse der römischen Antike* (C.H. Beck 1997) 74–84; Jan Willem Tellegen, 'The Reliability of Quintilian for Roman Law: The *causa Curiana*' in Olga Tellegen-Couperus (ed), *Quintilian and the Law* (Leuven University Press 2003) 191–200; Agnieszka Kacprzak, *Tra logica e giurisprudenza. Argumentum a simili nei topici di Cicerone* (University of Warsaw 2012); Barbara Cortese, 'Tra "aequitas" e "ius" nella causa Curiana' (2019) 67 Iura 49–77.

9.2 The Minor Importance of Interpretative Issues under the ius praetorium

9.3 Interpretation of Wills under the ius novum:

Jean Gaudemet, 'L'empereur – l'interprète du droit' in Wolfgang Kunkel and Hans Julius Wolff (ed), *Festschrift Ernst Rabel II* (Mohr Siebeck 1954) 170–203; Hans Josef Wieling, *Testamentsauslegung im römischen Recht* (C.H. Beck 1972); Antonio Palma, *Humanior interpretatio.,Humanitas' nell'interpretazione e nella normazione da Adriano ai Severi* (Giappichelli 1992); Antonio Palma, *Benignior interpretatio: benignitas nella giurisprudenza e nella normazione da Adriano ai Severi* (Giappichelli 1997); Andreas Staffhorst, *Die Teilnichtigkeit von Rechtsgeschäften im klassischen römischen Recht* (Duncker & Humblot 2006); Veronika Wankerl, *Appello ad principem. Urteilsstil und Urteilstechnik in kaiserlichen Berufungsentscheidungen (Augustus bis Caracalla)* (C.H. Beck 2009); Martin Avenarius, '*Benignior interpretatio*: Origin and Transformation of a Rule of Construction in the Law of Succession' (2010) 6 Roman Legal Tradition 1–21; Tobias Kleiter, *Entscheidungskorrekturen mit unbestimmter Wertung durch die klassische römische Jurisprudenz* (C.H. Beck 2010); Ulrike Babusiaux, *Papinians Quaestiones. Zur rhetorischen Methode eines spätklassischen Juristen* (C.H. Beck 2011); Mariagrazia Rizzi, *Imperator cognoscens decrevit. Profili e contenuti dell'attività giudiziaria imperiale in età classica* (Giuffrè 2012); Alessia Spina, *Ricerche sulla successione testamentaria nei responsa di Cervidio Scevola* (Giuffrè 2012); Arndt Christoph Hendel, 'D. 28,4,3 Marcellus *libro* 29 *digestorum*. Zum Sicherheitsgedanken bei der *benignior interpretatio*' (2013) 130 ZRG rom. 419–431; Jakob F. Stagl, 'Glanz der Rhetorik und Elend der Logik in einer Entscheidung Marc Aurels (Marcell. D. 28,4,3pr.–1)' in Rena van den Bergh and others (eds), *Essays Laurens Winkel II* (Unisa Press 2014) 871–880; Alessia Spina, *Ricerche sulla successione testamentaria nei responsa di Cervidio Scevola* (Giuffrè 2012); Aitor Blanco-Perez, 'Appealing for the Emperor's Justice: Provincial Petitions and Imperial Responses Prior to Late Antiquity' in Katell Berthelot, Natalie Dohrmann and Capucine Nemo-Pekelman (eds), *Legal Engagement. The Reception of Roman Law and Tribunals by Jews and other Inhabitants of the Empire* (École française de Rome 2021) 159–174.

Index of Sources

Literary sources
Cic.Brut.196., 251, 252
Cic.Brut.197., 252
Cic.inv.2.122., 251
Liv.3.34.6., 15

Legal sources before Justinian
Law of the twelve tables (lex duodecim tabularum)
V.3., 109, 110, 194, 274
V.4., 28, 31, 36
V.9-10., 63

Gaius, Institutiones
Inst.Gai.1.1., 22
Inst.Gai.1.4., 24
Inst.Gai.1.55., 31
Inst.Gai.1.115., 116
Inst.Gai.1.115a., 116
Inst.Gai.1.119., 35
Inst.Gai.1.132., 35
Inst.Gai.1.155., 115
Inst.Gai.1.157., 81
Inst.Gai.1.176., 80
Inst.Gai.1.185., 81
Inst.Gai.1.189., 79–80
Inst.Gai.1.194., 82
Inst.Gai.2.52., 69
Inst.Gai.2.53., 69–70
Inst.Gai.2.55., 70–1
Inst.Gai.2.57., 71
Inst.Gai.2.87., 30
Inst.Gai.2.101., 110
Inst.Gai.2.103., 112
Inst.Gai.2.104., 112–13
Inst.Gai.2.111., 85

Inst.Gai.2.112., 117
Inst.Gai.2.116., 117–18
Inst.Gai.2.117., 118
Inst.Gai.2.119., 134–5
Inst.Gai.2.120., 135
Inst.Gai.2.121., 136
Inst.Gai.2.121–122., 136–7
Inst.Gai.2.123., 159, 159–60
Inst.Gai.2.124., 164–5
Inst.Gai.2.125., 172
Inst.Gai.2.126., 172
Inst.Gai.2.127., 159
Inst.Gai.2.128., 164
Inst.Gai.2.130., 165
Inst.Gai.2.131., 165–6
Inst.Gai.2.133., 167
Inst.Gai.2.135., 171
Inst.Gai.2.144., 129–30
Inst.Gai.2.145., 125
Inst.Gai.2.147., 132
Inst.Gai.2.151., 130
Inst.Gai.2.151a., 137–8
Inst.Gai2.153., 78
Inst.Gai.2.154., 78
Inst.Gai.2.155., 79
Inst.Gai.2.157., 67
Inst.Gai.2.158., 72
Inst.Gai.2.162., 67
Inst.Gai.2.163., 72
Inst.Gai.2.165., 68
Inst.Gai.2.167., 68, 72
Inst.Gai.2.174., 122
Inst.Gai.2.179., 122–3
Inst.Gai.2.180., 123
Inst.Gai.2.181., 124–5
Inst.Gai.2.186., 77

Inst.Gai.2.192., 195
Inst.Gai.2.193., 195–6
Inst.Gai.2.194., 195
Inst.Gai.2.196., 196
Inst.Gai.2.197., 220
Inst.Gai.2.201., 196
Inst.Gai.2.202., 197
Inst.Gai.2.206., 86
Inst.Gai.2.209., 198
Inst.Gai.2.210., 198
Inst.Gai.2.216., 199
Inst.Gai.2.217., 199–200
Inst.Gai.2.218., 220
Inst.Gai.2.221., 200
Inst.Gai.2.224., 211
Inst.Gai.2.225., 211
Inst.Gai.2.226., 212
Inst.Gai.2.229., 203
Inst.Gai.2.235., 208
Inst.Gai.2.238., 208–9
Inst.Gai.2.249., 224
Inst.Gai.2.250., 229–30
Inst.Gai.2.251., 234
Inst.Gai.2.252., 234–5
Inst.Gai.2.254., 238, 240–1
Inst.Gai.2.255–256., 238–9
Inst.Gai.2.257., 239–40
Inst.Gai.2.258., 241
Inst.Gai.2.270., 226
Inst.Gai.2.277., 228
Inst.Gai.2.281., 224
Inst.Gai.2.285., 225, 243
Inst.Gai.2.286–286a., 225
Inst.Gai.2.286a., 242–3
Inst.Gai.2.287., 225, 243
Inst.Gai.2.288., 226
Inst.Gai.3.2., 32
Inst.Gai.3.3., 38
Inst.Gai.3.7., 33
Inst.Gai.3.10., 36
Inst.Gai.3.11., 37
Inst.Gai.3.12., 37
Inst.Gai.3.14., 39
Inst.Gai.3.16., 37
Inst.Gai.3.17., 39–40
Inst.Gai.3.26., 41
Inst.Gai.3.27., 44
Inst.Gai.3.29., 44

Inst.Gai.3.30., 44
Inst.Gai.3.36., 47
Inst.Gai.3.37., 48
Inst.Gai.3.78., 75
Inst.Gai.3.154a., 62
Inst.Gai.3.154b., 62
Inst.Gai.4.16., 95–6
Inst.Gai.4.34., 74
Inst.Gai.4.92., 97
Inst.Gai.4.93., 96–7
Inst.Gai.4.112., 60–1

Epitome Ulpiani
UE 15.1., 89
UE 16.1., 89–90
UE 16.1a., 90
UE 16.2., 89

Corpus iuris civilis
Institutiones
Inst.2.23.1., 222–3
Inst.2.25pr., 142–3
Inst.3.3.2., 50–1
Inst.3.3.3., 51
Inst.3.4pr., 55

Digesta
D.1.1.1.3., 21
D.1.1.7pr., 25
D.1.1.7.1., 23
D.1.1.11., 21–2
D.1.3.14., 155
D.1.3.15., 155
D.1.3.16., 155
D.1.4.1pr., 1, 24
D.5.2.2., 186
D.5.2.3., 185–6
D.5.2.6.1., 186–7
D.5.2.8.14., 190–1
D.5.2.8.16., 187
D.5.2.15.2., 188
D.5.2.17.1., 186
D.5.2.23pr., 189
D.5.2.24., 188
D.5.2.28., 190
D.5.2.29.4., 187
D.5.3.9., 98
D.5.3.11pr., 100

INDEX OF SOURCES

D.5.3.13.13., 99
D.5.3.20.6–6d., 101–3
D.5.3.20.9., 106
D.5.3.20.11., 103–4
D.5.3.20.17., 104
D.5.3.20.21., 104–5
D.5.3.23pr., 105
D.5.5.1., 101
D.22.1.3.3., 231
D.28.1.4., 114
D.28.1.6pr., 114
D.28.1.12., 126
D.28.1.20pr., 117
D.28.1.21pr., 119
D.28.1.21.1., 129
D.28.1.23., 140
D.28.2.2., 253
D.28.2.3.6., 160
D.28.2.11., 31–2
D.28.2.29pr., 166
D.28.2.29.12., 167–8
D.28.2.29.13., 168
D.28.3.13., 169
D.28.4.3., 267, 268–9
D.28.5.1pr., 6
D.28.5.1.1., 248
D.28.5.1.4., 128
D.28.5.1.5., 249
D.28.5.4pr., 162
D.28.5.4.1., 162
D.28.5.9.2., 250
D.28.5.9.13., 128
D.28.5.13.1., 120
D.28.5.13.2., 121
D.28.5.13.4., 120–1
D.28.5.31pr., 84
D.28.5.34., 118
D.28.5.67., 66
D.28.5.79pr., 128
D.28.5.93.1., 270
D.28.6.2.1., 123
D.28.6.2.4., 124
D.28.7.1., 119, 163
D.28.7.6., 119
D.28.7.11., 161
D.29.1.1pr., 148
D.29.1.2., 154
D.29.1.6., 150

D.29.1.15.1., 149
D.29.1.15.2., 153
D.29.1.15.4., 151
D.29.1.20.1., 152
D.29.1.26pr., 153
D.29.1.34pr., 154
D.29.1.38.1., 263–4
D.29.1.40pr., 149
D.29.1.42., 152
D.29.2.6pr., 83
D.29.2.6.1., 83
D.29.2.53.1., 64
D.29.3.4., 139
D.29.7.1., 146–7
D.29.7.2.2., 154
D.29.7.3pr., 145
D.29.7.3.2., 144–5
D.29.7.8pr., 144
D.29.7.8.1., 227
D.29.7.10., 145–6
D.29.7.13.1., 146
D.29.7.20., 249
D.30.36pr., 255
D.30.41.1–2., 210
D.30.78., 226
D.30.103., 245
D.30.114.2., 228
D.30.114.14., 233
D.30.114.15., 232
D.30.116pr., 194
D.31.32.6., 233–4
D.31.47., 254
D.31.67.9., 260
D.31.67.10., 261
D.31.81., 227
D.32.1.1., 224
D.32.2., 227
D.32.19., 201
D.34.3.16., 198–9
D.34.5.24., 262
D.34.7.1pr., 209
D.34.7.1.1., 209
D.34.8.1., 141
D.34.9.3., 91
D.34.9.12., 92
D.35.1.1.1–3., 202
D.35.1.7pr., 206
D.35.1.17pr., 256–7

D.35.1.17.1., 257
D.35.1.17.2., 257–8
D.35.1.24., 205
D.35.1.62.2., 222
D.35.1.83., 163
D.35.1.102., 264
D.35.1.112.2., 253–4
D.35.2.1pr., 212–13
D.35.2.59.1., 245–6
D.35.2.73.5., 213, 214
D.36.1.1.1–2., 235–6
D.36.1.1.3., 237
D.36.1.1.5., 237
D.36.1.30., 266
D.36.1.63., 230
D.36.1.78., 262–3
D.36.1.80.5., 231
D.36.2.5pr., 204
D.36.2.5.1–2., 204
D.36.2.5.4., 204
D.36.2.5.5., 205
D.36.3.1pr., 216
D.36.3.1.2., 217–18
D.36.3.1.14., 217
D.36.4.1.4., 216–17
D.36.4.5pr., 218
D.36.4.10., 218
D.37.1.6.1., 46
D.37.4.1pr., 173
D.37.4.1.1., 178
D.37.4.3.11., 173–4
D.37.4.8pr., 174
D.37.4.20.2., 183
D.37.5.1pr., 181
D.37.5.1.1., 182
D.37.5.5.6., 183–4
D.37.5.15pr., 182
D.37.6.1pr., 175
D.37.6.3.2., 176
D.37.8.1pr., 179
D.37.8.1.1., 180

D.37.11.1.8., 131–2
D.37.11.1.10., 138
D.37.11.2.1., 170
D.37.11.2.4., 133
D.38.6.1.1., 40
D.38.6.5pr., 49
D.38.6.5.2., 41
D.38.7.2.4., 42
D.38.8.1pr., 45
D.38.9.1pr., 73
D.38.10.4.2., 43
D.38.11.1pr-1., 45–6
D.38.17.1.9., 55
D.38.17.2.20., 53
D.38.17.2.21., 54
D.38.17.6.1., 56
D.42.5.31pr., 76
D.42.5.31.3, 76
D.42.6.1.1., 77
D.43.2.1pr-1., 99–100
D.43.3.1.1–2., 215
D.48.19.38.7., 140
D.48.20.7.4., 90–1
D.49.15.5.1., 126
D.49.15.22pr., 127
D.50.16.64., 28
D.50.16.120., 109
D.50.16.138., 86
D.50.16.142., 65
D.50.16.195.1., 28–9
D.50.16.195.2., 29, 31
D.50.16.195.5., 38
D.50.17.7., 61
D.50.17.62., 60

Codex
C.2.3.26., 63
C.3.36.6., 63
C.6.51.1.1b., 87–8
C.9.23.3., 141

Index of Places and Persons

Africa, 143
Africanus (Sextus Caecilius Africanus – jurist), 221
Alexander Severus (Marcus Aurelius Severus Alexander – Emperor), 19
Alexandria, 3, 162
Antoninus Caracalla *see* Caracalla
Antoninus Pius (Titus Aelius Hadrianus Antoninus Augustus Pius – Emperor), 19, 91, 135, 138, 153, 172, 173, 184
Antonius Silvanus, 1–3, 6
Aquilius (Gaius Aquilius Gallus – jurist), 166
Aristo, 206
Arrian (Arrianus – jurist), 100
Atilicinus (jurist), 198, 199, 201, 202
Augustus (Gaius Julius Caesar Octavianus – Emperor), 13, 16, 17, 19, 20, 26, 87, 93, 94, 95, 139, 142, 143, 156, 222, 223, 228, 246

Caesar (Gaius Iulius Caesar), 148
Caracalla (Marcus Aurelius Severus Antoninus – Emperor), 19, 87, 232, 233, 266, 270, 271
Carthage, 15
Cassius (Gaius Cassius Longinus – jurist), 19, 160
Cato Licinianus (Marcus Porcius Cato), 209
Cato the Elder (Marcus Porcius Cato), 209
Celsus (Publius Iuventus Celsus – jurist), 19, 99, 101, 102, 128, 209, 250
Cicero (Marcus Tullius Cicero), 251, 252
Claudius (Tiberius Claudius Caesar Augustus Germanicus – Emperor), 140
Constantine I (Flavius Valerius Constantinus – Emperor), 13, 20

Diocletian (Marcus Aurelius Gaius Valerius Diocletianus – Emperor), 4, 16, 19, 20
Domitian (Titus Flavius Domitianus – Emperor), 148

Egypt, 3
Elagabalus (Marcus Aurelius Antoninus – Emperor), 19

Gaius (jurist), 7, 8, 19, 24, 35, 38, 62, 71, 110, 112, 114, 118, 123, 125, 135, 136, 137, 173, 196, 198, 208, 212, 221, 224, 226, 257

Hadrian (Publius Aelius Hadrianus – Emperor), 4, 17–19, 23, 49, 50, 71, 102, 116, 117, 131, 152, 154, 179, 190, 243, 244, 245, 276

Javolenus (Gaius Octavius Tidius Tossianus Lucius Iavolenus Priscus – jurist), 19
Julian (Lucius Octavius Cornelius Publius Salvius Iulianus Aemilianus – jurist), 18, 19, 49, 124, 141, 145, 152, 153, 160, 161, 170, 176, 179, 183, 184, 206, 221, 222, 249
Julius Nepos (Emperor), 20
Justinian I. (Flavius Petrus Sabbatius Iustinianus – Emperor), 3, 4–7, 13, 18, 20, 57, 88, 142, 247

Kaser, Max, 7, 10

Labeo (Marcus Antistius Labeo – jurist), 19, 255
Livy (Titus Livius), 15
Lucius Lentulus, 143
Lucius Licinius Crassus, 252

Macer (Aemilius Macer – jurist), 153
Marcellus (Ulpius Marcellus – jurist), 19, 91, 268, 269
Marcian (Aelius Marcianus – jurist), 186, 266
Marcus Aurelius (Marcus Aurelius Antoninus Augustus – Emperor), 19, 55, 261, 267–9
Mauritania, 2
Maximian (Marcus Aurelius Valerius Maximianus – Emperor), 19
Modestinus (Herennius Modestinus – jurist), 19, 43, 234

Neratius (Lucius Neratius Priscus – jurist), 19, 206
Nero (Nero Claudius Caesar Augustus Germanicus – Emperor), 220, 236
Nerva (Marcus Cocceius Nerva – jurist), 19, 101, 102, 148, 198, 199, 201, 202

Octavian *see* Augustus

Papinian (Aemilius Papinianus – jurist), 19, 26, 92, 129, 146, 154, 231, 261, 265
Paul (Iulius Paulus – jurist), 18, 19, 46, 56, 57, 66, 86, 144, 149, 155, 163, 190, 230, 264, 271
Pomponius (Sextus Pomponius – jurist), 19, 66, 202
Proculus (Sempronius Proculus – jurist), 19, 100, 160, 254, 255

Quintus Mucius (Quintus Mucius Scaevola – jurist), 206, 251

Rabel, Ernst, 35, 111
Rome, 12–16, 18, 22, 81

Sabinus (Masurius Sabius – jurist), 19, 128, 129, 160, 220, 266
Scaevola (Quintus Cervidius Scaevola – jurist), 19, 166, 232, 262
Schulz, Fritz, 10
Septimius Severus (Lucius Septimius Severus Pertinax – Emperor), 17, 19, 232, 233, 266, 270, 271
Sulla (Lucius Cornelius Sulla Felix), 16, 126, 140

Tiberius (Tiberius Iulius Caesar Augustus – Emperor), 140
Titus (Titus Flavius Vespasianus – Emperor), 148
Trajan (Marcus Ulpius Traianus – Emperor), 19, 102, 142, 149
Trebatius Testa (Gaius Trebatius Testa – jurist), 143
Tryphoninus (Claudius Tryphoninus – jurist), 183

Ulpian (Domitius Ulpianus – jurist), 18, 19, 21, 24, 25, 38, 45, 55, 73, 100, 103, 107, 119, 120, 121, 150, 151, 153, 180, 188, 210, 253

Vespasian (Titus Flavius Vespasianus – Emperor), 25, 237

Index of Subjects

accept the estate *see* aditio hereditatis
accept the inheritance (cretio), 68, 83
accruing, 64–6, 92–3, 172–3
acquire the estate *see* aditio hereditatis
acquisition of estate, 72, 93
acquisition of inheritance, 9–10, 62, 68
act of mancipatio, 159
act per aes et libram *see* mancipation
actio, 74
actio ex testamento, 196–7
action of rei vindicatio, 195
actiones poenales *see* penal actions
actions for theft (actio furti), 60–1
actions on inheritance (hereditatis petitio), 94, 97, 100, 101, 104, 106, 107, 108, 136
aditio hereditatis, 57, 68, 72–3, 76, 80–1, 203
adoption, 43
adulterium *see* adultery
adultery (adulterium), 85
aequitas (equity), 22, 46, 175, 180, 181, 236, 269
aerarium populi Romani *see* public treasury
agere per formulas *see* formulary procedure
agnatic kinship, 36–8, 43, 44, 54, 58, 115
agnatus proximus (nearest agnate), 28–9, 36, 39, 44, 48, 52, 55, 58, 80, 251
alieni iuris, 30, 35, 83, 173
ambiguitas (ambiguity), 251
ambiguity *see* ambiguitas
appeal proceedings (appellatio), 18
appellatio *see* appeal proceedings
application for bonorum possessio *see* request for bonorum possessio
appointment of an heir (institutio heredis), 9, 117–19, 127, 130, 131, 146, 150, 184, 192, 249, 250

auctoritas of the guardian *see* consent of the guardian
auctoritas patrum, 24
auctoritas prudentium, 26
Augustan marital laws *see* marital legislation

bad faith, 71, 103–6, 107
balance-holder, 113, 134
benignitas, 253, 262, 263, 267–9
blood kinship *see* cognatic kinship
bona caduca, 191, 243
bona fides, 69–70
bona vacantia *see* vacant estate
bonorum emptor, 76
bonorum possessio (estate possession), 10, 40–1, 71–3, 99–100, 175, 275–6
bonorum possessio ab intestato, 40, 44, 47, 73, 187
bonorum possessio commisso per alium edicto, 174
bonorum possessio contra tabulas, 171, 180–1, 190
bonorum possessio cum re, 47, 138
bonorum possessio secundum tabulas, 86, 131, 139, 156, 170, 215
bonorum possessio sine re, 47–8
bonorum possessor (estate owner), 74–5, 99–101, 136, 181, 215, 236

caducum, 85–7, 90
caelibes *see* unmarried
capacitas *see* capacity to obtain
capacity to be sued, 98
capacity to draw up a will (testamenti factio), 114, 127, 137, 224, 276
capacity to inherit, 79

capacity to obtain (capacitas), 84–9, 225–6
capitis deminutio maxima, 125, 133–4
capitis deminutio minima, 44
capitis deminutio, 36, 42
captivity, 125–7
causa Curiana, 251
cautelary jurisprudence, 113, 192, 206, 276
cautelary practice, 117, 124, 146, 166
cautio, 202, 216–7
cautio legatorum servandorum causa, 216
cautio Muciana, 206–7
child-in-power, 30–2, 35–6, 58, 78, 83, 115, 132, 224
childless (orbi), 86, 87, 221, 225, 243, 245
christianity, 20
circumventing laws (fraus legis), 245
citizen, 84, 125–6, 132
citizenship, 3, 23, 25, 31, 125, 133, 224
civil successor, 73, 82
civil war, 16
civitas *see* community
claim for bonorum possessio *see* request for bonorum possessio
clandestine fideicommissa, 245–6
classes of heirs of intestacy, 40
    unde cognati, 43, 44, 50, 52
    unde legitimi, 42, 50, 54, 56–7
    unde liberi, 41, 50
    unde vir et uxor, 46
Codex Iustinianus, 4–5
codicillary clause, 147
codicilli *see* codicils
codicils (codicilli), 142, 144, 147, 154–5, 230, 249, 260, 262–3
coëmptio, 116–7
coercion, 239, 241–3
cognatic kinship (natural kinship), 43–5, 52, 53–4, 58, 182, 192
cognitio extra ordinem, 26–7, 107, 142, 155, 246
co-heirs, 65, 66, 87, 120, 128, 188
collatio bonorum, 175–6, 179–80
community of co-heirs (consortium), 62, 274
community (civitas), 22, 29
compilers, 6
condemnatio, 74
condemnatio pecuniaria, 98, 197
condicio *see* condition

condition (condicio), 118–19, 122, 150–1, 161–2, 168, 170, 201, 203–6, 254
coniunctio, 65–6
consanguinitas, 36, 39, 52
consent of the guardian, 80, 115, 137
consilium (imperial council), 18, 143
consortium *see* community of co-heirs
constitutio Antoniniana, 25
constitutio *see* constitution
constitution (constitutio), 4, 23–4, 26
consul, 24, 223
conubium, 31
Corpus iuris civilis *see* Justinian's compilation
creditor, 64
creditors of an estate, 71–3, 75–7, 93, 188–9, 233, 236, 240
cretio *see* accept the inheritance

damnum iniuria datum, 60
daughter under the paternal power (filia familias), 33, 38, 164
debts of the estate, 63, 79, 240
decedent's death, 68
decree issued by the Senate *see* senatusconsultum
decretum (decision), 25, 190
denuntiatio litis, 104, 107
dies cedens, 203–7
dies certus, 202
dies incertus, 202
dies veniens, 203, 206, 216–17
Digest (digesta), 3–6, 20
direct heir (suus heres), 9, 31–2, 41, 48, 62, 64, 67, 75, 78, 174
disinheritance (exheredatio), 158, 169
division of inheritance, 63
dolus *see* malice
dos *see* dowry
dowry (dos), 45

edict *see* edictum
edictum (edict), 16, 25, 40, 141, 184, 277
edictum de legatis praestandis, 181, 190
edictum perpetuum, 18, 179
eligible applicant *see* request for bonorum possessio
emancipated son (emancipatus), 41, 48–9, 171, 175, 179–80, 182, 189–90

INDEX OF SUBJECTS

emancipatio, 32, 34–5, 41, 44, 58, 111, 167
emancipatus *see* emancipated son
emperor *see* princeps
epistula *see* letter
equity *see* aequitas
estate, 120
exceptio doli *see* malice
exheredatio *see* disinheritance
extraneous heir (heres extraneus), 67, 72, 75

falsa causa, 257
falsa demonstratio non nocet (false description), 255–6, 259
false description *see* falsa demonstratio non nocet
familiae emptor, 112
family entail, 232
family inheritance, 28, 158
favor testamenti, 262
fiction, 74–5, 101, 126, 205
fideicommissa, 10, 142–6, 222–4, 260, 266, 276
fideicommissary, 229, 234–5, 241–2
fideiussio *see* surety
filia familias *see* daughter under the paternal power
filius familias *see* son under the paternal power
fiscal procedure, 106
fiscus, 87, 90–2, 101–2, 107, 127, 140, 221, 228, 237, 243–6, 266–9
form (formlessness, strict formalism), 110, 112, 118–19, 125, 129–30, 135–7, 142, 144, 147–9, 151, 154, 156, 192, 200, 207, 219, 221–4, 245–7, 249–50, 259–60, 273, 275–6
formal promise *see* cautio
formula, 16, 97
formulary procedure (agere per formulas), 94, 97–8, 107
fraus legi *see* circumventing laws
freedom, 81, 125, 132
freedom of testation, 110, 158, 192, 213, 214
furiosus *see* insane

Gaius' Institutes, 8–10, 247
gens *see* gentiles
gentiles (gens), 39–40, 80
governor *see* praeses provinciae

grandfather, 30, 33–4, 36, 42, 49, 168, 179, 264
grandmother, 51
grandson, 29, 32–4, 50, 164, 167–9
grant the creditors bonorum possession, 71–2, 75–6
guardian, 81, 116, 136
guardianship *see* tutela
guardianship of women *see* tutela mulieris

heir (heres), 117–8, 122, 234–5
heredatis petitio *see* actions on inheritance
hereditary prescriptive acquisition, 69–71
hereditas iacens (lying estate), 69
heres extraneus *see* extraneous heir
heres necessarius, 67, 77–8, 79
heres suus *see* child-in-power
heres *see* heir
household cult, 70
humanitas, 252–4, 263, 266–7
husband, 33

imperial chancellery, 19, 25
imperial council *see* consilium
imperial instructions (mandatum), 148–9
imperial legislation *see* ius novum
imperial treasury *see* fiscus
imperium proconsulare, 17, 25
inaugural law *see* lex de imperio
incapacitas *see* lack of capacity to obtain
incapacity to own property *see* patria potestas
indignitas *see* unworthy of the estate
indignus *see* unworthy of the estate
infringements of personality rights (actio iniuriarum), 61
inheritance tax (lex Iulia de vicesima hereditatum), 139–40, 276
insane (furiosus), 125, 132, 134
institutio ex certa re, 128, 150, 230–1
institutio heredis *see* appointment of an heir
intentio, 74
interdict, 99–101, 215–6
interdictum quod legatorum, 215
interlocutio *see* interlocutory decision
interlocutory decision (interlocution), 25
interpolation criticism, 6
interpretatio *see* interpretation
interpretation (interpretatio), 65–7, 107, 129–30, 146–7, 183, 233, 248, 253, 258, 275

intestacy, 8, 28–9, 33, 37–40, 111, 121, 130, 145, 183, 187, 227–8, 275
intestate succession *see* intestacy
invalidity of the will, 125, 134, 142, 147, 156, 160, 166, 182, 184, 187
iudex *see* judge
ius agendi cum senatu, 24
ius antiquum, 53–4, 57, 275
ius civile, 22–3, 25–7, 38, 47, 58, 110, 131, 133–4, 142, 159, 208, 244, 265, 270–2, 275
ius gentium, 22
ius honorarium *see* ius praetorium
ius liberorum *see* right of three children
ius naturale, 21
ius novum, 23, 26, 53–4, 84, 142–3, 222–3, 244, 259, 265, 271, 275
ius praetorium, 23, 26, 40, 47, 58–9, 73, 94, 133–5, 142, 170–1, 185, 214–15, 219, 259
ius Quiritium *see* law of the Quirites
ius respondendi *see* right to give authoritative opinions
ius singular, 154, 155, 273–5, 277
ius trium liberorum *see* right of three children

joint liability of the heirs, 64, 71, 78, 93, 104, 234–6, 239–40
judge, 15, 74–5, 96–8, 163, 187
jurists, 4–5, 11, 16–21, 113, 143, 247, 252, 275–6, 277
Justinian's compilation, 3–4, 7–8, 20

lack of capacity to obtain (incapacitas), 87, 89
Late Antiquity, 13
law of the Quirites, 22, 95, 96, 98, 112, 195, 196
law of the twelve tables (lex duodecim tabularum), 14, 16, 27, 29, 35–7, 39–40, 57–8, 63, 64, 80, 109, 115, 211, 274, 275–6
layers of law, 11–12, 21, 23, 27, 27, 84, 107, 144, 147, 156, 192, 246–7, 272–5, 277
legacy (legatum), 8, 30, 110–11, 181, 184, 194, 195, 225, 256, 257–8, 277
legacy per damnationem, 196, 200
legacy per praeceptionem, 199, 200, 220, 220–1
legacy per vindicationem, 195, 196, 200, 219, 221
legacy sinendi modo, 198, 200

legal capacity to act *see* legal capacity
legal capacity, 79, 133
legal opinions (responsum), 17
legal proceedings apud iudicem, 15
legal proceedings in iure, 15
legatarius *see* legatee
legatee (legatarius), 194–8, 203–6, 217, 226, 240, 267
legatum *see* legacy
legatum per damnationem *see* legacy per damnationem
legatum per praeceptionem *see* legacy per praeceptionem
legatum per vindicationem *see* legacy per vindicationem
legatum sinendi modo *see* legacy sinendi modo
leges Liciniae Sextiae, 15
legis actiones procedure, 94, 95, 108
letter (epistula), 25
lex Atilia, 81, 82
lex Claudia, 81
lex Cornelia de falsis, 140
lex Cornelia de iurisdictione, 16
lex Cornelia testamentaria nummaria, 140
lex Cornelia, 115, 126–7, 140–1
lex de imperio (inaugural law), 25
lex duodecim tabularum *see* law of the twelve tables
lex Falcidia, 212–14, 238, 266, 276
lex Furia, 211
lex Iulia de adulteriis coercendis, 84
lex Iulia de maritandis ordinibus, 84–5, 221
lex Iulia de vicesima hereditatum (inheritance tax), 276
lex Iulia et Papia, 82, 85–7, 89, 130, 139–40, 221, 225, 242–3, 276
lex Iulia et Titia, 81, 82
lex Iunia Vellaea, 167–9
lex Papia Poppea nuptialis, 84
lex regia, 24
lex Voconia, 212
lex, 25
loss of the testamenti factio, 125
lying estate *see* hereditas iacens

making of a testament, 113, 117, 130, 132, 146, 159

malice (dolus), 99, 136, 138
mancipatio *see* mancipation
mancipation, 34, 111, 113, 116, 118, 134, 156
mancipatory will (testamentum per aes et libram), 111–13, 119, 130–1, 248, 250
mandatum *see* imperial instructions
manumission, 12, 34, 63, 78, 83, 109, 111, 190, 211
manus *see* marital power
marital legislation, 51, 82, 84, 90, 93, 116, 192, 221
marital power (manus), 38, 115
marriage (matrimonium), 21, 31, 33, 43, 45, 51–2
marriage bans, 85
mater familias *see* woman sui iuris
minors, 124–5, 132
modality (modus), 201, 203
mother, 50–1, 54–5, 232

natural kinship *see* cognatic kinship
nearest agnate *see* agnatus proximus
nemo pro parte testatus, 61, 64, 121, 150, 183
non-Romans, 23, 31
nova clausula Iuliani, 42, 49–50, 58–9, 179–80, 276
novellae *see* Novels
Novels (novellae), 4
nuncupatio *see* mancipation

obligation to marry, 84–5, 221
oratio principis, 24
orbi *see* childless
over-indebtedness, 76–7, 242

pactum, 63
Pandectae *see* Digest
partial invalidity of a will, 268
partial validity of the will, 180
partiary legacy, 240
partitio legata *see* partiary legacy
pater familias, 29–32, 36, 82–3, 125–6
paternal power *see* patria potestas
patria potestas, 30, 39
pecuniary condemnation *see* condemnatio pecuniara
penal actions (actiones poenales), 61
penal legacy, 208

pietas, 185, 264
plebiscite (plebiscitum), 25–6
plebiscitum *see* plebiscite
plus nuncupatum quam scriptum, 249, 260
pontifex *see* priest
posthumous child *see* postumus
postliminium, 126
postumus, 166, 170, 251
power of the pater familias *see* patria potestas
power structures, 32
praefectus praetorio, 18
praeses provinciae (governor), 16–18, 27
praeterire, 159–61, 167–9, 171, 182, 190
praetor fideicommissarius, 223
praetor for foreigners *see* praetor peregrinus
praetor of the city *see* praetor urbanus
praetor peregrinus (praetor for foreigners), 15–6
praetor urbanus (praetor of the city), 15–16
praetor, 14–18, 17–18, 23, 26–7, 40, 71–2, 96, 139, 202, 275
praetorian law *see* ius praetorium
priest, 14
princeps (emperor), 16–18, 24, 26, 102, 155
Principate, 13, 16–17, 19, 23, 26, 39, 276
principium, 5
principle of representation, 33, 178–9
procedural oath, 95–7
procedure per sponsionem, 95–7
Proculians (school of jurists), 160, 200, 221
property, 8, 62, 69, 95, 111, 128, 196
protection against forgery, 139
province, 16–17, 81, 187
pubertas *see* puberty
puberty (pubertas), 122–3, 125, 231
public treasury (aerarium populi Romani), 87, 91, 243
Punic Wars, 15

quaestio perpetua, 140
quanti ea res est, 107
querela inofficiosi testamenti, 185, 191, 193

regula Catoniana, 209–210, 277
rei vindicatio *see* action of rei vindicatio
remarriage, 85, 222
renunciation of a right, 56

renunciation of inheritance, 68, 72, 75, 78, 130, 216–17, 237
Republic, 13, 14, 24, 26, 81, 277
request for bonorum possessio, 40, 54, 57, 74, 83, 131, 133, 137–8, 173, 177, 182, 189, 245
request of the creditors of the estate *see* grant the creditors bonorum possessio
res mancipi, 35
rescript (rescriptum), 18, 25, 64, 91, 135–6, 153, 172, 173, 233, 261
rescriptum *see* rescript
responsum *see* legal opinions
revocation of the will, 129–30, 137, 149–50
right of three children, 51, 81–2, 90, 117
right to give authoritative opinions, 17, 26
Roman legal writing, 3, 11, 20

Sabinians (school of jurists), 160, 221
sale of the estate (venditio bonorum), 75, 77, 78, 233
satisdatio, 76, 216
seal, 130, 134, 139, 140
security *see* cautio; *see also* satisdatio
semel heres, semper heres, 118, 151, 228
Senate, 16, 24, 92
senatusconsultum Iuventianum, 101, 107, 155, 274, 277
senatusconsultum Libonianum, 140, 141
senatusconsultum Neronianum, 139, 196, 219, 221
senatusconsultum Orfitianum, 55–7, 277
senatusconsultum Pegasianum, 237–8, 242–3
senatusconsultum Plancianum, 245–6
senatusconsultum Tertullianum, 50, 52, 53, 263, 277
senatusconsultum Trebellianum, 235, 237, 238–9
senatusconsultum, 18, 24, 26, 58, 71, 116, 117, 210, 243, 276
separatio bonorum, 77, 79
share of the estate, 176–7, 232
share of the inheritance, 63–4, 66–7, 86, 184
sine manu wife *see* woman sui iuris
singular fideicommissum, 241, 271
slave, 30, 35, 77, 78, 83–4, 126, 224
societas ercto non cito, 62
soldier's will, 9, 142, 147–8, 154–5, 260, 263–4

sole heir, 120, 128, 231, 262–3
son under the paternal power (filius familias), 29, 31–4, 38, 161, 166, 182
spousal inheritance law, 45, 88
spouse, 89
stipulation (stipulatio), 76, 206, 216, 235, 236, 240
stirpital representation, 33, 37, 49
subscriptio, 25
substitute for the pupillus (substitutio pupillaris), 122, 124, 251, 263
substitute heir (substitutio), 122–5, 141, 160–1
substitutio pupillaris *see* substitute for the pupillus
substitutio *see* substitute heir
surety (fideiussio), 76
surrogatio, 104
suus heres *see* direct heir

testamentary document, 133–4, 150, 159, 182, 249, 251
testamentary heir, 61, 136, 145, 161, 174, 188, 227
testamentary order of succession, 237
testamenti factio *see* capacity to draw up a will
testamentum *see* will
testamentum calatis comitiis, 110
testamentum in procinctu, 110
testamentum militis *see* soldier's will
testamentum paganorum, 148
testamentum per aes et libram *see* mancipatory will
testator, 8, 37, 51, 113, 121, 146–7, 186, 249–51, 257
the Institutes of Gaius *see* Gaius' Institutes
transfer of actions, 236, 239–40, 243
tribune of the plebs, 14, 17, 24
tribunicia potestas *see* tribune of the plebs
tutela (guardianship), 79–81, 115
tutela mulieris (guardianship of women), 82
tutor *see* guardian

unde *see* classes of heirs of intestacy
under paternal power *see* alieni iuris
universal fideicommissum, 230, 238–9
universal succession, 61, 127

unmarried (caelibes), 86, 87, 221, 225, 243, 245
unworthy of the estate (indignitas), 90–3, 138, 191, 268
usucapio pro herede *see* hereditary prescriptive acquisition
usucaption of an estate *see* hereditary prescriptive acquisition

vacant estate (bona vacantia), 127, 228
vacant inheritance *see* vacant succession
vacant succession, 73, 83
venditio bonorum *see* sale of the estate
venditio hereditatis, 234

vindicatio caducorum, 87, 91, 101, 106, 107
voluntatis quaestio, 250

wax tablets, 1, 112, 134
widow, 45
wife, 38, 45
will (testamentum), 1, 92, 109, 111–12
witness, 109, 113, 117, 119–20, 132, 134–5, 139–40, 249
woman (her position), 38, 50–1, 80–2, 115–17, 136–7
woman sui iuris, 30, 45, 80, 114–15, 117
worthiness to inherit, 84–5

EU Authorised Representative:
Easy Access System Europe Mustamäe tee 50, 10621 Tallinn, Estonia
gpsr.requests@easproject.com

Printed and bound by CPI Group (UK) Ltd, Croydon, CR0 4YY
25/03/2026
02077951-0010